TENNYSON'S POEMS:
NEW TEXTUAL PARALLELS

Tennyson's Poems:
New Textual Parallels

R. H. Winnick

https://www.openbookpublishers.com

Copyright © 2019 by R. H. Winnick

This work is licensed under a Creative Commons Attribution 4.0 International license (CC BY 4.0). This license allows you to share, copy, distribute and transmit the work; to adapt the work and to make commercial use of the work provided that attribution is made to the author (but not in any way which suggests that the author endorses you or your use of the work). Attribution should include the following information:

R. H. Winnick, *Tennyson's Poems: New Textual Parallels*. Cambridge, UK: Open Book Publishers, 2019. https://doi.org/10.11647/OBP.0161

In order to access detailed and updated information on the license, please visit https://www.openbookpublishers.com/product/944#copyright

Further details about CC BY licenses are available at http://creativecommons.org/licenses/by/4.0/

Digital material and resources associated with this volume are available at https://www.openbookpublishers.com/product/944#resources

Every effort has been made to identify and contact copyright holders and any omission or error will be corrected if notification is made to the publisher.

ISBN Paperback: 978-1-78374-661-3
ISBN Hardback: 978-1-78374-662-0
ISBN Digital (PDF): 978-1-78374-663-7
ISBN Digital ebook (epub): 978-1-78374-664-4
ISBN Digital ebook (mobi): 978-1-78374-665-1
DOI: 10.11647/OBP.0161

Cover image: 'Alfred, Lord Tennyson' by Herbert Rose Barraud. Carbon print, ca. 1888, NPG x26788 © National Portrait Gallery, London.

Cover design by Anna Gatti.

All paper used by Open Book Publishers is SFI (Sustainable Forestry Initiative) and PEFC (Programme for the Endorsement of Forest Certification Schemes) Certified.

For Christopher Ricks

Contents

Numbers and alphanumerics (such as '1A') before poem titles are those assigned by Christopher Ricks in his 1987 edition of Tennyson's complete poems (see Preface). An asterisk following a poem number indicates that the poem appears in both the selected and the complete Ricks edition; its absence, that the poem appears only in the latter.

Preface		1
1A	Three Translations of Horace	17
1	Translation of Claudian's 'Rape of Proserpine'	18
2	The Devil and the Lady	24
3	Armageddon	30
4	The Coach of Death, A Fragment	35
5	Memory [Memory! dear enchanter!]	36
8	Remorse	37
9	The Dell of E—	37
10	Anthony and Cleopatra	39
16	'Did not thy roseate lips outvie'	39
26	On Sublimity	39
27	Time: An Ode	41
30	The Walk at Midnight	41
45	'Oh! ye wild winds, that roar and rave'	42
46	Babylon	42
47	Love [Almighty Love!]	43
48	Exhortation to the Greeks	44
50	'Come hither, canst thou tell me if this skull'	44

51	The Dying Man to His Friend	45
54A	'The musky air was mute'	45
55	The Outcast	45
58A	The Invasion of Russia by Napoleon Buonaparte	46
59	Playfellow Winds	48
61	Home	48
62	'Among some Nations Fate hath placed too far'	48
63	To Poesy [O God, make this age great]	49
64	The Lark	49
67	Timbuctoo	49
73*	Mariana	50
75	Madeline	50
78*	Supposed Confessions of a Second-Rate Sensitive Mind	51
79	The Burial of Love	53
83	Recollections of the Arabian Nights	53
84	Ode to Memory	53
87	Adeline	56
88*	A Character	57
91	The Poet	58
95	Hero to Leander	60
99	The Grasshopper	60
101	Chorus, in an Unpublished Drama, Written Very Early	60
106	To a Lady Sleeping	61
107	Sonnet [Could I outwear my present state of woe]	62
108	Sonnet [Though Night hath climbed her peak of highest noon]	63
109	Sonnet [Shall the hag Evil die with child of Good]	63
110	Sonnet [The pallid thunderstricken sigh for gain]	65
124	Amy	65
126	Memory [Ay me!]	65
127	Ode: O Bosky Brook	66
128	Perdidi Diem	68
130	Sense and Conscience	69
132	'In deep and solemn dreams'	70
140	Lines on Cambridge of 1830	70
143	A Fragment [Where is the Giant of the Sun]	71
144	'O wake ere I grow jealous of sweet Sleep'	71

145	'The constant spirit of the world exults'	71
146	Sonnet [When that rank heat of evil's tropic day]	72
151	Sonnet [There are three things which fill my heart with sighs]	72
153	The Lover's Tale	73
155	'My life is full of weary days'	75
158	'If I were loved, as I desire to be'	75
159*	The Lady of Shalott	75
160*	Mariana in the South	77
161	Eleänore	78
162	The Miller's Daughter	81
163*	Fatima	81
164*	Œnone	83
166*	To — . With the Following Poem [The Palace of Art]	85
167*	The Palace of Art	86
169	The Hesperides	88
170*	The Lotos-Eaters	88
171	Rosalind	89
172	'My Rosalind, my Rosalind'	89
173*	A Dream of Fair Women	90
174	Song [Who can say]	91
175	Margaret	91
176	Kate	91
179	To — [As when with downcast eyes]	93
185	Sonnet [Alas! how weary are my human eyes]	94
190	'Pierced through with knotted thorns of barren pain'	94
192	The Ruined Kiln	95
193	The Progress of Spring	95
194	'Hail Briton!'	96
200	Early Spring [1833]	97
207	The Ante-Chamber	98
208	The Gardener's Daughter; Or, The Pictures	98
209*	The Two Voices	99
210*	St Simeon Stylites	104
212	St Agnes' Eve	104
214	'Hark! the dogs howl!'	104
215	Whispers	105

216*	On a Mourner	106
217*	Ulysses	107
218*	Tithon	109
219	Tiresias	110
220	Semele	112
223	Youth	112
225*	The Epic [Morte d'Arthur]	112
227*	'Oh! that 'twere possible'	113
233	'Fair is that cottage in its place'	114
238	'I loving Freedom for herself'	114
240	The Blackbird	114
241*	The Day-Dream	115
246	Lady Clara Vere de Vere	118
250	Sonnet [Ah, fade not yet from out the green arcades]	118
251	To Rosa	119
254	Three Sonnets to a Coquette	119
255	Sonnet [How thought you that this thing could captivate?]	119
257	The Voyage	119
259	The Flight	122
263	'The tenth of April! is it not?'	123
265*	A Farewell	123
267	Will Waterproof's Lyrical Monologue	123
270	Amphion	124
271*	Locksley Hall	124
275*	Edwin Morris or, The Lake	126
276*	The Golden Year	127
276A	'Wherefore, in these dark ages of the Press'	128
277*	The Vision of Sin	129
279	Love and Duty	132
285B	The Wanderer	132
286*	The Princess, A Medley	133
289	To — , After Reading a Life and Letters	145
290	The Losing of the Child	147
291	The Sailor Boy	147
296*	In Memoriam A. H. H.	148
297	To the Vicar of Shiplake	185

299*	To the Queen	185
300	'Little bosom not yet cold'	186
301*	To E. L., on His Travels in Greece	186
306	The Third of February, 1852	187
307	Hands All Round! [1852]	187
308	Suggested by Reading an Article in a Newspaper	187
310*	Will	188
311*	The Daisy	189
312*	To the Rev. F. D. Maurice	189
313	The Brook	190
316*	Maud, A Monodrama	192
317	The Letters	197
324*	Tithonus	198
329	Ode Sung at the Opening of the International Exhibition	198
330*	Enoch Arden	199
337	Aylmer's Field 1793	202
339	A Dedication	205
353	The Higher Pantheism	205
355	Lucretius	205
363	To the Rev. W. H. Brookfield	206
367	Prefatory Sonnet to the 'Nineteenth Century'	207
377*	Prefatory Poem to My Brother's Sonnets	207
383	De Profundis	208
386	Sir John Oldcastle, Lord Cobham	208
390	Prologue to General Hamley [The Charge of the Heavy Brigade]	209
392	Epilogue [The Charge of the Heavy Brigade]	209
394*	To Virgil	209
395	The Throstle	210
398*	To E. FitzGerald	210
399	Poets and their Bibliographies	210
400*	The Dead Prophet	210
407	Freedom	211
410	The Fleet	211
413	Vastness	211
415	The Ancient Sage	212

417*	Locksley Hall Sixty Years After	212
420	Demeter and Persephone	212
424	Happy, The Leper's Bride	214
425*	To Mary Boyle	214
426*	Far — Far — Away	215
427*	To the Marquis of Dufferin and Ava	215
431	Merlin and the Gleam	216
441	The Death of Œnone	217
443	St Telemachus	217
454	Kapiolani	218
462*	Crossing the Bar	218

Idylls of the King

464*	The Coming of Arthur	218
465*	Gareth and Lynette	219
466*	The Marriage of Geraint	220
467*	Geraint and Enid	221
468*	Balin and Balan	221
469*	Merlin and Vivien	222
470*	Lancelot and Elaine	222
471*	The Holy Grail	223
472*	Pelleas and Ettarre	223
473*	The Last Tournament	224
474*	Guinevere	226
475*	The Passing of Arthur	226

Alphabetical Index of Tennyson Poems Discussed	227
Index of Antecedent Writers and Works Discussed	233

Preface

The most recent major edition of Tennyson's complete poems, the three-volume second (1987) edited by Christopher Ricks,[1] cites more than twelve hundred instances in which phrases and short passages of as few as two or three and as many as several words therein are similar or identical to those occurring in prior works by other hands.[2] Thanks to the proliferation of digitized texts and the related development of powerful search tools over the three decades since that edition was produced, it has become possible to search for such textual parallels far more widely and effectively than ever before and to find, in Tennyson's case, hundreds more. Like those previously identified, each of these new instances may be deemed an allusion (meant to be recognized as such and pointing, for definable purposes, to a particular antecedent text), an echo (conscious or not, deliberate or not, meant to be noticed or not, meaningful or not), or merely accidental. Unless accidental, these new

---

1 *The Poems of Tennyson; in three volumes; second edition incorporating the Trinity College manuscripts*, ed. by Christopher Ricks (Harlow, Essex: Longman, 1987). Along with the first, one-volume edn (Longman, 1969), Ricks edited *Tennyson: A Selected Edition incorporating the Trinity College manuscripts* (Longman, 1989), a revised edn of which was published by Pearson Longman in 2007 and reissued by Routledge in 2014.

2 I base this figure on W. David Shaw's count of the textual parallels (all of which Shaw calls 'allusions') cited by Ricks in his 1969 edn of Tennyson's poems. As Shaw writes in *Tennyson's Style* (Ithaca and London: Cornell University Press, 1976), p. 27: 'The greatest number of allusions are to the Bible (a total of 272), followed, in order, by Milton, 213; Shakespeare, 155; Shelley, 129; Keats, 86; Horace, 57; Malory, 47; Virgil, 44; Lucretius, 38; Homer, 37; Gray, 29; Spenser, 27; Pope, 26; Wordsworth, 25; Ovid, 20. (I have omitted poets with fewer than twenty references.)' Shaw's count of these textual parallels totals 1205.

textual parallels may not only tell us more about Tennyson's reading but shed further light on his thematic intentions and artistic technique.[3]

Not surprisingly given his lifelong sensitivity to what he took to be, and what at times were in fact, questions about the originality of his work—beginning with an unsigned review of his recently published *Poems* (Moxon, 1833) in the *New Monthly Magazine* accusing him of having 'filled half his pages with the most glaring imitations';[4] and including, thirteen years later, Sir Edward Bulwer-Lytton's scornful reference to the 'borrowed notes' and 'purloin'd conceits' of 'School-Miss Alfred' in *The New Timon. A Romance of London* (Colburn, 1846)—Tennyson himself usually and often vehemently denied (with occasional exceptions, most of them noted in the Eversley edition of his poems and plays)[5] that his poems contained any conscious and deliberate echoes of any such prior works at all. The most galling attack, and the one that prompted his most intense and sustained response, came late in his life, long after he was named Poet Laureate, long after his verse had won him fame, fortune, and all but universal admiration, and, ironically, from a scholar-critic who claimed to hold him and his poetry in high regard.

When John Churton Collins published the first of three installments of 'A New Study of Tennyson' in the January 1880 issue of *The Cornhill Magazine*[6]—including in it, based on his wide reading and prodigious

---

3   In his preface to the second, three-volume edn, Ricks writes (p. xix): 'The footnotes cite many parallel passages. As in any annotated edition these illustrate a range of possible likenesses. At one end is conscious allusion to another poet; then unconscious reminiscence; then phrasing which is only an analogue and not a source. Some of the instances cited here are probably analogues, not sources, but they are cited because Tennyson's phrasing can be illuminated by the comparison.' Ricks's comments are also applicable to the textual parallels cited in this study.

4   'The Faults of Recent Poets', *New Monthly Magazine*, vol. 37, no. 145 (Jan. 1833), 69–74 (70); cited by Edgar Finley Shannon, Jr., in *Tennyson and the Reviewers: A Study of His Literary Reputation and of the Influence of the Critics upon His Poetry 1827–1851* (Cambridge, Mass.: Harvard University Press, 1952), p. 38.

5   *The Works of Tennyson*, 9 vols., annotated by Alfred Tennyson, edited by his elder son Hallam Tennyson (London: Macmillan, 1907–8); hereinafter cited as *Eversley*.

6   John Churton Collins, 'A New Study of Tennyson', *The Cornhill Magazine*, vol. 41, no. 241 (Jan. 1880), 36–50. Part II appeared under the same title in *The Cornhill*, vol. 42, no. 247 (July 1880), 17–35; and Part III in *The Cornhill*, vol. 44, no. 259 (July 1881), 87–106. Collins's *Cornhill* articles were later incorporated into his *Illustrations of Tennyson* (London: Chatto & Windus, 1891), which, as discussed below, added more instances of Tennyson's supposed echoes and borrowings. Other subsequent compilations of such echoes and borrowings include Wilfred P. Mustard, *Classical*

if imperfect memory, nearly a hundred instances in which Tennyson seemed to him to have derived phrases, lines, passages, even whole poems from an assortment of earlier, mostly classical authors—Tennyson filled the margins of his copy[7] with comments generally ranging from denial to outrage. Alongside two lines from his *Mariana*, said by Collins to have been adapted from two lines, 'scarcely less beautiful', of the Latin poet Cinna, Tennyson wrote: 'I read this for the first time'; alongside five others, 'not known to me';[8] alongside six, 'nonsense'; alongside three, 'no', or 'no, close as it seems'; alongside five, '!!' or '!!!'; and so on. (In three instances, it should be noted, Tennyson's marginal comment was 'possibly'.) If, as seems unlikely, he took the trouble to both read and mark up parts two and three of Collins's *Cornhill* pieces, his copies and any marginal comments they contained seem not to have survived.

Tennyson's annoyance with Collins, and insistence on the originality of his poems, found further expression in some of his subsequent correspondence and conversation.

In an 1882 letter to S. E. Dawson, author of a study on one of those poems,[9] he wrote:

> I thank you for your able and thoughtful essay on *The Princess*. [...] Your explanatory notes are very much to the purpose, and I do not object to your finding parallelisms. They must always occur. A man (a Chinese scholar) some time ago wrote to me saying that in an unknown, untranslated Chinese poem there were two whole lines of mine almost

---

Echoes in Tennyson (New York and London: Macmillan, 1904); G. G. Loane, 'Echoes in Tennyson,' in his *Echoes in Tennyson, and Other Essays* (London: Stockwell, n.d. [1928]), pp. 3–11; and E. A. Mooney, Jr., 'Tennyson's Earliest Shakspere Parallels', *Shakespeare Association Bulletin*, vol. 15, no. 2 (Apr. 1940), 118–24.

7   Preserved in the Tennyson collection of the Central Library, Lincoln; summarized by H. P. Sucksmith in 'Tennyson on the Nature of His Own Poetic Genius: Some Recently Discovered Marginalia', *Renaissance and Modern Studies*, vol. 11, no. 1 (1967), 84–89; and also selectively cited in the Ricks editions of Tennyson's poems.

8   In at least two instances, as Ricks points out, Tennyson denied prior knowledge of a source cited by Collins, then later, in the notes to *Eversley*, cited it himself. Alongside Collins's citation of Callimachus, *Lavacrum Palladis*, line 72, as the source of line 24 of *Œnone*, Tennyson wrote: 'not known to me'; but the same line of Callimachus is cited in connection with the same line of *Œnone* in *Eversley*, vol. 1, p. 360. Similarly, alongside Collins's suggestion of *Inferno* xv 95–96 as the source of the refrain 'Turn, Fortune, turn thy wheel' in lines 347–58 of *The Marriage of Geraint*, Tennyson wrote '!!!'; but the same lines are cited in *Eversley*, vol. 5, p. 470.

9   S. E. Dawson, *A Study; with Critical and Explanatory Notes, of Alfred Tennyson's Poem The Princess* (Montreal: Dawson Brothers, 1882).

word for word.[10] Why not? Are not human eyes all over the world looking at the same objects, and must there not consequently be coincidences of thought and impressions and expressions? It is scarcely possible for any one to say or write anything in this late time of the world to which, in the rest of the literature of the world, a parallel could not somewhere be found. But when you say that this passage or that was suggested by Wordsworth or Shelley or another, I demur; and more, I wholly disagree.

and added:

[T]here is, I fear, a prosaic set growing up among us, editors of booklets, book-worms, index-hunters, or men of great memories and no imagination, who *impute themselves* to the poet, and so believe that *he*, too, has no imagination, but is for ever poking his nose between the pages of some old volume in order to see what he can appropriate. They will not allow one to say 'Ring the bell' without finding that we have taken it from Sir P. Sidney, or even to use such a simple expression as the ocean 'Roars', without finding out the precise verse in Homer or Horace from which we have plagiarised it (fact).[11]

'He was always very sensitive to the remarks of the critics, whether they attacked his powers of observation or denied him any originality', wrote one friend a few years after the poet's death.

One especially annoyed him by suggesting sources from which he had copied or borrowed similes and expressions, often mentioning writers whom Tennyson declared that he had never read or heard of, and quite ignoring the fact that the same thought can strike various people at different times, and that it is not necessary to hunt for the source of all that a poet gives us, if only we will allow that poet some powers of imagination of his own.

---

10   The man, an English missionary in China, was the Rev. Arthur Evans Moule, to whom, on 6 Jan. 1880, Tennyson had sent a letter reading in its entirety: 'Dear Sir I thank you for your book and your quotation from the Chinese Poet. No man can write a single passage to which a parallel one may not be found somewhere in the literature of the world. Yours very faithfully A. Tennyson'. From *The Letters of Alfred Lord Tennyson*, ed. by Cecil Y. Lang and Edgar F. Shannon, Jr., vol. 3 (Cambridge, Mass.: Harvard University Press, 1990), p. 183.

11   The letter, dated 21 Nov. 1882, first appeared in vol. 1 of Hallam's two-volume *Alfred Lord Tennyson, a Memoir By His Son* (London: Macmillan, 1897; hereinafter, '*Memoir*'), pp. 256–57, and again, with minor textual variations, in *Eversley*, vol. 4, pp. 238–42.

'They allow me nothing,' he once said to me. 'For instance, "The deep moans round with many voices." "The deep," Byron; "moans," Horace; "many voices," Homer; and so on.'[12]

Another, recounting a visit to Farringford with her husband in January 1892 (Tennyson died that October), wrote:

> Next day we walked up at about 12.20 to accompany him in his morning walk. Montagu and he were in front, Hallam Tennyson and I behind. Montagu tells me how he was indignant with Z. for charging him with general plagiarism, in particular about Lactantius and other classics, 'of whom,' he said, 'I haven't read a word.' Also, of taking from Sophocles, 'whom I never read since I was a young man'; and of his owing his 'moanings of the sea' to Horace's *gementis litora Bospori*. Some one charged him with having stolen the 'In Memoriam' metre from some very old poet of whom he had never heard.[13]

In an earlier but still late conversation, the translator, literary historian, and critic Edmund Gosse, one of whose books Collins had savaged in print since their last meeting,[14] visited the Tennysons at Aldworth in 1888. In one account by Gosse, as recorded by his biographer,

> He arrived in the afternoon and was sent out into the garden, where he found a large party; tea spread out at a trestle table, Tennyson at one end of it, and an empty chair near the other. To this he crept, hoping to escape notice, but in vain. Tennyson boomed out at him, 'Well, Gosse, would you like to know what I think of Churton Collins?' This was worse than anything he had anticipated. He managed to mumble that he would. 'I

---

12 Rev. H. D. Rawnsley, *Memories of the Tennysons* (Glasgow: MacLehose, 1900), pp. 138–39. Hallam recorded a similar complaint in *Memoir*, vol. 2, p. 385: 'He himself had been "most absurdly accused of plagiarizing," e.g. "The moanings of the homeless sea," "moanings" from Horace, "homeless" from Shelley. "As if no one else had heard the sea moan except Horace."'

13 The account, by Mrs. Montagu Butler, appears as 'Visit to Farringford, January 1892' in *Tennyson and His Friends*, ed. by Hallam Tennyson (London: Macmillan, 1911), pp. 216–21.

14 Collins's review of Gosse's *From Shakespeare to Pope: An Inquiry Into the Causes and Phenomena of the Rise of Classical Poetry in England* (Cambridge: Cambridge University Press, 1885) ran in *The Quarterly Review*, vol. 163, no. 326 (Oct. 1886), 289–329. See the discussion of this episode in Anthony Kearney, *John Churton Collins: The Louse on the Locks of Literature* (Edinburgh: Scottish Academic Press, 1986), pp. 52–69.

think,' Tennyson went on, 'he's a Louse on the Locks of Literature.' The phrase from such a source was infinitely restoring.[15]

In another, contained in an August 1888 letter to his wife—the discrepancy first noticed and reported by Ricks[16]—Gosse wrote that Tennyson had asked him 'How's Churton Collins?' and without waiting for an answer added: 'Would you like to know what I think of him?' When Gosse said he would, Tennyson continued: 'Well! He's a jackass. That's what he is. But don't say I said so.'[17] Whatever Tennyson's actual words, the first of the two phrases stuck, even supplying the subtitle of Anthony Kearney's solid and sympathetic biography of Collins, published in 1986.[18]

Tennyson's continuing ire was understandable and not entirely unwarranted. Rather than recording in a matter-of-fact, nonjudgmental manner the many instances he had identified in which Tennyson phrases, lines, and passages seemed to him to echo or be borrowed from a broad range of mostly classical poets, Collins added insult to what Tennyson could only perceive as injury by implying, while claiming to think no such thing, that the textual parallels to be found in his poems showed Tennyson often to be at best (where foreign-language works were involved) a gifted translator of Greek, Roman, and Italian literature and at worst (where they were not) a plagiarist on a grand scale.

Collins began Part I of his *Cornhill* study—the one to which Tennyson would add his marginal comments—with a long paragraph ostensibly about not Tennyson but Virgil:

> Those who may happen to be familiar with the *Saturnalia* of Macrobius will remember that one of the most delightful episodes in that

---

15 Evan Charteris, *The Life and Letters of Sir Edmund Gosse* (London: William Heinemann, 1931), pp. 196–97.

16 In *Notes and Queries*, vol. 208 (Mar. 1963), 112–13.

17 The possibility that Gosse changed Tennyson's words to better wound Collins is discussed by Ann Thwaite in her *Edmund Gosse: A Literary Landscape, 1849–1928* (London: Secker & Warburg, 1984), pp. 295–97.

18 See note 14. See also Kearney, 'Making Tennyson a Classic: Churton Collins' *Illustrations of Tennyson* in Context', *Victorian Poetry*, vol. 30, no. 1 (Spring 1992), 75–82; Phyllis Grosskurth, 'Churton Collins: Scourge of the Late Victorians', *University of Toronto Quarterly*, vol. 34, no. 3 (Apr. 1965), 254–68; and William H. Pritchard, 'John Churton Collins: Forgotten Man of Letters', *Yale Review*, vol. 90, no. 4 (Oct. 2008), 87–105.

pleasant work are [sic] the two books in which Eustathius and Furius Albinus estimate the extent of Virgil's obligations to his predecessors. Eustathius having concluded a long and elaborate review of the passages in the Greek poets of which the great Roman had availed himself, Furius Albinus proceeds to trace him through Latin literature. He was half afraid, he said, to produce the formidable list of passages appropriated by the poet, because he might be exposing his favourite 'to the censure of the malignant and unlearned.' Remembering, however, that such parallels as he was about to point out have been common to poets of all ages, and haughtily observing that what Virgil condescended to borrow became him much more than the original owner—to say nothing of that owner becoming in some cases immortalised by the theft—Furius plunges into his theme. Between them these Langbaines of the fifth century made Conington very uncomfortable towards the end of the nineteenth; but if their disclosures have materially impaired Virgil's claims to originality, they have illustrated his faultless taste, his nice artistic sense, his delicate touch, his consummate literary skill. They initiated a new branch of study, they divulged a fruitful secret.[19]

He began the next with an affirmation by denial:

Without going so far as the thief in *Albumazar*, when he says,
> This poet is that poet's plagiary,
> And he a third's till they all end in Homer,
it is still interesting and necessary to remember that there have appeared in all literatures, at a certain point in their development, a class of poets who are essentially imitative and reflective.

And, three sentences later, he came down to cases:

Torquato Tasso, [Thomas] Gray, and Mr. Tennyson are, perhaps, the most striking types in the modern world. Of all these Virgil, Tasso, and the Laureate are undoubtedly the most distinguished.

What poet as sensitive to any questioning of his originality as was Tennyson would not have been deeply offended by these comments?[20]

---

19 Collins, *A New Study*, Part I, 36. Gerard Langbaine (1656–92), author of *An Account of the English Dramatic Poets* (1691); John Conington (1825–69), English classical scholar and translator of the *Aeneid*.

20 Or by others that followed, as on page 37,
    Mr. Tennyson has now, by general consent, taken his place among English classics; he too will have, like Virgil and Tasso, his critics and his commentators; and, unless we are much mistaken, one of the most important and fruitful departments of their labour will be that

Collins concluded Part I of his study with a paragraph once again claiming to find no fault with Tennyson's compositional practices. It began:

> Here we must pause, though we have by no means exhausted our list of these interesting and instructive parallel passages. It would be absurd and presumptuous to conclude that any of the similarities which have been pointed out were deliberate or even conscious imitations. In Mr. Tennyson's own noble words, we moderns are 'the heirs of all the ages.'[21] We live amid wealth as prodigally piled up as the massive and innumerable treasure-trove of Spenser's 'rich strond.'

---

of tracing his obligations to his predecessors, of illustrating his wondrous assimilative skill, his tact, his taste, his learning.

page 39,

The noble verses which open *In Memoriam* are obviously a transfusion, so to speak, of some verses of Lord Herbert's brother, George Herbert, who appears to be a favourite with the Laureate. A comparison of Herbert's first stanza with the opening of Mr. Tennyson's poem will at once illustrate the fine art of the latter poet, and the peculiar manner in which he has, more or less unconsciously no doubt, availed himself of his predecessor's poem.

page 40,

It would of course be absurd to assert that these resemblances are conscious imitations, but, as they lie within the compass of [the first] forty-four lines [of *In Memoriam*], they are at least curious enough to be pointed out.

page 43,

The whole of this piece is little else than a translation of the noble passage about the mood in which man is fitted for communion with his God in Jeremy Taylor's Fifth Golden Grove Sermon.

page 45,

For the fine idea at the end of *Œnone*, it would seem also that he is indebted to another of the Elizabethan dramatists, and, with due deference to the genius of the later poet [Tennyson], how feebly do his verses echo the massive majesty of Shakespeare's greatest follower [Webster]!

page 47,

In truth, the Poet Laureate's debts to Homer and Virgil would make in themselves an interesting dissertation. In *Eleänore* he has laid both Sappho and Horace under contribution. To the latter he is indebted for the beautiful picture and the suggestive touch in 'His bow-string slackened[,] languid love, / Leaning his cheek upon his hand, &c.' [...] To the former he is indebted for all the passage which succeeds 'My heart a charmed slumber keeps,' which is an *almost literal translation* of the greater part of Sappho's incomparable ode, filtered perhaps through Catullus.

and page 48:

The adaptations from Theocritus in the passage beginning 'All the land .... smelt of the coming summer,' to the end of the paragraph, in *The Gardener's Daughter*, must be obvious to every scholar.

21   A modification and misapplication of Tennyson's ironic lines 177–78 in *Locksley Hall*: 'Mated with a squalid savage—what to me were sun or clime? / I the heir of all the ages, in the foremost files of time—'.

In parts two and three of *A New Study* and in his *Illustrations of Tennyson*, Collins continued to document what he regarded as Tennyson's debt to his predecessors and to do so in ways that, if he read them, Tennyson could only have deemed more wormwood. Collins came closest to an outright accusation of plagiarism in the penultimate chapter of *Illustrations*, where, on page 163, he arrived at Tennyson's late poem *Columbus*, written and published in 1880:

> With regard to this poem a serious charge of plagiarism was brought against the poet by Mr. Eric Mackay, who pointed out that it is little more than an adaptation of a poem entitled *Columbus at Seville* written by a Mr. Joseph Ellis, and published by Pickering in 1869, and in 1876. A comparison between Tennyson's poem and Mr. Ellis's certainly seems to prove beyond doubt that the Poet Laureate not only got the whole framework of his poem from Mr. Ellis's, but has appropriated many of Mr. Ellis's ideas and details. If the resemblances between the poems are coincidences, it would be difficult to match coincidences so extraordinary in the whole history of literary parallels. Of one thing there can be no doubt, that the first edition of Mr. Ellis's poem appeared eleven years, and the second four years, before Tennyson's.

Was Tennyson, then, despite his denials, a serial plagiarist? Did Collins, despite his assertions to the contrary, think him so? As to the first question what can, I think, be said is that Tennyson's repeated insistence that he only rarely consciously and deliberately borrowed anything from anyone is as questionable as Collins's repeated insistence that he believed the same thing.[22] Based on the enormous number of textual parallels to prior works to be found in Tennyson's poems—those previously identified, plus those first reported in this study—a fundamental and lifelong aspect of Tennyson's art would seem to have been his habit of echoing any work, ancient or modern, which he had read and at least half-consciously recalled, that his creative intelligence

---

22 In a footnote on pp. xxxvii–xxxviii of the Introduction to his revised edn of *The Early Poems of Alfred Lord Tennyson* (London: Methuen, 1901), Collins continued to insist that his writings on Tennyson, including in *Illustrations*, did not constitute a charge of plagiarism: 'And may I here take the opportunity of pointing out that nothing could have been farther from my intention in that book than what has so often been most unfairly attributed to it, namely, an attempt to show that a charge of plagiarism might be justly urged against Tennyson. No honest critic, who had even cursorily inspected the book, could so utterly misrepresent its purpose.'

told him would enhance the resonance or deepen the meaning of his poems.

These textual parallels do not, in my view, reflect a lack of imagination or a want of originality, but an imagination of enormous range and power that regarded everything he had ever read, as well as the world around him, the people he knew, the people he loved (or didn't), and his own personal and emotional experience, as the raw material of his art. If Tennyson's lifelong practice of crafting poems in this manner left and leaves him susceptible, however unjustly, to the charge of plagiarism, so be it. The fact remains that in doing so, Tennyson masterfully created some of the most memorable and original poems ever written in the English language.[23] That this is so has often been observed, beginning with Arthur Hallam,

> Originality of observation seems to cost nothing to our author's liberal genius; he lavishes images of exquisite accuracy and elaborate splendour, as a common writer throws about metaphorical truisms, and exhausted tropes.[24]

and also, among others, by John Wilson Croker, reviewing Tennyson's *Poems* (1833):

> We pass by several songs, sonnets, and small pieces, all of singular merit, to arrive at a class, we may call them, of three poems derived from mythical sources — Œnone, the Hesperides, and the Lotos-eaters. But

---

23 Among the best examinations of Tennyson's allusive practices and purposes, Collins's insinuations, and related topics is the chapter on Tennyson in Christopher Ricks, *Allusion to the Poets* (Oxford: Oxford University Press, 2002), pp. 179–216 — first published as 'Tennyson Inheriting the Earth' in *Studies in Tennyson*, ed. by Hallam Tennyson (London: Macmillan, 1981), pp. 66–104. See also Robert Pattison, *Tennyson and Tradition* (Cambridge, Mass. and London: Harvard University Press, 1979), esp. chap. 1, 'Tennyson and the Uses of Tradition', pp. 1–14; Theodore Redpath, 'Tennyson and the Literature of Greece and Rome' in *Studies in Tennyson*, pp. 105–30; Robert Douglas-Fairhurst, 'Shakespeare's Weeds: Tennyson, Elegy and Allusion', in *Victorian Shakespeare*, ed. by Gail Marshall and Adrian Poole, 2 vols. (Basingstoke: Palgrave Macmillan, 2004), vol. 2, pp. 114–30; Douglas-Fairhurst's 'Introduction' in *Tennyson Among the Poets: Bicentenary Essays*, ed. by Robert Douglas-Fairhurst and Seamus Perry (Oxford: Oxford University Press, 2009), pp. 1–13, esp. pp. 5–7; and, in the same volume, Christopher Decker, 'Tennyson's Limitations', pp. 57–75.

24 'On Some of the Characteristics of Modern Poetry, and on the Lyrical Poems of Alfred Tennyson', *The Englishman's Magazine*, vol. 1, no. 5 (Aug. 1831), 616–28, reviewing Tennyson's *Poems, Chiefly Lyrical* (1830).

though the subjects are derived from classical antiquity, Mr. Tennyson treats them with so much originality that he makes them exclusively his own.[25]

by Robert Browning,

> 'Tennyson suspected of plagiarism!' I once heard Browning say, when this subject was mentioned: 'Why, you might as well suspect the Rothschilds of picking pockets'.[26]

by Robert Pattison,

> If Tennyson is in fact another Vergil, he is so because he treats his sources in the same way the Roman poet treats his: as the evidences of a plastic tradition to be evolved through the cultural process of poetry. The author of the *Aeneid* ransacked ancient culture to produce a distinct and wholly original epitome of the world as he saw it. Tennyson used the tradition in exactly this Vergilian way.[27]

and by Theodore Redpath:

> Tennyson could, I believe, have afforded to rest on his real originality; but it is, I suppose, understandable that he should have been sufficiently moved to permit himself to call Churton Collins 'a louse on the locks of literature' or 'a jackass', whichever, if either, was the description of Collins that he communicated to Edmund Gosse at that tea-party at Aldworth in the summer of 1886.[28]

As for Collins, what matters about his work on Tennyson more than his questioning of Tennyson's originality is the extraordinary range of his reading in classical and modern literature and his seeming ability to recall and compare to every poem in the Tennyson canon everything he had ever read. Tennyson disputed or dismissed nearly all of Collins's findings (those, at least, in the first *Cornhill* article), and others, myself included, may deem some of those findings less than convincing. But Collins's accomplishment in identifying so many credible examples

---

25 J. W. Croker, 'Poems by Alfred Tennyson', *The Quarterly Review*, vol. 49, no. 97 (Apr. 1833), 81–96. Repr. in *Tennyson: The Critical Heritage*, ed. by John D. Jump (London: Routledge & Kegan Paul, 1967), pp. 66–83.

26 Quoted by W. E. H. Lecky in *Memoir*, vol. 2, p. 204; also by Ricks in *Allusion to the Poets*, p. 179.

27 Pattison, *Tennyson and Tradition*, pp. 2–3.

28 Redpath, 'Tennyson and the Literature of Greece and Rome', p. 111.

of Tennyson's textual parallels—and in doing so a century before the arrival of digitized texts and online search tools—can only be called remarkable.

In this study, having made extensive use of those digitized texts and search tools to complement my own far less than photographic memory, I am pleased to present my findings. In purely quantitative terms, out of the total of nearly five hundred poems to which Christopher Ricks assigned numeric or alphanumeric designations in his three-volume edition of Tennyson, some one hundred eighty contain one or more phrases or short passages bearing a strong, previously undocumented resemblance to, and in most instances exactly matching, corresponding phrases and passages in poems, plays, and other works by Tennyson's literary and other predecessors (including the King James Version of the Bible) from classical to modern times. The total number of phrases and short passages in Tennyson poems newly found to have one or more such textual antecedents—including antecedents matching Tennyson's actual language more closely than any previously adduced—is just over seven hundred fifty. And, reflecting the fact that many of these phrases and short passages occur verbatim or very nearly so two or more times in works that predate him, the total number of textual antecedents discussed in this study is double that number, or more than fifteen hundred items.

Most of the poets and others to whose works (in English, sometimes in Greek, Latin, or Italian, often in translation) these newly identified textual parallels appear to point are already familiar names in Tennyson editions and studies: Blake, Byron, Campbell, Coleridge, Cowper, Dante, Dryden, Homer, Horace, Keats, Macpherson/Ossian, Milton, James Montgomery, Robert Montgomery, Moore, Ovid, Petrarch, Pope, Scott, Shakespeare, Shelley, Southey, Spenser, Thomson, Virgil, Thomas Warton, Wordsworth, and Young, to name just a few.[29]

But many others whose works also appear to be recognizably, often perfectly, and sometimes repeatedly echoed in the new examples have

---

29   For a full-length study focused entirely on Tennyson's echoes of, and borrowings from, a single canonical author, see Jayne Thomas, *Tennyson Echoing Wordsworth* (Edinburgh: Edinburgh University Press, 2019). Thomas argues that Wordsworth both informs and deforms Tennyson's major poetry, but is integral to the later poet's sense of his own poetic identity.

made few if any prior appearances in such editions and studies. They include, among others, Anna Lætitia (née Aikin) Barbauld, Richard Blackmore, Erasmus Darwin, Michael Drayton, Charles Abraham Elton, Thomas Gisborne, Letitia Elizabeth Landon, John Langhorne, John Ogilvie, Richard Polwhele, Eleanor Anne Porden, Mary Robinson, Charlotte Smith, John Wilson (except, writing as 'Christopher North', as a critic of Tennyson's poetry) and, in particular, Felicia Hemans, recognizable echoes of whose lyric and narrative poems—be they conscious and deliberate, accidental, or somewhere in between—occur in Tennyson's, by my count, just over forty times.

Given the large number of textual parallels noted in this study, an extended analysis of the critical significance of each one was clearly out of the question. I have therefore in most instances based my approach to such parallels on that usually taken by Ricks in his complete and selected editions. As in those editions, however, where a given textual parallel called for more extensive discussion, my comments on it are accordingly expanded. I hope and expect that Tennyson scholars will have more to say about many of these new textual parallels and what they signify in future Tennyson studies.

In cases where two or more antecedent poems, plays, or other works contain phrases or short passages with equally plausible claims to having suggested or supplied corresponding language in a Tennyson poem, I have presented up to several such antecedent instances, in chronological order, without arbitrarily selecting or preferring one over others. Readers may decide for themselves which if any of the quoted examples Tennyson is likely to have had in mind.

Also, in many instances—particularly those involving less familiar and readily available pre-Tennyson ('pre-T.') poems—rather than quoting only the specific words of an antecedent phrase, I have aimed to provide enough text from its own and sometimes neighboring lines to give readers a better sense of its immediate context and why Tennyson may have found it of interest or relevance in writing his own poem.

Numbers before the titles of Tennyson poems are those assigned by Ricks. An asterisk following a poem number indicates that the poem appears in both the selected (one-volume) and the complete (three-volume) Ricks editions; the absence of an asterisk, that it appears only in the latter. Dates in parentheses following the titles of Tennyson poems indicate when, if known, he wrote the poem in question (*wr*); or, if not, when it was first published (*pub*). Dates given for antecedent works discussed are of first publication, not composition. Unless otherwise stated, all books cited were first published in London. All emphasis in quoted text is original, not added.

Books known to have been in the library of Tennyson's father, George Clayton Tennyson, at Somersby or owned and/or read by the poet himself and later acquired by or deposited in the Tennyson Research Centre, City Library, Lincoln, England, as listed in volume one of *Tennyson in Lincoln: A Catalogue of the Collections in the Research Centre* compiled by Nancie Campbell (Lincoln: Tennyson Society, 1971) — hereinafter '*Lincoln*' — are identified as such. It should be kept in mind, however, that as the Cataloguer's Notes on pp. xv–xvi of that volume point out, many of the books once owned by Tennyson or members of his family were dispersed during or after his lifetime,[30] and that some of the books held by the Centre when the catalogue was prepared were subsequently sold; so that a book's absence from the catalogue or the collection should not be taken to mean that Tennyson could not once have owned and/or read it and echoed it in his work.

R. H. Winnick
Princeton, New Jersey

---

30 An entry (Item 2595) in the section of *Lincoln* devoted to the library of T.'s poet-brother Charles Tennyson (later Charles Tennyson Turner) is instructive. It lists as one of that library's holdings vol. 2 of the two-volume 1829 Whittaker edn of the works of Theocritus, Bion, and Moschus, in Greek and Latin, then quotes a note written by Charles on that volume's inside front board: 'Charles Turner, Friday 14 January, 1848. 2 volumes bought of Alfred, at his clearing off of duplicate and old books, some time ago.' Another entry (Item 86) in the section of *Lincoln* devoted to the library of George Clayton Tennyson is similarly instructive. It lists one of the several partial or complete edns of the works of Cicero in that library, then quotes a note, also presumably by Charles, on the fly-leaf of vol. 1: 'E. libris G. C. Tennyson, Coll. St. Johan. Cantabr. E. libris Alfred Tennyson. Trin. Coll. Cantabr. E. libris Caroli [i.e., Charles] Turner, taken with a lot of others, in a clearance of old books, of which partly, Alfred had duplicates.'

The Textual Parallels

1A Three Translations of Horace[1] (*wr* c. 1822)

i 8. 'And this praetexta's purple shade'. While the *purple* of his translation comes directly from line 7 (*'per hoc inane purpurae decus precor'*) of Horace's fifth epode, which 'concerns the preparation for the ritual murder of a young boy, kidnapped by the witch Canidia',[2] T.'s *purple shade* suggests he may also have had in mind Wordsworth's *An Evening Walk, Addressed to a Young Lady*, lines 102–3 of which read, in the poem as published in the 1793 and subsequent versions, 'There, objects, by the searching beams betrayed, / Come forth, and here retire in purple shade'; or perhaps Mary Robinson's *Sight. Inscribed to John Taylor, Esq. Oculist to His Majesty.* (also first published in 1793) 52–54: 'Then what to him avails the varying year, / The orient morn, or evening's purple shade, / That robes Creation in a garb of rest?'

ii 27. 'The mazy dance—the power of love.' For *mazy dance*, cp. Thomas Moore, *Lalla Rookh: An Oriental Tale* (1817), Part I ('The Veiled Prophet of Khorassan'), p. 60: 'He sees a group of female forms advance, / Some chain'd together in the mazy dance'.[3]

iii 5. 'And red right-arm of mighty Jove'. As Ricks notes, Pollard compares Milton's *Paradise Lost* ii 174: 'His red right hand.'[4] But cp. also Byron's *Translation From Horace*—his rendering of a passage in Horace's

---

1 Among the several works by Horace in George Clayton Tennyson's library at Somersby (Items 162 through 166 in *Lincoln*) were the two-volume fourth (1760) Hitch edn of *The Works of Horace; translated into English prose with the original Latin, begun by David Watson and revised by S. Patrick*, with 'A. Tennyson' written inside the front board of vol. 1; and the four-volume 1767 Flexney edn of Horace's *Works, translated into verse; with notes by Christopher Smart*. T. himself owned eight partial or complete edns of Horace (Items 1186 through 1193 in *Lincoln*), six in Latin and two in translation, the latter edited by Theodore Martin (1860) and by Sir Stephen E. De Vere (1888).
2 A. Pollard, 'Three Horace Translations by Tennyson', *Tennyson Research Bulletin*, vol. 4, no. 1 (1982), 16–24.
3 Based on the entries in *Lincoln*, T. owned several partial or complete edns of Moore's poems (Items 1621 through 1626), including vol. 2 only of the ten-volume 1840–41 Longman edn of *The Poetical Works of Thomas Moore, collected by himself*, in which *Lalla Rookh* occupied vol. 6; and all ten volumes of Longman's 1853–54 edn, in which *Lalla Rookh* occupied the same volume. None of the edns of Moore reported in *Lincoln* predate T.'s poem.
4 Unless otherwise indicated, all citations of *Paradise Lost* herein refer to the second, 1674 version. T.'s library contained nine edns of Milton's poetical works (Items 1596 through 1604 in *Lincoln*). The library of T.'s brother Charles (see preface, note 30)

Odes III iii, first published in *Hours of Idleness* (1807) — with, in line 9: 'Ay, and the red right arm of Jove'.

iii *80*. 'In evil hour'. Ricks notes that the phrase occurs in *Paradise Lost* ix 1067–68 ('O *Eve*, in evil hour thou didst give eare / To that false Worm'). It also occurs in *PL* ix 780–81: 'So saying, her rash hand in evil hour / Forth reaching to the Fruit, she pluck'd, she eat'; and in works by several later poets.[5]

iii *83–85*. 'Again should sound the battle's jar: / The neighing steed, the clattering car / Again should hurry to the war.' The lines may reflect T.'s reading of Byron's *Childe Harold's Pilgrimage*, Canto III (1816) xxv 1–4: 'And there was mounting in hot haste: the steed, / The mustering squadron, and the clattering car, / Went pouring forward with impetuous speed, / And swiftly forming in the ranks of war'.[6]

1 Translation of Claudian's 'Rape of Proserpine' (*wr* c. 1820–23)

1. 'The gloomy chariot of the God of night'. Cp. Rev. Joseph Beaumont, *Psyche, or, Loves mysterie in XX. canto's: displaying the intercourse betwixt Christ and the soule.* (1648) VIII cclix, beginning: 'Then to her gloomy Chariot she went, / Which of a poisnous Vapour framed was'. In a later, revised and enlarged version of the same poem (1702), *gloomy chariot* occurs in VIII cclxxxvi 1–2: 'Then to her gloomy Chariot she went, / A Chariot framéd of a pois'nous Steam'.

---

    also contained a complete (1839) one-volume edn of Milton's *Poetical Works* [Item 2530 in *Lincoln*], on the fly-leaf of which T. at some point wrote 'Alfred Tennyson'.

5   Including, among others, John Philips in *Cyder, A Poem in Two Books* (1708), Book II, 462–64: 'What shall we say / Of rash *Elpenor*, who in evil Hour / Dry'd an immeasurable Bowl'; from the 1788 Dodsley edn of his poems that T.'s father owned (Item 5 in *Lincoln*), Mark Akenside in *Hymn to the Naiads* (1746), Ode XVIII. *To the Right Honourable Francis Earl of Huntingdon*, 28: 'By flattering minstrels paid in evil hour'; Eleanor Anne (later 'Franklin') Porden in *The Veils; or the Triumph of Constancy. A Poem, in Six Books* (1815), Book II, 216–19: 'He ceased: in evil hour the listening throng / Their praises of this artful speech prolong; / In evil hour, this plan the monarch chose, / And bade his warriors snatch a short repose.'; and Byron, *A Very Mournful Ballad on the Siege and Conquest of Alhama* (1818), 46–47: 'By thee were slain, in evil hour, / The Abencerrage, Granada's flower'.

6   The three-volume 1819 Murray edn of Byron's *Works*, with *Childe Harold* I through IV in vol. 1, was at Somersby (Item 67 in *Lincoln*).

2. 'And the wan stars that sickened at the sight'. Ricks cites *Paradise Lost* x 412, 'the blasted Starrs lookt wan'; and Pope's *Dunciad* (1742 version) iv 636, 'The sickening stars'. But *the wan stars* itself occurs in Erasmus Darwin's *The Botanic Garden* (1791), Part I ('The Economy of Vegetation'), Canto I, line 134, 'The wan stars glimmering through its silver train'; in line 317, 'The wan stars danced between', of Coleridge's *The Rime of the Ancient Mariner* (1800 version); in Shelley's *Alastor, or, The Spirit of Solitude* (1816) 554, 'Beneath the wan stars and descending moon'; and in his *Laon and Cythna* (1817) — revised and reissued as *The Revolt of Islam* (1818), where the phrase also occurs — III xviii 5, 'Soon the wan stars came forth'.

3. 'And the dark nuptials of the infernal King'. The preface of Thomas Noble's 1808 translation of Book I of the *Argonautica* of Gaius Valerius Flaccus has, on pp. xxi–xxii, for *'Tristes thalamos, infestaque cerno / Omnia, vipereos ipsi tibi surgere crines!'* (from Book VII, lines 249–50), 'Now all is woe! — dark nuptials meet my eyes! / E'en 'mid thy tresses writhing snakes arise!'

7–8. 'Seraphic transports through my bosom roll, / All Phoebus fills my heart and fires my soul.' For *seraphic transports*, cp. Thomas Otway, *Alcibiades, A Tragedy* (1675) II i: "Tis the improvement of the part divine, / When souls in their Seraphick transports joyn'; and Rev. Thomas Raffles, *The Messiah* (1814) — a prose translation from the German of Friedrich Gottlieb Klopstock's epic *Der Messias* (1748–73) — vol. 3, p. 174: 'Low and tremulous the song began; but soon the angelic harps inspired the soul with seraphic transports, and struck to tones of deepest, loudest, sublimest harmony.'

27–28. 'Ye mighty Demons, whose tremendous sway / The shadowy tribes of airy Ghosts obey'. For *the shadowy tribes*, cp. William Collins, *Ode on the Poetical Character* (1746) 47–48: 'All the shad'wy Tribes of Mind / In braided Dance their Murmurs join'd'; and, from Rev. Thomas Grinfield's translation of *Aeneid* vi (1815), p. 230: 'The' [sic] astonish'd chief starts at the sudden view, / And asks the cause, unknowing; what yon stream, / And what the shadowy tribes that crowd her marge'.

For *airy ghosts*, cp. Dryden's *Æneis* (1697) vi 540–41: 'Still may the Dog the wand'ring Troops constrain / Of Airy Ghosts, and vex the guilty

Train'; and, from vol. 2 of the spurious but widely read *Poems of Ossian, Originally Translated by James Macpherson, Esq., Attempted in English Verse By the Late Rev. John Shackleton* (1817), *The Songs of Selma* 129–30: 'What shall I offer in your praise / Your airy ghosts to cheer?'

31. 'Whom livid Styx with lurid torrent bounds'. Cp. *styx livida* in the first-century epic *Thebaid* of Statius, i 57: '*tuque umbrifero styx livida fundo*';[7] or, in lines 83–84 of Pope's 1712 translation of the passage in which it occurs: 'Thou, sable Styx! whose livid streams are roll'd / Thro' dreary coasts, which I tho' blind behold'. Even closer to T.'s language are the closing lines of John Dart's 1720 translation of Tibullus's Book III, Elegy III: 'Where livid *Styx* rolls on his lazy Tide, / By dreary Confines bound on every Side.'

36. 'The dread Arcana of the Stygian reign'. Cp. Edward Richard Poole, *Byzantium: A Dramatic Poem* (1823), p. 71 (Gennadius speaking): 'His grave—a wilderness of thought; and that / Which flourished once— barren, for ever lost: / Now, would'st thou penetrate the dread arcana, speak?'

48. 'Of every God upon his glittering throne'. Cp., from Michael Drayton's *Pastorals* (1619), *Pastoral I: The First Eglogue* 39–40: 'Before the Footstoole of whose glittering Throne, / Those thy high Orders severally are placed'; Homer's *Odyssey* as translated by Alexander Pope, William Broome, and Elijah Fenton (1726) viii 25–26: 'Then from his glittering throne Alcinoüs rose: / Attend, he cry'd, while we our will disclose.';[8] and Moore's *Lalla Rookh*, Part I, p. 19: 'The Young all dazzled by the

---

[7] T. owned the 1822 Rodwell edn of *P[ublius]. Papinii Statii Opera, sedula recensione accurata* [The Works of Statius], ed. by John Carey (Item 2108 in *Lincoln*), which included the *Thebaid*, the *Silvae*, and the incomplete *Achilleid*.

[8] Based on the entries in *Lincoln*, George Clayton Tennyson and T. between them owned nearly twenty edns of Homer, roughly evenly divided between Greek only, Greek and Latin, and English only versions. Translations into English included, among others, those by George Chapman (Item 1172 in *Lincoln*), Charles Merivale (Item 1174), Andrew Lang, Walter Leaf, and Ernest Myers (Item 1175), and Henry Alford (Item 1177). Judging from *Lincoln* alone, neither T. nor his father owned the Pope–Broome–Fenton *Odyssey*, despite its many echoes in T.'s poems. Although the entry in *Lincoln* (Item 2483) gives no indication of T.'s having read it, the library of T.'s brother Charles as catalogued had vol. 1 only of the two-volume 1820 Chiswick edn of that translation.

plumes and lances, / The glittering throne, and Haram's half-caught glances'.

49. 'Should lead a dull and melancholy life'. Robert Burton's *The Anatomy of Melancholy* (1621) has, in Part I, Section 2, Subsection 5 ('Bad Air a cause of Melancholy'): 'but if it be a turbulent, rough, cloudy, stormy weather, men are sad, lumpish, and much dejected, angry, waspish, dull, and melancholy.'[9] Cp. also William Law's *A Serious Call to a Devout and Holy Life* (1729), chap. 11: 'That instead of making our lives dull and melancholy, [these rules of holy living unto God] will render them full of content and strong satisfactions.' Poetic instances of *dull and melancholy* include Stephen Duck's *The Thresher's Labour* (1730; rev. 1736) 60–61: 'Tis all a dull and melancholy Scene, / Fit only to provoke the Muse's Spleen'; and, from his *Tales in Verse* (1812), Rev. George Crabbe's *Tale X. The Lover's Journey.* 6–7: 'Again they sicken, and on every view / Cast their own dull and melancholy hue'.[10]

54. 'And fill the wide abyss with loud alarms'. For the latter phrase Ricks cites Dryden's *Cymon and Iphigenia* (1700) 399, 'The Country rings around with loud Alarms', but the phrase also occurs a total of five times in Books VII (lines 64 and 855) and VIII (lines 579, 721, and 926) of Dryden's *Æneis*; again in Book IV, line 358, of his *Georgics* (both 1697); and, among other works by other hands, in Pope's *Rape of the Lock* (1714) v 48, and twice in his *Iliad* (1715–20), in xvi 691 and 771.

55. 'The haggard train of midnight Furies meet'. Among other instances of *haggard train*, cp. Samuel Whyte's *Elegy I* (1770) 25–28, 'To some such drear and solemn scene, / Some friendly power direct my way, / Where pale Misfortune's haggard train, / Sad luxury! delight to stray.'; and Thomas Dermody's *Ode to Terror* (1789), which begins 'Hark! how the troubled air, / Resounds the scream of wan Despair, — / While Terror, ghastly spirit, huge and tall, / Array'd in sable robe, and mourning pall, / Attended by her haggard train / Of murd'rous sprites, and goblins

---

9   George Clayton Tennyson's library at Somersby had the two-volume eleventh (1806) Vernor, Hood and Sharpe edn of Burton's work (Item 63 in *Lincoln*).

10 As recorded in *Lincoln* (Item 2443), Charles Tennyson's library had vol. 2 only of the two-volume second (1812) Hatchard edn of Crabbe's *Tales*, with 'Alfred Tennyson' written on the title page. In that edn, *Tale X. The Lover's Journey.* was printed in vol. 1.

drear / In sullen grandeur stalks along the plain, / While Nature starts, and Pity pleads in vain.'

For *midnight Furies*, cp. Francis Hoyland's *Rural Happiness, An Elegy* (1763) xii 1–2: 'Thrice happy swains! your silent hours / These midnight Furies ne'er molest'.

60. 'The gleaming Pine shoots forth a dismal light'. After what seems to have been the first occurrence of *dismal light* in Abraham Cowley's *Davideis, a Sacred Poem of the Troubles of David* (1656) iv 556–57: 'As when a wrathful *Dragons* dismal light / Strikes suddenly some warlike *Eagles* sight',[11] the phrase became something of a cliché, occurring, for example, three times in Sir Richard Blackmore's *Prince Arthur* (1695) and once each in Wordsworth's *Salisbury Plain* (1794) 95–96: 'again the desert groans, / A dismal light its farthest bounds illumes'; and Sir Walter Scott's *Rokeby* (1813) xxxiv 6: 'But soon shall dawn a dismal light!'

61–62. 'Around her head the snaky volumes rise / And dart their tongues of flame and roll their gory eyes.' For *snaky volumes*, cp. Henry James Pye's *Alfred: An Epic Poem* (1801) iv 729–30: 'There Cambria's griffin, on the azure field, / In snaky volumes writhes around the shield'; in vol. 2 of his *Fables*, Richard Wharton's *Cambuscan, An Heroic Poem, In Six Books* (1805)—his version of Chaucer's *Squire's Tale*—with, on p. 20: 'Of copper was the roof; and round its rim / Four snaky volumes cast a fiery gleam'; Margaret Holford's anonymously published *Wallace; or, The Fight of Falkirk; A Metrical Romance* (1809) III xlv 3: 'There envy's snaky volumes rest'; and Porden's *The Veils* iii 93: 'There giant Draco's snaky volumes roll'.

64. 'And Earth's fell offspring burst their brazen chain'. Ricks cites *Paradise Lost* x 697, 'Bursting thir brazen Dungeon'; but cp. also the instances of *brazen chain* itself in Blackmore's *King Arthur: An Heroick Poem in Twelve Books* (1697) iii 9–10: 'On this sharp Rock did the dire Fiend remain / Bound with a vast, unweildy, brazen chain.'; Sir Charles Abraham Elton's *Elegy XIV, after Propertius* (1810) 13–16: 'Let brazen bonds my shackled arms restrain, / Or Danae's iron tower my prison

---

11 Charles Tennyson's library had the three-volume (1802–6) Heath edn of Cowley's *Works* (Item 2439 in *Lincoln*), with 'A. Tennyson' on the fly-leaf of vol. 1 and the *Davideis* in vol. 2.

be; / For thee, my life! I'd burst the brazen chain, / And break through Danae's iron tower to thee'; and *Revolt of Islam* iii 1270–71: 'I gnawed my brazen chain, and sought to sever / Its adamantine links, that I might die'.

70. 'And dared the forkèd terrors of the sky'. Ricks cites Shelley's *Prologue to Hellas* (1822) 145, 'the hundred-forkèd snake'; but cp. also Coleridge's *Dura Navis* (1787) 12–16: 'Whilst total darkness overspreads the skies; / Save when the lightnings darting wingéd Fate / Quick bursting from the pitchy clouds between / In forkéd Terror, and destructive state / Shall shew with double gloom the horrid scene?'

74. 'Those awful hands which make the world their own'. Cp. Pope's *Iliad* xx 23–24, 'What moves the God who Heav'n and earth commands, / And grasps the thunder in his awful hands'; Isaac Watts, *To Her Majesty* (1721) 62–63: 'for by thine awful hands / Heaven rules the waves, and thunders o'er the lands'; and the sonnet by Henry Kirke White—appearing in vol. 2 of his posthumous *Poetical Remains* (1807) edited by Robert Southey—beginning: 'What art thou, MIGHTY ONE! and where thy seat? / Thou broodest on the calm that cheers the lands. / And thou dost bear within thine awful hands, / The rolling thunders and the lightnings fleet.' T. may also have had in mind William Blake's *Jerusalem, The Emanation of the Giant Albion* (1804–20) plate 48, lines 30–32, reading in part: 'With awful hands, she took / A Moment of Time, drawing it out with many tears & afflictions, / And many sorrows'.

113–14. 'Himself the God of terrors, reared on high, / Sits throned in shades of midnight majesty'. For the latter phrase, cp. Samuel Rogers, *The Voyage of Columbus* (1810), Canto VII ('The New World') 41–42: 'Here blue savannas fade into the sky. / There forests frown in midnight majesty'.[12]

119–20. 'The bellowing beast that guards the gates of Hell / Repressed the thunder of his triple yell'. Cp. Allan Ramsay, *The Miser and Minos* (1760) 29–30, where, when the Miser arrives in Hades, having swum across the river Styx to avoid paying Charon's fare, 'the three-pow'd dog

---

[12] The 1812 Cadell and Davies edn of Rogers's *Poems*, including this one, was at Somersby (Item 285 in *Lincoln*).

of hell / Gowl'd terrible a triple yell'; W. L. Lewis's 1767 translation of Statius's *Thebaid* vii 782–83, *'audio iam rapidae cursum Stygis atraque Ditis / flumina tergeminosque mali custodis hiatus'*, as (lines 1053–54): 'E'en now I hear the Porter's triple Yell, / Hoarse-sounding *Styx*, and all the Streams of Hell'; and, also referring to Cerberus, lines 510–11 of J. J. Howard's 1807 translation of a passage in Book VII of Ovid's *Metamorphoses*: 'With rabid anger swol'n, a triple yell / Fill'd all the air'.

124. 'His hoarse waves slumbered on his noiseless bed'. For *hoarse waves*, cp. Francis Fawkes's translation (1760) of Grammaticus Musaeus's *De Herone et Leandro* as *The Loves of Hero and Leander*, 318–19: 'Guard well its light, when wintry tempests roar, / And hoarse waves break tumultuous on the shore'; Thomas Gray's translation (written 1737; published 1814) *From Tasso [La Gerusalemme Liberata]* XIV xxxii 5–6: 'Nor yet in prospect rose the distant shore; / Scarce the hoarse waves from far were heard to roar'; and Francis Hodgson's *The Friends* (1818) IV liii 5–6: 'Through black Cayuga's rocks, the indignant tide / Rears its hoarse waves on high, repulsed from either side.'

2 The Devil and the Lady (*wr* c. 1823–25)

I i 3–5. 'while the arrowy bolt / With ravaging course athwart the dark immense / Comes rushing on its wings of fire'. For *dark immense*, Ricks cites *Paradise Lost* ii 829: 'the void immense'. But cp. also, by Mrs. F. Ryves, *Cumbrian Legends; or, Tales of Other Times* (Edinburgh, 1812), which begins with an *Address* in verse reading in part (lines 7–11): 'and when, on every side, / Flames the red flash, and flows th' ensanguined tide, / Creeps th' insidious drug, and speeds the poniard wide;— / Nature looks up, and thro' the dark immense, / Beholds one ray to glad the sick'ning sense: —'.

I i 7–8. 'Gives answer to his brother winds that rave / From the three corners of the lurid sky.' Pre-T. instances of *lurid sky* occur in chap. 4 of Shelley's early Gothic novella *Zastrozzi, a Romance* (1810): 'The lurid sky was tinged with a yellowish lustre'; and in scene 3 of Byron's closet drama *Heaven and Earth: A Mystery* (1823): 'Hark! hark! the sea-birds cry! / In clouds they overspread the lurid sky'. Another such instance occurs in Rev. George Woodley's *Mount-Edgcumbe* (1804) 157–60: 'Oft too, when hoary Etna whirls on high / Whole burning rocks, that brave the lurid sky, / The firy seas that from its bosom flow, / In cureless ruin lay the vales below!'

I i 58. 'A murrain take thine ill timed pleasantry.' Cp. 'The powerful hold in deep remembrance an ill-timed pleasantry', an oft-repeated adage translating Tacitus's *Annales* v 2: *'Facetiarum apud praepotentes in longum memoria est'*.[13]

I i 84–85. 'I'd dive i' the sea, / I'd ride the chariot of the rocking winds'. Cp. *Psalm* civ 3: 'Who layeth the beams of his chambers in the waters: who maketh the clouds his chariot: who walketh upon the wings of the wind';[14] Milton's *Il Penseroso* (1645) 121–26: 'Thus night oft see me in thy pale career, / Till civil-suited Morn appeer, / Not trickt and frounc't as she was wont, / With the Attick Boy to hunt, / But Cherchef't in a comly Cloud, / While rocking Winds are Piping loud'; and Christopher Smart's *On the Immensity of the Supreme Being: A Poetical Essay* (1751) 111–15: 'What are yon tow'rs / The work of lab'ring man and clumsy art / Seen with the ring-dove's nest—on that tall beech / Her pensile house the feather'd Artist builds— / The rocking winds molest her not'.

I i 87. 'Or from the hornèd corners of the moon'. Cp. *Macbeth* III v 23–24 (Hecate speaking): 'Upon the corner of the moon / There hangs a vap'rous drop profound'.[15] Also Milton's *Comus* (1634) 1012–17: 'But now my task is smoothly don, / I can fly, or I can run / Quickly to the green earths end, / Where the bow'd welkin slow doth bend, / And from thence can soar as soon / To the corners of the Moon.'

I i 90–92. 'Of the Ecliptic and the spangled Lyre / Or that dim star which in Boötes' Wain / Shines nightly'. In Edward Young's *Imperium Pelagi. A*

---

13   George Clayton Tennyson's library at Somersby had three edns of Tacitus, two in Latin (both signed by T.) and one in French (Items 335 through 337 in *Lincoln*). T. himself owned a three-volume Latin edn published in Paris in 1760 (Item 2157 in *Lincoln*), on the fly-leaf of vol. 1 of which he wrote 'Alfred Tennyson, Trin. Coll. Cambridge.'
14   All scriptural quotations herein, including this one, are based on the King James Version of the Bible.
15   All Shakespeare quotations herein, and all associated line numbers, are based on the text in *The Riverside Shakespeare*, ed. by G. Blakemore Evans (Boston: Houghton Mifflin, 1997).

Naval Lyric. (1730), cp. stanza iii of *The Merchant. Ode the First. Strain the Fifth*: 'Here no demand for Fancy's wing; / Plain Truth's illustrious: as I sing, / O hear yon spangled harp repeat my lay! / Yon starry lyre has caught the sound, / And spreads it to the planets round, / Who best can tell where ends Britannia's sway.'

I ii 26. 'In all his sinews like a sensitive plant'. T. may have had in mind any or all of at least four poems about the readily anthropomorphized perennial herb *Mimosa pudica*, the so-called 'sensitive plant', a species notable for the tendency of its leaves to fold if touched, shaken, or otherwise disturbed: the first of the four, James Perry's *Mimosa: or, the Sensitive Plant* (1779):

> Enamour'd of your melting eye,
> It grows more stiff, erect, and high,
>   As you approach the place.
> You feel the *thrill* in every *part*;
> It sends the *tremor* to your heart,
>   And *shrinks* before your face.
>
>   (lines 13–18)

the second, William Cowper's *The Poet, The Oyster, and Sensitive Plant* (1782), where the plant takes umbrage at an envious oyster:

> The plant he meant grew not far off,
> And felt the sneer with scorn enough:
> Was hurt, disgusted, mortified,
> And with asperity replied:—
>
>   (lines 17–20)[16]

the third, Darwin's *Botanic Garden*, Part II ('The Loves of the Plants'), with, in Canto I of that Part, a paean to the 'chaste Mimosa':

> Weak with nice sense, the chaste Mimosa stands,
> From each rude touch withdraws her timid hands;
> Oft as light clouds o'er-pass the Summer-glade,
> Alarm'd she trembles at the moving shade;
> And feels, alive through all her tender form,
> The whisper'd murmurs of the gathering storm;
> Shuts her sweet eye-lids to approaching night;

---

16 This poem was among those reprinted in vol. 1 of the two-volume 1808 Johnson edn of *Poems, by William Cowper*, which was at Somersby (Item 90 in *Lincoln*).

> And hails with freshen'd charms the rising light.
> (lines 267–74)

and the fourth, Shelley's 311-line *The Sensitive Plant* (1820):

> For the Sensitive Plant has no bright flower;
> Radiance and odour are not its dower;
> It loves, even like Love, its deep heart is full,
> It desires what it has not, the Beautiful!
> (lines 74–77)[17]

I iv 7–8. 'How in thy tedious absence shall I chide / The lazy motion of the lagging hours?' For *lagging hours*, cp. Shelley's fragmentary *Melody to a Scene of Former Times* (1810) 34: 'Oh! lagging hours how slow you fly!'; and his *Sensitive Plant* (see previous entry) 95–96: 'Whilst the lagging hours of the day went by / Like windless clouds o'er a tender sky.' Other instances of the phrase occur in William Pattison's *Abelard to Eloisa* (1728) 53–56: 'Amid the blaze of day, the dusk of night, / My Eloisa rises to my sight: / Veil'd, as in Paraclete's secluded towers, / The wretched mourner counts the lagging hours'; and in Richard Alfred Davenport's *Sonnet to Ianthe* (1800) 1–2: 'Loveliest and best belov'd, sever'd from thee / How oft the lagging hours I sorely chide'.

I iv 75–76. 'I have wandered far / From the utmost Arctic to its opposite'. In George Moore's *The Minstrel's Tale: And Other Poems* (1826), cp. *Ocean*, p. 69: 'The new-made waves acknowledged his controul, / From utmost arctic to antarctic pole'. The date of Moore's volume (reviewed in the September 1826 issue of, among other periodicals, *The New Monthly Magazine*) suggests that T. may still have been working on *The Devil and the Lady* when it appeared.[18]

I iv 123–24. 'Thou shrunken, sapless, wizen Grasshopper / Consuming the green promise of my youth.' Cp. Letitia Elizabeth Landon (often signing herself 'L.E.L.'), *Fragment* ('A solitude / Of green and silent beauty') 20–24, speaking of 'dark pines, which in the spring / Send

---

17 Shelley's poem first appeared in the 1820 Ollier edn of *Prometheus Unbound: a lyrical drama in four acts; with other poems*, T.'s copy of which (Item 2028 in *Lincoln*) has on its fly-leaf 'A. Tennyson, Trinity College, Cambridge.'
18 Unless, as here, otherwise indicated, all mentions of 'Moore' in this study refer to Thomas Moore, not to George or Dugald.

forth sweet odours, even as they felt / As parents do, rejoicing o'er their children / In the green promise of their youthful shoots, / The spreading of their fresh and fragrant leaves.'[19]

I iv 133. 'He bears a charmèd life and will outlast me'. Ricks notes that J. McCue compares the line to *Macbeth* V viii 12–13, where Macbeth claims to 'bear a charmed life, which must not yield / To one of woman born.' But cp. also Southey, *The Curse of Kehama* (1810) viii 117–18: 'He bears a charmed life, which may defy / All weapons'; and Scott's historical novel *Rob Roy* (1817), where in chap. 13 Miss Vernon says of the unscrupulous Raleigh Osbaldistone: 'He bears a charmed life; you cannot assail him without endangering other lives, and wider destruction.'

I v 93–94. 'Why wilt thou crouch and bow and lick the dust / Whereon thy consort treads?' Ricks cites *Paradise Lost* ix 526: 'Fawning, and lick'd the ground whereon she trod'; but cp. also *Isaiah* xlix 23: 'And kings shall be thy nursing fathers, and their queens thy nursing mothers: they shall bow down to thee with their face toward the earth, and lick up the dust of thy feet; and thou shalt know that I am the LORD: for they shall not be ashamed that wait for me.'

I v 119–20. 'I do beseech thee leave me to my thoughts / And solitude.' Cp. John Fletcher and Philip Massinger's *The False One* (1647) II iii, in which Caesar tells Antony, Dolabella, and Sceva: 'Go to your rests, and follow your own wisdoms, / And leave me to my thoughts';[20] M[atthew]. G[regory]. ('Monk') Lewis's *The Castle Spectre, a Drama in Five Acts* (1798) II iii (Percy speaking): 'Silence, fellow! — Leave me to my thoughts!'; and David Garrick's farce *The Lying Valet* (1821) I i, in which Gayless says: 'Prithee leave me to my thoughts' and Sharp replies: 'Leave you! No, not in such bad company, I'll assure you.'

---

19   Landon's fragment first appeared in the *Literary Gazette, and Journal of the Belles Lettres*, vol. 7, no. 352 (18 Oct. 1823), 667, next in 1828.

20   Formerly believed to have been written by Francis Beaumont and Fletcher, *The False One* was first published in the Beaumont and Fletcher folio of 1647. The ten-volume 1778 Evans edn of *The Dramatick Works of Beaumont and Fletcher* (Item 23 in *Lincoln*), with T.'s name written on the fly-leaf or inside front cover of three of the ten (1, 3, and 10), was at Somersby. *The False One*, still misattributed to *Beaumont* and Fletcher, is in vol. 4. (The publication date of '1788' for this edn indicated in *Lincoln* appears to be a typographical error.)

I v 163–64. 'Dost mutter? how? / Would you outface the devil, Insolence?' Cp. Thomas Heywood, *The Fair Maid of the West* (1631) I iii (Mr. Spencer speaking): 'No, sir. Could you outface the devil, / We do not fear your roaring.'; and, by the otherwise anonymous 'G. L.', *The Noble and Renowned History of Guy Earl of Warwick*, the 1821 Chiswick edition of which has, in chap. 11, on p. 89: 'Why, here is a face may well outface the devil.'

I v 207–8. 'and the keen ploughshare / Shall trench deep furrows in the inverted sky'. Cp. lines 1–2 of an alternate, possibly early, version of Shakespeare's *Sonnet 2*: 'When forty winters shall besiege thy brow / And trench deep furrows in that lovely field'.

I v 224–26. 'methinks in good truth I have hemmed in / My proposition with a sweeping circle / Of insurmountable improbabilities.' For the latter phrase, cp. James Northcote, *Memoirs of Sir Joshua Reynolds* (1813), where *insurmountable improbabilities* occurs, on p. 327, in the postscript of a letter by Reynolds concerning the authenticity of a portrait of Milton then in his possession: 'If to this it is urged, that it is too much to expect all those suppositions will be granted, we can only say, let the supposition be made of its being a forgery, and then see what insurmountable improbabilities will immediately present themselves.'

III ii 78. 'The mighty waste of moaning waters lay'. The earliest instance of *mighty waste* may be found in Samuel Daniel's *Musophilus* (1599) 145–46, speaking of Chaucer: 'Yet what a time hath he wrested from Time, / And wonne vpon the mighty waste of dayes'; followed by Drayton's *Poly-Olbion* (1612), *The Sixteenth Song* 91–92: 'Which now deuowring Time, in his so mighty waste, / Demolishing those walls, hath vtterly defac't'.; Wordsworth's *Descriptive Sketches* (1793) 408: 'A mighty waste of mist the valley fills'; John Langhorne's *The Correspondence of Theodosius and Constantia* (1796), Letter XIV: 'Mark in the mighty waste of seas and skies, / Magnificence Divine.'; Thomas Love Peacock's *Rhododaphne, or The Thessalian Spell* (1818) v 230–31: 'Through the mighty waste of waves / Speeds the vessel swift and free'; Joanna Baillie's *Christopher Columbus* (1821) xliv 2: 'The mighty waste of welt'ring waters rose'; and Felicia Hemans's *The Forest Sanctuary* (1825) I vi 8–9: 'What part hath mortal name, where God alone / Speaks to the mighty waste, and through its heart is known?'

3 Armageddon (*wr* c. 1824–27)

i 1. 'Spirit of Prophecy whose mighty grasp'. Cp. *Revelation* xix 10, ending: 'for the testimony of Jesus is the spirit of prophecy.' Also, in Blake's *All Religions Are One* (1788), Principle 5: 'The Religions of all Nations are derived from each Nation's different reception of the Poetic Genius, which is everywhere call'd the Spirit of Prophecy'; and twice in Book I of his *Milton* (1808), both on p. 23: 'He is the Spirit of Prophecy, the ever apparent Elias.' (line 71); and 'Every one is a fallen Son of the Spirit of Prophecy' (line 75).

i 2–4. 'whose capacious soul / Can people the illimitable abyss / Of vast and fathomless futurity'. Pre-T. instances of *capacious soul* include, among others, John Oldham, *An Ode of Anacreon, Paraphras'd. The Cup.* (1683) 1–4: 'Make me a Bowl, a mighty Bowl, / Large, as my capacious Soul, / Vast, as my thirst is; let it have / Depth enough to be my Grave'; Blackmore, *Prince Arthur* I i 634–35 (spoken by the Fury Persecution, and referring to '*Rome*, proud *Rome*'): 'To her wide Breast, and vast capacious Soul, / I often Torrents of black Poison rowl'; the Pope–Broome–Fenton *Odyssey* xix 325–26: 'But your wise lord, (in whose capacious soul / High schemes of pow'r in just succession roll)'; the fourth of William Hazlitt's *Lectures on the English Poets* (1818), in which he observes that 'The capacious soul of Shakspeare had an intuitive and mighty sympathy with whatever could enter into the heart of man in all possible circumstances'; and — in a poem published while T. may still have been working on *Armageddon* — Robert Pollok's *The Course of Time* (1827) iv 636–37: 'Take one example, to our purpose quite. / A man of rank, and of capacious soul' — the man being Lord Byron.

As to *people the illimitable abyss*, cp. *Paradise Lost* ii 402–5, Satan speaking: 'But first whom shall we send / In search of this new world, whom shall we find / Sufficient? who shall tempt with wandring feet / The dark unbottom'd infinite Abyss', and vii 210–11: 'On heav'nly ground they stood, and from the shore / They view'd the vast immeasurable Abyss'; the Pope–Broome–Fenton *Odyssey* xx 74–75: 'Snatch me, ye whirlwinds! far from human race, / Tost thro' the void illimitable space'; and Shelley's *Prometheus Unbound* I i 368–70: 'And my commission is to lead them here, / Or what more subtle, foul, or savage fiends / People the abyss, and leave them to their task.'

As to *vast and fathomless futurity*, cp. Young, *The Complaint: or, Night-Thoughts on Life, Death, & Immortality* (1742–45), Night Sixth ('The Infidel Reclaimed. Part I.') 250: 'The vast Unseen! the Future fathomless!' Whether or not T. read it or an account of it, the phrase 'fathomless futurity' itself occurs in the second sentence of the sermon delivered by John Henry Newman at St. Clement's, Oxford, on Sunday, 2 January 1825: 'We are called upon to reflect more seriously on the flight of time — on the shortness of life — and the still shorter space which remains for us before the day of death — and of the immense and boundless and fathomless futurity which lies stretched out beyond it.'[21]

i 5–9. 'With all the Giant Figures that shall pace / The dimness of its stage, – whose subtle ken / Can throng the doubly-darkened firmament / Of Time to come with all its burning stars / At awful intervals.' Cp. Thomas Heywood, *The Golden Age. Or The liues of Iupiter and Saturne, with the deifying of the heathen gods* (1611) III i (Saturn speaking): 'I am all sad, / All horrou[r] and afrightment, since the slaughter / And tragick murder of my first borne *Ops*, / Continued in the vnnaturall massacre / Of three yong Princes: not a day hath left me / Without distast, no night but double darkned / With terrour and confused melancholy'.

i 32. 'Never set sun with such portentous glare'. Cp., among other instances of the latter phrase, Rev. John Ogilvie's *Rona, A Poem, in Seven Books* (1777), Book VI, p. 172: 'As on the cloud (when with portentous glare / Dire forms tremendous ride the vault of air)'; William Hamilton Drummond, *The Battle of Trafalgar, a Heroic Poem* (Belfast, 1806) ii 403–4: 'The glowing timbers shoot portentous glare, / The wheeled artillery thunder in the air'; and Southey's *Curse of Kehama* i 20–23: 'For lo! ten thousand torches flame and flare / Upon the midnight air, / Blotting the lights of heaven / With one portentous glare.'

---

21 Quoted from John Henry Newman, *Sermons 1824–1843*, ed. by Francis J. McGrath, vol. 5, *Sermons preached at St Clement's, Oxford, 1824–1826 and Two Charity Sermons, 1827* (Oxford: Clarendon, 2012), p. 154.

i *33–34.* 'when Earth / First drunk the light of his prolific ray.' Cp. Young, *A Paraphrase on Part of the Book of Job* (1719) 201–2: 'Adopted by the sun, in blaze of day, / They ripen under his prolific ray.' Subsequent instances of *prolific ray*, themselves prolific, occur in James Thomson's *On a Country Life* (1720) 25–26: 'In the sweet Spring the sun's prolific ray / Does painted flowers to the mild air display'; Robert Dodsley's *Public Virtue: A Poem in Three Books* (Dublin, 1754), Book I ('Agriculture') ii 79: 'Turn it to catch the sun's prolific ray'; and William Hayley's *An Essay on History; in Three Epistles to Edward Gibbon, Esq.* (1780), Epistle II, 184–85: 'Thy Favour, like the Sun's prolific ray, / Brought the keen Scribe of Florence into Day'.

i *39.* 'His ineffectual, intercepted beams'. Ricks cites *Hamlet* I v 90, 'uneffectual fire'; but cp. also Blackmore, *A Paraphrase On The Book of Job* (1700), chap. 37, lines 51–56: 'Sometimes the Lord of Nature in the Air / Hangs evening Clouds, his Sable Canvas, where / His Pencil dipt in Heav'nly Colours, made / Of intercepted Sunbeams mixt with Shade, / Of temper'd Ether, and refracted Light, / Paints his fair Rainbow, charming to the Sight.' And, by Rev. Charles Swan in *Gaston; or, The Heir of Foiz: A Tragedy. With Other Poems* (1823), his *The False One*, Canto II, p. 169, with: 'The vapoury vault of Heaven, when the full cloud / Hangs darkling, touched by intercepted beams / Of broken light.'

i *69–70.* 'and drove / The buoyant life-drops back into my heart.' Cp. Langhorne, *Verses in Memory of a Lady. Written at Sandgate Castle, MDCCLXVIII.* (1768) 27–28: 'Oh! had ye known how Souls to Souls impart / Their Fire, or mix'd the Life-drops of the Heart!' Cp. also Felicia Hemans, *The Siege of Valencia* (1823), scene i, p. 113: 'That passionate tears should wash it from the earth, / Or e'en the life-drops of a bleeding heart'; and, reflecting her penchant for self-borrowing, her *Greek Funeral Chant or Myriologue* (1825) 37–38: 'And thou wert lying low the while, the life-drops from thy heart / Fast gushing like a mountain-spring!—and couldst thou thus depart?'

i *83–84.* 'The streams, whose imperceptible advance, / Lingering in slow meanders'. For the latter phrase, cp. Blackmore, *Prince Arthur* I ii 380–81: 'Upon the Crystal River's flowry side, / That winding did in slow Meanders glide'; Thomas Chatterton, *The Death of Nicou. An African*

Eclogue (1770) 1–2: 'On Tiber's banks, Tiber, whose waters glide / In slow meanders down to Gaigra's side'; and Robinson, *Ode on Adversity* (1791) 9–10: 'The shallow rivers o'er their pebbly way, / In slow meanders murmuring play'.

i *87–88*. 'now, as instinct with life, / Ran like the lightning's wing'. Cp. Young's *Complaint*, Night Ninth ('The Consolation') 859: 'Let Thought, awaken'd, take the Lightning's Wing'; Rev. William Thompson's *Sickness. A Poem. In Three Books.* (1745) ii 562–64: 'Callirhoe shriek'd; and from the gaping wound, / Quick as the lightning's wing, the reeking knife / Wrench'd'; in William Julius Mickle's translation of Luís Vaz de Camões's epic *Os Lusiadas* (1572) as *The Lusiad; or, The Discovery of India. An Epic Poem.* (Oxford, 1776), Book IX, line 523: 'Fleet is her flight, the lightning's wing she rides'; and, in the same section of the poem that begins with a reference to Byron's 'capacious soul' as noted above, Pollok's *Course of Time* iv 688: 'And wove his garland of the lightning's wing'.

i *88–90*. 'and dashed upon / The curvature of their green banks a wreath / Of lengthened foam'. For the latter phrase Ricks cites Keats, *Endymion* (1818) ii 348: 'lengthened wave'. But cp. also the American Thomas Odiorne's *Ethic Strains, On Subjects Sublime and Beautiful* (Boston, 1821) II ii 75–78: 'So, in a clear and tranquil winter-morn, / When air is dense, and snows the ground adorn, / Emerging smoke from chimney's top ascends, / And, in a lengthen'd foam, convolving blends'.

i *125*. 'And darkness almost palpable.' Ricks cites the phrase 'palpable darkness' in *Paradise Lost* xii 188, from a passage on the plagues of Egypt: 'Darkness must overshadow all his bounds, / Palpable darkness, and blot out three dayes'. But cp. also John Marston's *Satire II* (1598) 21–22: 'O darkness palpable! Egypt's black night! / My wit is stricken blind, hath lost his sight'; Pope's *Dunciad* iii 173: 'Fast by, in darkness palpable inshrin'd'; and Coleridge's *The Destiny of Nations. A Vision.* (1817) 292–94: 'Moaning she fled, and entered the Profound / That leads with downward windings to the Cave / Of Darkness palpable, Desert of Death'.

If not from Marston, Milton himself may have borrowed the phrase from Rev. Isaac Ambrose's *Ultima, The Last Things* (1650), where a passage on p. 135 of the chapter entitled *Hels horrour* reads in part:

> Could men have a sight of hell whiles they live on earth, I doubt not their hearts would tremble in their bosomes : yet view it in a way of meditation, and see what you find ? are there not wonderfull engines, sharpe and sore instruments of revenge, *fiery Brimstone, pitchy Sulphur, red hot chains, flaming whips, scorching darkness?* will you any more? *the worm is immortall, cold intolerable, stench indurable, fire unquenchable, darkness palpable:* This is that prison of the damned[.]

In any case, the ultimate, scriptural source of the phrase—also from a passage on the plagues of Egypt—is *Exodus* x 21, reading, in the Vulgate, 'tenebrae tam densae ut palpari queant' and, in the King James Version, 'And the LORD said unto Moses, Stretch out thine hand toward heaven, that there may be darkness over the land of Egypt, even darkness which may be felt.'

i 133. 'Full opposite within the livid West'. Ricks cites Thomson's *Winter* (1726) 224: 'the livid east'. But cp. also, from James Alexander Linen's *Poems, in the Scots and English Dialect, on Various Occasions* (Edinburgh, 1815), *The Aged Mourner comforted* 3–4: 'No storms loud from the livid west / Sent snowy show'rs'.

ii 24. 'With such a vast circumference of thought'. Ricks cites Shelley's *Epipsychidion* (1821) 550: 'Within that calm circumference of bliss'. But cp. also *Paradise Lost* vi 255–56: 'his ample Shield / A vast circumference'; Coleridge, *Reflections on having Left a Place of Retirement* (1796) 39–41: 'God, methought, / Had built him there a Temple: the whole World / Seem'd *imag'd* in its vast circumference'; Wordsworth, *Yew-Trees* (1815) 9–10: 'Of vast circumference and gloom profound / This solitary tree!'; and Keats, *Otho the Great: A Tragedy in Five Acts* (1819) III ii 38–39: 'Though heaven's choir / Should in a vast circumference descend'.

ii 52–54. 'Immeasurable Solicitude and Awe, / And solemn Adoration and high Faith, / Were traced on his imperishable front'. For *immeasurable solitude*, cp. Charles Brockden Brown, *Wieland; or The Transformation: An American Tale* (New York, 1798; London, 1822), chap. 9, p. 95: 'I feel no reluctance, my friends[,] to be thus explicit. Time was, when these emotions would be hidden with immeasurable solicitude, from every human eye. Alas! these airy and fleeting impulses of shame are gone.'

For *imperishable front*, cp. Shelley, *Queen Mab: A Philosophical Poem* (1813) vii 183–84: 'The dampness of the grave / Bathed my imperishable front.'

4 The Coach of Death, A Fragment (*wr* c. 1823–28)

31–32. 'To draw strange comfort from the earth, / Strange beauties from the sky.' For *strange comfort*, cp. Pope's *Essay on Man* (1734), Epistle II, 271–72: 'See some strange comfort ev'ry state attend, / And pride bestow'd on all, a common friend'.

For *strange beauties*, cp., in John Dowland's *Second Book of Songs or Ayres* (1600), his *Eyes and Hearts* 1–2: 'Now cease, my wandring eies, / Strange beauties to admire'; and, in Thomas Campion's *The Lords' Masque* (1613), stanza ii of the song beginning 'Woo her, and win her, he that can!': 'Mix your words with music then, / That they the more may enter; / Bold assaults are fit for men, / That on strange beauties venter.'

101. 'Vast wastes of starless glooms were spread'. Ricks cites *Revolt of Islam* X xliii 1: 'a starless and a moonless gloom'. But cp. also Wordsworth's *Salisbury Plain* xlviii 429–32: 'reason's ray, / What does it more than while the tempests rise, / With starless glooms and sounds of loud dismay, / Reveal with still-born glimpse the terrors of our way?'

121–28. 'With a silver sound the wheels went round, / The wheels of burning flame; / Of beryl, and of amethyst / Was the spiritual frame. / Their steeds were strong exceedingly: / And rich was their attire: / Before them flowed a fiery stream; / They broke the ground with hoofs of fire.' For lines 122–24, Ricks cites the Messiah's chariot in *Paradise Lost* vi 755–56: 'the wheels / Of Beril, and careering Fires between'. But for the passage as a whole see also *Daniel* vii 9–10: 'I beheld till the thrones were cast down, and the Ancient of days did sit, whose garment was white as snow, and the hair of his head like the pure wool: his throne was like the fiery flame, and his wheels as burning fire. A fiery stream issued and came forth from before him'.

For *hoofs of fire*, cp. also, by the fourth-century soldier-historian Ammianus Marcellinus, the *Res Gestae*, where a passage in Book XIV, chapter 6, reads in part: *'quidam per ampla spatia urbis [...] sine periculi metu properantes equos uelut publicos, ignitis quod dicitur calcibus agitant'*; or, in J. C. Rolfe's 1940 translation: 'certain persons hasten without fear of danger through the broad streets of the city and over the upturned stones of the pavements as if they were driving post-horses with hoofs of fire (as the saying is)'.

155. 'The arks of during adamant'. Ricks cites *Paradise Lost* iii 45, 'But cloud instead and ever-during dark', and vii 206, 'Her ever-during gates, harmonious sound'. But the phrase *during adamant* itself may be found in at least two places: Howard's *Metamorphoses* xv 1010–11: 'There wilt thou written find thy offspring's fate / On ever-during adamant'; and John Weever's *The Mirror of Martyrs, or, The life and death of that thrice valiant Capitaine, and most godly Martyre Sir John Old-castle knight, Lord Cobham* (1601) 787–89: 'My Destinies are set in parlament, / Aboue their heades a curious frame of stone: / Marble below, and during Adamant'.

159–60. 'The black bitumen howled beneath / In dreadful sympathy.' Cp. *Revolt of Islam* I xxvi 7–8: 'All thoughts within his mind waged mutual war / In dreadful sympathy'.

173. 'Amid a waste of spiral fires'. Ricks cites *Paradise Lost* i 222–23: 'the flames / Drivn backward slope thir pointing spires'; and ii 1013, 'Springs upward like a Pyramid of fire'. But cp. also Henry Ingram, *The Flower of Wye* (1815), Canto VI, p. 286: 'Now spiral fires ascend, and thro' the air / Are heard the feeble accents of Despair.'

5 Memory [Memory! dear enchanter!] (*wr* 1824–26)

15–16. 'Fruits which time hath shaken / From off their parent bough'. Cp. Philips's *Cyder*, Book I, 276–77: 'Let Art correct thy Breed: from Parent Bough / A Cyon meetly sever'; Mary Leapor, *The Enquiry* (1748) 59: 'Pluck off yon Acorn from its Parent Bough'; and Thomson's *Winter* 60–61: 'The falling Fruits, / Thro' the still Night, forsake the Parent-Bough'.

49–50. 'From age's frosty mansion, / So cheerless and so chill?' Cp. John Heywood's early-Tudor interlude *The Play of the Weather* (1533) 37–42: 'And firste—as became—our father, moste aunctent, / With berde white as snow, his lockes both cold and hore, / Hath ent'red such mater as served his entent, / Laudinge his frosty mansion in the firmament / To aire and yerth as thinge moste precious, / Pourginge all humours that are contagious.'

8 Remorse (*pub* 1827)

17. 'Remorse, with soul-felt agony'. Cp., by the Anglo-Irish poet Mary Tighe, *Good Friday, 1790* (1811), stanza ii: 'For on this day the Godhead died, / (Amazing thought!) for me! / Pierced were his hands, his feet, his side: / His soul felt agony.' Also, by the American James Athearn Jones, *Bonaparte* (New York, 1820) section I, lines 5–9: 'Where / The eye discern'd a home of man, or saw / A human dweller, there were hearts that mourn'd / O'er tombless corses—there were eyes that wept / In soul-felt agony.'; and, from Grinfield's *The Omnipresence of God: with Other Sacred Poems* (Bristol, 1824), *Jesus Christ, the Comforter of Disquietude* xiii 3–4: 'We bleed with guilt: His blood like balm, / The soul-felt agony can calm'.

21–22. 'An hopeless outcast, born to die / A living death eternally!' Cp. Thomson, *Tancred and Sigismunda, A Tragedy* (1745) I vi (Tancred speaking): 'Then, then, to love me, when I seem'd of fortune / The hopeless outcast, when I had no friend'.

9 The Dell of E— (*pub* 1827)

8–9. 'And far–far off the heights were seen to shine / In clear relief against the sapphire sky'. Cp., among other instances of the latter phrase, John Stewart, *The Pleasures of Love* (1806) 454–55, 'Or mark Coanza clear, soft-gliding by, / Reflect the orange grove, the sapphire sky'; Wordsworth, *The Excursion* (1814), Book II ('The Solitary') 854: 'Clouds of all tincture, rocks and sapphire sky'; Hemans, *The Voice of Spring* (1823) 56–57: 'There were voices that rung through the sapphire sky, / And had not a sound of mortality!'; and, also by Hemans, *The Sicilian Captive* (1825) 43–44: 'Doth not thy shadow wrap my soul?–in silence let me die, / In a voiceless dream of thy silvery founts, and thy pure, deep sapphire sky'.

12. 'And glistening 'neath each lone entangled glade'. In *The Newcastle Magazine*, n.s., vol. 1, no. 4 (Apr. 1822), pp. 198–99, cp. 'Poetical Illustrations of Northumbrian Traditions, no. 2., *The Seeker*. Part I', by

'A Strolling Player' elsewhere identified as 'A. B.', 78–82: 'From Font to Cambois who can tell / How many a deep entangled glade, / Green vale, and wild wood's grateful shade, / And castled crag, and hoary pile, / With fretted roof and cloister'd aisle?'; and by Sydney Owenson, Lady Morgan, from her anonymously published *The Mohawks; a Satirical Poem with Notes* (also 1822), *Dedication. Freely Imitated From Horace, Book I, Ode XII.*, lines 97–98: 'Like plants close buried in the shade / Of some entangled murky glade'.

45. 'Where once, throughout the impenetrable wood'. Ricks cites *Paradise Lost* ix 1086, from a passage reading: 'O might I here / In solitude live savage, in some glade / Obscur'd, where highest Woods impenetrable / To Starr or Sun-light, spread thir umbrage broad'. But cp. also, from his *Walks in a Forest, and Other Poems* (1794), Thomas Gisborne's *Walk the Third. Summer.—Moonlight*, p. 25: 'Cross we this knoll, / And meet them as they circle round the skirts / Of that impenetrable wood.';[22] and Scott's *Marmion: A Tale of Flodden Field* (Edinburgh, 1808) VI xxxiv 12–13: 'The stubborn spear-men still made good / Their dark impenetrable wood'.[23] All three passages may ultimately be traceable to Statius's *Thebaid* x 85: '*nulli penetrabilis astro, lucus iners*' [a grove penetrable by no star]; and, less directly, to the opening lines of Dante's *Inferno*: '*Nel mezzo del cammin di nostra vita / mi ritrovai per una selva oscura, / ché la diritta via era smarrita.*' [Midway on the journey of our life / I found myself in a dark wood, / For the direct way had been lost.][24]

---

22   The seventh (1808) Cadell and Davies edn of Gisborne's *Walks in a Forest; or, Poems descriptive of scenery and incidents characteristic of a forest at different seasons of the year*, was at Somersby (Item 128 in *Lincoln*).
23   The seventh Constable edn (Edinburgh, 1811) of Scott's *Marmion*, with 'A. Tennyson' on the overleaf, was at Somersby (Item 305 in *Lincoln*).
24   As catalogued in *Lincoln* (Items 94 and 95), George Clayton Tennyson's library held two partial edns of Dante: *The Divina Commedia of Dante Alighieri: consisting of the Inferno, Purgatorio, and Paradiso. Translated into English verse, with preliminary essays, notes, and illustrations, by the Rev. Henry Boyd* (Cadell and Davies, 1802), vol. 2 only, lacking vols. 1 and 3; and, edited by Rev. Henry Francis Cary, *The Vision; or, Hell, Purgatory, and Paradise, of Dante Alighieri* (Taylor, 1814), vols. 2 and 3 only, lacking vol. 1. T. himself owned a dozen more (Items 816 through 827 in *Lincoln*), in Italian and/or English, including translations by Cary (Taylor, 1831)—this edn complete; John A. Carlyle (Chapman and Hall, 1849); C. B. Cayley (Longman, 1854); and Arthur John Butler (Macmillan, 1885, 1890, and 1892).

10 Anthony and Cleopatra (*pub* 1827)

5. 'But wear not thou the conqueror's chain'. Ricks cites *Antony and Cleopatra* IV xiv 61–62 (Antony speaking): 'Than she which by her death our Caesar tells, / "I am conqueror of myself."' But cp. also the several pre-T. instances of *conqueror's chain* itself, in Moore, *Sublime Was the Warning* (1808) 2–3: 'And grand was the moment when Spaniards awoke / Into life and revenge from the conqueror's chain'; Rev. Peregrine Bingham, *The Pains of Memory* (1811) Book I ('The Effects of Memory on Minds which are not afflicted with the Consciousness of Guilt') xii 33–36: 'Shall they, sweet objects of our earliest care, / Angelic forms, Britannia's matchless Fair, / Their heroes see retreating from the plain, / Mourn their disgrace, and wear a conqueror's chain?'; *Childe Harold* I lxxxv 9: 'None hugged a Conqueror's chain, save fallen Chivalry!'; and Hemans, *Owen Glyndwr's War-Song* (1822) 31–32: 'But who the torrent-wave compels / A conqueror's chain to bear?'

16 'Did not thy roseate lips outvie' (*pub* 1827)

25. 'Borne through the boundless waste of air'. Ricks cites Gray's *Couplet about Birds* (1814): 'There pipes the woodlark, and the song-thrush there / Scatters his loose notes in the waste of air.' But cp. also Ogilvie's *Providence: An Allegorical Poem in Three Books* (1764) i 595–96: 'Not an insect-wing / Weak-waving whisper'd in the waste of air.'; his *Solitude: or, the Elysium of the Poets, a Vision* (1765) 389, speaking of Shakespeare: 'Graceful he moved, and scann'd the waste of air'; and Anna Lætitia Barbauld, *To Mrs. P— —, With some Drawings of Birds and Insects* (1773) 37–38: 'Thro' the wide waste of air he darts his sight, / And holds his sounding pinions pois'd for flight'.

26 On Sublimity (*pub* 1827)

1. 'O tell me not of vales in tenderest green'. Cp. Gray's *Ode on the Pleasure Arising from Vicissitude* (1775) i 7–8, where April 'lightly o'er the living scene / Scatters his freshest, tenderest green.'[25] But the conjunction

---

25 Gray's ode was first published in *The Poems of Mr. Gray* (Dublin: Chamberlaine, 1775), a copy of which was at Somersby (Item 133 in *Lincoln*). It was also reprinted

of *vales* and *tenderest green* in T.'s poem suggests that it may be a reply to the opening lines of John Wilson's *Solitude*, from his *The City of the Plague, and Other Poems* (Edinburgh, 1816): 'O vale of visionary rest! / — Hush'd as the grave it lies / With heaving banks of tenderest green, / Yet brightly, happily serene, / As cloud-vale of the sleepy west / Reposing on the skies.'

8. 'What time grey eve is fading into night'. Ricks cites *Lycidas* 28: 'What time the Gray-fly winds her sultry horn'. But cp. also, from his *Poems On Various Subjects* (Carlisle, 1798), R[obert]. Anderson of Carlisle's *Sonnet XIX. To Eliza.* 9–10: 'As, press'd with care, I sought the peaceful shade, / What time grey Eve stole o'er the dewy plain'; and Marcus Rainsford, *The Revolution, Or, Britain Delivered. A Poem, in Ten Cantos* (1800), Canto VI, p. 245: 'The Tower's dire walls receive the virtuous train, / What time grey eve gives place to twilight's reign'.

15. 'Through windows rich with gorgeous blazonry'. Cp., in R[obert]. Potter's *The Tragedies of Æschylus Translated* (Norwich, 1777), *The Seven Chiefs Against Thebes* II iii: 'The gorgeous blazonry of arms'; and Hemans, *The Abencerrage* (1819) iii 55–56: 'Shields, gold-emboss'd, and pennons floating far, / And all the gorgeous blazonry of war'.

23. 'And more than mortal music meets mine ear'. Ricks cites *Il Penseroso* 120: 'Where more is meant than meets the ear'. But cp. also Cowper's *Table Talk* (1782) 737: 'With more than mortal music on his tongue';[26] and, from Mary Wollstonecraft's *Letters Written During a Short Residence in Sweden, Norway, and Denmark* (1796), Letter 2, paragraph 10: 'The waters murmur, and fall with more than mortal music, and spirits of peace walk abroad to calm the agitated breast.'

31. 'I love the starry spangled heaven'. Among several prior instances of similar expressions—as one commentator has noted, 'this was the common poetical decoration of the firmament'[27]—cp. *The Taming of the Shrew* IV v 31 (Petruchio speaking), 'What stars do spangle heaven with such beauty'; and *Paradise Lost* vii 383–84: 'With thousand thousand

---

in (among others) the fifth (1854) Williams edn of Gray's *Poetical Works* (Item 1045 in *Lincoln*).

26 In the 1808 Johnson edn of Cowper's *Poems* (see note 16), this poem is in vol. 1.

27 Henry J. Todd, in his edn of *The Poetical Works of Milton*, vol. 7 (1809), p. 153n.

Starres, that then appeer'd / Spangling the Hemisphere'. But T.'s next line, 'A canopy with fiery gems o'erspread', suggests that he may have owed 'the starry spangled heaven' as well as 'canopy' to a reading of Josuah Sylvester's translation (1604) of Guillaume de Saluste Du Bartas's *La Sepmaine; ou, Creation du Monde* (1578) as *Du Bartas His Diuine Weekes and Workes*, where—in 'First Weeke: or, Birth of the World'—*The Second Day of the First Weeke* 1171–72 read: 'Could prop as sure so many waves on high / Above the Heav'ns' Star-spangled Canopy.'

32. 'A canopy with fiery gems o'erspread'. While the *canopy* in T.'s line may have been suggested by Sylvester (see above), T. may have owed *fiery gems* to Howard's *Metamorphoses*, where Book II begins: 'By towering columns bright with burnish'd gold, / And fiery gems, which blaz'd their light around'. The phrase may ultimately be traceable to Statius's *Thebaid* xii 527–28, with *'ignea gemmis / cingula'*—girdles of fiery gems, the war booty Theseus brought back from his battles with the Amazons.

27 Time: An Ode (*pub* 1827)

67. '"Live, when, wrapt in sullen shade["]'. Ricks cites Scott, *The Vision of Don Roderick* (1811) II i: 'All sleeps in sullen shade'. But cp. also, among other instances of the phrase, Henry King's *St. Valentine's Day* (1657) 5–6, 'And I should to custome prove a retrograde / Did I still dote upon my sullen shade.'; Dryden's *Æneis* vi 616, 'With tears he first approach'd the sullen shade'; Southey's *Sonnet 1* (1794) 1–4: 'Go Valentine and tell that lovely maid / Whom Fancy still will pourtray to my sight, / How her Bard lingers in this sullen shade, / This dreary gloom of dull monastic night.'; and, its final clause exactly matching T.'s, William Falconer's *The Shipwreck* (1762) i 817–18, where Morn 'comes not in refulgent pomp array'd, / But sternly frowning, wrapt in sullen shade'.

30 The Walk at Midnight (*pub* 1827)

8. 'Arrested by the wandering owl.' The latter phrase occurs in several pre-T. translations of Ovid's *Epistulae* 2.118, '*Et cecinit maestum devia carmen avis*', as 'and the wandering owl complained in mournful notes.'

25–26. 'Then, to the thickly-crowded mart / The eager sons of interest press'. Cp. Thomson's *Summer* (1727) 1389–90: 'And in whose breast, enthusiastic, burns / Virtue, the sons of interest deem romance'.

29–30. 'Then, wealth aloft in state displays / The glittering of her gilded cars'. For the latter phrase Ricks cites Milton's *Comus* 95: 'And the gilded Car of Day'. But cp. also, among other instances, the Pope–Broome–Fenton *Odyssey* iv 11–12: 'With steeds, and gilded cars, a gorgeous train / Attend the nymph to *Phthia*'s distant reign.'; Pope's *First Satire of the Second Book of Horace, Imitated* (1733) 107: 'Dash the proud Gamester in his gilded car'; and Charlotte Smith's *Apostrophe to an Old Tree* (1797) 29–30: 'The crouds around her gilded car that hung, / Bent the lithe knee, and troul'd the honey'd tongue'.

Though it does not occur as such in Tennyson's line or poem, the phrase *glittering car* or *cars* does do so in several pre-T. poems, including twice in Pope's *Iliad*, v 298–99: 'And now both heroes mount the glittering car; / The bounding coursers rush amidst the war.', and xi 255–56: 'The chief she found amidst the ranks of war, / Close to the bulwarks on his glittering car.'; twice in John Hoole's translation of Tasso, *Jerusalem Delivered* (1763), xviii 34, 'Had rode triumphant on his glittering car', and xx 404–5: 'Now came Rinaldo where, with martial air, / Appear'd Armida in her glittering car.'; and in Darwin's *Botanic Garden* II i 219–20: 'So shines with silver guards the Georgian star, / And drives on Night's blue arch his glittering car'.

45 'Oh! ye wild winds, that roar and rave' (*pub* 1827)

7. 'When through the dark immense of air'. Ricks cites *Paradise Lost* ii 829, 'through the void immense', and *Queen Mab* ii 39, 'the immense of Heaven'. But cp. also, once again, the prefatory *Address* of Mrs. Ryves's *Cumbrian Legends*, lines 10–11, cited above: 'Nature looks up, and, thro' the dark immense, / Beholds one ray to glad the sick'ning sense'.

46 Babylon (*pub* 1827)

26. 'But their loins shall be loosed, and their hearts shall be sunk'. To the poem's several previously noted scriptural echoes may be added *Daniel* v 6: 'Then the king's countenance was changed, and his thoughts

troubled him, so that the joints of his loins were loosed, and his knees smote one against another.'

47 Love [Almighty Love!] (*pub* 1827)

31. 'Alike confess thy magic sway'. Cp. Robert Burns, *Song — My Peggy's Charms* (1787) 11–12: 'Who but owns their magic sway! / Who but knows they all decay!';[28] and Ingram's *Flower of Wye*, Canto V, p. 198: '"But I display'd a test, whose magic sway / Chas'd ev'ry doubt, and op'd the road to day"'. Cp. also Thomas Babington Macaulay's *Pompeii* (1819), which, as stated on the title page of the pamphlet in which it was printed, had obtained — as would T.'s *Timbuctoo* in 1829 — the Chancellor's Medal at the Cambridge commencement in July 1819, and lines 259–60 of which read: 'The wand of eloquence, whose magic sway / The sceptres and the swords of earth obey'. (Note that *sway/obey* is also the rhyme pair in lines 31–32 of T.'s poem.)

32. 'Thy soul-enchanting voice obey!' The title work of Edward Moxon's *The Prospect, and Other Poems* (1826) has, on page 53, 'Her cheerful smile, her soul-enchanting voice, / Taught e'en repining envy to rejoice.' Other instances of *soul-enchanting* minus *voice* occur in Edmund Spenser's *An Hymne in Honour of Beautie* (1596) ii 13–14: 'To admiration of that heavenly light, / From whence proceeds such soule enchaunting might.'; in the sonnet by William Herbert, third Earl of Pembroke, beginning 'Dear, when I think upon my first sad fall' (1660) 5–6: 'Rock't into endless heavenly Trances, by / Thy soul inchanting-Graces harmony'; in Coleridge's *Monody on the Death of Chatterton* (1790) 13–15: 'Is this the land of liberal Hearts! / Is this the land, where Genius ne'er in vain / Pour'd forth her soul-enchanting strain?'; in Robinson's *Sonnet to Amicus* (1791), which begins: 'Whoe'er thou art, whose soul-enchanting song / Steals on the sullen ear of pensive woe'; and in James Montgomery's *The West-Indies. A Poem, in Four Parts. Written in Honour of the Abolition of the African Slave Trade, by the British Legislature, in 1807.* (1809), Part III,

---

28 George Clayton Tennyson owned the four-volume sixth (1809) Cadell and Davies edn of Burns's *Works* (Item 61 in *Lincoln*), in which T. wrote 'Alfred Tennyson' on the fly-leaf of vol. 1 and this poem was reprinted in vol. 4. T. himself owned three other, later edns of Burns's works (Items 672, 673, 674).

205–6, 'He sees no beauty in the heaven serene, / No soul-enchanting sweetness in the scene'.

35. 'Wingest thy shaft of pleasing dread'. Instances of the oxymoron include (among others) Thomson's *Winter* 109, 'With what a pleasing dread they swell the soul!'; James Beattie's *The Minstrel; or, the Progress of Genius* (1771) Book I, 480–81, 'Listening, with pleasing dread, to the deep roar / Of the wide-weltering waves.';[29] from her Gothic novel *The Romance of the Forest* (Dublin, 1791), Ann Radcliffe's poem *Night* 5–6: '*These* paint with fleeting shapes the dream of sleep, / *These* swell the waking soul with pleasing dread'; and Wilson's *The Isle of Palms* (Edinburgh, 1812) iv 40–41, 'The loneliness of Nature's reign adorning / With a calm majesty and pleasing dread'.

48 Exhortation to the Greeks (*pub* 1827)

19–20. 'Remember the night, when, in shrieks of affright, / The fleets of the East in your ocean were sunk'. For *shrieks of affright*, cp. Samuel Johnson's *Irene, A Tragedy* (1749) I i (Leontius speaking): 'From ev'ry palace burst a mingled clamour, / The dread dissonance of barb'rous triumph, / Shrieks of affright, and wailings of distress.'; from his *Tales of Wonder* (1801), M. G. Lewis's *The Cloud-King* 67–68: 'Yet long in her ears rang the shrieks of affright, / Which pour'd for her danger the page Amorayn.'; and Charles Peers, *The Siege of Jerusalem* (1823), Book IX, p. 198: 'Shrieks of affright, of anguish, and despair'. Peers's poem was inscribed 'To Henry Hallam, Esq.', father of Arthur Hallam, 'By His Attached Friend, The Author'; and his *Christ's Lamentation Over Jerusalem* was named the Seatonian Prize Poem at Cambridge in 1805—either or both of which may have brought *The Siege of Jerusalem* to T.'s attention.

50 'Come hither, canst thou tell me if this skull' (*wr* c. 1824–26)

24. 'The soul had fled its cold receptacle.' Cp. G. H. C. Egestorff's verse translation of Klopstock's *Der Messias* as *Klopstock's Messiah, A Poem in Twenty Cantos*, vol. 1 (Hamburg, 1821; London, 1826), with two instances

---

[29] The 1806 Mawman edn of *The Minstrel* was at Somersby (Item 22 in *Lincoln*).

of *cold receptacle*: first in ii 183–84: 'While with his withered arms he clasps the cold / Receptacle of the child's now mouldering bones'; and again in vii 995–96: 'O Herod, by the Royal bones of David, / Whose cold receptacle trembles with concern'.

51 The Dying Man to His Friend (*wr* c. 1824–26)

5–6. 'Fare thee well! my soul is fleeting / To the radiant realms of day'. Cp., from his *Poems on Various Subjects* (Edinburgh, 1780), William Cameron's *Lyric Odes II.2*, lines 8–9: 'Swift as thought they wing their way / Through the radiant realms of day'; and, in *The Evangelical Magazine and Missionary Chronicle*, vol. 4 (1826), p. 145, *The Universal Hallelujah*, by the otherwise anonymous 'H. E.', stanza v: 'Silenc'd ev'ry dark foreboding, / 'Midst the radiant realms of day, / Doubts no more, the heart corroding, / Strew with frequent thorns the way.'

54A 'The musky air was mute' (*wr* c. 1824–27)

3–4. 'Her small and naked foot / Shook the pale dewdrop from the drooping blade.' For the latter phrase, cp. *Fergusson and Burns; or the Poet's Reverie. Part II.*, by the also otherwise anonymous 'C. B.', as collected by James Burnet—after its initial appearance in *Blackwood's Edinburgh Magazine*, vol. 12, no. 69 (Oct. 1822), 498–500—in *The Royal Scottish Minstrelsy: being a Collection of Loyal Effusions occasioned by the Visit of His Most Gracious Majesty George IV. to Scotland, August 15, 1822* (Leith, 1824), pp. 166–81. In this imaginary dialogue between the late poets Robert Fergusson (died 1774) and Robert Burns (died 1796), Burns is given to say of 'the Poet', in lines 53 to 58, 'His loves in life sae deep are fixt, / Their embers smoulder in the next; / Yet nane could meet me here this e'en— / My Mary's shade, my living Jean— / Mair welcome, Fergusson, than you— / Sae meets the drooping blade the dew.'

55 The Outcast (*wr* 1826)

7. 'Unreal shapes of twilight shades'. Among others instances of *unreal shapes*, cp. Helen Maria Williams's *Duncan, An Ode* (1791) 33–34: 'Then unreal shapes appear / By the blue unhallow'd flame'; Rev. William Herbert's *Ode to Despair* (1804) 1–4: 'O thou, the fiend to Death allied, /

Who sit'st by weeping Sorrow's side, / And bid'st unreal shapes arise / Of monsterous port and giant size'; Southey's epic *Madoc* (1805, revised 1812) xvii ('The Deliverance') 90–92: 'and she stood / With open lips that breathed not, and fixed eyes, / Watching the unreal shapes'; and Shelley's *Sonnet ('Lift not the Painted Veil')* (1824) 1–2: 'Lift not the painted veil which those who live / Call Life: though unreal shapes be pictured there'. In *The Banquet* (1818), his translation of Plato's *Symposium*, Shelley had previously written: 'What then shall we imagine to be the aspect of the supreme beauty itself, simple, pure, uncontaminated with the intermixture of human flesh and colours, and all other idle and unreal shapes attendant on mortality; the divine, the original, the supreme, the monoeidic beautiful itself?'

58A The Invasion of Russia by Napoleon Buonaparte (*wr* c. 1824–28)

3. 'And fast and far along the spangling snow'. Cp. *Queen Mab* iv 35–37: 'The stars are quenched / In darkness, and the pure and spangling snow / Gleams faintly through the gloom that gathers round!'; and, in lines 61–62 of the same poem: 'And the bright beams of frosty morning dance / Along the spangling snow.'

7. 'The fiery glancing of thine eye shall quail'. Cp. Macpherson/Ossian's *Fingal* (1761) III xv 1–2: 'His gloomy chiefs with fiery-glancing eyes / FINGAL surveys—his chiefs of battle rise.'[30]

26. 'In his wide hall stood fixed to bloodless stone'. For *bloodless stone*, cp. *silicem sine sanguine* in Ovid's *Metamorphoses*, Book V, 248–49: '*oraque regis / Ore Medusaeo silicem sine sanguine fecit*' [Then exposing the head of Medusa to the king, he changed his face into a bloodless stone].[31]

---

30 As catalogued, vol. 1 only of the two-volume (1809) Suttaby edn of Macpherson/Ossian's *Poems*, with *Fingal* and with 'A. Tennyson' on its fly-leaf, was at Somersby (Item 244 in *Lincoln*).

31 The fifth (1822) Whittaker edn of *Ovid's Metamorphoses, Translated into English Prose; with the Latin Text* [...] *and Notes in English. For the Use of Schools, as well as Private Gentlemen*—from which this translation is quoted—was at Somersby (Item 245 in *Lincoln*), as was the second Williams edn (Eton, 1815) of *Electa ex Ovidio et Tibullo in usum Regiae Scholiae Etoniensis* [Selections from Ovid and Tibullus used at Eton]

36. 'As Moscow burst upon the raptured eye'. Among other instances of the latter phrase, cp. Thomson's *Spring* (1728) 110–12: 'where the raptured eye / Hurries from joy to joy, and, hid beneath / The fair profusion, yellow Autumn spies—'; and his *Summer* 1408–9: 'Here let us sweep / The boundless landscape,—now the raptured eye, / Exulting swift, to huge Augusta send'. Cp. also Thomas Campbell's *Hymn* ('When Jordan hushed his waters still') (1795) 17–18: 'Oh, Zion, lift thy raptured eye, / The long-expected hour is nigh—'; also by Campbell, *The Pleasures of Hope* (1799) Part I, 15–16: 'What potent spirit guides the raptured eye / To pierce the shades of dim futurity?'; and James Hogg's *Mador of the Moor* (Edinburgh, 1816) v 3–4: 'Amid bewildered waves of silvery light / That maze the mind and toil the raptured eye.'

45–46. 'Far along / Rang the glad shouting through the haggard throng'. Cp. Charles Phillips's *The Emerald Isle*, the sixth (1818) edition of which has, on p. 56: 'Oft had they joined, perhaps, the haggard throng, / Bearing the now neglected fleece along'.

47. 'A deep, dark flush of momentary bloom'. In George Herbert's *The Temple* (1633), cp. *Repentance*, stanza i: 'Lord, I confesse my sinne is great; / Great is my sinne. Oh! gently treat / With thy quick flow'r, thy momentarie bloom; / Whose life still pressing / Is one undressing, / A steadie aiming at a tombe.'; and Edward Lovibond, *To the Thames* (1785) 13–16: 'What, if chance sweet evening ray, / Or western gale of vernal day, / Momentary bloom renews, / Heavy with unfertile dews'.

75. 'The humid couch upon the tentless mould'. For *humid couch*, cp. Thomson, *Edward and Eleanora. A Tragedy*. (1739) III iv (Daraxa speaking): 'Here flow'd her Tears afresh; with burning Lip, / She press'd the humid Couch, and wept again.'; and, in her *Elegiac Sonnets and Other Poems* (1784), Charlotte Smith's sonnet 75 ('Where the wild woods and pathless forests frown') 6–7: 'With pale capricious light the Summer Moon / Chequers his humid couch'. No *humid couch* or *tentless mould*,

---

(Item 246) with the names of George Clayton, Alfred, and Frederick Tennyson on the title page. The library of T.'s brother Charles also contained an 1813 Latin edn of Ovid with 'Alfred Tennyson' on its title page (Item 2539 in *Lincoln*).

but Byron's *Lara, A Tale* (1814) II 944 has 'The tentless rest beneath the humid sky'.

59 Playfellow Winds (*wr* c. 1827–28)

4–5. 'my cheek white / As my own hope's quenched ashes.' Cp. stanza v of Elton's *Elegy VIII* (1810), after Propertius: 'When flames the pyre, and I am embers made, / My relics to an earthen shell convey; / Then plant a laurel that the tomb may shade / Where my quench'd ashes rest, and grave the lay'.

61 Home (*wr* 1828)

4. 'Leagues of sounding foam?' Cp. Falconer's *The Shipwreck* iii 550–51: 'Amaz'd he saw her, o'er the sounding foam / Upborne, to right and left distracted roam.'; and Macpherson/Ossian's *Death: A Poem* (1805) 359–61: 'Thus water-fowl upon the sable flood, / Now here, now there, their floating bodies shew, / But then are lost amidst the sounding foam'.

62 'Among some Nations Fate hath placed too far' (*wr* 1828)

6. 'Striking the dark of crannied caverns dim'. Cp. John Wright, *The Retrospect; or Youthful Scenes* (1825) ii 537–40: 'He thence through manhood traced the broken dream, / Till sad it sickened into autumn wan; / Reclined in crannied cavern's twilight gleam, / Thus would his descant flow o'er the lone rushing stream:—'.

11–12. 'One throne there is, round whose unshaken base / The myriad feet of all on Earth might move'. Among other pre-T. instances of *unshaken base*, cp. Cowper's *The Nativity* (1801) 155–58: 'Upon my meanness, poverty, and guilt, / The trophy of thy glory shall be built; / My self-disdain shall be th' unshaken base, / And my deformity, its fairest grace'; Blackmore's *Prince Arthur* I iv 780–81: 'Pois'd on their own unshaken Base they view, / All the Vicissitudes, that Time can shew.'; and *Childe Harold* II x 1–2: 'Here let me sit upon this massy stone, / The marble column's yet unshaken base'.

13–14. 'One King into whose everlasting face / All eyes might look and live, his name is Love.' Cp. Henry Vaughan, *The Night* (1650) 1–3: 'Through that pure *Virgin-shrine*, / That sacred vail drawn o'r thy glorious noon / That men might look and live as Glo-worms shine'.

63 To Poesy [O God, make this age great] (*wr* 1828)

7–8. 'A long day's dawn, when Poesy shall bind / Falsehood beneath the altar of great Truth'. Cp. *Queen Mab* vi 35–38: 'The truths of their pure lips, that never die, / Shall bind the scorpion falsehood with a wreath / Of ever-living flame / Until the monster sting itself to death.'

64 The Lark (*wr* 1828)

4. 'Athwart the bloomy morn.' Cp. Rev. Moses Browne, *Piscatory Eclogues* (1729) I. *The Weather* 133–34: 'But now with me dispend the louring Night, / 'Till bloomy Morn renew the cheering Light'; Thomas Warton, *The Pleasures of Melancholy. Written in the Year 1745.* (1747) 130–31, 'Yet more delightful to my pensive mind / Is thy return, than bloomy Morn's approach'; and John Corry, *Elegy to Maria M.* (1797) 1–2: 'Celestial Venus shines with fainter light, / And bloomy Morn proclaims approaching Day'.

67 Timbuctoo (*wr* c. 1824–29)

36. 'Unto the fearful summoning without'. Cp. *Hamlet* I i 148–49 (Horatio speaking): 'And then it started like a guilty thing / Upon a fearful summons.'

103–4. 'The clear Galaxy / Shorn of its hoary lustre, wonderful'. Cp. the title work in Charles A. Allnatt's *Poverty: A Poem. With several others, on various subjects, chiefly Religious and Moral* (Shrewsbury, 1801) 41–42: 'Eighty long winters have profusely shed / A hoary lustre round his aged head'.

140–42. 'Where is he that borne / Adown the sloping of an arrowy stream / Could link his shallop to the fleeting edge'. Ricks cites *Childe Harold* III lxxi 3: 'arrowy Rhone'. But cp. also David Carey, *To the Aurora*

Borealis (1807) 13–14: 'Your fiery course, your arrowy stream, / Gigantic hosts that proudly ride!'

73* Mariana (*pub* 1830)

13–14. 'Her tears fell with the dews at even; / Her tears fell ere the dews were dried'. Collins notes,[32] as does Ricks, that T.'s 'gray-eyed morn' in line 31, 'Till cold winds woke the gray-eyed morn', echoes *Romeo and Juliet* II iii 1 (Friar Laurence speaking): 'The grey-ey'd morn smiles on the frowning night'. Neither notes that T.'s line 14 echoes lines 5–6 of the same speech: 'Now ere the sun advance his burning eye, / The day to cheer and night's dank dew to dry'.

38. 'A sluice with blackened waters slept'. Cp. *Queen Mab* iv 26–27: 'Cloud upon cloud, in dark and deepening mass, / Roll o'er the blackened waters'.

43–44. 'For leagues no other tree did mark / The level waste, the rounding gray.' Cp. James Grahame, *The Sabbath* (Edinburgh, 1804) 268–71: 'Or far in moors, remote from house or hut, / Where animated nature seems extinct, / Where even the hum of wandering bee ne'er breaks / The quiet slumber of the level waste'.

63–64. 'the mouse / Behind the mouldering wainscot shrieked'. Among other pre-T. translations of the Homeric parody *Batrachomyomachia* [The battle of the frogs and mice], cp. Thomas Parnell's version (1717) 135–36: 'Loud shrieks the mouse, his shrieks the shores repeat; / The nibbling nation learn their heroe's fate'. Other versions in which a mouse is said to *shriek* include those by George Chapman (1624), Samuel Wesley (1726), and William Cowper (1791).

75 Madeline (*pub* 1830)

5. 'Sudden glances, sweet and strange'. For the former phrase, cp. Watts, *Stanzas to Lady Sunderland at Tunbridge Wells, 1712* 15–16: 'His lightning

---

32 In *Illustrations*, p. 27; and in *Early Poems*, p. 7, though in the latter he misquotes Shakespeare's line.

strikes with less surprise / Than sudden glances from her eyes.'; for the latter, *Prometheus Unbound* III iii 74–75: 'It seems in truth the fairest shell of Ocean: / Its sound must be at once both sweet and strange.'

28–29. 'A subtle, sudden flame, / By veering passion fanned'. Cp. the Prologue to Richard Cumberland's otherwise lost *The Princess of Parma* (1778) 29–30: 'There under Folly's colors gaily rides, / Where humor points, or veering passion guides.';[33] and Pye's *Alfred* v 143–44: 'While tears, and prayers, and threats, alternate strove, / As the wild gust of veering passion drove.'

78* Supposed Confessions of a Second-Rate Sensitive Mind (*pub* 1830)

Title. In her *Hours of Solitude: A Collection of Original Poems* (1805), cp. Charlotte Dacre's *The Vanity of Hope*, stanza ii: 'Oh! I wish my sad eyes could discover / A being of nature refin'd, / What rapture to prove him a lover, / A lover of sensitive mind!' Cp. also, from Mary Ann Browne's *Mont Blanc, and Other Poems* (1827), the final stanza of *I Speak Not of Beauty*, which would seem to be in response to Dacre's poem: 'Oh! give me the maid with a heart that can feel, / Whose soul with the chain of affection is twin'd, / And a brow on which pity hath set her soft seal; – / Oh! give me the maid with a sensitive mind.'

1–2. 'O God! my God! have mercy now. / I faint, I fall.' Ricks cites Shelley's *Indian Serenade* (1822) 18: 'I faint! I fail!' But cp. also the instances of T.'s phrase itself in lines 27–28 of Paris's song in the opening scene of William Congreve's *The Judgment of Paris* (1701): 'I faint, I fall! O take me hence, / Ere Ecstasie invades my aking Sense'; in line 19 of Charles Wesley's *Jesus, Lover of My Soul* (1740): 'Lo! I sink, I faint, I fall—'; and, twice, in Darwin's *Botanic Garden*: once in II ii 331–32: '"I faint, I fall!" —*at noon* the Beauty cried, / "Weep o'er my tomb, ye Nymphs!" —and sunk and died.'; and again in II iv 263–64: '"I faint!—I fall!—ah, me!—sensations chill / "Shoot through my bones, my shuddering bosom thrill!"'

---

33 Which prologue survived thanks to its inclusion in the 1789 and subsequent edns of Vicesimus Knox's *Elegant Extracts, or Useful and Entertaining Pieces of Poetry, selected for the improvement of Youth*, and in other contemporary verse collections.

22. 'And women smile with saint-like glances'. Cp., by F[rancis]. S[utherland]. Egerton, first Earl of Ellesmere, *Boyle Farm. A Poem.* (1827), p. 45: 'But most I love to turn and gaze / On all that mimic day displays, / On eyes that watch that fiery levin, / And saint-like glances turn'd to heaven'.[34]

49. 'Scarce outward signs of joy arise'. In her *Metrical Legends of Exalted Character* (1821), cp. Joanna Baillie's *The Legend of Lady Griseld Baillie* xliii 1–2: 'These ye may guess, for well the show / And outward signs of joy we know.' Cp. also John Wesley's *Explanatory Notes on the Whole Bible* (1754–65), where, commenting on the phrase *in laughter* in Proverbs xiv 13 ('Even in laughter the heart is sorrowful; and the end of that mirth is heaviness.'), he writes: 'The outward signs of joy are often mixed with real sorrow.'

83–86. 'What Devil had the heart to scathe / Flowers thou hadst reared — to brush the dew / From thine own lily, when thy grave / Was deep, my mother, in the clay?' In his 1785 edition of Milton's *Poems upon Several Occasions*, Thomas Warton commented, also appositely for T.'s poem, on line 50, 'And from the boughs brush off the evil dew', of Milton's masque *Arcades* (1634):

> The expression and idea are Shakesperian, but in a different sense and application. Caliban says [in *The Tempest* I ii 321–22], As WICKED DEW as e'er my mother BRUSH'D / With raven's feather from unwholsom fen, &c. Compare [*Paradise Lost* v 428–29]: —From off the [boughs] each morn / We BRUSH mellifluous DEWS.— The phrase hung on the mind of Gray [in *Elegy Written in a Country Churchyard* 99], BRUSHING with hasty steps the DEW AWAY.

96–97. 'Unpiloted i' the echoing dance / Of reboant whirlwinds'. Cp. Jonathan Swift's Latin poem *Carberiae Rupes* (1723) and William Dunkin's English translation, *Carbery Rocks*—both published in the 1735 collected edition of Swift's poems—the former with *reboant* (Latin for *loudly reverberating*) in line 25, '*Littora littoribus reboant*'; and the latter with *whirling winds* in line 9: 'For, long the whirling winds and beating tides / Had scoop'd a vault into its nether sides.' As Ricks reports, T.'s is the earliest example of *reboant* noted in the *OED*.

---

34   T. may also have seen the poem in *The Literary Gazette*, where it appeared in issue no. 563 for 3 Nov. 1827, on pages 715–16.

180–82. 'Let Thy dove/Shadow me over, and my sins/Be unremembered'. Echoing but inverting *Hamlet* III i 87–89 (Hamlet speaking): 'Soft you now, / The fair Ophelia. Nymph, in thy orisons / Be all my sins rememb'red.'

79 The Burial of Love (*pub* 1830)

2. 'Palecold his lips'. Cp. Shakespeare's *Titus Andronicus* V iii 153 (Lucius speaking): 'O, take this warm kiss on thy pale cold lips'.

83 Recollections of the Arabian Nights (*pub* 1830)

81. 'A sudden splendour from behind'. Instances of *sudden splendour* occur in Parnell's *Piety; or, The Vision* (1721) 6: 'A sudden splendour seem'd to kindle day'; Rev. Thomas Maurice's *The Lotos of Egypt* (1805) xvii 3–4, 'But mark,—slow rising near the distant pole, / A sudden splendour all her shores illumes.'; Porden's *The Veils* iii 20: 'A sudden splendour fills the vaulted room'; and James Montgomery's *Greenland* (1819) i 241–42: 'Or if a sudden splendour kindled joy, / 'Twas but a meteor dazzling to destroy'.

90. 'Distinct with vivid stars inlaid'. Cp. Thomson's *Winter* 88, 'The vivid stars shine out, in radiant Files'; Crabbe's *Inebriety* (1775), Part the First, 62: 'The vivid stars shoot lustre through the sky';[35] and Cowper's *Adam: a sacred drama* (1810) I i, 'There lovely flowers profuse / Appear as vivid stars'.

84 Ode to Memory (*pub* 1830)

1–4. 'Thou who stealest fire, / From the fountains of the past, / To glorify the present; oh, haste, / Visit my low desire!' Instances of the latter phrase occur in Pope, *Elegy to the Memory of an Unfortunate Lady* (1717) 11–12: 'Why bade ye else, ye Powers! her soul aspire / Above the vulgar flight of low desire' (and note the presence of *Memory* in both titles); Oliver Goldsmith, *The Traveller. Or, a Prospect of Society* (1764) 363–74:

---

35 As catalogued in *Lincoln* (Item 792), T. owned an incomplete set (lacking vol. 6) of the eight-volume (1834) Murray edn of Crabbe's *Poetical Works*, in which *Inebriety* was reprinted in vol. 2.

'Ye powers of truth, that bid my soul aspire, / Far from my bosom drive the low desire';[36] Robinson, *Sonnet Introductory* from her *Sappho and Phaon* (1796) 5–8: 'Well may the mind, with tuneful numbers grac'd, / To Fame's immortal attributes aspire, / Above the treach'rous spells of low desire, / That wound the sense, by vulgar joys debas'd.'; and Byron, *The Giaour* (1813) 1132–35: 'Yes, Love indeed is light from heaven; / A spark of that immortal fire / With angels shared, by Alla given, / To lift from earth our low desire.'

13–14. 'Even as a maid, whose stately brow / The dew-impearlèd winds of dawn have kissed'. For *dew-impearlèd* Collins cites, as does Ricks with the qualification 'possibly', sonnet 53 ('Cleere *Ankor*, on whose siluer-sanded shore') of Drayton's *Ideas Mirrour* (1594), line 8: 'Amongst the dainty dew-empearled flowers'. But cp. also Rev. William Mason's *Elfrida, A Dramatic Poem. Written on the Model of the Ancient Greek Tragedy* (1752), p. 20: 'Where'er thou art, enchanting Maid, / Thou soon wilt smile in Harewood's shade: / Soon will thy fairy feet be seen, / Printing this dew impearled green'; and line 15 of Rev. William Pooley's untitled poem beginning 'Hence Melancholy, pensive maid' (1761): 'Whilst on the dew impearled plain'.

15–17. 'When, she, as thou, / Stays on her floating locks the lovely freight / Of overflowing blooms'. Instances of *floating locks* include, among others, Macpherson/Ossian's *Cath-Loda* (1763), p. 185: 'A moonbeam glittered on a rock; in the midst, stood a stately form; a form with floating locks, like Lochlin's white-bosomed maids.'; in her *Cumbrian Legends*, Mrs. Ryves's *Music of the Chase* 94–95: 'The night retires; her floating locks, unshorn, / Hang in soft shadow on the drowsy morn'; from Wilson's *City of the Plague* II iv: 'Those floating locks blench'd by the ocean storms'; and *Revolt of Islam* I lx 6–7: 'Which thro' her floating locks and gathered cloak, / Glances of soul-dissolving glory, shone'. All may be traceable ultimately to Martial's *Epigrams* IV xlii, *Ad Flaccum* [To Flaccus] 7–8, speaking (as does the entire poem) of his favorite

---

36 As catalogued in *Lincoln*, T. owned two edns of Goldsmith's works, both containing *The Traveller*, but both published years after the appearance of this poem. The earlier of the two was the 1836 Daly edn of *The Poetical Works of Oliver Goldsmith*, on the fly-leaf of which T. wrote 'A. Tennyson March 1847' (Item 1018 in *Lincoln*).

Amazonicus: *'Lumina sideribus certent mollesque flagellent / Colla comae'* [Let his eyes rival the stars, and his floating locks play upon his neck].[37]

30. 'Thou leddest by the hand thine infant Hope.' For the latter phrase cp., from her 1784 collection, Charlotte Smith's sonnet 45, *On leaving a part of Sussex*, 2–3: 'My early vows were paid to Nature's shrine, / When thoughtless joy, and infant hope were mine'; and—note his capitalization of 'Hope'—Coleridge's *On Receiving an Account that his Only Sister's Death was Inevitable* (1791) 5–6: 'Ah! how has Disappointment pour'd the tear / O'er infant Hope destroy'd by early frost!'

35–36. 'Was cloven with the million stars which tremble / O'er the deep mind of dauntless infancy.' Among the excerpts of previously unpublished Dermody poems included in James Grant Raymond's two-volume *Life of Thomas Dermody* (1806) is one (in vol. 2, p. 57) on the ill-fated Thomas Chatterton reading in part: '"Ev'n now, when Taste pretends to spread her sway, / Behold the master of the wondrous lay, / In dauntless infancy a finish'd bard, / Despair his portion, prisons his reward!["]'

39. 'Those spirit-thrilling eyes so keen and beautiful'. Cp. *Revolt of Islam* VII iv 4–7: 'But she was calm and sad, musing alway / On loftiest enterprise, till on a day / The Tyrant heard her singing to her lute / A wild, and sad, and spirit-thrilling lay'.

48. 'Thou comest not with shows of flaunting vines'. Ricks cites *Comus* 545, 'flaunting Hony-suckle'. But cp. also Jacob George Strutt's translation (1814) of Claudian's *Rape of Proserpine*, Book II, 134–35: 'Low ivies crept around, and flaunting vines / Bound their smooth tendrils to majestic elms.'

65–66. 'Pour round mine ears the livelong bleat / Of the thick-fleecèd sheep from wattled folds'. For the latter line both Collins and Ricks cite *Comus* 344, 'The folded flocks pen'd in their watled cotes'. But cp. also William Beckford of Somerley, *A Descriptive Account of the Island*

---

[37] Prose translation by H. G. Bohn (1890). The three-volume 1823 Valpy edn of Martial's *Epigrammata*, with 'A. Tennyson' on the inside front board of vol. 1, was at Somersby (Item 220 in *Lincoln*).

of Jamaica (1790), vol. 1 (of 2), p. 396: 'While in their wattled folds the shepherds keep, / Nor dread the sweeping storm, their fleecy sheep'.

85–86. 'Place it, where sweetest sunlight falls / Upon the storied walls'. Both Collins and Ricks cite *Il Penseroso* 159–60, with 'storied Windows' — Ricks adding '(and "light")'. But cp. also Elton, *The Duke's Feast* (1810) xxi 121–22: 'His arms in musing thought the merchant folds, / And, touch'd with sadness, views the storied walls'; as well as John Thomas Hope's Newdigate Prize-winning *The Arch of Titus* (1824), published in *Oxford English Prize Poems* (Oxford, 1828), pp. 169–71: 'Yet linger not! within the circling space / The storied walls more radiant beauties grace'.

87 Adeline (*pub* 1830)

11–13. 'Whence that aery bloom of thine, / Like a lily which the sun / Looks through in his sad decline'. Cp. Cowper, *To Mary* (1803) 33–34: 'Partakers of thy sad decline, / Thy hands their little force resign'.[38]

26–27. 'Do beating hearts of salient springs / Keep measure with thine own?' Ricks notes that *salient springs* occurs in Wordsworth's *The Borderers*, adding that it was written in 1797 but not published until 1842. Another poem with the same phrase that T. could have seen before writing his own was Charles Lloyd's *Stanzas, written 10th, 11th, and 12th November, 1819* (1821), stanza xxxii of which begins: 'I had a store of joy within me then;— / An inexhaustible and salient spring'.

Cp. also the comment of Edmund Burke as (mis)quoted and misconstrued by Robert Carruthers in the introductory essay of *The Poetry of Milton's Prose* (1827), p. xxxi: 'Milton's mind never could have grown old: it had what Burke terms "a living salient spring of action," which only death could contract or shut up.' What Burke had actually written, in *Letters to a Noble Lord* (1796), was 'He had in himself a salient, living spring of generous and manly action', referring not to Milton but to his own late son.

31–32. 'With what voice the violet woos / To his heart the silver dews?' Cp. Samuel Boyse's *Cambuscan, or the Squire's Tale* (1741) — a 'modernising'

---

38 T.'s library as catalogued in *Lincoln* had vol. 2 only of the three-volume (1830–31) Pickering edn of *The Poetical Works of William Cowper* (Item 789). *To Mary* was in vol. 3.

of Chaucer's tale completed by Joseph Sterling after Boyse's death—
419–20: 'The Rose of Tigris, Sarra's Violet woos, / And with this mystic
Ring her valu'd Friendship sues!' Cp. also the anonymous *Broomeholme
Priory, or The Loves of Albert and Agnes. A Poem, In Four Books.* (1801),
Book IV, 85–86, where, speaking of the snow-drop in winter, the poet
writes: 'The violet woos it as a beauteous bride, / And springs in sweetest
fragrance by its side'.

88* A Character (*wr* c. 1829–30)

1–4. 'With a half-glance upon the sky / At night he said, "The wanderings /
Of this most intricate Universe / Teach me the nothingness of things."'
Cp. Shelley's preface to *Prometheus Unbound*, where he comments
on line 67 of Sophocles's *Oedipus Rex* ('πολλὰς δ᾽ ὁδοὺς ἐλθόντα
φροντίδος πλάνοις'): '"Coming to many paths in the wanderings
of careful thought." [...] What a picture does this line suggest of the
mind as a wilderness of intricate paths, wide as the universe'.[39] See also
a passage from Homily 8 on *1 Corinthians* iii 1–3 by the Early Church
father John Chrysostom: 'And yet one might think that even without
words experience itself is sufficient to teach you the nothingness of
things present, and their utter meanness.'

7–9. 'He spake of beauty: that the dull / Saw no divinity in grass, / Life
in dead stones, or spirit in air'. T.'s lines may have been suggested by
either or both of two sermons by the English theologian John Owen
(1616–83), an edition of whose works, edited by Thomas Russell, was
published in 1826. As to *divinity in grass*, in *The Everlasting Covenant, The
Believer's Support Under Distress*, a sermon preached in 1669 and first
published in 1756, Owen wrote:

> Why, saith [David, in *2 Samuel* xxiii], 'He shall be as the light of the
> morning, when the sun riseth, even a morning without clouds; as the

---

39 As catalogued in *Lincoln* (Items 320, 321, and 322), George Clayton Tennyson's
library had three partial or complete edns of Sophocles in either or both Greek and
Latin, in one of which—R. F. P. Brunck's 1809, Greek-only edn—T. wrote 'Alfred
Tennyson' on the fly-leaf of vol. 2. T.'s own library had five more (Items 2075
through 2079 in *Lincoln*) in Greek, Latin, and/or English; and that of T.'s brother
Charles had the seven-volume (1822–25) Fleischer edn (Item 2580) with Greek text
and Latin notes, on the title page of vol. 7 of which T. also wrote his name.

tender grass springing out of the earth by clear shining after rain.' [...] You know the reason of the allusion: when the grass hath been long dried, and there comes a great rain upon it, and clear shining upon that rain, how will the grass spring up! There was to be a great drought upon the church; but Christ comes, and he was as the rain, and as the sun shining upon the rain; then there was a springing up with great glory, and unto great fruitfulness.

As to *life in dead stones*, this was among the topics addressed in Owen's sermon entitled *The Branch of the Lord, the Beauty of Zion*, preached and first published in 1650:

> [I]f all the most skilfull Workmen in the world should go to the pit of Nature, by their own strength to hew out stones for this building, they will never with all their skill and diligence, lay one stone upon it. There is Life required to those stones, which none can give but Christ. The Father hath given into his hand alone, to give life eternall to whom he will, John 17:2. He alone can turn stones into children of Abraham. To him is committed all dispensation of quickning power. He brings us from the dust of death, and no man hath quickned his own soul. With spiritual power, all spiritual life is vested in Christ. If dead stones live, it must be, by hearing the voyce of the Son of God.

20–22. 'He canvassed human mysteries, / And trod on silk, as if the winds / Blew his own praises in his eyes'. For *trod on silk*, cp. Edward and Henry Leigh's *Select and Choyce Observations, Containing All the Romane Emperours* (1657), in which, on p. 245, the emperor Diocletian is said to have been 'the first who wore cloath of gold, trod on silk and purple embellished with pearls; and (next after *Caligula* and *Domitian*) was the first, who would be sued unto as a god, though (saith *Aur[elius]. Victor*) he carried himself liker a Father, than a Tyrant.'

91 The Poet (*pub* 1830)

1–2. 'The poet in a golden clime was born, / With golden stars above'. For *golden clime* Ricks cites *Endymion* iii 455, 'She did so breathe ambrosia; so immerse / My fine existence in a golden clime', but cp. also Rogers, *The Pleasures of Memory* (1792), Part II, 126–27: 'May range, at will, bright Fancy's golden clime, / Or, musing, mount where Science sits sublime';[40]

---

40   As stated above (note 12), Rogers's *Poems* (1812), which included this one, was at Somersby.

and, from Blake's *Songs of Experience* (1794), *Ah! Sun-flower* 3: 'Seeking after that sweet golden clime'.

For *golden stars*, cp. Dryden's *Æneis* xi 1211–12: 'A shout, that struck the golden stars, ensu'd: / Despair and rage, and languish'd fight renew'd'; and his *Georgic II* 466: 'And golden stars flew up to light the skies'. Cp. also *Revolt of Islam* VI xxx 265–70: 'for now / A power, a thirst, a knowledge, which below / All thoughts, like light beyond the atmosphere, / Clothing its clouds with grace, doth ever flow, / Came on us, as we sate in silence there, / Beneath the golden stars of the clear azure air.'; as well as Shelley's *Letter to Maria Gisborne* (1824) 258–60: 'Whether the moon, into her chamber gone, / Leaves midnight to the golden stars, or wan / Climbs with diminished beams the azure steep'.

9–10. 'with echoing feet he threaded / The secretest walks of fame'. For *secretest* both Collins and Ricks cite *Macbeth* III iv 126: 'the secret'st man of blood'. But cp. also Sir Philip Sidney's 1595 treatise *An Apology for Poetry*, also known as *The Defence of Poesy*, which speaks of its power to 'plant goodness even in the secretest cabinet of our souls'; as well as *Endymion* ii 572: 'And that of all things 'tis kept secretest.'

For *walks of fame*, see, in Langhorne's *The Fables of Flora* (1771), the first stanza of *Fable II. The Evening Primrose*: 'There are that love the shades of life, / And shun the splendid walks of Fame; / There are who hold it rueful strife, / To risque AMBITION's losing game'; and, by the Irish-born American James M'Henry, *The Pleasures of Friendship* (Pittsburgh, 1822; Philadelphia, 1825), Part II, 399–402: 'Or should our LIVING BARDS your thoughts engage, / Whose varied strains delight th' admiring age. / Lo! FRIENDSHIP warms them with her noblest flame; / To aid each other in the walks of fame.'

11–12. 'The viewless arrows of his thoughts were headed / And winged with flame'. Ricks notes that the poem *To Poesy [Religion be thy sword]* co-written by T. and Arthur Hallam has, in lines 5–6, 'Oh might I be an arrow in thy hand, / And not of viewless flight, but trailing flame'; and cites Keats's *Ode to a Nightingale* (1819) 33: 'But on the viewless wings of Poesy'. But cp. also Hoole's *Jerusalem Delivered* vii 589–91: 'the fiery bolts of heaven; / The viewless arrows that in tainted air / Disease and plagues to frighted mortals bear'; and, though also published in 1830, Lewis Evans's *The Pleasures of Benevolence* i 3–4: 'The midnight pest that walks in ghastly power, / The viewless arrows of the noontide hour'.

95 Hero to Leander (*pub* 1830)

38–39. 'Leander! go not yet. / The pleasant stars have set'. Cp. Thomas Wyatt, *Complaint of the Absence of His Love* (1557) 70–71: 'The lively streams of pleasant stars that under it doth glide; / Wherein the beams of love do still increase their heat'.

99 The Grasshopper (*pub* 1830)

34 and 40. 'What hast thou to do with evil'. Ricks cites *Comus* 122: 'What hath night to do with sleep?' But cp. also *Revolt of Islam* II xx 4–6: 'And one more daring raised his steel anew / To pierce the Stranger: "What hast thou to do / With me, poor wretch?"'; and 'What hast thou to do with me, thou meddlesome watchman?', line 1 of the anonymous translation of the Latin epigram from the *Carmina Priapea* (variously numbered xvi and xvii and sometimes attributed to Martial) that begins *'Quid mecum tibi, circitor moleste?'*

Scriptural analogues of the phrase include *Judges* xi 12: 'And Jephthah sent messengers unto the king of the children of Ammon, saying, What hast thou to do with me, that thou art come against me to fight in my land?'; *2 Kings* ix 19: 'And Jehu answered, What hast thou to do with peace? turn thee behind me.'; as well as *Matthew* viii 29: 'And, behold, they cried out, saying, What have we to do with thee, Jesus, thou Son of God? art thou come hither to torment us before the time?'

101 Chorus, in an Unpublished Drama, Written Very Early (*pub* 1830)

9–10, 19–20, and 29–30. 'are full of strange / Astonishment and boundless change.' Ricks notes that T.'s refrain was suggested by Shelley's *On Death* (1816) 23–24: "All that is great and all that is strange / In the boundless realm of unending change".' As for *strange astonishment*, cp. also Spenser's *Two Cantos of Mutabilitie* (1609), VI xvi 1–3: 'Eftsoons the son of Maia forth he sent / Down to the Circle of the Moon, to know / The cause of this so strange Astonishment'; Joseph Cottle's *Alfred, an Epic Poem* (1800) v 36: 'Whilst strange astonishment the master fill'd';

and Pollok's *Course of Time* i 288–89: 'Of wonder full and strange astonishment, / At what in yonder den of darkness dwells'.

21–22. 'Each sun which from the centre flings / Grand music and redundant fire'. Cp., from the first (1817) edition of Charles Symmons's translation of *The Æneis of Virgil*, vol. 2, Book XI: 'To damp with prudence war's redundant fire'. In an article on that edition in *The Monthly Review* lxxxv (July 1818), the reviewer, on p. 249, condemned Symmons's choice of 'redundant' in rendering Virgil's *'Cautius ut saevo velles te credere Marti'* (xi 153) as 'a very injudicious epithet, and ill suited to the first unrestrained overflow of the father's sorrows', the apparent result of which was that the offending word was removed and the line rewritten in the second (1820) edition. The presence of 'redundant fire' in T.'s poem suggests, however, that he had seen it in Symmons's first edition—or in *The Monthly Review*.

27. 'The lawless comets as they glare'. Cp. Joseph Thurston, *The Fall; in Four Books* (1732) ii 32: 'So lawless comets strike th' astonish'd eye, / So sure prognosticate a ruin nigh'; and William Duckett, *Grecian Liberty: An Ode* (1822) 40–41: 'Like lawless comets in their course, / Urg'd by the impulse of blind force'.[41]

28. 'And thunder through the sapphire deeps'. Cp. Darwin's *Botanic Garden* I ii 119–20: 'HENCE with diffusive SALT old Ocean steeps / His emerald shallows, and his sapphire deeps.'

106 To a Lady Sleeping (*pub* 1830)

2. 'Through whose dim brain the wingèd dreams are borne'. For *dim brain*, cp. *Prometheus Unbound* II i 66: 'Like music which makes giddy the dim brain'; and, also by Shelley, *The Witch of Atlas* (1824) v 5: 'Dark—the dim brain whirls dizzy with delight'.

For *wingèd dreams*, cp. the lyric *Weep No More*, lines 7–8, in the Fletcher–Massinger–Nathan Field tragicomedy *The Queen of Corinth* (1647) III ii: 'Joys as wingèd dreams fly fast, / Why should sadness longer last?'; and

---

41 Duckett's poem was published in, and apparently only in, *The Monthly Magazine; or, British Register* vol. 54, no. 375 (1 Dec. 1822), 428–29.

Moore, *Love's Young Dream* (1811) 29: "'Twas morning's winged dream'. The phrase may ultimately be traceable to the *Hecuba* of Euripides, lines 70–71, 'ὢ πότνια Χθών, / μελανοπτερύγων μῆτερ ὀνείρων', reading, in John Potter's *Archæologia Græca, or The antiquities of Greece* (1697 and all later editions): 'Hail, reverend *Earth,* from whose prolifick Womb / Sable wing'd Dreams derive their Birth.'

8. 'Though long ago listening the poisèd lark'. Cp. Tobias Smollett, *Ode to Independence*—also known as *Independence: An Ode*—(1773) 106: 'Where the poised lark his evening ditty chants'; and John Stewart, *The Pleasures of Love* (1806), Part II, 55–56: 'See the blithe kids o'er scented herbage rove, / And the poised lark attune his hymn of love.'

9. 'With eyes dropt downward through the blue serene'. Ricks notes that *blue serene* is a traditional phrase occurring twice in Shelley, once in *Revolt of Islam* I iv 5: 'Beneath that opening spot of blue serene'; and again in line 46 of the unfinished *The Woodman and the Nightingale,* published posthumously in 1824: 'Chequering the sunlight of the blue serene'. Other instances of the phrase occur in Thomson's *Winter* 301: 'Clear Frost succeeds, and thro' the blew Serene, / For Sight too fine, th'Ætherial Nitre flies'; Thomas Warton's *Pleasures of Melancholy* 8–10: 'But when the skies / Unclouded shine, and thro' the blue serene / Pale Cynthia rolls her silver-axled car'; and Charlotte Smith's sonnet 80 (*To the Invisible Moon*) 3: 'To watch thee, gliding thro' the blue serene'.

107 Sonnet [Could I outwear my present state of woe] (*pub* 1830)

1. 'Could I outwear my present state of woe'. Cp. *Paradise Lost* v 542–43: 'O fall / From what high state of bliss into what woe!', as well as the iterated refrain 'And a [first/second/third/fourth/fifth/sixth/seventh] Age passed over & a State of dismal woe' in Blake's *Milton* (1810), lines 10, 13, 16, 19, 21, 23, and 27.

13–14. 'This to itself hath drawn the frozen rain / From my cold eyes and melted it again.' Cp. *Inferno* xxxiii 109–50, where, in the ninth circle, Dante promises to remove the frozen tears from one sinner's face in exchange for his name. When the sinner identifies himself as the treacherous Fra Alberigo, who, after an argument, had his own cousin and the cousin's son assassinated while on a conciliatory visit to his house, Dante breaks that promise.

108 Sonnet [Though Night hath climbed her peak of highest noon] *(pub 1830)*

8. 'Basing thy throne above the world's annoy.' For the latter phrase Ricks cites Keble's *The Christian Year* (1827), where poem 53, *Third Sunday After Trinity*, stanza vii, has 'earth's annoy'. But the phrase itself occurs in Thomas Edwards's *Narcissus* (1595), L'Envoy ii 9: 'Aie me pretie wanton boy, / What a sire did hatch thee forth, / To shew thee of the worlds annoy'; in Joseph Hall's *Elegy on Dr. Whitaker* (1596) viii 4: 'And all agreed to work the worlds annoy'; and in Francis Rous the Elder's *Thule, or Vertues Historie* (1598) vi 251: 'Freed from these troubles and the worlds annoy'. Hall's elegy was reissued among the miscellaneous poems in his *Satires* (Chiswick, 1824), pp. 169–73.

14. 'An honourable eld shall come upon thee.' For *honourable eld* Ricks cites Thomson's *Castle of Indolence* (1748) II xxxi, 'venerable eld'. But the phrase itself occurs in Spenser's *The Faerie Queene* (1590) I viii st. 47: 'Her crafty head was altogether bald, / And as in hate of honorable eld, / Was ouergrowne with scurfe and filthy scald';[42] as well as in Reginald Heber's *Morte D'Arthur: A Fragment*—posthumously published in *The Life of Sir Reginald Heber, D.D.* (also 1830)—III xxxvi 4: 'And the fair peace of honourable eld'.

109 Sonnet [Shall the hag Evil die with child of Good] *(pub 1830)*

4. 'Hateful with hanging cheeks, a withered brood'. For *hanging cheeks*, cp. Ben Jonson's *Volpone; or, The Foxe* (1607) I i 56–59 (Mosca speaking): 'Would you once close / Those filthy eyes of yours, that flow with slime, /

---

[42] George Clayton Tennyson's library at Somersby had the 1590 Ponsonbie edn of *The Faerie Queene* (Item 326 in *Lincoln*)—from which these lines are quoted—with 'A. Tennyson' inscribed on the inside front board and on the back of the second fly-leaf.

Like two frog-pits; and those same hanging cheeks, / Cover'd with hide, instead of skin'. Directly or indirectly T. and Jonson both echo *Satire X* of Juvenal, *hanging cheeks* being a literal translation of *'pendentesque genas'* in line 193 of that poem.[43]

5. 'Though hourly pastured on the salient blood?' In *Poems on Several Occasions* (1748) by the otherwise anonymous 'H. G.', cp. *All is Vanity, Eccles. i.2*, lines 29–30: 'Mid-night debauches fire the salient blood / And dart fell poison through the vital flood.' Cp. also, in the November 1774 issue of *Monthly Miscellany*, 280–81, a poeticized version, signed 'TOGATUS, Cambridge', of Richard Steele's *The Story of Inkle and Yarico* (1767)—itself based on Richard Ligon's *A True and Exact History of Barbados* (1657)—in *The Spectator*, vol. 1, no. 11, for 13 March 1711. Lines 98–99 of the poem by TOGATUS read: 'The salient blood its sprightly course disdains, / And curdling freezes in her icy veins'.

8–9. 'and in the solitude / Of middle space confound them'. For *middle space*, cp. line 3 of *Faerie Queene* II ii st. 20, 'And cruel combat ioynd in middle space'; line 4 of *FQ* II iv st. 32, 'Hath now fast bound, me met in middle space.'; Dryden's *Æneis*, with a total of seven instances in books 6, 8, 10, 11, and 12; Hogg's *Mador of the Moor*, Introduction, lines 10–13: 'O that some spirit at the midnight noon / Aloft would bear me, middle space, to see / Thy thousand branches gleaming to the moon, / By shadowy hill, gray rock, and fairy lea'; and Keats, *Imitation of Spenser* (1817) 9: 'And, in its middle space, a sky that never lowers.' The phrase occurs in several other poems, most involving military situations.

14. 'Nor blot with floating shades the solar light.' Cp., in Langhorne's *The Visions of Fancy. In Four Elegies.* (1762), *Elegy III*, line 34: 'While floating shades of dusky night descend'; and Shelley's *Alastor* 123–24: 'nor, when the moon / Filled the mysterious halls with floating shades'.

---

43   George Clayton Tennyson's library had three edns of Juvenal's *Satires*, two in Latin—Items 184 (with 'Alfred Tennyson' on the title page) and 185 (with 'A. Tennyson, Somersby in agro Lincolniensi Lindseinsique divisione' on the fly-leaf) in *Lincoln*—and one (Item 186) in Latin and English (1777) with Thomas Sheridan's prose translation (but without *hanging cheeks*).

110 Sonnet [The pallid thunderstricken sigh for gain] (*pub* 1830)

2. 'Down an ideal stream they ever float'. Cp. Mason, *Ode I. On Leaving St. John's College, Cambridge, 1746* (1797) 7–8: 'Shall teach th' ideal stream to flow / Like gentle Camus, soft and slow'.

4–6. 'while wistfully they strain / Weak eyes upon the glistering sands that robe / The understream.' For *glistering sand(s)*, cp. Drayton's *Poly-Olbion, The Fifteenth Song* 267: 'Gilds with his glistering sands the ouer-pamper'd shore'; and Joseph Beaumont's *Psyche* XV cccxxiii 1–4: 'A thousand greedy *Hands* their zeal have fill'd / With this most *privileg'd Earth*, and held it more / Golden than all the *glistering Sand* which swell'd / The fame of *Ganges* or of *Indus's* shoar'.

124 Amy (*wr* c. 1828–30)

5. 'The silver tongues of featherfooted rumour'. Cp. Catullus, *Carmina* 58b, line 5: '*adde huc plumipedas uolatilesque*' [add to this the featherfooted and swift]. In English verse, *featherfooted* occurs as a hyphenated compound in James Shirley's *The Triumph of Peace* (1634) *Song IX*, lines 9–10: 'Ye feather-footed Hours run / To dress the chariot of the Sun'; in Aaron Hill's *Advice to the Poets* (1731) p. 32: 'Fancy's light *Dwarfs!* whose feather-footed Strains, / Dance, in wild Windings, through a *Waste* of Brains!'; and in Joseph Warton's *Ode to Sleep* (1748) 1–2: 'O Gentle, feather-footed Sleep, / In drowsy Dews my Temples steep'.

18. 'Or snowdrop burst to life'. Cp. Rev. Luke Booker, *The Snowdrop* (1789) 1–2: 'Impatient for the coming Spring, / A Snowdrop burst its leafy cell'.

126 Memory [Ay me!] (*wr* c. 1826–27)

3–4. 'Those fair eyes in my inmost frame / Are subtle shafts of pierceant flame.' For T.'s *pierceant* Ricks cites Spenser's 'persant' in *Faerie Queene* I x st. 47; and Keats's 'perceant' in *Lamia* (1820) ii 301. But for *faire eyes, flame,* and *persant* in proximity, cp. also *FQ* II iii st. 23: 'In her faire eyes two living lamps did flame, / Kindled above at th' Hevenly Makers light, / And darted fyrie beames out of the same, / So passing persant, and so wondrous bright'.

127 Ode: O Bosky Brook (*wr* c. 1823–27)

9. 'Of sallows, whitening to the fitful breeze'. Ricks cites Shelley's *Rosalind and Helen: A Modern Eclogue* (1819) 959: 'fitful breezes'. But cp. also Scott, *The Lady of the Lake* (1810) i 3: 'And down the fitful breeze thy numbers flung'; and Wordsworth, *Written In a Blank Leaf of Macpherson's Ossian* (1827) 1–2: 'Oft have I caught, upon a fitful breeze, / Fragments of far-off melodies'.

15. 'Watching the red hour of the dying Sun'. In John Clare, *The Shepherd's Calendar* (1827), cp. *March* 151–52: 'Now love-teazed maidens, from the droning wheel, / At the red hour of sun-set, slily steal'.

20. 'Varied with steadfast shades the glimmering plain'. For the latter phrase, cp. Wordsworth, *Water-Fowl* (1827) 22–23: ''tis themselves, / Their own fair forms, upon the glimmering plain'.

52. 'In tremulous darts of slender light'. Cp. Edward Fairfax's translation of Tasso under the title *Godfrey of Bulloigne, or, Jerusalem Delivered* (1600) VIII xxv 7–8: 'And through the Darkness to my feeble Sight / Appear'd the Twinkling of a slender Light.'[44]

54. 'Or on the screaming waste of desolate heath'. For the latter phrase, cp. Shelley's *Zastrozzi*, chap. 1: 'It was still dark, when they stopped at a small inn, on a remote and desolate heath'; his other early Gothic novella *St. Irvyne; or, The Rosicrucian* (1811), where the phrase occurs twice; and Scott's novel *The Pirate* (1822), chap. 2: 'At other times [...] this unhappy man would wrap himself in a dark-coloured sea-cloak, and wander out along the stormy beach, or upon the desolate heath, indulging his

---

44 T.'s library had the two-volume fifth (1817) Knight edn of Fairfax's *Godfrey of Bulloigne*, now subtitled *The Recovery of Jerusalem* (Item 2162 in Lincoln), with 'A. Tennyson' on the inside front board of vol. 1 and with 'Alfred Tennyson from R.J.T.'—probably, as Robert Pattison notes in *Tennyson and Tradition*, p. 171, R. J. Tennant, a close friend of T.'s from their Cambridge years to the early 1830s—on both title pages. As catalogued in *Lincoln* (Item 338), George Clayton Tennyson's library had only vols. 2, 3, and 4 of the four-volume Seguin edn (Avignone, 1816) of *La Gerusalemme liberata*.

own gloomy and wayward reveries'. Although Shakespeare himself does not use the phrase, critical commentaries on *Macbeth* and *King Lear* commonly speak of their opening scene and third act, respectively, as taking place on a desolate heath.

56. 'Or in close pastures soft as dewy sleep'. For the latter phrase Ricks cites Shelley's *Adonais* (1821) 61, 'He lies, as if in dewy sleep he lay', and his posthumously published *Ginevra* (1824) 127–28, 'until the dewy sleep is shaken / From every living heart'. But cp. also, among other instances of the phrase, *Paradise Lost* ix 1044–45: 'till dewy sleep / Oppressed them, wearied with their amorous play'; and, from *Ovid's Epistles: with his Amours* (1729), the much-reprinted translation 'By an unknown Hand' of his *Elegy XIII. To the Morning, not to make Haste* 67–68: 'See how the Moon does her *Endimion* keep / In Night conceal'd, and drown'd in dewy Sleep?'

61–62. 'the bright boss / Of thine own Halo's dusky shield'. For the latter phrase, cp. *Fingal* iv 131–32, 'And on his stately side the dusky shield / The King beheld', and elsewhere in the Macpherson/Ossian pseudo-canon.

64–65. 'The margin of the dun and dappled field / Of vagrant waves'. Cp. John Dyer, *The Ruins of Rome* (1740) 485: 'Through silver channels glide the vagrant waves'.

67. 'With such a lustrous chord of solemn sheen'. From Wordsworth's *Ecclesiastical Sketches* (1822), cp. poem XXXIII (*Inside of King's College Chapel, Cambridge*) 5–8: 'Martyr, or King, or sainted Eremite, / Whoe'er ye be, that thus, yourselves unseen, / Imbue your prison-bars with solemn sheen / Shine on, until ye fade with coming Night!—'.

72. 'Blossoming round the everduring walls'. For the latter phrase, cp. Philip Bracebridge Homer, *Observations On a Short Tour Made in the Summer of 1803, to the Western Highlands of Scotland* (1804), where lines 13–14 of the poem beginning 'Here let me stand' on p. 29 read: 'From rock to rock his tumbling torrent falls, / And thund'ring shakes these ever-during walls'.

78. '(What time the white West glares with sickening ray)'. In *Poems on Subjects Chiefly Devotional* (1760) by 'Theodosia' (Anne Steele), cp. *A Dying Saviour*, stanza iv: 'And didst thou bleed, for sinners bleed? /

And could the sun behold the deed? / No, he withdrew his sickening ray, / And darkness veil'd the mourning day.' Among other instances of *sickening* (or *sick'ning*) *ray*, cp., in Mrs. Elizabeth Singer Rowe's *Friendship in Death: in Twenty Letters from the Dead to the Living* (1728), Letter 1 of 'Letters to the Author By Another Hand', ending: 'Thy sick'ning ray, and venerable gloom, / Shew life's last scene, the solitary tomb'; and John Anster, *The Times: A Reverie* (Edinburgh, 1819) iv 103–5: 'While through the open roof the mid-day sun / Shone visible a God, and with the blaze / Of brightness mock'd the taper's sickening ray!'

81. 'The lighthouse glowing from the secret rock'. Cp. Fairfax's *Godfrey of Bulloigne* II lxviii 1–2: 'Yet still we sail while prosperous blows the wind, / Till on some secret rock unwares we light'; the Pope–Broome–Fenton *Odyssey* iv 879: 'Safe from the secret rock and adverse storm'; and Richard Savage, *The Genius of Liberty* (1738) 67–68: 'E'en now thy fancied perils fill her mind; / The secret rock, rough wave, and rising wind'.

128 Perdidi Diem (*wr* c. 1826–27)

11. 'Wounding with dreadful rays that solid gloom'. One pre-T. instance of *dreadful rays* occurs in Watts's *Reliquiae Juveniles. Miscellaneous Thoughts in Prose and Verse.* (1734), where the untitled poem on p. 142 begins: 'Let *Astrapé* forbear to blaze / As Lightning does, with dreadful Rays'; another, in Mickle's *Lusiad* i 663–64: 'From his black ships the sudden lightnings blaze, / And o'er old Ocean flash their dreadful rays'.

Pre-T. instances of *solid gloom* include, in Watts's *Horae Lyricae* (1706 and subsequent editions), *To the Dear Memory of my Honoured Friend* Thomas Gunston *Esq.* 370–71: 'But not one Beam can reach the darksome Grave, / Or pierce the solid Gloom that fills the Cave'; and Thomson's *Winter* 195–96: 'The weary clouds, / Slow-meeting, mingle into solid gloom.'

24 and 33. 'Young ravens fallen from their cherishing nest' and 'With sleep-compelling down of her most glossy breast.' Cp. Cowper's *A Fable* (1780), which begins: 'A raven, while with glossy breast / Her new-laid eggs she fondly press'd'.[45] Other instances of *glossy breast* occur in

---

45 In the two-volume (1808) Johnson edn of Cowper's *Poems* (see note 16), this poem is in vol. 1.

Charlotte Smith's *Studies by the Sea* (1804) 95–100: 'But with instinctive love is drest / The Eider's downy cradle; where / The mother-bird, her glossy breast / Devotes, and with maternal care, / And plumeless bosom, stems the toiling seas / That foam round the tempestuous Orcades.'; and in Wordsworth's *To a Small Celandine* (1807) 29–30: 'Spreading out thy glossy breast / Like a careless Prodigal'.

130 Sense and Conscience (*wr* c. 1826–27)

40–41. 'Nor barbèd fire of spears, nor deadliest draught / Could drive him to the death'. For *barbèd fire* Ricks cites line 99 of *Adonais*, 'And dull the barbèd fire against his frozen cheek'. T. may have owed *deadliest draught* to *The Dance of the Consumptives* in the *Remains of Henry Kirke White*, where the line containing the phrase, spoken by Melancholy and addressed to Consumption, first occurs in vol. 1, p. 320, of the 1808 edition: 'Hist, sister, hist! who comes here; / Oh, I know her by that tear, / By that blue eye's languid glare, / By her skin, and by her hair: / She is mine, / And she is thine, / Now thy deadliest draught prepare.'; or to John Imlah's *May Flowers. Poems and Songs: Some in the Scottish Dialect* (1827), in which the poem called *To* .... has, in stanza iv, lines 5–8: 'But oh! the bitterness and gall— / 'Tis mine the very dregs to drain; / And this the deadliest draught of all— / We never meet again!'

52–53. 'Long time he lay and slept: his awful brows / Pillowed on violet-woven mosses deep'. Cp. Thomas Warton's *Pleasures of Melancholy* 190–91: 'When from her vi'let-woven couch awak'd / By frolic Zephyr's hand'.

79. 'How changed from that fair vision which, clad in light'. Ricks cites *Paradise Lost* i 84–87: 'But O how fall'n! how chang'd / From him, who in the happy Realms of Light / Cloth'd with transcendent brightness didst outshine / Myriads though bright.' But cp. also instances of the phrase *clad in light* itself, in lines 45–48 of Nahum Tate's 'White-LILY' (1689) translating a Latin poem, *Lilium Candidum*, from Book IV of Cowley's *Plantarum* or *Book of Plants* (1668): 'Nature on many Flow'rs beside / Bestows a muddy white; / On me she plac'd her greatest Pride, / All over clad in Light.'; in Rev. Henry Boyd's translation (1806) of Petrarch's *The Triumph of Chastity* 97–98: 'A sky-descended legion, clad in light /

Of glorious panoply, contemning mortal might'; in Hemans's *Morning* (1808) 1–2: 'Now rosy morning clad in light / Dispels the darkling clouds of night'; in James Montgomery's *Greenland* iii 25: 'Till morning comes, but comes not clad in light'; and, from Sir John Bowring's *Matins and Vespers with Hymns and Occasional Devotional Pieces* (1823), in his *Fourth Week. Winter. Sunday Morning*, 49: ' —O Thou eternal Being! clad in light'.

132 'In deep and solemn dreams' (*wr* c. 1825–26)

43. 'We have waked the matin bird'. For the latter phrase, cp. William Lisle Bowles, *Hope* (1789), which begins: 'As one who, long by wasting sickness worn, / Weary has watched the lingering night, and heard / Unmoved the carol of the matin bird / Salute his lonely porch'; Coleridge's sonnet on La Fayette (1794) 3–4: 'Within his cage the imprison'd Matin Bird / Swells the full chorus with a generous song'; and Byron's *Mazeppa* (1819) 296–98: 'And not an insect's shrill small horn, / Nor matin bird's new voice was borne / From herb nor thicket.'

59–60. 'And the hollow dark I dread / Closes round my friendless head'. For *hollow dark*—which also occurs in T.'s poem 173, *A Dream of Fair Women*, lines 17–18: 'Those far-renownèd brides of ancient song / Peopled the hollow dark, like burning stars'—Ricks cites Keats's *Fall of Hyperion* i 455, 'And stretch'd her white arm through the hollow dark', noting, however, that it was not published until 1856. But the phrase also occurs in *Paradise Lost* ii 951–54: 'At length a universal hubbub wilde / Of stunning sounds and voices all confus'd / Born through the hollow dark assaults his eare / With loudest vehemence'.

140 Lines on Cambridge of 1830 (*wr* c. 1830)

8–9. 'Nor yet your solemn organ-pipes that blow / Melodious thunders through your vacant courts'. Cp. Edwin Atherstone, *A Midsummer Day's Dream* (1824) part 3 ('Dream Continued'), p. 104: 'and the sun above / Pour'd out his voice as if the infinitude / Of space were fill'd with deep, melodious thunders.'[46]

---

46 See also the instances of *melodious thunder* singular cited in the discussion of T.'s poem 220, *Semele*, lines 12–13, on p. 112 below.

143 A Fragment [Where is the Giant of the Sun] (*wr* c. 1830)

10. 'Broadbased amid the fleeting sands'. For the latter phrase, cp. Thomas May's translation (1631) of Lucan's *Pharsalia* ix 548–49: 'But since compos'd of loose, and fleeting sands / Resisting not, it bides'. Cp. also, in its close-to-final lines, Allan Ramsay's *Health, a Poem* (Edinburgh, 1724) 389–90: 'Where fleeting sands ne'er yield t'industrious toil, / The golden sheaf, or plants for wine and oil'; and, in vol. 3 of his posthumous *Works* (1753), Aaron Hill's *To Clio*, stanza xii: 'But, as it is, our fleeting sands so fast / *Ebb* to their *end*, and lead us to *decay*; / That e're we learn to *see*, our daylight's past, / And, like a melting *mist*, life shrinks away.'

Hazlitt's essay *On a Sun-Dial*, in *The New Monthly Magazine*, vol. 20, no. 82 (Oct. 1827), 352–58, says of the hour-glass:

> The philosopher in his cell, the cottager at her spinning-wheel must, however, find an invaluable acquisition in this 'companion of the lonely hour,' as it has been called [by Robert Bloomfield], which not only serves to tell how the time goes, but to fill up its vacancies. What a treasure must not the little box seem to hold, as if it were a sacred deposit of the very grains and fleeting sands of life!

144 'O wake ere I grow jealous of sweet Sleep' (*wr* c. 1830)

6. 'My shadowed Memory!' Cp. Henry Trevanion, *The Influence of Apathy* (1827) 15–16: 'Raise on the shadowed memory of my mind / The phantom feelings that delude mankind'.

145 'The constant spirit of the world exults' (*wr* c. 1830)

9. 'But some high-thoughted moods and moulds of mind'. Cp., in Bartholomew Griffin's *Sonnets to Fidessa* (1596), Sonnet 1 (*'Fidessa fair! long live a happy maiden!'*) 3: 'High-thoughted, like to her, with bounty laden'; Moore's *Shall the Harp Then Be Silent*—also known as *Grattan's Lamentation*—(1815) 23–24: 'In whose high-thoughted daring, the fire, and the force, / And the yet untamed spring of her spirit are shown?';

his *Remonstrance* (1820) 12: 'Is for high-thoughted spirits like thine to command?'; and Keats's *Lamia* ii 115: 'She set herself, high-thoughted, how to dress / The misery in fit magnificence'.

146 Sonnet [When that rank heat of evil's tropic day] (*wr* by 1834)

8. 'Thy looks, thy words, were ... and rain to me'. The missing word in the source *Heath MS* and *Allen MS* indicated by the ellipsis in Ricks may have been *dew*, as in *1 Kings* xvii 1: 'And Elijah the Tishbite, who was of the inhabitants of Gilead, said unto Ahab, As the Lord God of Israel liveth, before whom I stand, there shall not be dew nor rain these years, but according to my word.'; as in George Herbert's *The Flower*, from *The Temple* (1633), 43–44: 'I once more smell the dew and rain, / And relish versing'; and as in James Montgomery's *Instruction* (1819) 17–20: 'As dew and rain, as light and air, / From heaven Instruction came, / The waste of Nature to repair, / Kindle a sacred flame'. T.'s lines 10–11, 'Far on within the temple of the mind / I seemed to hear God speaking audibly', further suggest that T. may have been thinking of *1 Kings* or of either or both Herbert's and Montgomery's poems. If, as Sir Charles Tennyson surmised in 1931 (see Ricks's headnote to the poem) the friend to whom the poem was addressed may have been Arthur Hallam, the lacuna may reflect T.'s belated realization that 'Thy looks, thy words, were dew and rain to me' could have been construed, by Hallam or others, as inappropriate, even sacrilegious — and may explain why the poem remained unpublished during T.'s lifetime.

151 Sonnet [There are three things which fill my heart with sighs] (*wr* 1830)

14. 'And dazzled to the heart with glorious pain.' Cp. Anne Finch, Countess of Winchilsea, *Clarinda's Indifference at Parting with Her Beauty* (1713) 22–23: 'When didst thou e'er a pleasing rule obtain? / A glorious empire's but a glorious pain.'; and (also 1713) Young's *Epistle to Lord*

Lansdowne 222–23: 'Who hears the godlike Montezuma groan, / And does not wish the glorious pain his own?'

153 The Lover's Tale (*wr* c. 1827–28)

i 6. 'Oh! pleasant breast of waters, quiet bay'. Cp. *Childe Harold* III lvi 1–4: 'The castled crag of Drachenfels / Frowns o'er the wide and winding Rhine, / Whose breast of waters broadly swells / Between the banks which bear the vine'.

i 7–9. 'Like to a quiet mind in the loud world, / Where the chafed breakers of the outer sea / Sank powerless'. In James Miller's *St Baldred of the Bass, A Pictish Legend* [...] *with other Poems and Ballads* (Edinburgh, 1824), cp. *The Lost Drave of Dunbar; or the Witch of Keith*, p. 258: 'As evermore the rock-chafed breakers fell / With roaring deafening noise.'

i 53–54. 'Beneath a low-browed cavern, where the tide / Plashed, sapping its worn ribs'. For *low-browed*, Ricks cites Milton's *L'Allegro* (1645) 8: 'low-brow'd Rocks'. But cp. also M. G. Lewis's *The Castle Spectre* IV i (Osmond speaking): 'Methought I wandered through the low-browed caverns, where repose the reliques of my ancestors!'

i 58. 'Mixt with the gorgeous west the lighthouse shone'. Ricks cites *Paradise Lost* ii 3: 'the gorgeous East'. But *the gorgeous west* itself occurs in Wilson's *Isle of Palms* iii 518–22: 'And say! what wanteth now the Isle of Palms, / To make it happy as those Isles of rest / (When eve the sky becalms / Like a subsiding sea) / That hang resplendent mid the gorgeous west', as well as in two poems collected in *Cambridge Prize Poems: Being a collection of the English poems which have obtained The Chancellor's Gold Medal* [as had T.'s *Timbuctoo* in 1829] *in the University of Cambridge* (1847). One of these was *Evening*, by T.'s friend Thomas Babington Macaulay (of Trinity, winner for 1821), with, in lines 33–34, 'And view the Sun, descending to his rest, / Lead his bright triumph down the gorgeous West'; and the other *Palmyra*, by T.'s acquaintance John Bright (of St. John's, winner for 1822), with, in lines 106–7, 'And view a summer's sun sink down to rest / Behind the mountains of the gorgeous west'.

i 298. '"A day for Gods to stoop," she answered'. Cp. *Isaiah* xlvi 1–2, referring to two Babylonian deities: 'Bel boweth down, Nebo stoopeth, their idols were upon the beasts, and upon the cattle: your carriages were heavy loaden; they are a burden to the weary beast. They stoop, they bow down together; they could not deliver the burden, but themselves are gone into captivity.' Cp. also, in Sir Richard Fanshawe's translation of Camões's epic as *The Lusiad, or, Portugals Historicall Poem* (1655) IX xx 6–7: 'For, with *his shafts* it is, she makes the *high* / GODS, stoop to the *base ground*'; Henry Grenfield's *God in the Creature* (1686), Sermon I, 167–68: 'Humility outwondring Miracle? / God stoops to man; and Heaven unto Hell.'; and chap. 3 of Charles Lamb's children's book *The Adventures of Ulysses* (1808):

> And well [Circe] might speak of [the Sirens], for often she had joined her own enchanting voice to theirs, while she has sat in the flowery meads, mingled with the Sirens and the Water Nymphs, gathering their potent herbs and drugs of magic quality: their singing altogether has made the gods stoop, and [quoting from Berowne's speech in *Love's Labours Lost*, IV iii 342] 'heaven drowsy with the harmony.'

i 327–28. 'A land of promise flowing with the milk / And honey of delicious memories!' Cp. *Deuteronomy* xxvi 9: 'And he hath brought us into this place, and hath given us this land, even a land that floweth with milk and honey.'

i 437–38. 'And a peculiar treasure, brooking not / Exchange or currency'. Cp. *Exodus* xix 5: 'Now therefore, if ye will obey my voice indeed, and keep my covenant, then ye shall be a peculiar treasure unto me above all people: for all the earth is mine'.

i 734. 'There on the depth of an unfathomed woe'. Cp. Hemans's *Sicilian Captive*, where, in line 20, the captive girl's eyelashes 'Half-veiled a depth of unfathomed woe'.

ii 135–37. 'All I had loved, and my dull agony, / Ideally to her transferred, became / Anguish intolerable.' The latter phrase occurs twice in Cowper's *Iliad* (1791): first in xi 327–29: 'But when the wound grew dry, and the blood ceased, / Anguish intolerable undermined / Then all the might of Atreus' royal son.'; and again in xix 446–49: 'He gnash'd his teeth, fire glimmer'd in his eyes, / Anguish intolerable wrung his heart / And fury against Troy, while he put on / His glorious arms, the labour of a God.'

155 'My life is full of weary days' (*pub* 1832)

1. 'My life is full of weary days'. Cp. *Endymion* i 910–12: 'How sickening, how dark the dreadful leisure / Of weary days, made deeper exquisite, / By a fore-knowledge of unslumbrous night!'

158 'If I were loved, as I desire to be' (*pub* 1832)

13. 'Flung leagues of roaring foam into the gorge'. Cp. Macpherson/Ossian's *Fingal* (second, 1762 edn), Book V, p. 71: 'Beside a stream of roaring foam his cave is in a rock.'

159* The Lady of Shalott (*wr* c. 1831–32)

56. 'An abbot on an ambling pad'. Cp. Ramsay's *Health* 311–12: 'The race delights him, horses are his care, / And a stout ambling pad his easiest chair.'; Thomas Betterton's 'character' of *The Wife of Bath* in a 'modernis'd' version, by several hands, of *The Canterbury Tales* (Dublin, 1742), p. 22: 'Upon an ambling Pad at Ease she sat, / Jingling the Bit, and slack'd her Pace to chat.'; and John Collins, *To-Morrow* (1804) 5: 'With an ambling pad-pony to pace o'er the lawn'.

82–84. 'The gemmy bridle glittered free, / Like to some branch of stars we see / Hung in the golden Galaxy.' Ricks notes that details of the appearance of T.'s knight echo those in *Faerie Queene* I vii st. 29 ff. But the passage may also owe something to Phillips's *The Emerald Isle*, beginning with the sixth (1818) edition, p. 121: 'Art thou the festal hall of state, / Where once the lovely and the great, / The stars of peace, the swords of honour, / Cheer'd by the ever gracious eye / Of ERIN's native majesty, / Glitter'd, a golden galaxy, / Around the great o'CONOR!'

91. 'All in the blue unclouded weather'. Cp. Wordsworth, *The Green Linnet* (1807) 3–4: 'With brightest sunshine round me spread / Of spring's unclouded weather'.

96–98. 'As often through the purple night, / Below the starry clusters bright, / Some bearded meteor, trailing light'. Three echoes in as many lines. The phrase *purple night* may point to Shelley's *Lines Written in the Bay of Lerici* (1822) 5–6, referring to the moon: 'Balanc'd on her wings of light, / Hover'd in the purple night'; *starry clusters*, to the title work in John Struthers's *The Peasant's Death; or, A Visit to the House of Mourning: and Other Poems* (Glasgow, 1806) lines 122–23, 'Out to the night she looks; / there all is drear, / No silver moon nor starry clusters rise'; *some bearded meteor*, to the Duke's speech in John Ford's tragedy *Love's Sacrifice* (1633) IV i 42–46: 'Forbear; the ashy paleness of my cheek / Is scarletted in ruddy flakes of wrath; / And like some bearded meteor shall suck up, / With swiftest terror, all those dusky mists / That overcloud compassion in our breast.' The image of a comet as a *bearded meteor* may be traceable to Aeschylus, *Agamemnon* 306, with 'φλογὸς μέγαν πώγωνα' [a mighty beard of flame].[47]

102–3. 'From underneath his helmet flowed / His coal-black curls as on he rode'. Cp., in Barry Cornwall (pseudonym of Bryan Waller Procter), *English Songs: and Other Small Poems* (1832), Dramatic Fragment 22 ('Loss of Strength') 1–4: 'When I was young, I was as hot as wrath, / Swift like the wind, and thoughtless. My hair fell / In coal-black curls upon my brawny neck, / And sunshine filled my eyes.'

127. 'And down the river's dim expanse'. Cp. Pye's *Alfred* v 417–18: 'At morn roll up the mountain steep, and crown, / With clouds of dim expanse, the upland down'; Moore's *Fragment of a Mythological Hymn to Love* (1806) 9–10: 'No form of beauty sooth'd thine eye, / As through the dim expanse it wander'd wide'; and *Revolt of Islam* I xxiii 8–9: 'Over the starry deep that gleams below / A vast and dim expanse, as o'er the waves we go.'

---

47 George Clayton Tennyson's library had two edns of Aeschylus (Items 3 and 4 in *Lincoln*), both in Greek and Latin, the earlier of the two (1745) having 'A. Tennyson' on the inside front board of vol. 2, and the later (1782–1801) having 'Alfred Tennyson' on the inside front board of vol. 1. T.'s own library had eleven edns of Aeschylus's works (Items 377 through 387 in *Lincoln*), the translators, transcribers, or commentators of which included Carl Jacob Blomfield (1826), F. A. Paley (1861 and 1870), Anna Swanwick (1873 and 1886), Robert Browning (1877), and John F. Davies (1885).

160* Mariana in the South (*wr* 1830–31)

3. 'Close-latticed to the brooding heat'. In *Miscellany Poems and Translations By Oxford Hands* (1685), cp.—among its anonymous *Pindarick Odes By the same Hand*—*Ode I* v 1–7: 'How much beyond our wonder's He / Deriv'd of Earthly Pedigree / That did from no less Monsters the wild Nation free / For when Ambition, the base Ferment of the Soul, / Threw into a Calenture the Senseless All; / Which by it's curst ill-brooding Heat, / Did in each muddy Brain a Python-plot beget'.

31–32. 'And on the liquid mirror glowed / The clear perfection of her face.' For *liquid mirror* Ricks cites *Alastor* 462: ('Nor aught else in the liquid mirror laves / Its portraiture'). For *clear perfection*, cp. Thomson's *Winter* 57: 'And into clear perfection, gradual bliss'.

44. 'And runlets babbling down the glen.' Both 'runlets babbling' and line 51's 'the babble of the stream' may recall Robert Blair's *The Grave* (1743) 507–8, 'Here the warm Lover, leaving the cool Shade, / The Telltale Echo, and the babbling Stream'; as well as Southey's *To a Brook near the Village of Corston* (1794), beginning 'As thus I bend me o'er thy babbling stream', and Hemans's *To My Brother and Sister, in the Country. Written in London.* (1808) 25–26: 'Or stray beside the babbling stream, / Where Luna sheds her placid beam'.

77–78. 'And flaming downward over all / From heat to heat the day decreased'. Cp. Young's *A Poem on the Last Day* (Oxford, 1713), Book II, 227–28: 'Crown'd with that Majesty, which form'd the World, / And the Grand Rebel flaming downward hurl'd.'; and Ingram's *Matilda, A Tale of the Crusades* (1830), Book I, p. 35: 'Fierce as that sun, which flam'd with downward ray / Her glowing heart, to wild extremes a prey'.

90–92. 'Large Hesper glittered on her tears, / And deepening through the silent spheres / Heaven over Heaven rose the night.' For line 90, both Collins and Ricks cite Keats's abandoned epic *Hyperion* (1820) ii 5–6: 'a den where no insulting light / Could glimmer on their tears', Ricks also citing Thomson's *Autumn* (1730) 200–1, where Lavinia's eyes 'like the dewy star / Of evening, shone in tears'. Line 91, in turn, echoes lines 28–30 of the *Hymn on the Seasons* (also 1730) with which Thomson's *magnum opus* ends: 'But wandering oft, with brute unconscious gaze, /

Man marks not THEE; marks not the mighty hand / That, ever-busy, wheels the silent spheres'.

161 Eleänore (*pub* 1832)

6. 'Far off from human neighbourhood'. Cp. Wordsworth, *The White Doe of Rylstone* (1815) 174–75: 'Or melancholy's sickly mood, / Still shy of human neighbourhood'; Southey, *The Poet's Pilgrimage to Waterloo* (1816), Part the First ('The Journey'), III ('The Field of Battle') xliv 5–6: 'Forsook again the solitary wood, / For their old home and human neighbourhood'; and *Endymion* i 621–22: 'till the stings / Of human neighbourhood envenom all'.

9–10. 'Thy bounteous forehead was not fanned / With breezes from our oaken glades'. For the latter phrase, cp., from his *Translations From Claudian* (1823), Rev. Henry Howard's rendering of Claudian's *Epithalamium on the Marriage of Honorius and Maria* 12–13: 'And when the forest's oaken glades / In "panting speed" thy courser treads'; and Christopher Wordsworth's *The Druids*—winner of the Chancellor's Gold Medal at Cambridge for 1827, two years before T.'s *Timbuctoo* did so—138–39: "Tis morn again: now quit the steep to rove / Through oaken glades and pass along the grove.'

11–12. 'But thou wert nursed in some delicious land / Of lavish lights, and floating shades'. For *delicious land*, cp. Drayton's *To the Virginian Voyage* (1606), stanza viii: 'When as the Lushious smell / Of that delicious Land, / Above the Seas that flowes, / The cleere Wind throwes, / Your Hearts to swell / Approaching the deare Strand.' Other instances of the same phrase occur in *Purchas His Pilgrimage* (1613) VII v, saying 'Of Zeilan' [Ceylon]: 'The Indians call it *Tenarisim*, or the delitious land, and some are of opinion, that this was Paradise'; in Coleridge's *The Silver Thimble* (1796) 11–12: 'Such things, I thought, one might not hope to meet / Save in the dear delicious land of Faery!'; and in *Childe Harold* I xv 1–2: 'Oh, Christ! it is a goodly sight to see / What Heaven hath done for this delicious land!'

For *floating shades*, Ricks cites *Alastor* 124: 'Filled the mysterious halls with floating shades'. But cp. also, in Langhorne's *The Visions of Fancy.*

In Four Elegies. (1762), *Elegy III* 36–39: '"Thus glide the pensive moments, o'er the vale / "While floating shades of dusky night descend: / "Not left untold the lover's tender tale, / "Nor unenjoy'd the heart-enlarging friend.["]'

16. 'From old well-heads of haunted rills'. Cp. M'Henry's *The Bard of Erin* (Belfast, 1808) 43–44: 'Bold, wild, sublime, as are his native hills, / But soft, and tender, like his haunted rills'; John Stewart's *Ode (The Niliad)* (1810) 1–4: 'O ye on Inspiration's hills, / Thessalian-born, of song divine, / Where gush the thousand haunted rills / The laurell'd groves among that shine'; and Thomas Pringle's *The Emigrants* (1824) xxxii 1–4: 'How can they part? — The lake, the woods, the hills, / Speak to their pensive hearts of early days; / Remembrance woos them from the haunted rills, / And hallows every spot their eye surveys'.

29–30. 'With the hum of swarming bees / Into dreamful slumber lulled.' For *dreamful slumber*, cp. John Marston's *Parasitaster; or, The Fawn* (1606; reprinted by J. W. Dilke in *Old English Plays; being a Selection from the Early Dramatic Writers*, vol. 2, 1814), with, in Act I, scene ii (on p. 316 of Dilke's edition), a speech by Hercules reading in part: 'Dear sleep and lust, I thank you; but for you, / Mortal, till now I scarce had known myself. / Thou grateful poison, sleek mischief Flattery, / Thou dreamful slumber (that doth fall on kings / As soft and soon as their first holy oil) / Be thou for ever damn'd'. Cp. also Blake, *The [First] Book of Urizen* (1794) 199–201: 'In a horrible, dreamful slumber, / Like the linkèd infernal chain, / A vast Spine writh'd in torment'.

49–50. 'The luxuriant symmetry / Of thy floating gracefulness'. Cp. the anonymous *The Modern Gyges. A Tale of Trials.* in *Blackwood's Edinburgh Magazine*, vol. 25, no. 149 (Feb. 1829), 239: 'The setting sun threw its golden radiance through the half-closed Venetian blinds and diffused a rich glow of light around the brilliant and matchless proportions of this lovely woman. In luxuriant symmetry of form she fully equalled the Grecian Venus of the Florence gallery'.

73–74. 'Slowly, as from a cloud of gold, / Comes out thy deep ambrosial smile.' For the latter phrase, cp. Samuel Pattison's *To Peace* (1792), which begins: 'Thou beauteous angel of our isle; / Array'd with each ambrosial smile'; from his *Poems* (Cambridge, 1797), Charles Newton's *Regular Lyric Ode*, which ends: 'Venus propitious hears my vows, / For me she leaves her fav'rite Isle: / With her own rosy Wreath she decks my brows, / And lends my Chloe's lips her own ambrosial Smile.'; and, from the February 1820 issue of *The Gentlemen's Magazine*, 160–62, Raleigh Trevelyan's *On the Ten Commandments* 81–82: 'Till (whilst along the sev'nfold bound'ry, Morn, / In Sabbath's dawn ambrosial smile, is born).'

89. 'As though a star, in inmost heaven set'. Cp. Young's *Poem on the Last Day*, Book I, 91–92: 'From inmost Heaven incessant thunders roll / And the strong echo bound from pole to pole.'; Southey's *Hymn to the Penates* (1796) 7–8: 'whether, as sages deem, / Ye dwell in inmost Heaven'; and, in lines 157–58 of the same poem: 'PENATES! some there are / Who say, that not in the inmost heaven ye dwell'.

130–31. 'And a languid fire creeps / Through my veins to all my frame'. Ricks notes that T. himself compared lines 122–44 to Sappho's *Fragment 2* (now generally known as *Fragment 31*) beginning 'φαίνεταί μοι κῆνος ἴσος θέοισιν' [That man seems to me to be equal to the gods]; lines 130–31 may be traced specifically to the fragment's line reading: 'δ᾽ αὐτίκα χρῶι πῦρ ὑπαδεδρόμηκεν' [and instantly a subtle fire has overrun my flesh].

But cp. also the several pre-T. instances of *languid fire* itself, including in Hill's *An Ode; on Occasion of Mr. Handel's great Te Deum* (1733) v 1–4: 'Ah! give thy passport to the nation's pray'r; / Ne'er did religion's languid fire / Burn fainter—never more require / The aid of such a fam'd enliv'ner's care'; in Parnell's *Epigram* beginning 'The greatest gifts that Nature does bestow' (1780), lines 13–14: 'The Love of Friends is found a languid Fire, / That glares but faintly, and will soon expire'; in Southey's *Sonnet* beginning 'A wrinkled crabbed Man they picture thee / Old Winter' (1800), line 13: 'Pausing at times to move the languid fire'; and in Boyd's 1802 translation of Dante's *Paradiso*, Canto XXVI, stanza xxiii, beginning: '"Four thousand times the Sun in ARIES rode, / And thence an hundred times the chill abode / Of dim AQUARIUS blanch'd his languid fire'.[48]

---

[48] In Boyd's translation (see note 24), the phrase occurs in vol. 3.

162 The Miller's Daughter (*wr* c. 1832)

51–52. 'And see the minnows everywhere / In crystal eddies glance and poise'. Another phrase previously occurring in a Cambridge University prize poem, *crystal eddies* comes midway through William Gibson's *Conscience*, winner of the Seatonian award in 1772: 'Whence are his fears? see! where the reeking flood, / In crystal eddies curling once along, / Now glows with human blood'. Cp. also, in what appears to be the only other pre-T. instance of the phrase—and one clearly echoing Gibson—John Pinkerton's *Rimes* (1781), with, in *Ode VI. The Prophecy of Tweed.* 37: 'No more shall blood our crystal eddies stain'.

163* Fatima (*pub* 1832)

1. 'O Love, Love, Love! O withering might!' Cp. the first quatrain of Shakespeare's *Sonnet 126*: 'O Thou my louely Boy who in thy power, / Doest hould times fickle glasse, his sickle, hower: / Who hast by wayning growne, and therein shou'st, / Thy louers withering, as thy sweet selfe grow'st.'; and, in 1804's *Poetical Register*, T. Robertson's *The Fallen Oaks* 9–10: 'Oaks, ye beheld Time's withering might, / Rush, in the waste of years array'd'.[49]

6. 'Lo, parched and withered, deaf and blind'. Pre-T. instances of *parched and withered* include, among others, Christopher Harvey's *Schola cordis*[50] (1647) Ode 29 (*The watering of the Heart*) iii 1–4: 'See how the seed, which thou did'st sow / Lies parch'd, and wither'd, will not grow / Without some moisture, and mine heart hath none, / That it can truly call its owne'; Sir Thomas Urquhart's 1663 translation from the French of Rabelais's *Pantagruel* (1532), chap. 2 ('Of the Nativity of the most dread and redoubted Pantagruel'):

> But that we may fully understand the cause and reason of the name of *Pantagruel*, which at his Baptism was given him, you are to remark, that in that year there was so great a drought over all the countrey of *Affrick*,

---

[49] Fully cited: *The Poetical Register, and Repository of Fugitive Poetry, for 1804* (Rivington, 1806), pp. 55–57.

[50] Full title: *Schola cordis, or, The heart of it self, gone away from God brought back againe to him & instructed by him in 47 emblems*. Harvey's co-authors were Benedictus van Haeften and Francis Quarles.

that there past thirty and six moneths, three weeks, foure dayes, thirteen houres, and a little more without raine, but with a heat so vehement, that the whole earth was parched and withered by it[.]

and Wordsworth's *Excursion* iv 1095–97: 'will showers of grace, / When in the sky no promise may be seen, / Fall to refresh a parched and withered land?'

13–14. 'I looked athwart the burning drouth / Of that long desert to the south.' For *burning drouth*, cp. *Ane Poeme of Tyme*, attributed to King James VI of Scotland (the future King James I of England and Ireland) and collected, along with four others similarly attributed, in vol. 3 of *Chronicle of Scottish Poetry: From the Thirteenth Century, to the Union of the Crowns*, ed. by James Sibbald (Edinburgh, 1802), pp. 488–89. Stanza ii reads in part: 'The balmie dew throw burning drouth he dryis, / Quhilk made the soil to savour sweit, and smell / By dewe that on the nicht before down fell'.

17. 'A thousand little shafts of flame'. Cp. Rev. Richard Hole's *Ode to Terror* (1792) 96: 'They wing the lightning's shafts of flame'; in his *Odes of Anacreon* (1800), Moore's translation of *Ode XIII*, lines 11–12: 'He slung his quiver's golden frame, / He took his bow, his shafts of flame'; and Francis Wrangham's translation (1817), from Petrarch's *Laura*, of sonnet 149 (*'Amor che 'ncende 'l cor d' ardente zelo'*) 1–2: '''Tis Love's caprice to freeze the bosom now / With bolts of ice, with shafts of flame now burn'. The phrase *shafts of flame* also occurs in George Waddington's *Columbus* — which in 1813 won (as would T.'s *Timbuctoo* sixteen years later) the Chancellor's Medal at the Cambridge commencement — 291–92: 'But not at him, ye fiends of vengeance, aim / Your poison'd weapons and your shafts of flame'.

33. 'And, isled in sudden seas of light'. Cp. Phineas Fletcher's allegorical epic *The Purple Island* (1633) X v 1: 'But those twinne Loves, which from thy seas of light / To us on earth derive their lesser streams'; Watts's *The Incomprehensible* (1706) 19–20: 'Faith shall direct her humble flight, / Through all the trackless seas of light'; and Hill's *The Fanciad* (1743) — full title: *The Fanciad. An heroic poem. In six cantos. To His Grace the Duke of Marlborough, on the turn of his genius to arms.* — Canto III, lines 5–6: 'But starts from Thought, — involv'd in Seas of Light! / And hears soft Angels, whisp'ring, on his Right.'

34. 'My heart, pierced through with fierce delight'. Pre-T. instances of the latter phrase include, among others, Wyatt's *In Spain* (c. 1539) 51–52: 'As doth th' accumbred sprite the thoughtful throes discover, / Of fierce delight, of fervent love, that in our hearts we cover'; George Stepney's *The Nature of Dreams* (c. 1700) 25–26: 'Unguarded then she melts, acts fierce delight, / And curses the returns of envious light'; Pope's *Iliad* xxiii 961–62: 'Lowering they meet, tremendous to the sight; / Each Argive bosom beats with fierce delight.'; Dyer's *Ruins of Rome* 154: 'When drunk with rule she will'd the fierce delight'; and Scott's *The Lord of the Isles* (1815) IV xx 1–2: 'Oh, War! thou hast thy fierce delight, / Thy gleams of joy, intensely bright!'

164* Œnone (*wr* 1830–32)

3. 'The swimming vapour slopes athwart the glen'. For *swimming vapour*, cp. Egestorff's *Messiah* I xi 615–19, speaking of Rachel: 'With wonder and amazement she beholds / The ever-varying aspect of this new, / Profound and ever-fathomless creation, / Not conscious of the near affinity / Between the swimming vapour and herself'; and I xii 1108–11: 'And the immortal soul perfected soar'd / Aloft, still higher tow'rd the heaven of heav'ns, / A rising beam of morning, cumbent less / Than swimming vapour, fleet as passing thought.'

66–68. 'and while I looked / And listened, the full-flowing river of speech / Came down upon my heart.' In Plato's *Timaeus*, the speaker describes (at 75d) how the gods provided the human head with mouth, jawbone, teeth, tongue, and lips both to enable food to enter the body and to enable 'the river of speech [...] the fairest and noblest of all streams', to flow out of it.[51] Three centuries later, in *Academica* II xxxviii, Cicero famously referred to Aristotle as *'flumen orationis aureum fundens'* [pouring forth a golden stream of eloquence],[52] a metaphor recurring minus the adjective in *Inferno* i 79–80, where Dante asks the spirit who

---

51 As catalogued in *Lincoln*, T.'s library contained eight edns of Plato (Items 1790 through 1797), in Greek only, Greek and Latin, Greek and English, and English only, all of the English translations—including this by Benjamin Jowett—postdating T.'s poem.

52 George Clayton Tennyson's library contained five partial or complete edns of Cicero's works (Items 82 through 86 of *Lincoln*), on the fly-leaf or front board of two of which T. wrote his name.

will guide him through the underworld: *'Or se' tu quel Virgilio e quella fonte / che spandi di parlar si largo fiume?'* [And are you then that Virgil and that fountain / From which has flowed so great a river of speech?][53]

119–20. 'Still she spake on and still she spake of power, / "Which in all action is the end of all["]'. T. may have had in mind the opening passage of Aristotle's *Nicomachean Ethics*, which as translated by Thomas Taylor (1811) concludes: 'Hence, if there is one certain end of all actions, this will be the practical good; but if there are many ends, these will be practical goods.'

198–201. 'Ah me, my mountain shepherd, that my arms / Were wound about thee, and my hot lips prest / Close, close to thine in that quick-falling dew / Of fruitful kisses'. For the latter phrase, cp. line 25—'So fruitful Kisses fell where Venus flew'—of Fenton's *Basium I* (1717), translating the first of a suite of nineteen neo-Latin love lyrics by 'Johannes Secundus' (Jan Everaerts) first published as the *Liber Basiorum* [Book of Kisses] in Utrecht in 1541. Fenton's *fruitful kisses* translates *'fecundis oscula'* in line 17 of the Latin poem.

205–8. 'My tall dark pines, that plumed the craggy ledge / High over the blue gorge, and all between / The snowy peak and snow-white cataract / Fostered the callow eaglet'. For the latter phrase, cp. Laurence Eusden's *To Charles Lord Halifax. Occasioned by Translating into Latin Two Poems by His Lordship and Mr. Stepney* (1709) 18–19: 'The callow eaglet wisely takes his rest / Safe in the covert of a downy nest'; Jacob Jones, Jun.'s *Sonnet to Clare, the Northamptonshire Peasant-Poet* (1824) 9–12: 'Such sight, the callow eaglet of the north / Scarce bore, too near his earliest vision plying, / When his full sun of fame burst sudden forth, / His reeling eye, its giddy glory trying.'; and John Bree's *Saint Herbert's Isle: A Legendary Poem* (1832) II vii 6–9: 'She sought the concord of the silent steep, / Till the wild glede would round her wail and flit, / Or wolf-cub bay the yet unfolded sheep, / Or callow eaglet scream from its high-roosted keep.'

215. 'Between the loud stream and the trembling stars'. For *the loud stream*, cp. Macpherson/Ossian's *Temora* (1773 edn), vol. 2, Book VII, p.

---

53 In his edn of the *Inferno* (Oxford: Oxford University Press, 1996), Robert M. Durling notes of these lines: 'That Vergil's poetry was like a great river was a traditional topic in ancient and medieval literary criticism.'

147: '"Beneath the moss-covered rock of Lona, near his own loud stream; grey in his locks of age, dwells Clonmal king of harps.["]';[54] and *Alastor* 548–50, 'Mid toppling stones, black gulphs and yawning caves, / Whose windings gave ten thousand various tongues / To the loud stream'.

For *the trembling stars*—here and in line 28 of T.'s *On a Mourner* (poem 216, on p. 106), 'Through silence and the trembling stars'—cp. Young's *Complaint*, Night Ninth, 944–47: 'The trembling stars / See crimes gigantic, stalking through the gloom / With front erect, that hide their head by day, / And making night still darker by their deeds.'; as well as Hemans's *Imelda* (1825) 61–62: 'When trembling stars look'd silvery in their wane, / And heavy flowers yet slumber'd, once again'.

230. 'Sealed it with kisses? watered it with tears?' On the first question, cp. *Romeo and Juliet* V iii 113–15 (Romeo speaking): 'Arms, take your last embrace! and, lips, O you / The doors of breath, seal with a righteous kiss / A dateless bargain to engrossing death!'; and, also by Shakespeare, *Venus and Adonis* 515–16: 'Which purchase if thou make, for fear of slips, / Set thy seal manual on my wax-red lips.' On the second, cp. *Psalm* vi 6, 'I am weary with my groaning; all the night make I my bed to swim; I water my couch with my tears'; William Davenant's *Gondibert* (1651) IV xxiv 3–4: 'Go gather cypress for thy brother's urn, / And learn of me to water it with tears.'; and, in Blake's *Songs of Experience* (1794), *A Poison Tree* 5–6: 'And I waterd it in fears, / Night & morning with my tears'.

263. 'That, wheresoe'er I am by night and day'. Cp. Wordsworth's *Ode: Intimations of Immortality from Recollections of Early Childhood* (1807) 7–9: 'Turn wheresoe'er I may, / By night or day, / The things which I have seen I now can see no more.'

166* To — . With the Following Poem [The Palace of Art] (*pub* 1832)

4. 'A spacious garden full of flowering weeds'. Cp. *Hamlet* I ii 133–37, 'How [weary], stale, flat, and unprofitable / Seem to me all the uses of this world! / Fie on't, ah fie! 'tis an unweeded garden / That grows to seed, things rank and gross in nature / Possess it merely.'; Coleridge,

---

54 In the first (1763) edn of *Temora*, *stream* was modified not by *loud* but *blue*.

France: An Ode (1798) i 11–12: 'How oft, pursuing fancies holy, / My moonlight way o'er flowering weeds I wound, / Inspired, beyond the guess of folly, / By each rude shape and wild unconquerable sound!'; and *Adonais* xlix 1–6: 'Go thou to Rome,—at once the Paradise, / The grave, the city, and the wilderness; / And where its wrecks like shattered mountains rise, / And flowering weeds, and fragrant copses dress / The bones of Desolation's nakedness / Pass'.

5. 'A glorious Devil, large in heart and brain'. For the former phrase, cp. Andelocia's speech in Part II of Thomas Dekker's two-part comedy *The Honest Whore* (1630), Act IV, scene i: 'O me, what hell is this? fiends, tempt me not. / Thou glorious devil, hence. O now I see, / This fruit is thine, thou hast deformèd me'; and Zenocia's speech in the Fletcher–Massinger tragicomedy *The Custom of the Country* (1647), also in Act IV, scene i: 'Not fair, not to be liked, thou glorious Devil, / Thou varnisht piece of Lust, thou painted Fury!'

6–7. 'That did love Beauty only, (Beauty seen / In all varieties of mould and mind)'. In David Macbeth Moir's *The Legend of Genevieve: With Other Tales and Poems* (1825), cp. *Mary's Mount* vii 7–10: 'In mould and mind by far excelling, / Or Cleopatra on the wave / Of Cydnus vanquishing the brave, / Or Troy's resplendent Helen!'

167* The Palace of Art (*wr* c. 1831–32)

5–6. 'A huge crag-platform, smooth as burnished brass / I chose.' Cp. Scott, *The Lay of the Last Minstrel* (1805), where, in a note to the line (I xxvii 5) reading 'On Minto-crags the moon-beams glint', he writes that in the Teviot valley 'A small platform, on a projecting crag, commanding a most beautiful prospect, is termed *Barnhills' Bed*.'[55]

53–56. 'Full of long-sounding corridors it was, / That over-vaulted grateful gloom, / Through which the livelong day my soul did pass, / Well-pleased, from room to room.' One early pre-T. instance of *grateful gloom* occurs in Maurice's *Hagley: a Descriptive Poem* (Oxford, 1776), p.

---

55 The ninth (1808) Longman edn, with 'Alfred Tennyson' on the fly-leaf, was at Somersby (Item 304 in *Lincoln*).

19: 'To that lone *Dell*, beneath the deep'ned shade, / Where down the valley bursts the rude cascade; / Whose rugged sides — with hoary moss o'er grown, / Deck'd with huge fragments of romantic stone, / Grotesque and wild — with verdure never bloom, / But o'er the senses shed a grateful gloom'. Other, subsequent ones occur in Anna Seward's 'poetical novel' *Louisa* (1784), the first of whose four verse epistles has, on p. 5: 'Soon then did Cheerfulness the morn illume, / And Peace descend with Evening's grateful gloom'; in Helen Maria Williams, *A Paraphrase on Psalm lxxiv. 16, 17* (1786)—sometimes reprinted as *The Benevolence of God*—lines 9–14: 'Or when, in paler tints array'd, / The evening slowly spreads her shade; / That soothing shade, that grateful gloom, / Can, more than day's enliv'ning bloom, / Still every fond and vain desire, / And calmer, purer, thoughts inspire'; in William Sotheby's translation (1800) of Virgil's *Georgic III* 183–84: 'Through Silarus' groves, or where dark ilex sheds / The grateful gloom that o'er Alburnus spreads'; and in Alexander Yeman's *The Fisherman's Hut, in the Highlands of Scotland* (1807), Part II, 117–18: 'Come forth in bright, tho' pensive, grateful gloom, / Yon stone to raise, to mark the poet's tomb'.

69. 'One showed an iron coast and angry waves.' For *iron coast*, cp. Thomas Downey, *Pleasures of the Naval Life* (1813), Canto I, p. 37: 'Then, flitting fast by Dorset's iron coast, / With jutting rocks and beetling cliffs embossed'; and George Woodley, *Cornubia* (1819) III ii 5–7: ''Tis all an iron coast; and hapless he / Whose bark too closely, 'midst the tempest's pow'r / Tends to the shore'.

For *angry waves*, cp., in Rev. William Diaper's *Nereides: or Sea-Eclogues* (1712), *Eclogue II*, 29–32: 'When fatal Rocks have split the broken Ship, / And shrieking Mortals sink into the Deep, / If *Laron* hears the Cry, he often saves, / And buoys the floating Wretch amidst the angry Waves.'; in Mary Matilda Betham's *Elegies and Other Small Poems* (Ipswich, 1797), her *Translation* [from Metastasio's *Cantata Dello Stesso*] 1–4: 'Whilst zephyr sooth[e]s the angry waves / Of Ocean into rest, / Each vessel is in safety borne, / And every pilot blest.'; Southey's *The Spanish Armada* (1798) 37–38: 'And hark! the angry Winds arise, / Old Ocean heaves his angry Waves'; Porden's *The Veils*, Book IV ('The Sea') 272–73: 'At once the angry waves forget to roar, / Their calm as wondrous as their rage before'; and, from the same, 292–93: 'The angry waves retire, and safe they land, / Tho' faint with toil, on the subaqueous strand.'

169 The Hesperides (*wr* c. 1830)

75. 'Wandering waters unto wandering waters call'. Cp., in *A Collection of Select Epigrams* (1757), Broome's *To Belinda at the Bath* 9–10: 'No more the Po! whose wand'ring waters stray / In mazy errors, thro' the starry way'; and, in Isaac D'Israeli's *Mejnoun and Leila, The Arabian Petrarch and Laura* (1799), Part I ('The Land of Cashmere') 5–6: 'A music wild thy wandering waters pour / By coral banks, and many a glowing shore.'

170* The Lotos-Eaters (*wr* 1830–32)

6. 'Breathing like one that hath a weary dream.' Cp. Burns, *Song V. Again rejoicing nature sees*—also known as *Composed in Spring*—(1786) iii 3: 'But life to me's a weary dream'; *Childe Harold* III iv 5–7, 'Yet, though a dreary strain, to this I cling / So that it wean me from the weary dream / Of selfish grief or gladness'; and in *Blackwood's Edinburgh Magazine* vol. 13, no. 76 (May 1823), 548—also later reprinted in *The Poetical Album; and Register of Modern Fugitive Poetry*, ed. by Alaric A. Watts (1828)—Moir (as 'Δ'), *Sunset Thoughts* 15–16: 'Oh! who would live those visions o'er, all brilliant though they seem, / Since Earth is but a desert shore, and Life a weary dream!'

17. 'and, dewed with showery drops'. Cp. John Gay's rendering into English verse of portions of Ovid's *Metamorphoses* ix (1717; repr. 1813), in which a section called 'The Translation of Lychas into a Rock' has, in lines 25–26: 'So showery drops, when chilly tempests blow, / Thicken at first, then whiten into snow'.

62. 'And make perpetual moan'. Cp. Byron's *Darkness* (1816) 52: 'But with a piteous and perpetual moan'; and Shelley's *Revolt of Islam* VII xxv 8–9: 'Day after day, and sitting there alone, / Vexed the inconstant waves with my perpetual moan'.

116. 'but all hath suffered change'. Cp. Ariel's Song in *The Tempest* I ii 397–402: 'Full fadom five thy father lies, / Of his bones are coral made: / Those are pearls that were his eyes: / Nothing of him that doth fade, / But doth suffer a sea-change / Into something rich and strange'; *Paradise Lost* x 211–14: 'then, pitying how they stood / Before him naked to the air,

that now / Must suffer change, disdain'd not to begin / Thenceforth the form of servant to assume'; and Dryden's *Of the Pythagorean Philosophy. From Ovid's Metamorphoses, Book XV* (1700) 672–73: 'All suffer Change; and we, that are of Soul / And Body mix'd, are Members of the whole.'

128. 'There *is* confusion worse than death'. Alluding, it would seem, to Byron's *Mazeppa* 562–66: 'But a confusion worse than such: / I own that I should deem it much, / Dying, to feel the same again; / And yet I do suppose we must / Feel far more ere we turn to dust.'

152. 'Where the wallowing monster spouted his foam-fountains in the sea.' Cp. John Leyden, *The Mermaid* (1803) stanza xii: '"Unwarp, unwind his oozy coils, / Sea-green sisters of the main, / And in the gulf where ocean boils, / The unwieldy wallowing monster chain.'

171 Rosalind (*wr* c. 1831)

29. 'Like sunshine on a dancing rill'. Cp. Mason, *Il Pacifico* (1748) 57–58: 'By scooped valley, heaped hill, / Level river, dancing rill'.

32. 'From excess of swift delight.'—in a poem repeatedly likening Rosalind to a falcon. Cp. Blake, *Visions of the Daughters of Albion* (1793) 14: 'Over the waves she went in wing'd exulting swift delight'; and Shelley—translating Homer but with Blake's poem also clearly in mind—*Hymn to Mercury* (1824) lxxiv 1: 'These words were wingèd with his swift delight'.

172 'My Rosalind, my Rosalind' (*wr* c. 1831)

13–14. 'All the petty shocks and fears / That trouble life in early years'. Cp. Shakespeare, *A Lover's Complaint* 272–73, 'And sweetens in the suffring pangues it beares, / The *Alloes* of all forces, shockes and feares'.

32–33. 'Think you hearts are tennisballs, / To play with, wanton Rosalind?' Cp. Shakespeare's *Henry V*, Act I, scene ii, in which the Dauphin mocks King Henry by sending him, in response to Henry's French claims, a box of tennis balls.

173* A Dream of Fair Women (*wr* 1831–32)

5–8. 'Dan Chaucer, the first warbler, whose sweet breath / Preluded those melodious bursts that fill / The spacious times of great Elizabeth / With sounds that echo still.' In praising Chaucer, T. seeks further to honor England's *first warbler* by applying to him a phrase that Chaucer himself applies, in lines 5–7 of the *Canterbury Tales*' General Prologue, to the god of the West Wind: 'Whan Zephirus eek with his sweete breeth / Inspired hath in every holt and heeth / The tendre croppes'.

13–16. 'In every land / I saw, wherever light illumineth, / Beauty and anguish walking hand in hand / The downward slope to death.' Cp. Bowles, *Bereavement* (1789) 5–9: ''Twas the voice of Hope. / Of love and social scenes, it seemed to speak, / Of truth, of friendship, of affection meek; / That, oh! poor friend, might to life's downward slope / Lead us in peace, and bless our latest hours.'

29–30. 'And high shrine-doors burst through with heated blasts / That run before the fluttering tongues of fire'. Cp. *Acts* ii 1–3: 'And when the day of Pentecost was fully come, they were all with one accord in one place. And suddenly there came a sound from heaven as of a rushing mighty wind, and it filled all the house where they were sitting. And there appeared unto them cloven tongues like as of fire, and it sat upon each of them.'

45–47. 'And once my arm was lifted to hew down / A cavalier from off his saddle-bow, / That bore a lady from a leaguered town'. For the latter phrase, cp. Pope's *Iliad* xviii 593–94: 'Two mighty hosts a leaguer'd town embrace, / And one would pillage, one would burn, the place.'

69–70. 'Growths of jasmine turned / Their humid arms festooning tree to tree'. For *humid arms*, cp. *umeris umida* in another dream poem, Ovid's *Hero Leandro*, Epistle XIX of his *Epistulae Heroidum*. Writing to Leander, Hero in lines 57–60 tells her lover, fatally it will prove, how she dreams he will once again swim across the Hellespont to be with her: '*forsitan invitus mecum tamen, improbe, dormis / et, quamquam non vis ipse venire, venis. / nam modo te videor prope iam spectare natantem, / bracchia nunc umeris umida ferre meis*' [Then in dreams I find you by my side, and perhaps much against your will, you are induced to come. For sometimes I seem to see you swimming near the shore, sometimes you recline your humid arms on my shoulders].

The same phrase occurs in a more naturalistic setting in John Bowdler's collection of *Poems Divine and Moral* (1821), where, on p. 460, a poem called *The Seasons*, by 'an American Lady',[56] begins: 'I love the rising grace, the varied charms, / Which on the Earth's enamell'd bosom play, / When Nature bursts from April's humid arms / And springs impatient to the Ides of May.'

174 Song [Who can say] (*pub* 1832)

4–7. 'Who can tell / Why to smell / The violet, recalls the dewy prime / Of youth and buried time?' Cp. Wordsworth's *The Female Vagrant* (1798) 25, which recalls 'The cowslip-gathering at May's dewy prime'; and James Montgomery's *Youth Renewed* (1826) 7–10, which similarly recalls 'Childhood, its smiles and tears, / Youth, with its flush of years, / Its morning-clouds and dewy prime, / More exquisitely touch'd by Time.'

175 Margaret (*pub* 1832)

11–12. 'From all things outward you have won / A tearful grace'. For the latter phrase, cp. Susanna Pearson's *Sonnet, to Peter Pindar, Esq.* (1790) 5–8: 'Desist, and sweep the pensive chords again, / Whose magic sounds awake the tearful grace, / Win from affliction half her secret pain, / And lull the agony they cannot chase'.

176 Kate (*wr* c. 1832)

3. 'Her rapid laughters wild and shrill'. For the latter phrase, cp. Scott's *Lay of the Last Minstrel* III iii 4: 'But the Page shouted wild and shrill'; and, also by Scott, *The Monks of Bangor's March* (1817) iii 4: 'Heard the war-cry wild and shrill'. Cp. also Hemans's *The Captive Knight* (1824), in

---

56   Previously published under the title *Love of Nature* in *The New-York Magazine; or, Literary Repository* (New York, 1796), 495, and there signed 'Ethelinde'.

which the refrain in lines 5–6, 'Cease awhile, clarion! Clarion, wild and shrill, / Cease! let them hear the captive's voice — be still!' is repeated in three of the poem's next four stanzas; and, from her *Legends of the North, or the Feudal Christmas* (1825), Mrs. Henry Rolls's *Ninth Day* 3: 'And the wind whistles, wild and shrill'.

7. 'For Kate hath an unbridled tongue'. Ricks cites *The Tempest* II ii 49–50: 'But none of us car'd for Kate; / For she had a tongue with a tang'. But cp. also, among instances of *unbridled tongue* itself, Sir Walter Raleigh's *Instructions to His Sonne And to Posterity* (1632), chap. 4: 'as *Euripides* truely affirmeth, Every unbridled tongue in the end shall finde itselfe unfortunate'; and, in vol. 1 of his edition of *The Tragedies of Euripides* (Oxford, 1823), R. Potter's translation of *The Bacchae* 411–13: 'When the rude unbridled tongue / Vents the mad and wayward thought, / Vengeance is its destin'd end'.

17. 'Kate saith "the world is void of might."' Instances of the latter phrase occur in Fairfax's *Godfrey of Bulloigne* XX lxxxiii 6: 'Though every limb were weak, faint, void of might'; in Sylvester's translation from the French of Odet de la Noue's *Paradoxe que les adversitez sont plus necessaires que les prosperités* as *A Paradox Against Libertie* (1594) 215–16: 'Regarding all these griefes, which men so much affright, / As Babyfearing buggs, and scar-crowes voyd of might'; and in Scott's *The Bride of Triermain* (1813) xxxviii 14–15: 'Vapid all and void of might / Hiding half her charms from sight.'

18. 'Kate said "the men are gilded flies."' Instances of *gilded fly* or *flies* occur in *King Lear* IV vi 110–13 (Lear to Gloucester): 'Adultery? / Thou shalt not die. Die for adultery? No, / The wren goes to't, and the small gilded fly / Does lecher in my sight.'; Cowper's *The Task* (1785) vi 921–22: 'He cannot skim the ground like summer birds / Pursuing gilded flies';[57] and *Queen Mab* iii 106–8: 'Those gilded flies / That, basking in the sunshine of a court, / Fatten on its corruption!' Cp. also the *gilded flies* in the Beaumont–Massinger comedy *The Elder Brother* (1637) IV iii, where

---

57   As previously stated (see note 38), T. library as catalogued in *Lincoln* had vol. 2 of the three-volume Pickering edn of Cowper's *Works*, the one containing *The Task*.

the bookish Charles, determined to duel his scheming younger brother for the hand of his beloved Angellina though he has never before held a sword, declares: 'Teach me to fight; I willing am to learn. / Are ye all gilded flies? nothing but show in ye?';[58] and those in William Hazlitt's *The Spirit of the Age: or Contemporary Portraits* (1825), where, in the essay on Jeremy Bentham, Hazlitt mentions a recently published 'romance' called (he says) *Hunter's Captivity among the North American Indians* that includes an account 'of the huge spiders that prey on bluebottles and gilded flies in green pathless forests'.[59]

23-24. 'And wearing on my swarthy brows / The garland of new-wreathed emprise'. Instances of *swarthy brows* occur in Howard's *Metamorphoses* ii 30-32: 'Crown'd with a flowery garland Spring appear'd: / Chaplets of grain the swarthy brows adorn'd / Of naked Summer'; in Hogg's parody of Scott, *Wat o' the Cleugh* (1817) II xix 3-4: 'But a darker, gloomier veil was wore / On the swarthy brows of Lammermore!'; and in J. H. Wiffen's translation of *Jerusalem Delivered* (1824-25) XX xlii 7-9: 'and, knitting to a frown / His swarthy brows, rushed forward to requite / Shame with incensed disdain, and with revenge despite.'

179 To — [As when with downcast eyes] (*pub* 1832)

5-6. 'If one but speaks or hems or stirs his chair, / Ever the wonder waxeth more and more'. Cp. the anonymous *A Song Setting Forth the Good Effects of the Spring*—composed c. 1307-27, beginning 'Lenten ys come with love to toune', and collected by Joseph Ritson in *Ancient Songs and Ballads* (1829)—reading in part: 'Wormes woweth under cloude, / Wymmen waxeth wounder proude' (that is, worms woo under ground [clod], women put on amazing airs).

---

58 In the ten-volume (1778) Evans edn of *The Dramatick Works of Francis Beaumont and John Fletcher* cited in note 20, *The Elder Brother* was in vol. 2.

59 The 1825 Colburn edn of Hazlitt's *The Spirit of the Age* was at Somersby (Item 142 in *Lincoln*). The actual title of the work to which Hazlitt refers, written by John D[unn]. Hunter and published in London in 1823, was *Memoirs of a Captivity among the Indians of North America, From Childhood to the Age of Nineteen*.

185 Sonnet [Alas! how weary are my human eyes] (*wr* c. 1830–32)

11–12. 'And all the infinite variety / Of the dear world will vary evermore.' Cp. *Antony and Cleopatra* II ii 234–35 (Enobarbus speaking): 'Age cannot wither her, nor custom stale / Her infinite variety'; and, in Blake's *All Religions are One* (1788), Principle 2: 'As all men are alike in Outward Form; so, and with the same infinite variety, all are alike in the Poetic Genius.'

190 'Pierced through with knotted thorns of barren pain' (*wr* c. 1832)

22. 'My soul was but the eternal mystic lamp'. Among other instances of the latter phrase, cp. Southey's *Joan of Arc, an Epic Poem* (Bristol, 1796) iii 275–76: 'On the altar burns that mystic lamp whose flame / May not be quench'd'; Landon's *The Fate of Adelaide, A Swiss Romantic Tale* (1821) II vii 29–30: 'Aladdin, who possest / The mystic lamp'; as well as A. G. H. Hollingsworth's *Rebecca; or, the Times of Primitive Christianity* (1832), Canto IV ('The Tribunal'), p. 303: 'And let these prayers stream forth an incens'd cloud, / Kindled by Thy Great Spirit's mystic lamp'.

23. 'Wounding with dreadful rays the solid dark'. For *dreadful rays*, cp. William Pittis, *An epistolary poem to N. Tate, Esquire, and the poet laureat to His Majesty, occasioned by the taking of Namur* (1696) 133–34: 'But! oh what matchless Heroe's that, who's arms / Reflect such dreadful Rays, and horrid Charms?'; Watts, *Passion and Reason* (1742) 1–2: 'Let *Astrapé* forbear to blaze, / As Lightning does, with dreadful Rays'; and Mickle's *Lusiad* i 663–64: 'From his black ships the sudden lightnings blaze, / And o'er old Ocean flash their dreadful rays'.

32. 'Which the wide-weltering sea somewhere enwombs'. For *wide-weltering*, cp., among other instances, Beattie's *The Minstrel* 477–79: 'Thence musing onward to the sounding shore, / The lone enthusiast oft would take his way, / Listening with pleasing dread to the deep roar / Of the wide-weltering waves'; and Gisborne's *Conscience* (1798) 53–54: 'Lo, as secure he quits the unplunder'd dead, / Wide-weltering seas of fire before him spread'.

For *enwombs*, cp. Donne's *A Funerall Elegie* (1611) 41–42: 'Or as the Affrique Niger streame enwombs / It selfe into the earth'.

192 The Ruined Kiln (*wr* c. 1831–33)

3. 'Then basked the filmy stubbles warm and bare'. In Henry Hudson's *The Hours* (1817), cp. *Idyll I (Morning)*, p. 25: 'O'er filmy stubble blythe the fowler hies'.

193 The Progress of Spring (*wr* c. 1833)

48–49. 'Come, Spring! She comes, and Earth is glad / To roll her North below thy deepening dome'. In James and Edward Aston's *Pompeii, and Other Poems* (1828), cp. *To the Evening Star* 10–11: 'Or when thou shinest in yon deep'ning dome, / Let me by some lone lake or streamlet roam'.

57–58. 'Still round her forehead wheels the woodland dove, / And scatters on her throat the sparks of dew'. For the latter phrase, cp. Giles Fletcher, *Christ's Victorie and Triumph, in Heaven, in Earth, over and after Death* (1610), Part II, 230–32: 'The flow'rs-de-luce, and the round sparks of dew, / That hung upon their azure leaves, did shew / Like twinkling stars, that sparkle in the ev'ning blue'. Cp. also Hemans's *Night-Blowing Flowers* (1827) 13–14: 'Take ye no joy in the dayspring's birth, / When it kindles the sparks of dew?'; and her *The Palm-Tree* (also 1827) 21–22: 'Lamps, that from flowering branches hung, / On sparks of dew soft colour flung'.

71. 'I sat beneath a solitude of snow'. For the latter phrase, cp. Southey's *Thalaba the Destroyer* (1801) X xiii 98–99: 'And have you always had your dwelling here / Amid this solitude of snow?'

90–91. 'The still-fulfilling promise of a light / Narrowing the bounds of night.' For the latter phrase, cp. Ovid's *Metamorphoses* as translated by various hands (1717), with, on p. 120, Eusden's translation from Book IV of *Alcithöe and her Sisters transform'd to Bats*: 'Now from the Skies was shot a doubtful Light, / The Day declining to the Bounds of Night'; and, on p. 334 of the same volume, Congreve's from Book X of *The Story of Orpheus and Euridice*: 'They well-nigh now had pass'd the Bounds of Night, / And just approach'd the Margin of the Light'.

94–95. 'And new developments, whatever spark / Be struck from out the clash of warring wills'. The phrase *warring wills* previously occurred in Richard Polwhele's *The English Orator. A Didactic Poem.* (1786), Book II, lines 83–84: 'The Judgement's feeble Rule amidst a Crowd / Of warring Wills, and Passion's lawless Sway'. But here as in poem 209, *The Two Voices*, lines 106–8, as discussed on p. 100 below, T. may also have been thinking of two earlier antecedents, one by Prudentius, with *'fissa voluntas'*, and the other by Petrarch, with *'voglie divise'*, both phrases translatable as *divided* or *warring will(s)*.

In Prudentius's fifth-century allegory *Psychomachia*, lines 758–61 read: *'ergo cavete, viri, ne sit sententia discors / Sensibus in nostris, ne secta exotica tectis / nascatur conflata odiis, quia fissa voluntas / confundit variis arcana biformia fibris.'* [So beware, men, that there be no discordant thought among our sentiments, that no foreign faction arise in us from the occasion of hidden quarrels, for a divided will creates disorder in our inmost nature, making two parties in a heart at variance.]

In Petrarch's *Canzoniere* (1327)—and perhaps reflecting his reading of Prudentius—poem 128 (beginning *'Italia mia, benché 'l parlar sia indarno a le piaghe mortali'*), lines 55–56 read: *'Vostre voglie divise / guastan del mondo la piú bella parte'* [Your divided wills waste the world's most beautiful part].

98. 'From hoary deeps that belt the changeful West'. For the latter phrase, cp. Gisborne's *To F. G. On His Birthday. Supposed to be Spoken by Himself.* (1813) 7–10: 'If thunder from the changeful West / Blacken the rising wave; / Back to the port its speed is prest, / Before the tempest rave.'

99. 'Old Empires, dwellings of the kings of men'. The latter phrase occurs twice in Macpherson/Ossian's 1762 volume, once in *Carthon*: '"Art thou of the kings of men?"', and again in *Dar-Thula*: '"Thy fathers were not among the renowned, nor of the kings of men."'

194 'Hail Briton!' (*wr* 1831–33)

21–22. 'For Britain had an hour of rest; / But now her steps are swift and rash'.[60] For the latter phrase, cp., from Sylvester's *Du Bartas His Diuine*

---

60 A version of these lines forms the opening passage of T.'s poem 427, *To the Marquis of Dufferin and Ava* (written c. 1888–89), which reads: 'At times our Britain cannot rest, / At times her steps are swift and rash'.

Weekes and Workes, his translation of *Les Furies* (intended for 'The Third Part of the First Day of the Second Week') as *The Furies*, lines 718–19: 'Then, boyling *Wrath*, stern, cruell, swift, and rash, / That like a Boar her teeth doth grinde and gnash'; Elias Ashmole's *The Way to Bliss* (1658), Book II, chap. 2 ('Of Health'), p. 88: 'And if he be not swift and rash, but will have sober Patience, his own skill and labour shall be but little, and *Nature* her self very kindly will in her due time perform all, even all that *heavenly Workmanship*'; as well as James King's *A Poem on Leigh Park, The Seat of Sir George Thos. Staunton, Bart.* (1829), p. 39: 'Less swift and rash the Spirit of the storm / Rides the careering blast, when thunders form / In black array, to fling their bolts around, / And vollied lightnings fire the rending ground.'

50. 'Unfurnisht foreheads, iron lungs'. For the latter phrase, cp. Dryden's *Georgic II*, 61–62: 'Not though I were supply'd with Iron Lungs, / A hundred Mouths, fill'd with as many Tongues'; and his *Æneis* vi 850–51: 'Had I a hundred Mouths, a hundred Tongues, / And Throats of Brass, inspir'd with Iron Lungs'. See also the commentary on p. 211 below on T.'s poem 407, *Freedom*, lines 37–40, with another instance of *iron lungs* and another antecedent.

54. 'Despotic hearts reviling kings'. Cp. Pope's *Iliad* ii 261–62, speaking of Thersites: 'But chief he gloried with licentious style / To lash the great, and monarchs to revile.'

167. 'To hold the spirit of the Age'. Cp. Hazlitt's *The Spirit of the Age*. But T. may also have had in mind John Stuart Mill's similarly titled essay, first published in seven instalments in *The Examiner* from January to May 1831.

200 Early Spring [1833] (*wr* 1833)

1–2. 'Once more the Heavenly Power / Makes all things new'. Cp. *Revelation* xxi 5: 'And he that sat upon the throne said, Behold, I make all things new.'

27. 'My tricksy fancies range'. Noting line 30's 'From word to word', Ricks cites *The Merchant of Venice* III v 63, with 'a tricksy word'. But in her *Dramatic Scenes, Sonnets, and Others Poems* (1827), cp. also Mary

Russell Mitford's *Weston Grove* xi 5–6: 'By Shakspeare's tricksy fancy drest / Lord of the sword and of the jest'.

207 The Ante-Chamber (*wr* c. 1834)

51. 'Through one whole life an overflowing urn'. For the latter phrase, cp. Barbauld's *A Summer Evening's Meditation* (1773) 35–37: 'From what pure wells / Of milky light, what soft o'erflowing urn, / Are all these lamps so fill'd?'; and David Mallock's *The Well of Bethlehem* (1832) 37–38: 'Exulting to their leader, they in conscious pride return, / Bearing aloft, in blood-stain'd hands, the overflowing Urn!'

208 The Gardener's Daughter; Or, The Pictures (*wr* 1833–34)

18. 'Such touches are but embassies of love'. Among other instances of the latter phrase, cp. Mary, Lady Chudleigh, *The Song of the Three Children Paraphras'd* (1703) 95–98: 'Ye blest Inhabitants of Light, / Who from your shining Seats above, / Are often sent on Embassies of Love: / To distant Worlds you take your willing Flight'; Watts, *An Elegiac Ode On the Reverend Mr. T. Gouge* (1706) 225–26: 'How did our Souls start out to hear / The Embassies of Love he bore'; and, in James Howell's *Epistolæ Ho-Elianæ: Familiar Letters Domestick and Foreign* (quoting from the 1726 edn, rather than the orthographically erratic first edn of 1650), his introductory poem *'To the knowing Reader touching* Familiar Letters' 5–8: 'They are those wing'd *Postilions* that can fly / From the Antartic to the Artic Sky, / The Heralds and swift Harbingers that move / From East to West, on Embassies of Love'.

67. 'And vague desires, like fitful blasts of balm'. For *vague desires*, cp. John Cunningham's *The Contemplatist: A Night Piece* (1762), stanza xii: 'What are those wild, those wand'ring fires, / That o'er the moorland ran? / Vapours. How like the vague desires / That cheat the heart of Man!'; and the title work in John Walker Ord's *The Wandering Bard: and Other Poems* (Edinburgh, 1833) I xvi 13–16: 'There are no growing fears, nor vague desires, / Nor dread, nor doubt, nor madness borne in vain; / But, lifted on the clouds, love's heavenly fires, / Brighten the sacred shrines of heart and brain.'

For *fitful blasts*, cp. Macpherson/Ossian's *Dar-Thula* (1820 version) v 8–9: 'How sweetly doth her gentle voice transpire, / Between the fitful blasts of wildly-shrieking storm!'; and, ultimately, *'inaequales procellae'* [sudden storms] in Horace's *Odes* II ix 3.

209* The Two Voices (*wr* 1833)

10. '"An inner impulse rent the veil["]'. Cp. *Matthew* xxvii 51: 'And, behold, the veil of the temple was rent in twain from the top to the bottom; and the earth did quake, and the rocks rent'; and its echoes in Barbauld's *Epistle to William Wilberforce, Esq. On the Rejection of the Bill for Abolishing the Slave Trade* (1791) 5–6: 'With his deep groans assail'd her startled ear, / And rent the veil that hid his constant tear'; Wordsworth's *Elegiac Stanzas* on the death of Frederick William Goddard (1807) iv 1, 'If foresight could have rent the veil'; from Blake's *The Gates of Paradise* (c. 1810), *The Keys of the Gates* 20: 'I rent the Veil where the Dead dwell'; *Revolt of Islam* XII vi 6–8: 'the mighty veil / Which doth divide the living and the dead / Was almost rent, the world grew dim and pale'; and, by Sotheby, *Virgil's Tomb* (1818) 71–72: 'When the Cumean Maid's prophetic rhyme / Glanc'd on the unborn age, and rent the veil of Time.'

11–12. 'from head to tail / Came out clear plates of sapphire mail.' For the latter phrase, cp. George Croly, *Castor and Pollux* (1822) 4–6: 'What eyes are fix'd upon the cloudy veil, / Twin Warriors! to behold your sapphire mail, / Shooting its splendours through the rifted sky!'

56–57. 'But he: "What drug can make / A withered palsy cease to shake?"' Cp. *Matthew* ix 1–8 and *Mark* ii 1–12, in which (say the rubrics) 'Christ healeth one sick of the palsy'; and *Matthew* xii 9–14, *Mark* iii 1–6, and *Luke* vi 6–11, in which (say their rubrics) 'He healeth the withered hand.' T.'s phrase itself occurs in C. H. Johnson's *John the Baptist, A Prize Poem Recited in the Theatre, Oxford, in the year 1809*, reprinted in *The Poetical Register, and Repository of Fugitive Poetry, for 1810–1811* (1814), p. 457: 'Glad is the tale consenting tongues record; / "Messiah reigns, high deeds proclaim the Lord. / "The deaf can hear, the blind receive their sight, / "And withered Palsy springs with new delight["]'.

61–63. '"And men, through novel spheres of thought / Still moving after truth long sought, / Will learn new things when I am not."' Cp. Rogers,

To an Old Oak (1812) 16–20: 'Father of many a forest deep, / Whence many a navy thunder-fraught; / Erst in their acorn-cells asleep, / Soon destin'd o'er the world to sweep, / Opening new spheres of thought!'[61]

67–69. '"Not less swift souls that yearn for light, / Rapt after heaven's starry flight, / Would sweep the tracts of day and night.["]' For *swift souls*, cp. *spiriti veloci* in Dante's *Purgatorio* xxii 7–9: 'E io più lieve che per l'altre foci / m'andava, sì che sanz'alcun labore / seguiva in sù li spiriti veloci' [And I, climbing more lightly than on the other stairs, effortlessly followed the swift souls].

85–87. '"Or make that morn, from his cold crown / And crystal silence creeping down, / Flood with full daylight glebe and town?["]' The phrase *crystal silence* occurs twice in Shelley, once in *Ode to Naples, Epode I.a.* (1820) 17–21: 'The wreaths of stony myrtle, ivy and pine, / Like winter leaves o'ergrown by moulded snow, / Seemed only not to move and grow / Because the crystal silence of the air / Weighed on their life'; and again in *Witch of Atlas* xiv 1–4: 'The deep recesses of her odorous dwelling / Were stored with magic treasures—sounds of air, / Which had the power all spirits of compelling, / Folded in cells of crystal silence there'.

106–8. '"Sick art thou — a divided will / Still heaping on the fear of ill / The fear of men, a coward still.["]' T.'s phrase *divided will* previously occurred in Shelley's *Lines Written among the Euganean Hills* (1819) 19–23: 'And the dim low line before / Of a dark and distant shore / Still recedes, as ever still / Longing with divided will, / But no power to seek or shun'.

But here as in lines 94–95 of poem 193, *The Progress of Spring* (as discussed on p. 96 above), T. may also have been thinking (as may Shelley) of earlier poems by Prudentius and Petrarch, the former with '*fissa voluntas*' in his *Psychomachia* 760, and the latter with '*Vostre voglie divise*' in poem 128, line 55, of his *Canzoniere*—phrases translatable as, respectively, *divided will* and *Your divided wills*.

115. '"Go, vexèd Spirit, sleep in trust["]'. Instances and versions of *vexèd spirit* occur in Thomas Middleton's *A Yorkshire Tragedy* (1606) ii 38–39 (the Wife speaking): 'And so much unlike himself at first / As if some

---

61 From Rogers's *Poems* (1812); see note 12.

vexèd spirit had got his form upon him'; in Jonson's *Every Man Out of His Humour* (1616) I iii 86–87 (Macilente speaking): 'Peace, fool, get hence, and tell thy vexèd spirit, / Wealth in this age will scarcely look on merit'; and in Shakespeare's *King John* III i 17 (Constance speaking), 'With my vex'd spirits I cannot take a truce'. All may ultimately be traceable to *Ecclesiastes* iv 4: 'Again, I considered all travail, and every right work, that for this a man is envied of his neighbour. This is also vanity and vexation of spirit'.

143. 'But, having sown some generous seed'. The earliest poetic instance of *generous seed* may be that in *Metamorphoses* ix 280: '*inpleratque uterum generoso semine*' [and filled her womb with generous seed]. Later ones occur in G[eorge]. D[avies]. Harley's *A Legacy of Love* (1796) p. 260, line 4, 'The generous seed affection loves to sow'; and in Wordsworth's *Artegal and Elidure* (1815) 29–30: 'But, intermingled with the generous seed, / Grew many a poisonous weed'.

146. 'Not void of righteous self-applause'. For the latter phrase, cp. Young's *Complaint*, Night Sixth, 239, 'As flatulent with Fumes of Self-applause', and Night Seventh ('The Infidel Reclaimed. Part II.') 148–51: 'In *Self-applause* is Virtue's golden Prize; / No Self-applause attends it on *thy* Scheme; / Whence Self-applause? From Conscience of the Right? / And what is Right, but Means of Happiness?' Cp. also Goldsmith's *The Traveller* 279–80, 'The mind still turns where shifting fashion draws, / Nor weighs the solid worth of self-applause.'; and *Endymion* iii 12–14: 'With unladen breasts, / Save of blown self-applause, they proudly mount / To their spirit's perch'.

151–53. '"Whose eyes are dim with glorious tears, / When, soiled with noble dust, he hears / His country's war-song thrill his ears["]'. Pre-T. instances of *glorious tears* occur in Wordsworth's *Descriptive Sketches* (1793) 350–51: 'Confused the Marathonian tale appears, / While burn in his full eyes the glorious tears.'; and in Robert Montgomery's *The Messiah* (1832), Book V, p. 140: 'What toils and agonies, what glorious tears / And blessed pangs by penitence sublimed'.

For *noble dust*, cp., among other instances, *Hamlet* V i 202–4 (Hamlet speaking): 'To what base uses we may return, Horatio! Why may not imagination trace the noble dust of Alexander, till 'a find it stopping a bunghole?'

219. 'Like Stephen, an unquenchèd fire.' For the latter phrase, cp. *Faerie Queene* IV v st. 4: 'Her Husband *Vulcan* whylome for her sake, / When first he loued her with heart entire, / This pretious ornament they say did make, / And wrought in *Lemno* with vnquenched fire'. Also the Beaumont–Fletcher tragicomedy *A King and No King* (1619) IV iv 163–64 (Arbaces speaking): 'Let them be Seas, and I will drink them off, / And yet have unquencht fire left in my breast';[62] and Cowley's *Pyramus and Thisbe* (1628) xxii 1–4: 'As shee avoids the Lion, her desire / Bids her to stay, lest *Pyramus* should come, / And be devour'd by the sterne Lions ire, / So shee for ever burne in unquencht fire'.

229. 'I said, "I toil beneath the curse["]'. Cp. *Genesis* iii 17: 'And unto Adam he said, Because thou hast hearkened unto the voice of thy wife, and hast eaten of the tree, of which I commanded thee, saying, Thou shalt not eat of it: cursed is the ground for thy sake; in sorrow shalt thou eat of it all the days of thy life'; as well as v 29: 'And [Lamech] called his name Noah, saying, This same shall comfort us concerning our work and toil of our hands, because of the ground which the LORD hath cursed.'

266. '"These things are wrapt in doubt and dread["]'. Pre-T. instances of the latter phrase occur in line 5 of *Faerie Queene* III x st. 59: 'Matter of doubt and dread suspitious'; Smollett's *Ode to Independence* 101: 'Disquiet, Doubt, and Dread shall intervene'; Byron's *The Corsair* (1814) III vi 3–4: 'This fearful interval of doubt and dread, / When every hour might doom him worse than dead'; and Hemans's *The Brigand Leader and his Wife* (1827) 15–16: 'She will not shrink in doubt and dread, / When the balls whistle round thy head'.

275–76. 'In her still place the morning wept: / Touched by his feet the daisy slept.' Cp. Ebenezer Elliott's *To the Wood Anemone* (1820) 19–22: 'Or while the daisy slept, / Say, hast thou wak'd and wept, / Because thy lord, the lord of love and light, / Had left thy pensive smile?'[63]

---

[62] *A King and No King* is in vol. 1 of the edn of *The Dramatick Works of Beaumont and Fletcher* cited in note 20.

[63] *To the Wood Anemone* was first published in Elliott's *Peter Faultless to his Brother Simon, Tales of Night, in Rhyme, and Other Poems* (Edinburgh, 1820); but was not collected in the three-volume (1844) Steill edn of Elliott's *Poetical Works* that T. owned (Item 901 in *Lincoln*), and on the title page of vol. 1 of which he wrote 'A. Tennyson'.

330. 'Whose troubles number with his days'. Cp. *Job* xiv 1: 'Man that is born of a woman is of few days and full of trouble.'

331. '"A life of nothings, nothing-worth"'. Cp. the couplet of Shakespeare's *Sonnet 72* ('O Least the world should taske you to recite'): 'For I am shamd by that which I bring forth, / And so should you, to loue things nothing worth.'[64]

343–45. '"I cannot make this matter plain, / But I would shoot, howe'er in vain, / A random arrow from the brain.["]' T. echoes but rearranges and reassigns elements of Hole's *Arthur; or, the Northern Enchantment* (1789) vii 155–56: 'A random arrow pierc'd his courser's brain, / And crush'd beneath its weight he prest the plain.' — T.'s *random arrow* being shot by, not into, the speaker's brain; and Hole's noun *plain* (flatland) becoming T.'s adjective *plain* (easily understood).

379–81. '"Moreover, something is or seems, / That touches me with mystic gleams, / Like glimpses of forgotten dreams –["]'. For *mystic gleams*, cp. Wilson's *Isle of Palms* iii 325–27: 'But if they look—those mystic gleams, / The glory we adore in dreams, / May here in truth be found.' The phrase also occurs in an explicitly Christian context in Robert Montgomery's *The Omnipresence of the Deity* (1828), Part I, 111–12: 'Lightnings! that are the mystic gleams of God, / That glanc'd when on the sacred mount he trod'.

388–90. '"But thou," said I, "hast missed thy mark, / Who sought'st to wreck my mortal ark, / By making all the horizon dark.["]' For *mortal ark*—which recurs in *In Memoriam* xii 6 ('I leave this mortal ark behind')—cp. Otway's *The Atheist: or, The Second Part of the Souldiers Fortune* (1684) V iv (Beaugard's father speaking): 'A Minister of Peace to wounded Consciences; I come here by appointment with an Olive Branch in my mouth, to visit a mortal Ark toss'd and floating in flouds of its own Tears, for its own Frailties.'

451. 'I wondered at the bounteous hours'. Cp. Wordsworth's *Gipsies* (1807) 9–10: 'Twelve hours, twelve bounteous hours are gone, while I / Have been a Traveller under open sky'.

---

64 As discussed below, a couplet also echoed in T.'s poems 225 (*The Epic*), 271 (*Locksley Hall*), and 296 (*In Memoriam*).

210* St Simeon Stylites (*wr* 1833)

7. 'Battering the gates of heaven with storms of prayer'. Cp. Andrew Marvell, *Upon Appleton House* (1651) iv 7–8: 'As practising, in doors so strait, / To strain themselves through *Heavens Gate.*'⁶⁵ Cp. also the remarks of the Anglican cleric John Trapp on *Matthew* xxiv 20 in his *Commentary or Exposition Upon All the Books of the New Testament* (1656) chap. 4, p. 297:

> Christ saith not, Fight ye, but pray ye. To fight it boots not : for God hath resolved the lands ruine : But prayers are *Bombardae & instrumenta bellica Christianorum*, as *Luther* hath it, the great guns and artillery of Christians, whereby they may batter Heaven, and make a breach upon God himself.

and, from a variously numbered sermon preached by John Donne and posthumously published in 1661: '[P]rayer is the way which God hath given us to batter Heaven'.⁶⁶

212 St Agnes' Eve (*wr* 1833)

7–8. 'Still creeping with the creeping hours / That lead me to my Lord'. Cp. Shakespeare's *As You Like It* II vii 112 (Orlando speaking): 'Lose and neglect the creeping hours of time'; and Hazlitt's *On A Sun-Dial*, where the chimes in English churches are said to 'give a fillip to the lazy, creeping hours, and relieve the lassitude of country-places.'

214 'Hark! the dogs howl!' (*wr* c. 1833)

10. 'Lo! the broad Heavens cold and bare'. Among other instances of *broad heavens* (Homer's οὐρανὸν εὐρὺν), cp. the Pope–Broome–Fenton *Odyssey* viii 311–12: 'and how the sun, whose eye / Views the broad heavens, disclos'd the lawless joy.'; and John Mason Good's translation of Lucretius as *The Nature of Things: A Didactic Poem* (1805) ii 1108–10: 'Who grasp the reins that curb th' ENTIRE of THINGS, / Turn the broad

---

65 T. owned the 1816 Curll edn of Marvell's *Works* (Item 1528 in *Lincoln*).
66 First published as *A Sermon Preached at the Temple*, sermon 22 in vol. 3 of *XXVI Sermons (Never before Publish'd) Preached by that Learned and Reverend Divine John Donne, Doctor in Divinity, Late Dean of the Cathedral Church of St. Pauls, London* (1661), p. 304.

heavens, and pour through countless worlds / Th' ethereal fire that feeds their vital throngs –'.⁶⁷

15. 'Divideth like a broken wave –'. Pre-T. instances of *broken wave* include Joseph Addison's hymn beginning and generally known as 'How are Thy servants blest, O Lord!' (1712) 9–10: 'When by the dreadful tempest borne / High on the broken wave'; Dyer's *The Fleece* (1757), Book I, lines 10–12: 'So may the proud attempts of restless Gaul / From our strong borders, like a broken wave, / In empty foam retire.'; Cowper's *The Task* vi 155–56: 'Her silver globes, light as the foamy surf / That the wind severs from the broken wave';⁶⁸ and Gisborne's *Rothley Temple* (1815) xxii 1014: ' — "And falterest thou, like broken wave?" —'.

215 Whispers (*wr* 1833)

1. 'Tis not alone the warbling woods'. Instances of the latter phrase occur in William Thompson's *An Hymn to May* (1746) viii 3: 'By the mix'd music of the warbling woods'; Polwhele's *The Fall of Constantinople* (1822), Canto VI, 163–66: 'Far o'er the riches of the imperial realm, / Tho' meads and warbling woods with sweet accord / Breathed airs of dalliance, yet did slavery whelm / Its habitants with horrors of their lord!'; and White's *The Hermit of the Pacific, or The Horrors of Utter Solitude* (1822) 46–49: 'Lo, the grey morning climbs the eastern tow'r, / The dew-drop glistening in her op'ning eye / Now on the upland lawns salute the hour / That wakes the warbling woods to melody'.

2. 'The starred abysses of the sky'. Ricks cites *Prometheus Unbound* III iv 99, with 'The abysses of the sky'; and Macaulay's *Evening* 60, 'To pore into the wide abyss of sky'. But cp. also David Mallet, *The Excursion. A Poem. In Two Books.* (1728), Book II, line 206, 'While in these deep abysses of the Sky'; and James Montgomery's *Greenland* i 90, 'Sounding the blue abysses of the sky'.

---

67   George Clayton Tennyson's library at Somersby had the 1807 Clarendon edn of Lucretius's *De Rerum Natura* with translation and notes by Thomas Creech, originally published in 1682 (Item 208 in *Lincoln*); and the four-volume fifth Bell and Bradfute edn (Edinburgh, 1813) edited by Gilbert Wakefield (Item 209). T. himself owned four edns of Lucretius—Items 1437 through 1440 in *Lincoln*), including an 1821 edn of the Wakefield with 'Alfred Tennyson' on the fly-leaf.
68   See note 57 above regarding T.'s ownership of a volume containing *The Task*.

3. 'The silent hills, the stormy floods'. Instances of *silent hills* occur in *Fingal*, Book I: 'fly, Connal, to thy silent hills, where the spear of battle never shone' and elsewhere in the Macpherson/Ossian pseudo-canon; Coleridge's *Fears in Solitude* (1798) 34–35: 'What uproar and what strife may now be stirring / This way or that o'er these silent hills'; Southey's *Roderick, The Last of the Goths* (1814), Canto XXI ('The Fountain in the Forest'), p. 275: 'Shining upon the silent hills around'; and Grinfield's *Monitory Recollections on a New Year's Day* (1824) 14: 'In this rude solitude of silent hills'.

For *stormy floods*, cp., from the second, posthumous edition of Watts's *Collection of Hymns and Sacred Poems* (1779), *God's Dominion over the Sea*, stanza ii: 'If but a *Moses* wave Thy rod, / The sea divides, and owns its GOD; / The stormy floods their Maker knew, / And let His chosen armies thro'''; Campbell's *Pleasures of Hope* i 91–92: 'To thee the heart its trembling homage yields / On stormy floods, and carnage-cover'd fields'; and lines 789–90 of Wordsworth's translation of *Aeneid* Book I as first published in *The Philological Museum* (1832): '["]For He, the Castaway of stormy floods, / May roam through cities, or in savage woods.'''

216* On a Mourner (*wr* 1833)

1–2. 'Nature, so far as in her lies, / Imitates God'. Cp. Thomas Aquinas, *Summa Theologica* (1485), in the section of Part 1 addressing the question 'Whether the image of God is found in every man?': 'Since man is said to be the image of God by reason of his intellectual nature, he is the most perfectly like God according to that in which he can best imitate God in his intellectual nature.' Also, from Part 1, Contemplation III, section vii, of the English theologian John Norris's *Reason and Religion, or the Grounds and Measures of Devotion, consider'd from the nature of God* (1698): 'But tho' Nature imitates God, yet it happens here, as in most other imitations, the *Extract* comes far short of the *Original*'.

4. 'Counts nothing that she meets with base'. Cp. *Endymion* i 770–73: '"Peona! ever have I long'd to slake / My thirst for the world's praises: nothing base, / No merely slumberous phantasm, could unlace / The stubborn canvas for my voyage prepar'd — / Though now 'tis tatter'd["]';

and Thomas Hood's *Ode to Melancholy* (1827) 102–3: 'The same calm, quiet look she had, / As if the world held nothing base'.[69] Two decades later, T. would refer to Wordsworth in *To the Queen* (1851) as 'him that uttered nothing base'.

26. 'And when no mortal motion jars'. Cp. Sir Toby Belch's speech in *Twelfth Night* III iv 273–76: 'Why, man, he's a very devil, I have not seen such a firago. I had a pass with him, rapier, scabbard, and all; and he gives me the stuck in with such a mortal motion that it is inevitable'. Also Joseph Beaumont's *Psyche* VII cclviii 3–6: 'When lo the *Star* vouchsaf'd to be their guide, / And with a moderate pace its journy bend / To *Palestine;* that it might not outrun / Their Dromedaries' mortal motion.'; and, in Wilson's *City of the Plague* II ii, *Dirge* 21–22: 'Our lady's soft and gentle feet / O'er earth in mortal motion swim'.

217* Ulysses (*wr* 1833)

1. 'It little profits that an idle king'. The latter phrase occurs in *La Pucelle; or, The Maid of Orleans* (1796)—a version of Voltaire's unfinished satirical poem, published privately and anonymously but known to have been written by Catherine Maria Bury (née Dawson), Countess of Charleville—with, in Canto III, lines 78–79: 'A forceless Phantom, despicable thing, / Like Chilperic, that truly idle King.'

But T.'s use of the phrase—and his framing of the poem's dramatic situation around it—may also owe something to another, earlier poem: Gray's *The Bard*, a Pindaric ode first published in 1757[70] and beginning with another king suffering forced idleness: '"Ruin seize thee, ruthless King! / Confusion on thy banners wait, / Though fann'd by Conquest's crimson wing / They mock the air with idle state!["]'

---

69 T. owned the seven-volume Moxon edn (1862–63) of *The Works of Thomas Hood. Comic and serious, in prose and verse. Edited, with notes, by his son* (Item 1182 in *Lincoln*), in which *Ode to Melancholy* was in vol. 1.

70 In *Odes: by Mr. Gray, author of An elegy in a country church-yard* (Dublin, 1757). *The Bard* was subsequently reprinted in, among others, the 1775 and 1854 edns of his works owned, respectively, by T.'s father and T. himself (see note 25).

2. 'By this still hearth, among these barren crags'. For *barren crags*, cp. Samuel Johnson's essay in *The Rambler* no. 128 for 8 June 1751, reading in part: '[I]n the condition of men it frequently happens, that grief and anxiety lie hid under the golden robes of prosperity, and the gloom of calamity is cheered by secret radiations of hope and comfort; as in the works of nature the bog is sometimes covered with flowers, and the mine concealed in the barren crags.'[71] Cp. also, in Sotheby's *Farewell to Italy* (1818), *Genoa* x 1–4: 'Where Freedom? — crush'd beneath thy despot's throne: / Him, whose base hand the iron gates unclos'd / Where Alps with all her rocks the foe oppos'd: / Who fled 'mid barren crags to lurk unknown'.

5. 'That hoard, and sleep, and feed, and know not me'. Ricks notes the line's affinity to *Hamlet* IV iv 33–39, beginning: 'What is a man, / If his chief good and market of his time / Be but to sleep and feed?' For *know not me*, cp. *Jeremiah* ix 3: 'And they bend their tongues like their bow for lies: but they are not valiant for the truth upon the earth; for they proceed from evil to evil, and they know not me, saith the Lord'; as well as the titles of two plays by Thomas Heywood: *If you know not me, You know no bodie: Or, The troubles of Queene Elizabeth* (1605) and *The Second Part of, If you know not me, you know no bodie* (1606), both plays on the life and reign of the then-late monarch.

11. 'Vext the dim sea'. Cp. *Revolt of Islam* III xxxii 3–4: 'To mark if yet the starry giant dips / His zone in the dim sea'; and Moore's hymn *As Down in the Sunless Retreats* (1816) ii 1–2: 'As still to the star of its worship, though clouded, / The needle points faithfully o'er the dim sea'. An earlier hymn, Cowper's *Contentment* (1779), begins: 'Fierce passions discompose the mind, / As tempests vex the sea; / But calm content and peace we find, / When, Lord, we turn to thee.'

31. 'To follow knowledge like a sinking star'. For the latter phrase, cp. Hayley's *The Triumphs of Temper* (1781), Canto V, 115–16: 'And now Serena, from th' exalted car, / Look'd down, astonish'd, on each sinking star'; Burns's *Liberty.—A Fragment* (1816) 17: 'One quench'd in darkness,

---

71 T. owned the twelve-volume 1801 Baldwin edn of Johnson's *Works; with an essay on his life and genius by Arthur Murray* (Item 1264 in *Lincoln*), in which this *Rambler* essay appears in vol. 5.

like the sinking star'; Wordsworth's sonnet beginning 'I watch, and long have watched, with calm regret / Yon slowly-sinking star' (1819); and Eliza Acton's *Cards of Fortune* (1826) 117–18: 'A shatter'd gem; a sinking star,— / The mirrors of thy fortune are!'

41. 'In offices of tenderness'. Cp. Johnson's essay in *The Rambler* no. 99 for 26 February 1751: 'The necessities of our condition require a thousand offices of tenderness, which mere regard for the species will never dictate.'

45. 'There gloom the dark broad seas.' For the latter phrase, cp. Crabbe's *Sir Eustace Grey* (1807), set in a madhouse, where the Patient says in lines 212–19: 'At length a moment's sleep stole on — / Again came my commission'd foes; / Again through sea and land we're gone, / No peace, no respite, no repose: / Above the dark broad sea we rose, / We ran through bleak and frozen land; / I had no strength, their strength t' oppose, / An infant in a giant's hand.'[72]

47–48. 'That ever with a frolic welcome took / The thunder and the sunshine'. Cp. Robert Lloyd, *The Poet. An Epistle to C. Churchill.* (1774), p. 24: 'Then welcome frolic, welcome whim! / The world is all alike to *him*.'

218* Tithon (*wr* 1833)

2. 'The vapours weep their substance to the ground'.[73] In his *Poems* (Glasgow, 1815), cp. David Cameron's *Friendship. Written in Autumn.* 7–8: 'Through deepest groves the cold winds sweep, / That with the drizzling vapours weep'. In his *Dramatic Scenes and Other Poems* (1819), cp. also Barry Cornwall's *Stanzas*, the tenth of which (beginning 'For not alone with Alpine heights my soul') reads, in lines 4–6: 'Bursting in thundering billows 'gainst the steep; / The rainbow, that when summer vapours weep, / Arches the sky'.

51. 'In wild and airy whisperings'. Cp. George Croly, *Salathiel: A Story of the Past, the Present, and the Future* (New York and London, 1828), vol.

---

72 In Crabbe's *Poetical Works* (see note 35), *Sir Eustace Grey* was in vol. 2.
73 In T.'s *Tithonus*—first published in *The Cornhill Magazine*, vol. 1, no. 2 (Feb. 1860), 175–76—the line (also line 2) reads: 'The vapours weep their burthen to the ground'.

1, chap. 14, p. 162 of the second London ed.: 'The airy whisperings, the loneliness, the rich twilight, were the very food of mystery.'

56–57. 'Coldly thy rosy shadows bathe me, cold / Are all thy lights, and cold my wrinkled feet'.[74] Cp., by Eliza S. Francis, *Sir Wilibert de Waverley; or, the Bridal Eve* (1815) xxvi 3–4: 'When through the eastern portals wide, / Morn's rosy shadows lightly glide'; and Byron's *Sardanapalus, A Tragedy* (1821) I ii 42–46: 'Thou hast no more eyes than heart to make her crimson / Like to the dying day on Caucasus, / Where sunset tints the snow with rosy shadows, / And then reproach her with thine own cold blindness, / Which will not see it.'

219 Tiresias (*wr* c. 1833)

15. 'Through all its folds the multitudinous beast'. For the latter phrase cp. Smollett, *The History and Adventures of an Atom* (1740), vol. 2, pp. 66–67: 'but he escaped the weight of a more severe sentence in another tribunal, by retreating without beat of drum, into the territories of China, where he found an asylum, from whence he made divers ineffectual appeals to the multitudinous beast at Niphon.' The phrase may ultimately be traceable to Plato's *Republic*, Book IX, at 588c: 'Θηρίου ποικίλος καὶ πολυκέφαλος' [a beast diverse and many-headed].

93–95. 'Stony showers / Of that ear-stunning hail of Arês crash / Along the sounding walls.' Ricks notes that Cowley has 'stony shower' in his imitation of Pindar, *The Plagues of Egypt* (1656) stanza xi, where the lines in question, 200–3, read: 'And straight a stony shower / Of monstrous *Hail* does downward powre, / Such as ne're *Winter* yet brought forth, / From all her stormy *Magazins* of the *North*.' But cp. also Pope's *Iliad* xii 203–4: 'Thro' the long walls the stony showers were heard, / The blaze of flames, the flash of arms, appear'd'; Gray's translation of *Thebaid* vi (1775) 17–18: 'Who trust your arms shall raze the Tyrian towers, / And batter Cadmus' walls with stony showers';[75] and, in the *Poetical Register*,

---

74   These lines also occur in *Tithonus* as lines 66–67.
75   See note 25 regarding George Clayton Tennyson's ownership of the 1775 volume containing Gray's translation.

and Repository of Poetry, for 1802 (1803), *Chatterton's Poem Charity, Modernised from its Obsolete English By Anna Seward* vi 6–7: 'Again the lightnings flash, the Thunder roars, / And from the full Clouds burst the pattering, stony showers.'[76]

T.'s *ear-stunning* may have been suggested by a passage in Rev. H[enry]. H[art]. Milman's *Belshazzar: A Dramatic Poem* (1822), where Kalassan, High Priest of Bel, says on p. 109 in the Summit of the Temple scene: 'Roll on! I say,—roll on / My bridal music! the ear-stunning tambour— / Blaze forth my marriage fires!' The phrase also occurs in Drummond, *Bruce's Invasion of Ireland* (Dublin, 1826), Canto IV ('The Battle') 241–42: 'E'en the boldest recoil from the strokes of the Gael / That ring on their crests with an ear-stunning peal.'

For *sounding walls*, cp. Charles Hopkins, *The History of Love. A Poem: In a letter to a Lady.* (1695), in which his translation of *The Passion of Scylla for Minos, From the Eighth Book of Ovid's Metamorphoses* begins: 'A Tower with sounding Walls erected stands, / The sacred Fabrick of *Apollo's* Hands.'; and Thomas Aird's *The Captive of Fez* (1830) III v 47–48: 'To hordes dispersed that hear the sounding walls / Of crystal water from which Atlas falls'.

131–32. 'No stone is fitted in yon marble girth / Whose echo shall not tongue thy glorious doom'. For the latter phrase, cp. the Pope–Broome–Fenton *Odyssey* iv 289–90, 'Such, happy *Nestor!* was thy glorious doom; / Around thee full of years, thy offspring bloom'; George Lord Lyttelton, *Cato's Speech to Labienus. In the Ninth Book of Lucan.* (1775) 3–4: 'Whether to seek in arms a glorious doom / Or basely live, and [be] a king in Rome?';[77] *Revolt of Islam* IV vii 4–5: 'Then I bethought me of the glorious doom / Of those who sternly struggle to relume / The lamp of Hope o'er man's bewildered lot'; and Wiffen's *Jerusalem Delivered* (1821 text) IV xxxix 3–4: '"Kings—nations—tamed in battle kneel, and deem / "Their deed of vassalage a glorious doom,—["]'.

---

76 Chatterton's pseudo-archaic line 7, as first published in his *An Excelente Balade of Charitie* (1770), reads: 'And the full cloudes are braste attenes in stonen showers'.

77 The three-volume third (1776) Dodsley edn of *The Works of George Lord Lyttelton* was at Somersby (Item 212 in *Lincoln*), his translation of Cato's speech to Labienus in vol. 3.

220 Semele (*wr* c. 1835)

4–5. 'This mortal house is all too narrow / To enclose the wonder.' Cp. Spenser, *The Ruines of Time* (1591) 351–54: 'What booteth it to haue beene rich aliue? / What to be great? what to be gracious? / When after death no token doth suruiue, / Of former being in this mortall hous'; and *Antony and Cleopatra* V ii 51–52, where the doomed queen vows to follow her lover in death: 'I'll not sleep neither. This mortal house I'll ruin, / Do Caesar what he can.'

12–13. 'and melodious thunder / Wheels in circles.' For *melodious thunder* — which also occurs in line 27 of T.'s *The Poet's Mind* (poem 92, *pub* 1830 as among T.'s juvenilia), 'With a low melodious thunder'; in line 9 of his *Lines on Cambridge of 1830* (poem 140) as *melodious thunders*, as discussed on p. 70 above; and in *The Princess* (poem 286) ii 452, 'A long melodious thunder to the sound' — cp. Robert Montgomery's *Woman, The Angel of Life* (1833), Canto II, p. 96: 'Now, with wild melodious thunder / The vaulted pavement echoes under'.

223 Youth (*wr* 1833)

1. 'Youth, lapsing through fair solitudes'. Cp. Mallet's *Excursion* 324: 'Fair Solitudes! where all is Paradise'.

14. 'Summer through all her sleepy leaves'. Cp. Radcliffe's *Edwy. A Poem in Three Parts.* — posthumously published in vol. 4 of her *Works* (1833) — Part II, *The Fairie Court. A Summer's Night in Windsor Park*, p. 297: 'And sleepy leaves, scarce moved in air, / Or only swayed by breezes fleet, / With the lake's murmuring falls afar, / Made melody most sad and sweet.'

18. 'To snowy crofts and winding scars'. Cp. Wordsworth's *Peter Bell, a Tale in Verse* (1819) Part I, 196–97: 'And he had trudg'd through Yorkshire dales, / Among the rocks and winding *scars*'.

225* The Epic [Morte d'Arthur] (*wr* c. 1837–38)

38–39. 'these twelve books of mine / Were faint Homeric echoes, nothing-worth'. Here as elsewhere (see on p. 103 the commentary on line 331 of poem 209, and on p. 126 the commentary on line 148 of poem 271), the latter phrase echoes the couplet of Shakespeare's *Sonnet 72*: 'For I am shamd by that which I bring forth, / And so should you, to loue things nothing worth.'

227* 'Oh! that 'twere possible' (*wr* c. 1833–37)

23. 'Half the night I waste in sighs'. Prior instances of the latter phrase include Thomas Wyatt's *The mournful Lover to his Heart with Complaint that it will not break* (1557) 5: 'To waste in sighs were piteous death'; Ogilvie's *Rona*, Book II, p. 46: 'For thee, for thee, I waste in sighs away!'; and, in his *Miniature Lyrics* (Dublin, 1824), Thomas H. Bayly's *The Last Green Leaf* 13–16: 'We do not meet to *banish* thought; / Yet, though regrets will come *unsought*, / We will not waste in sighs of grief, / Life's ling'ring joy — *the last green leaf.*'

40. 'Wrapt in drifts of lurid smoke'. Cp. *Prometheus Unbound* II iv 150–52: 'That terrible Shadow floats / Up from its throne, as may the lurid smoke / Of earthquake-ruined cities o'er the sea.' The phrase also previously occurred in vol. 1 (1808) of the first, privately printed version of John Fitchett's *Alfred, a Poem*, Book VII, lines 1044–45: 'Volumes roll / Of lurid smoke, and fill the vaulted skies. —'.[78]

47–48. 'And on my heavy eyelids / My anguish hangs like shame.' Cp. Shakespeare's *Sonnet 61*, which begins: 'Is it thy wil, thy Image should keepe open / My heauy eielids to the weary night?'[79] Other instances of the same phrase occur in Dryden's *The Fire of London* ccxxv 4 — from his *Annus Mirabilis: The Year of Wonders, 1666* (1667) — 'Whose heavy eyelids yet were full of night'; in the pseudonymous Isaac Bickerstaff's *Leucothoe. A dramatic poem.* (1756) II ii 7: 'Dull, and more dull my heavy eyelids grow'; and in Jacob George Strutt's translation into English of a Latin poem by Milton entitled, as translated, *On the Fifth of November*,

---

[78] Fitchett's epic was completed after his death in 1838 by Robert Roscoe; a six-volume edn of the work now called *King Alfred, a Poem* — with the quoted passage now in lines 1044–45 of Book V — was published by Pickering in 1841–42.

[79] And which, as discussed below (see p. 197), is also echoed in section ii, lines 213–14, of T.'s *Maud*.

lines 90–92: 'But scarce had sleep his heavy eyelids clos'd, / When the dark prince of hell, man's deadliest foe, / Wrapt in a feigned shape before him stood.'[80]

233 'Fair is that cottage in its place' (*wr* c. 1834)

5. 'The dimpling eddies kiss the shore'. Pre-T. instances of *dimpling eddies* occur in Thomas Percy's *Cynthia: an Elegiac Poem* (1758) 18: 'That silent stream where dimpling eddies play'; in Dermody's *Carrol's Complaint* (1800) 13–16: 'Thou, a sea-nymph once, could skim / Gentle Ocean's burnish'd brim, / Once, thro' coral groves could stray, / And with the dimpling eddies play'; as well as in James Montgomery's *The Pelican Island* (1827) v 7: 'And dimpling eddies sparkled round their peaks'.

238 'I loving Freedom for herself' (*wr* 1832–34)

7–8. 'Lured by the cuckoo-tongue that loves / To babble its own name'. Cp. Mark Akenside, *To the Cuckoo* (1745) iii 1–4: 'I said "While Philomela's song / Proclaims the passion of the grove / It ill beseems a Cuckoo's tongue / Her charming language to reprove." —'.[81]

240 The Blackbird (*wr* c. 1833)

3. 'I keep smooth plats of fruitful ground'. Pre-T. instances of the latter phrase, variously spelled, include, in *Tottel's Miscellany* (1557), Henry Howard, Earl of Surrey's *The meanes to attain happy life* 1–5: 'Martial, the things that do attain / The happy life, be these, I finde. / The richesse left, not got with pain: / The frutefull ground: the quiet minde: / The egall frend, no grudge, no strife'; Spenser's *Muiopotmos: or The Fate of the Butterflie* (1590) 114: 'In Spring when flowres doo clothe the fruitfull

---

80 The quoted lines of Strutt's translation appear on p. 81 of *The Latin and Italian Poems of Milton. Translated into English Verse, by Jacob George Strutt* (Conder, 1814), the entire poem on pp. 76–90.

81 The 1788 Dodsley edn of Akenside's *The Pleasures of Imagination; and Other Poems*, including *To the Cuckoo*, was at Somersby (Item 5 in *Lincoln*). T. himself owned an undated copy of Cooke's Edition of Akenside's *Poetical Works; with the Life of the Author* (Item 399 in *Lincoln*), also containing the poem and identified as having been 'Formerly in the possession of Edmund Peel, Dec. 1828'.

ground'; Dryden's translation of Virgil's Fourth Eclogue (1716) 39–40: 'Great Cities shall with Walls be compass'd round; / And sharpen'd Shares shall vex the fruitful Ground'; as well as James Montgomery's *Sow in the Morn Thy Seed* (1832) stanza iii: 'The good, the fruitful ground, / Expect not here nor there; / O'er hill and dale, by plots, 'tis found: / Go forth, then, everywhere.'

241* The Day-Dream (*wr* c. 1830–38)

Prologue

3. 'While, dreaming on your damask cheek'. For the latter phrase, cp. *Twelfth Night* II iv 110–12 (Viola speaking): '[S]he never told her love, / But let concealment like a worm i' the bud / Feed on her damask cheek'. Other instances occur in Thomas Tickell's sentimental ballad *Lucy and Colin* (1725), in which the doomed Lucy is famously beautiful until (as stanza ii says), losing Colin's affections, 'luckless love and pining care / Impair'd her rosy hue, / Her coral lip, and damask cheek, / And eyes of glossy blue.'; Blair's *The Grave* 245: 'Whilst surfeited upon thy damask cheek'; Akenside's *Song* ('The shape alone let others prize') (1745) 5–6: 'A damask cheek, an ivory arm, / Shall ne'er my wishes win'; and Darwin's *Botanic Garden* II ii 369–70: 'Withers the damask cheek, unnerves the strong, / And drives with scorpion-lash the shrieking throng.'

6. 'I went through many wayward moods'. Cp. Lewis Theobald's *The Cave of Poverty, a Poem. Written in imitation of Shakespeare.* (1715) 307–10: 'Hence the gross Vulgar, who from outward Plight / Of inward Bearing found their rash Surmise, / Misdeem'd them Haggs, foul Sisters of the Night; / And thought their wayward Moods of Magick Rise'; in Cary's Dante, vol. 2, *Purgatory* xvi 87–89: 'the soul / Comes like a babe, that wantons sportively, / Weeping and laughing in [its] wayward moods';[82] and Wordsworth's *A Farewell* (1815) 41–42: 'And O most constant, yet most fickle Place, / Thou hast thy wayward moods'.

15–16. 'Then take the broidery-frame, and add / A crimson to the quaint Macaw'. Cp. Leigh Hunt's *The Story of Rimini* (1816) Canto III ('The Fatal

---

82 T. and his father both owned copies of Cary's translation; see note 24.

Passion') 296: 'While she sat busy at her broidery frame'; and Canto IV ('How the Bride returned to Ravenna') 113: 'For ever stooping o'er her broidery frame'.[83]

The Sleeping Palace

1–2. 'The varying year with blade and sheaf / Clothes and reclothes the happy plains'. Among other instances of the latter phrase, cp. Elizabeth Singer Rowe's *A Pastoral Elegy* (1696) 20–21: 'There the wing'd Choir in Loud and Artful strains / Transmit their Eccho's to the happy Plains'; in the 1702 edition of the Dryden–Tonson *Miscellany Poems*, the anonymous *The Blasted Swain* 56–57: 'Curst be the wretch that first did Gold dispense, / And robb'd the happy Plains of Innocence!'; Falconer's *The Shipwreck* i 748–49: 'Arabian sweets perfume the happy plains; / Above, beneath, around, inchantment reigns!'; Christopher Smart's translation of Horace's *Epode xiv* [elsewhere numbered *xvi*] in *The Works of Horace* vol. 2 (1767) p. 217: 'Circumfluent ocean waits us, — steer the fleet / To plains, the happy plains and blessed isle', translating lines 40–41 of the original: *'Nos manet Oceanus circumvagus: arva, beata / Petamus arva, divites et insulas'*;[84] and Wordsworth's *The Fountain* (1798) 59–60: 'I live and sing my idle songs / Upon these happy plains'.

15–16. 'The peacock in his laurel bower, / The parrot in his gilded wires.' For *laurel bower*, cp. B. T. H. Cole, *The Holy Wars. Seatonian Prize Poem.* (1808), p. 8: 'Monarchs and heroes shared the festal hour, / And Love and Beauty rear'd the laurel bower'; James Montgomery, *The World Before the Flood* (1813) Canto VI, p. 106: 'Then sang the Minstrel, in his laurel bower, / Of Nature's origin, and Music's power.'; and Hemans, *The Olive Tree* (1834) 1–4: 'The Palm — the Vine — the Cedar — each hath power / To bid fair Oriental shapes glance by, / And each quick glistening of the Laurel bower / Wafts Grecian images o'er Fancy's eye.'

For *gilded wires*, cp. Thomas Bailey, *Ireton* (1827) p. 19: 'The Lark, by nature taught to wing the air, / Flutters and strives, his native skies to

---

83 Charles Tennyson's library included the 1832 Moxon edn of Hunt's *Poetical Works* (Item 2488 at *Lincoln*), which included *The Story of Rimini* and in which 'Alfred Tennyson' is written on the inside front board.

84 As previously stated (see note 1), T.'s father owned Smart's four-volume translation of Horace.

share, / As much, when gilded wires confine his wings, As when from rustic twigs his durance springs'.

17. 'Roof-haunting martins warm their eggs'. Cp. Aristophanes, *The Wasps* as translated by William James Hickie (1820), p. 145: 'A mouse! No, by Jove, but some roof-haunting Heliast here, creeping from under the tiles.'

The Sleeping Beauty

19. 'The fragrant tresses are not stirred'. Cp. John Harington (as 'I. H.'), *The History of Polindor and Flostella* (1657), Book III, 9–10: 'Undrest those *Flowry* banks (which seem'd grown *proud* / Their fragrant *Tresses* th' honour were allow'd'; Good's verse translation of the scriptural *Song of Songs* (1803), p. 25: 'Beneath thy fragrant tresses, as they flow, / O'er thy fair cheeks pomegranate blossoms blow.'; as well as Landon's *Sir Thomas Lawrence* (1833) 17–20: 'And odours floated on the air, / As many a nymph had just unbound / The wreath that bound their raven hair, / And flung the fragrant tresses round.'

The Departure

13. 'And o'er them many a sliding star'. Ricks cites Dryden's *Palamon and Arcite* (1700) iii 129–33, including line 131 reading: 'Beneath the sliding sun thou runn'st thy race'. But cp. also Fairfax's *Godfrey of Bulloigne* XX xx 1–4: 'Upon the captain, when his speech was done, / It seemed a lamp and golden light down came, / As from night's azure mantle oft doth run / Or fall, a sliding star, or shining flame'.

L'Envoi

41–42. 'For since the time when Adam first / Embraced his Eve in happy hour'. Prior instances of the latter phrase occur in the Pope–Broome–Fenton *Odyssey* xix 23–24: 'In happy hour (pleas'd Euryclea cries) / Tutor'd by early woes, grow early wise!'; Porden's *The Veils* iii 829–30: '"When lo! in happy hour, a piercing scream / "Thrill'd thro' my frame, and rous'd me from my dream.["]'; Keats's *To George Felton Mathew* (1817) 78–79: 'Whence gush the streams of song: in happy hour /

Came chaste Diana from her shady bower'; Hemans's *The Abencerrage* iii 13–14: 'And thou, the warrior born in happy hour' / Valencia's lord, whose name alone was power'; and her *Siege of Valencia* vi 135–36: 'He that was born in happy hour for Spain / Pour'd forth his conquering spirit!'. In Southey's *Chronicle of the Cid* (1808), the phrase 'he who was born in happy hour' as an epithet for the title hero occurs six times.

246 Lady Clara Vere de Vere (*wr* c. 1835)

47–48. 'And, last, you fixed a vacant stare, / And slew him with your noble birth.' For *vacant stare*, cp. Cowper's *The Progress of Error* (1782) 205–6: 'Yet folly ever has a vacant stare, / A simp'ring count'nance, and a trifling air';[85] Gisborne's *Consolation* (1798) xxvii 7–8: 'The heartless smile betray'd its mimic air; / And languor sicken'd in the vacant stare.'; and Coleridge's *Destiny of Nations* 218–20: 'The Maid gazed wildly at the living wretch. / He, his head feebly turning, on the group / Looked with a vacant stare'.[86]

250 Sonnet [Ah, fade not yet from out the green arcades] (*wr* c. 1835–36)

1. 'Ah, fade not yet from out the green arcades'. Pre-T. instances of the latter phrase occur in Richard Glover, *The Atheniad* (1787) xix 514–18: 'In native windings from his Lydian fount / As various flow'd Maeander, here along / A level champaign, daisy-painted meads, / Or golden fields of Ceres, here through woods / In green arcades projecting o'er his banks'; in Hemans, *Modern Greece* (1817) xv 9–10: 'And from those green arcades a thousand tones / Wake with each breeze, whose voice through Nature's temple moans.'; in her *The Sunbeam* (1826) 9–10: 'To the solemn depths of the forest shades, / Thou art streaming on thro' their green

---

85 As stated above (see note 38), T.'s library as catalogued in *Lincoln* had only vol. 2 of the three-volume Pickering edn of Cowper's *Poetical Works*. *The Progress of Error* is in vol. 1.

86 The last of these is among the 'juvenile poems' by Coleridge reprinted in *Poetical Works of Coleridge, Shelley and Keats* (Paris, 1829), T.'s copy of which (Item 773 in *Lincoln*) has 'Alfred Tennyson' on the inside front board.

arcades'; as well as in Hood, *The Plea of the Midsummer Fairies* (1827) iii 5–7: 'And there were fountain springs to overflow / Their marble basins, — and cool green arcades / Of tall o'erarching sycamores'.

251 To Rosa (*wr* c. 1835–36)

1. 'Sole rose of beauty, loveliness complete'. Cp. Robert Montgomery's *Satan, A Poem* (1830), Book II, p. 155: 'And thus they dawn'd, the new-created pair; / In loveliness complete, with forms of light / Reflecting glory wheresoe'er they moved.'

254 Three Sonnets to a Coquette (*wr* c. 1836)

2. 'And singing airy trifles this or that'. A common literary phrase, *airy trifles* may be traceable to *Othello* III iii 322–24 (Iago speaking): 'Trifles light as air / Are to the jealous confirmations strong / As proofs of holy writ'.

255 Sonnet [How thought you that this thing could captivate?] (*wr* 1836)

12. 'An angel's form — a waiting-woman's heart'. Playing, it would seem, on the title of Selina Davenport's four-decker Gothic novel *An Angel's Form and a Devil's Heart* (1818).

257 The Voyage (*wr* c. 1836)

17–20. 'How oft we saw the Sun retire, / And burn the threshold of the night, / Fall from his Ocean-lane of fire, / And sleep beneath his pillared light!' Cp. *Exodus* xiii 21: 'And the LORD went before them by day in a pillar of a cloud, to lead them the way; and by night in a pillar of fire, to give them light; to go by day and night'; and, echoing that scriptural passage, Rev. Edward Smedley's *Prescience: or the Secrets of Divination* (1816) i 111–12: 'With steadier radiance gilds approaching night, / And fires his beacon flame of pillar'd light.' T. may have read, or reread, Smedley's poem in 1836 in connection with a request from T.'s friend

Richard Monckton Milnes, 1st Baron Houghton, to contribute a poem to a volume then being assembled for the benefit of the ailing Smedley, who died before it was published.[87]

29–32. 'Far ran the naked moon across / The houseless ocean's heaving field, / Or flying shone, the silver boss / Of her own halo's dusky shield'. For the latter phrase, cp. Macpherson/Ossian's *Sul-Malla of Lumon* in vol. 2 of *The Poems of Ossian* [...] *Attempted in English Verse by the Late Rev. John Shackleton*' (1817) 177–79: 'By night a dream to Ossian came— the shade / Of Trenmor shapeless stood. The dusky shield / On Selma's streamy rock he seem'd to strike.' Cp. also Henry Sewell Stokes, *The Lay of the Desert* (1830) clxiii 1–4: 'Alas! the mental orb is oft concealed / By one or other passion of the soul, / Just as the physical sun by dusky shield / Of stormy clouds that o'er the welkin roll'.

42. 'Gloomed the low coast and quivering brine'. Cp. Chatterton's *Elinoure and Juga* (1777) as excerpted and anonymously 'Modernized from Rowley's Poems' in *The Gentleman's Magazine* 48 (Nov. 1778) p. 534, i 6–7: 'Thus faintly spoke, with languishment of eyne, / Like drops of pearly dew glisten'd the quivering brine' (the latter line in Chatterton's pseudo-archaic style having originally read 'Lyche droppes of pearlie dew lemed the quyvryng brine').

43–44. 'With ashy rains, that spreading made / Fantastic plume or sable pine'. For *ashy rains*, cp.—anonymously published but known to have been written by the Franco-German polymath Constantine Samuel Rafinesque—*The World, or Instability. A Poem. In Twenty Parts.* (1836) Part IV ('The Earth and the Moon'), Subsection 1 ('Water, Fire and Land') 899–901: 'While from this very power, follows good, / The ashy rains of dust and gravel hard, / Soon crumble and become a fruitful soil'.

Line 44's *fantastic plume* previously occurred, also anonymously, in *The Tower and the Ivy, a Tale. Addressed to the Admirers of Shakespeare.*, first published in the October 1773 issue of *The London Magazine*,[88] pp.

---

87 Entitled *The Tribute*, edited by Lord Northampton, and published in 1837, the volume included, on pages 244 to 250, a poem of T.'s called *Stanzas* later incorporated into *Maud*.

88 Or perhaps first, but in any case nearly simultaneously, in *St. James's Chronicle or British Evening Post* for 19 Oct. 1773; then in the Nov. 1773 issue of *The Gentleman's*

512–13, lines 43–46: 'At last, with clust'ring foliage spread, / Above the top it rears its head, / There soon displays its hostile bloom, / And nods like some fantastic plume.'

45–46. 'By sands and steaming flats, and floods / Of mighty mouth, we scudded fast'. Cp. *Poly-Olbion, The Nineteenth Song* 191–92: 'Then *Woolstan* after him discouering *Dansig* found, / Where *Wixel*'s mighty mouth is powrd into the Sound'; and Porden's *The Arctic Expeditions* (1818) 85–86: 'Or find some gulf, deep, turbulent, and dark, / Earth's mighty mouth! suck in the struggling bark'.

51–52. 'At times the whole sea burned, at times / With wakes of fire we tore the dark'. For the first of the two lines, cp. *Rime of the Ancient Mariner*, Part II, 127–30: 'About, about, in reel and rout / The death-fires danced at night; / The water, like a witch's oils, / Burnt green, and blue, and white.' For the second, cp. N[icholas]. T[oms]. Carrington's *The Gamester* (1827) 5–6, speaking of a winter storm: 'Again the light / Swift tore the dark veil from the brow of night'.

54. 'From havens hid in fairy bowers'. Pre-T. instances of *fairy bowers* occur in Barbauld, *To Mr. C—ge* (1799), later republished as *To Mr. S. T. Coleridge. 1797.* (1825) 25–28: 'Here each mind / Of finer mould, acute and delicate, / In its high progress to eternal truth / Rests for a space, in fairy bowers entranced'; in Hemans, *The Abencerrage* i 7–8: 'Within thy pillared courts the grass waves high, / And all uncultured bloom thy fairy bowers.'; in Caroline Norton's *The Sorrows of Rosalie. A Tale.* (1829) xxi 5: 'Blossoms which, culled from youth's light fairy bowers', and her *I Would the World Were Mine* (also 1829) 3–5: 'where I alone / Might gather the buds that first were blown, / And weave a thousand fairy bowers'; as well as in Landon, *The Fairy of the Fountains* (1834) 407–8: 'Weary, weary had the hours / Passed within her fairy bowers'.

83. 'We loved the glories of the world'. Pre-T. instances of the latter phrase include George Wither's *Epithalamia: or Nuptiall Poems* (1612) 205–6: 'Let not these glories of the world deceave you / Nor her vaine favors of your selfe bereave you.'; Young's *Complaint*, Night Sixth, 753–54: 'But

---

Magazine. It was reprinted in the 1778 and 1783 edns of *The Muse's Mirrour*, both on pp. 102–5.

these Chimæras *touch* not thee, LORENZO! / The Glories of the World, thy sev'nfold *Shield*.'; and Night Ninth, 90–91: 'LORENZO! such the Glories of the World! / What is the World itself? *Thy* World? — A Grave.'; as well as Barbauld's *Summer Evening's Meditation* 119–22: 'the hour will come / When all these splendours bursting on my sight / Shall stand unveil'd, and to my ravished sense / Unlock the glories of the world unknown.'

87. 'Across the whirlwind's heart of peace'. While Ricks cites Wordsworth's *Excursion* iv 1146–47: 'And central peace, subsisting at the heart / Of endless agitation', cp. also his *Elegiac Stanzas* (beginning 'Who weeps for Strangers?')—written and privately but widely circulated in 1808 to raise funds for the orphaned children of a local couple, George and Sarah Green, who died in a snowstorm in March of that year — lines 21–24: 'But deeper lies the heart of peace / In quiet more profound; / The heart of quietness is here / Within this churchyard bound.'

259 The Flight (*wr* c. 1836?)

11. 'But I could wish yon moaning sea would rise and burst the shore'.[89] For *moaning sea*, cp. Hemans, *The Bride of the Greek Isle* (1825) 123–24: 'And there came by fits, thro' some wavy tree, / A sound and a gleam of the moaning sea.'; her *Italian Girl's Hymn to the Virgin* (1829) 1–2: 'In the deep hour of dreams, / Through the dark woods, and past the moaning sea'; as well as Robert Browning's *Paracelsus* (1835) Part II, line 535: 'When nights were still, and still the moaning sea'.[90]

13. 'For, one by one, the stars went down across the gleaming pane'. For the latter phrase, cp. the anonymous *Stanzas to the Lady Jane Grey, at Bradgate*—first published in *The London Magazine*, vol. 5 (Feb. 1822), 171–72, as part of a longer article entitled 'Bradgate Park, the Residence of Lady Jane Grey', signed 'E. H.', and widely reprinted thereafter — lines 1–4: 'This was thy home then, gentle Jane! / This thy green solitude;

---

89   The phrase *moaning sea* first occurs in a poem by T. in *Hero and Leander* (*pub* 1830) 28–29: 'No western odours wander / On the black and moaning sea'. After *The Flight*, it does so again in *The Passing of Arthur* (1869) 86–87: 'and far away / The phantom circle of a moaning sea'.
90   T. owned the first (1835) edn of *Paracelsus* (Item 643 in *Lincoln*), on the fly-leaf of which he wrote 'Alfred Tennyson'.

– and here / At evening, from thy gleaming pane, / Thine eye oft watch'd the dappled deer'.[91]

263 'The tenth of April! is it not?' (*wr* 1837)

2. 'Yet Nature wears her frozen robe.' Cp. John Aikin (signing himself 'J. B. A.'), *On Approaching My Home After Long Absence*, in *The Athenaeum* vol. 3 (Apr. 1808), 353, lines 5–6: 'Where winter's frozen robe of white, / Betraying oft the wanderer's sight'.

265* A Farewell (*wr* c. 1837)

9. 'But here will sigh thine alder tree'. Cp. Eusden, *Claudian's Court of Venus* (1714) — translating part of that fourth-century poet's wedding hymn for the emperor Honorius Augustus, *Epithalamium de nuptiis Honorii Augusti* — lines 42–43: 'The distant platanes seem to press more nigh, / And to the sighing alder alders sigh.' Cp. also, from his *Songs and Poems* (1834), Charles MacKay's *The Alder Tree* 10–12: 'Alder tree! O alder tree! / Is it a voice of sorrow / That sighs 'mong thy leaves in the silent night'.

267 Will Waterproof's Lyrical Monologue (*wr* c. 1837)

29–30. 'Old wishes, ghosts of broken plans, / And phantom hopes assemble'. For *phantom hopes*, cp. *The Story of Teribazus and Ariana* in Glover's *Leonidas*, sixth edn (1770) viii 228–29: 'Disperse, ye phantom hopes! Too long, torn heart, / Hast thou with grief contended.'; and, in his *Twelve Dramatic Sketches Founded on the Pastoral Poetry of Scotland* (1829), William Maxwell Hetherington's *The Ewe-Bughts*, scene ii, p. 95: 'Ye Phantom-hopes! that smiling twine / Rose-chaplets for the ardent brow, / I've hail'd your glittering splendours mine,— / Farewell your vain delusions now!'

---

91 In his *The Tourist's Guide, or Pencillings in England and on the Continent* (Philadelphia, 1847), John Henry Sherburne, an early biographer of John Paul Jones, claimed authorship of the poem.

270 Amphion (*wr* 'probably' c. 1837–38)

95. 'The vilest herb that runs to seed'. In his *Poems on Various Subjects* (1802), cp. Dermody's *A Fragment of Petronius Arbiter, Imitated* 3–4: 'The vilest herb keen hunger will not scorn, / Nor slight the berry blushing on the thorn', translating the first-century Roman's *'Vile olus, et duris haerentia mora rubetis, / Pugnantis stomachi composuêre famem.'*

271* Locksley Hall (*wr* 1837–38)

9. 'Many a night I saw the Pleiads, rising through the mellow shade'. Among instances of the latter phrase, cp. Rev. Henry Rowe's *Reflections on the Ruins of a Monastery* (1796), stanza xxiii: 'The subterranean dell wolves whelps invade, / Daws wheeling round the darken'd air inshroud, / Chatt'ring thro' feeble twilight's mellow shade, / Obscur'd the glimm'ring with a feather'd cloud.'; Baillie's *Evening* (1823) 103–4: 'And soft as that dim light and mellow shade, / Aërial music whisper'd from the glade'; and, in his *Poems* (Edinburgh, 1836), John Ramsay's *Lines to Eliza* 19–20: 'And when the dews of evening deck the blade, / And the lone redbreast tops the mellow shade'.

10. 'Glitter like a swarm of fire-flies tangled in a silver braid.' Cp. Darwin's *Botanic Garden* I iii 289–90, on the firefly nymph: 'Each tangled braid with glistening teeth unbinds, / And with the floating treasure musks the winds.'

27–28. 'And she turned — her bosom shaken with a sudden storm of sighs — / All the spirit deeply dawning in the dark of hazel eyes —'. For *storm of sighs*, cp. *un vento angoscioso di sospiri* in poem 17 of Petrarch's *Canzoniere*, which begins: *'Piovonmi amare lagrime dal viso / con un vento angoscioso di sospiri, / quando in voi adiven che gli occhi giri / per cui sola dal mondo i' son diviso.'* [Bitter tears pour down my face / with an anguished wind of sighs / when my eyes turn to you / through whom alone I am divided from the world.]

37. 'Many an evening by the waters did we watch the stately ships'. Instances of the latter phrase occur in Dyer's *The Fleece* (1757) i 172–75: 'To these thy naval streams, / Thy frequent towns superb of busy trade, / And ports magnific add, and stately ships / Innumerous.'; and in Robert

Lloyd's *The First Book of the Henriade. Translated from the French of M. De Voltaire* (1762) 391–92: 'The stately ships, their swelling sails unfurl'd, / Brought wealth and homage from the distant world'.

106. 'And the nations do but murmur, snarling at each other's heels.' Cp. *Childe Harold* IV cxxxix 1–3: 'And here the buzz of eager nations ran, / In murmur'd pity, or loud-roar'd applause, / As man was slaughter'd by his fellow man.'; and IV cxlii 1–3: 'But here, where Murder breathed her bloody steam; / And here, where buzzing nations choked the ways, / And roar'd or murmur'd like a mountain stream'.

132. 'Left me with the palsied heart, and left me with the jaundiced eye'. Pre-T. instances of *the palsied heart* include—from her collection *The Peacock at Home; and Other Poems* (1809)— Mrs. [Catherine Ann Turner] Dorset's *To a Friend, Who Asserted that Life Had No Pleasure After Early Youth* (1809) 9–10 (quoting the friend): '"To sordid selfishness a prey, / "The palsied heart forgets to feel["]'; Robert Montgomery's *Messiah*, Book V, p. 171: 'Each limb was marble, and the palsied heart / Throbb'd loud and quick with supernat'ral play!'; and Charles Gregory Sharpley's *The Coronation* (1838) V xxviii 5–7: 'Thou bland deceiver Poesy!— / O, who could wish the palsied heart, / That coldly seeks how false thou art'.

For *the jaundiced eye*, cp. Pope's *Essay on Criticism* (1711) II 358–59: 'All seems Infected that th'Infected spy, / As all looks yellow to the Jaundic'd Eye.'—lines ultimately traceable to a passage on the effects of jaundice in Book IV, lines 332–36, of Lucretius's *De Rerum Natura*.

143. 'Knowledge comes, but wisdom lingers, and he bears a laden breast'. The phrase *curis pectus*, roughly equivalent to *laden breast*, occurs often in Roman literature. In English, see, in his *Odes on Various Subjects* (1746), Joseph Warton's *Ode VI. Against Despair*, stanza ii of which begins: '"Haste with thy poison'd dagger, haste, / To pierce this sorrow-laden breast!["]'; Barry Cornwall's *Address to the Ocean* (1820) 10–12: 'At once, and on thy heavily laden breast / Fleets come and go, and shapes that have no life / Or motion, yet are moved and meet in strife.'; and, in his *Lyra Apostolica* (Derby, 1836), John Henry Newman's poem *Death*, lines 13–16: 'And may the Cross beside my bed / In its meet emblems rest; / And may the absolving words be said / To ease a laden breast.'

148. 'I am shamed through all my nature to have loved so slight a thing.' Pointing, as do other of T.'s poems—see on p. 103 the commentary on line 331 of poem 209 and on pp. 112–13 the commentary on lines 38–39 of poem 225—to the couplet of Shakespeare's *Sonnet 72*: 'For I am shamd by that which I bring forth, / And so should you, to loue things nothing worth.'

153. 'Here at least, where nature sickens, nothing.' Prior instances and versions of *nature sickens* occur in Blackmore's *Creation: A Philosophical Poem* (1712) ii 263–64: 'At length forsaken by the solar rays / See, drooping Nature sickens and decays'; Pope's *Essay on Man*, Epistle IV, 107–8: 'Why drew Marseilles' good bishop purer breath, / When Nature sicken'd, and each gale was death?'; Hayley's *The Triumphs of Temper* i 236–37: 'All Nature sickens; and her fairest flower, / Enchanting Woman, feels the baneful power'; as well as Macaulay's *Dies Irae* (1826) 15–16: 'Nature sickens with dismay, / Death may not retain his prey'.

154. 'Deep in yonder shining Orient, where my life began to beat'. Cp. poem 337 of Petrarch's *Canzoniere*, which begins *'Quel, che d'odore et di color vincea / l'odorifero et lucido oriente'* [That which in odor and color conquered the odoriferous and shining Orient].[92]

168. 'I will take some savage woman, she shall rear my dusky race.' Cp. James Montgomery's *The West-Indies*, Part I, 213–18: 'The blood of Romans, Saxons, Gauls and Danes, / Swell'd the rich fountain of the Briton's veins; / Unmingled streams a warmer life impart, / And quicker pulses to the Negro's heart: / A dusky race, beneath the evening sun, / Shall blend their spousal currents into one'.

275* Edwin Morris or, The Lake (*wr* 1839)

25–27. 'was he not / A full-celled honeycomb of eloquence / Stored from all flowers?' Cp. *Proverbs* xvi 24: 'Pleasant words are as an honeycomb, sweet to the soul, and health to the bones.'

---

92 As discussed below (p. 179), Petrarch's *lucido oriente* is also echoed in *In Memoriam* cv 24, 'What lightens in the lucid east'.

86–88. 'It is my shyness, or my self-distrust, / Or something of a wayward modern mind / Dissecting passion. Time will set me right.' For *wayward modern mind*, cp. Thomas Warton's *Verses on Reynolds's Painted Window at New-College* (1782) 5–6: 'Nor steal, by strokes of art with truth combin'd, / The fond illusions of my wayward mind!'; George Crabbe, *The Borough* (1810), *Letter X. Clubs and Social Meetings.* 329–30: 'If Man's warm Passions you can guide and bind, / And plant the Virtues in the wayward Mind';[93] James Montgomery's *The World Before the Flood*, Canto I, p. 14: 'Yet no delight the Minstrel's bosom knew, / None save the tones that from his harp he drew, / And the warm visions of a wayward mind, / Whose transient splendour left a gloom behind'; and Hemans's *The Charmed Picture* (1829) stanza ii: 'Oft in their meek blue light enshrined, / A blessing seems to be, / And sometimes there my wayward mind / A still reproach can see'.

For *Time will set me right*, cp. *Hamlet* I v 188–89: 'The time is out of joint—O cursed spite, / That ever I was born to set it right!'—Hamlet's sense that (however unwillingly) he must set the time right standing in contrast to the willingness of T.'s speaker to be set right by Time.

276* The Golden Year (*wr* 1839)

10. 'A tongue-tied Poet in the feverous days'. Cp. line 1 of Shakespeare's *Sonnet 85*: 'My toung-tide Muse in manners holds her still'.[94]

22. '"We sleep and wake and sleep, but all things move["]'. A line whose second hemistich echoes Heracleitus, the fifth-century BCE poet-philosopher of whom Socrates speaks at 402a of Plato's *Cratylus*: 'λέγει που Ἡράκλειτος ὅτι "πάντα χωρεῖ καὶ οὐδὲν μένει".' [Heracleitus says 'Everything moves and nothing is at rest'.]

57. 'Twere all as one to fix our hopes on Heaven'. Cp., in Southey's *Roderick*, Canto XVII ('Roderick and Siverian') 24–26: 'For Gaudiosa

---

93   In Crabbe's *Poetical Works* (see note 35), *The Borough* was in vol. 3.
94   T.'s library as catalogued held vol. 2 only—containing the *Sonnets* and *A Lover's Complaint*—of *A Collection of Poems, In Two Volumes; Being all the Miscellanies of Mr. William Shakespeare, which were Publish'd by himself in the Year 1609, and now correctly Printed from those Editions* (London: Bernard Lintott, [1709–10]). On its fly-leaf T. wrote 'A. Tennyson, Xmas Day 1838', and on its title page 'Alfred Tennyson' (Item 1998 in *Lincoln*).

and her Lord that hour / Let no misgiving thoughts intrude: she fix'd / Her hopes on him, and his were fixed on Heaven'; and, in Edward Bickersteth's *Christian Psalmody: A Collection of Above 700 Psalms, Hymns, and Spiritual Songs* (1833), hymn 304, stanza iv: 'Now a new scene of time begins, / Now fix thy hopes on heaven; / Seek pardon for thy former sins, / In Christ so freely given.'

59–60. 'With that he struck his staff against the rocks / And broke it'. Pointing to *Numbers* xx 11: 'And Moses lifted up his hand, and with his rod he smote the rock twice: and the water came out abundantly'. Cp. also, among literary instances of broken staffs, *The Tempest* V i 50–57, in which, near the play's end, Prospero declares:

> But this rough magic
> I here abjure; and, when I have requir'd
> Some heavenly music (which even now I do)
> To work mine end upon their senses that
> This airy charm is for, I'll break my staff,
> Bury it certain fadoms in the earth,
> And deeper than did ever plummet sound
> I'll drown my book.[95]

67–68. 'when every hour / Must sweat her sixty minutes to the death'. Cp. Shakespeare's *The Rape of Lucrece* 328–29: 'Who with a ling'ring stay his course doth let, / Till every minute pays the hour his debt.'

276A 'Wherefore, in these dark ages of the Press' (*wr* c. 1839)

11–13. 'when my name / Shot like a racketball from mouth to mouth / And bandied in the barren lips of fools'. For the latter phrase, cp. Francis

---

95 In English state trials, the breaking of his staff by the Lord-Steward historically signified that the proceeding over which he had presided was at an end, as in the trial of Lord Morley, for murder, before the House of Lords (18 Charles II. A.D. 1666). The record of the case in *Cobbett's Complete Collection of State Trials and Proceedings for High Treason and Other Crimes and Misdemeanors from the Earliest Period to the Present Time*, vol. 6 (1810), columns 769–86, ends: 'The Lord-Steward making a short speech of admonishment to the prisoner, told him he was discharged, paying his fees; and then dismissed the Court, and broke his staff.'

Quarles, *Sions Elegies* (1625), Threnodia III, Elegy 16, lines 9–12: 'Oh, how mine eyes, the rivers of mine eyes / O'reflow these barren lips, that can devise / No Dialect, that can expresse or borrow / Sufficient Metaphors, to shew my sorrow!'; and Akenside, *The Pleasures of Imagination* (1744), Book III, 186–90: 'Thy once formidable name / Shall grace her humble records, and be heard / In scoffs and mockery bandied from the lips / Of all the vengeful brotherhood around, / So oft the patient victims of thy scorn.'

50–53. 'And if I win false praise the shame is mine; / The grain of reputation which accrues / Will rot into the sapless blade, that bears / No ear but loathing'. For *sapless blade*, cp. the December *fit* of Samuel Thomson's *The Year in 12 Fits, ascribed to Damon.* (1799), stanza iv: 'The seely sheep, denied a shed, / By cold and hunger now haf dead, / Each, to procure the sapless blade, / The snow up-digs, / And find, thro' night, a cauld-rife bed / On frozen riggs.'[96]

277* The Vision of Sin (*wr* c. 1839–40)

22. 'Sleet of diamond-drift and pearly hail'. For the latter phrase, cp. Mason's *Elfrida*, pp. 36–37: 'Tell what time the Snow-drop cold / Its maiden whiteness may unfold, / When the golden harvest bend / When the ruddy fruits descend. / Then bids pale Winter wake, to pour / The pearly hail's translucent show'r'.

31. 'Purple gauzes, golden hazes, liquid mazes'. For *purple gauzes*, cp. Horace's *Odes*, Book IV, Ode XIII, 13–16: '*nec Coae referunt iam tibi purpurae / nec cari lapides tempora, quae semel / notis condita fastis / inclusit volucris dies.*' [Now neither silks of Coan purple nor precious jewels can bring back your lost youth.]

The phrase *liquid maze* singular or plural occurs in a handful of pre-T. works, one of them, from his *Nereides*, Diaper's *Eclogue XIII*, lines 96–97: 'I see a Nymph, who in the liquid maze / Now sporting dives, and with a Dolphin plays'; and another, Anne Bannerman's *The Spirit of the Air*

---

[96] Thomson's poem appeared in the second of his three books, *New Poems on a Variety of Different Subjects* (Belfast, 1799), p. 221.

(1800) x 1–4: 'But, far beyond the solar blaze, / Again I wing my rapid flight; / Again I cleave the liquid maze, / Exulting in immortal might'. Cp. also, in his *Table-Talk* (1821), Hazlitt's essay *On the Past and Future*:

> Without that face pale as the primrose with hyacinthine locks, for ever shunning and for ever haunting me, mocking my waking thoughts as in a dream, without that smile which my heart could never turn to scorn, without those eyes dark with their own lustre, still bent on mine, and drawing the soul into their liquid mazes like a sea of love, without that name trembling in fancy's ear, without that form gliding before me like Oread or Dryad in fabled groves, what should I do, how pass away the listless leaden-footed hours?[97]

32. 'Flung the torrent rainbow round'. Cp. Hemans, *The Meeting of the Bards* (1822) 7–8: 'And where the torrent's rainbow spray was cast, / And where dark lakes were heaving to the blast'.

40. 'Twisted hard in fierce embraces'. Pre-T. instances of *fierce embrace* singular occur in Pope's *Essay On Man*, Epistle III, 123–24, in a passage on sexual congress: 'Nor ends the pleasure with the fierce embrace; / They love themselves, a third time, in their race'; in Gray's *The Descent of Odin: An Ode* (1768), 63–64, 'In the caverns of the west, / By Odin's fierce embrace compressed';[98] and in Mickle's *Lusiad* x 627–29, speaking of 'the fleecy clouds': 'And now in fierce embrace with frozen air, / Their wombs comprest soon feel parturient throws / And white wing'd gales bear wide the teeming snows.'

43. 'Till, killed with some luxurious agony'. Cp. Bingham's *Pains of Memory* I xxiv 55–58: 'Oh, was it a trance of magic pow'r, / When in that last heart-rending hour / We mingled tear, we mingled sigh, / In love's luxurious agony?'

61. 'Who slowly rode across a withered heath'. Prior instances of the latter phrase occur in Coleridge's *Fears in Solitude* (1798) 17, 'Here he might lie on fern or wither'd heath'; Campbell's *Pleasures of Hope* ii 117–18, 'Though boundless snows the wither'd heath deform, / And the dim sun scarce wanders through the storm'; Charlotte Smith's *The Gossamer* (1800) 12–14: 'So vanish schemes of bliss, by Fancy made; / Which, fragile as the fleeting dews of morn, / Leave but the wither'd heath,

---

97 The 1821 Warren edn of *Table-Talk* was at Somersby (Item 143 in *Lincoln*).
98 For T.'s access to and ownership of works by Gray, see note 25.

and barren thorn!'; Scott's *Lady of the Lake* I xxvi 13–14, 'And withered heath and rushes dry / Supplied a russet canopy'; and—from Part I of his *Memorials of a Tour in Scotland, 1814*—Wordsworth's *The Brownie's Cell* (1820) ix 1–4: 'Spring finds not here a melancholy breast, / When she applies her annual test / To dead and living; when her breath / Quickens, as now, the withered heath'.

123–26. '"Drink, and let the parties rave: / They are filled with idle spleen; / Rising, falling, like a wave, / For they know not what they mean.["]' For the last of these lines, cp. *Luke* xxiii 34: 'Then said Jesus, Father, forgive them; for they know not what they do. And they parted his raiment, and cast lots.' Note, too, the echo—conscious or not, deliberate or not—of *parted his raiment* in line 123's *parties rave*.

135. '["]Greet her with applausive breath["]'. Cp. William Austin, *Atlas Under Olympus, an heroick poem* (1664), p. 41, lines 204–5: 'Could not th' applausive breath did so contest / To lift thee up higher then all the rest?'; and, in Hugh Downman's *Poems, Sacred to Love and Beauty* (Exeter, 1808), poem LXI (beginning 'Let others covet wealth or power') stanza iv: 'From bravest efforts who would swerve / Amid the crimson ranks of death, / When she excited every nerve, / The prize, her warm applausive breath.'

151–52. '"Chant me now some wicked stave, / Till thy drooping courage rise'. Instances of *drooping courage* singular or plural occur in Dryden's *Æneis* v 243–44: 'Then, on the Deck amidst his Mates appear'd, / And thus their drooping Courages he cheer'd'; Addison's *Cato* (1712) I ii: 'I'll animate the soldiers' drooping courage, / With love of freedom, and contempt of life'; and Edward Gibbon's *History of the Decline and Fall of the Roman Empire* (1776), vol. 1, chap. 6:

> The rebel ranks were broken; when the mother and grandmother of the Syrian prince, who, according to their eastern custom, had attended the army, threw themselves from their covered chariots, and, by exciting the compassion of the soldiers, endeavoured to animate their drooping courage.[99]

These and other instances of the phrase may ultimately be traceable to *adflictos animos* in a letter from Cicero to Atticus reading in part: '*idem,*

---

99 The twelve-volume 1802 Cadell edn of Gibbon was at Somersby (Item 127 in *Lincoln*); T. himself owned copies of two other, later edns published in, respectively, 1834 and 1862 (Items 990 and 991).

inquam, ego recreavi adflictos animos bonorum, unumquemque confirmans, excitans' [Well, as I say, it was I yet again who revived the drooping courage of the honest men, fortifying and raising them one by one].[100]

279 Love and Duty (*wr* c. 1840)

8–9. 'Sin itself be found / The cloudy porch oft opening on the Sun?' Cp. Dugald Moore, *The Bridal Night* (Glasgow, 1831), I xvii 1–2: 'The moon was now within a cloudy porch / Of night's old palace'.

10–11. 'And only he, this wonder, dead, become / Mere highway dust?' In Henry Killigrew, *Epigrams of Martial, Englished with some other pieces, ancient and modern* (1695), cp. Book III, *Epigram 5. To his Book*, lines 7–8: 'His Wife will thee into her Bosom Store, / Altho, with Highway-Dust, all cover'd o'er'; and Capel Lofft the Younger, *Ernest; or Political Regeneration* (1839), Book VIII, 71–72: 'But thou hast stifled many millions; / Stifled them with the common highway dust'.

25–26. 'Wait: my faith is large in Time, / And that which shapes it to some perfect end.' Cp. *Hamlet* V ii 10–11 (Hamlet speaking): 'There's a divinity that shapes our ends, / Rough-hew them how we will—'.

85–87. 'Should my Shadow cross thy thoughts / Too sadly for their peace, remand it thou / For calmer hours to Memory's darkest hold'. For the latter phrase, cp. Hemans, *The Last Song of Sappho* (1831) 29–30: 'Give to that crown, that burning crown, / Place in thy darkest hold!'

285B The Wanderer (*wr* c. 1845–46?)

1. 'The gleam of household sunshine ends'. Cp. Joseph Fawcett, *Change* (1798), p. 79, lines 3–4: 'Ah! where is now that hospitable blaze, / Whose household sunshine wont to gild his face'.

---

100 From Book I, Epistle 16, Marcus Tullius Cicero to his friend Titus Pomponius Atticus, sent from Rome in June/July 61 BCE. The letter's full text is available from many print and digital sources including, in both formats, Cicero, *Letters to Atticus* 1, ed. and translated by D. R. Shackleton Bailey, Loeb Classical Library (Cambridge, Mass.: Harvard University Press, 2015). I quote from the Loeb text and Shackleton Bailey's translation, but several other, earlier edns also translate *adflictos animos* as *drooping courage*. For edns of Cicero owned by George Clayton Tennyson and signed by T., see note 52.

286* The Princess, A Medley (*wr* 1839–47)

Prologue

[Prologue] 9. 'we were seven at Vivian-place.' Cp. Byron, *The Prisoner of Chillon* (1816) 17–18: 'We were seven—who now are one, / Six in youth, and one in age'. Both T.'s poem and Byron's echo the iterated 'We are seven' in Wordsworth's 1810 poem of that name.

[Prologue] 36. '"O noble heart who, being strait-besieged["]'. For the latter phrase, cp. Massinger's *The Duke of Milan* (1623) V i 37–41 (Eugenia speaking): 'Unless you would impute it as a Crime, / She was more fair than I, and had Discretion / Not to deliver up her Virgin Fort / (Though strait besieg'd with Flatteries, Vows, and Tears) / Until the Church had made it safe and lawful.'[101] Cp. also Joseph Beaumont's *Psyche* IX xviii 1–2: '*These* rescue lend us when sly *Danger* near / Our strait-besieged Soul or Body draws'.

[Prologue] 85–86. 'while the twanging violin / Struck up with Soldier-laddie'. Cp. the song variously called 'The Soldier Laddie' and 'Irish Soldier Laddie', with words by Sir Alexander Boswell (1775–1822). It begins: 'Come, rest ye here, Johnie, / what news frae the south? / Here's whey in a luggie / to slocken your drowth. / Our soldiers are landed, / my hopes are maist deeing, / I'm fear'd John to ask ye, / is Jamie in being?'

[Prologue] 99. 'A broken statue propt against the wall'. Although suggestive of the poems by Shelley and by Horace Smith both entitled *Ozymandias* and both published in 1818, the phrase *a broken statue* occurs not there but in Watts, *The Hero's School of Morality* (1709), which begins, *in medias res*: 'Thereon, amongst his travels, found / A broken statue on the ground'.

[Prologue] 222. 'Seven and yet one, like shadows in a dream.' In Barry Cornwall's *English Songs, and Other Small Poems* (1832), cp. *Song CLXV. Sister, I Cannot Read To-day*, lines 1–4: 'Sister, I cannot read to-day! / Before

---

101 As catalogued, T.'s library had vols. 1, 3, and 4 of the four-volume 1779 edn of Massinger's *Dramatick Works* (Item 1536 in *Lincoln*), in which T. wrote 'A. Tennyson' on the fly-leaf of vol. 1. Also as catalogued, the Somersby library had vols. 1 and 3 of the four-volume second (1813) Nicol edn of Massinger's *Plays* (Item 222). *The Duke of Milan* was in vol. 1 of both edns.

my eyes the letters stream; / Now, — one by one, — they fade away, / Like shadows in a dream'. See also the discussion below regarding echoes of *Hamlet* II ii 254–60 and other works in *The Princess* i 18.

[Prologue] *236–38.* 'and the women sang / Between the rougher voices of the men, / Like linnets in the pauses of the wind'. Cp. Radcliffe's *The Romance of the Forest; interspersed with some pieces of poetry* (Dublin, 1791; repr. Chiswick, 1823), chap. 1, p. 5: 'The voices had ceased, and all remained still for a quarter of an hour, when, between the pauses of the wind, he thought he distinguished the sobs and moaning of a female'. Cp. also, from *The Poetical Remains of the Late Dr. John Leyden* (1819), the Scottish orientalist's *Sonnet Written at Woodhouselee in 1802*, lines 1–5: 'Sweet Riv'let! as, in pensive mood reclin'd, / Thy lone voice talking to the night I hear, / Now swelling loud and louder on the ear, / Now sinking in the pauses of the wind, / A still sadness overspreads my mind'.

Part I

i 2. 'Of temper amorous, as the first of May'. Cp. *The history of the Earl of Warwick, sirnam'd the King-maker: containing his amours, and other memorable transactions. By the author of the Memoirs of the English court.* (1708) Among the purportedly genuine documents quoted at length by its author — Madame [Marie-Catherine] d'Aulnoy (c. 1650–1705), best known for her fairy tales and namer of that genre (*contes de fées*) — is Letter IV of 'The Princess of _____ to the Prince of *Hesse Darmstadt*', reading in part:

> Notwithstanding the Prince's Glorious Affair with the Princess of _____, he found it not amiss at his leisure hours, to unbend himself with the fair English Ladies; his Soul was Passionate, his Temper Amorous and Sweet; he pretended not to be one of those Hero's of *Romance*, that can subsist upon the bare Imagination of an absent Mistress, and who think it a Crime deserving Death, should they bestow the least Glance upon another.[102]

---

102 The letter also appeared in 1711 under the title *Court Intrigues, in a Collection of Original Letters, from the Island of the New* Atalantis, &c., pp. 138–63, with the quoted passage on p. 144.

i 4. 'For on my cradle shone the Northern star.' Cp. Margaret Hodson's *Margaret of Anjou, a Poem in Ten Cantos* (1816) VIII xxxv 1–4: '"Never, by heaven! Perish first / Each hope that on my cradle shone, / False hopes, by servile flatt'ry nurs'd / To feed a monarch's son!["]'.

i 9–10. 'and that one / Should come to fight with shadows and to fall.' T.'s *fight with shadows* may ultimately be traceable to Plato's *Apology* at 18d, in which σκιαμαχεῖν (from the Greek verb σκιαμαχέω, 'to fight against a shadow') occurs in a passage where Socrates says of his accusers: 'for I cannot have them up here, and examine them, and therefore I must simply fight with shadows in my own defense, and examine when there is no one who answers.'

Other echoes of Plato's phrase occur in John Fletcher's *The Faithful Shepherdess* (1609) V i (the Old Shepherd speaking): 'Stay a little while; / For, if the Morning's Mist do not beguile / My fight with Shadows, sure I see a Swain; / One of this jolly Troop's come back again.'; in Carrington's *Written on the Last Night of the Year 1819* (1820) 5–8: 'but kind Providence / Has mercifully thrown a veil across / The pregnant future, and to fear the worst / Is but to fight with shadows'; and in Mary Russell Mitford's *The Wedding Ring. A Dramatic Scene.*, where Sir Edward says (p. 61): 'for true men love not / To fight with shadows and for shadows!'[103]

i 12–13. 'And, truly, waking dreams were, more or less, / An old and strange affection of the house.' For *waking dreams*, cp. Coleridge, *Love* (1799) 5–8: 'Oft in my waking dreams do I / Live o'er again that happy hour, / When midway on the mount I lay, / Beside the ruined tower.'; and John Wilson (here signing himself 'Eremus'), *Waking Dreams: A Fragment* in *Blackwood's Edinburgh Magazine* vol. 2, no. 8 (Nov. 1817), 174–76, where the phrase occurs only in the title. Mary Shelley twice refers to her own *waking dreams* in the Introduction to the revised, one-volume 'popular' edition of *Frankenstein; or, The Modern Prometheus* published in 1831.

---

103 In Mitford's *Dramatic Scenes, Sonnets, and Other Poems* (1827). Mitford was best known for *Our Village: Sketches of Rural Character and Scenery*, several edns of which were published between 1824 and 1832, and four volumes of which (according to *Lincoln*, Item 1608) T. owned.

i *18*. 'And feel myself the shadow of a dream'; also iii *172*, 'And I myself the shadow of a dream'. Pointing to the exchange between Hamlet, Guildenstern, and Rosencrantz in *Hamlet* II ii 254–62:

> *Ham.* O God, I could be bounded in a nutshell, and count myself a king of infinite space — were it not that I have bad dreams.
> *Guil.* Which dreams indeed are ambition, for the very substance of the ambitious is merely the shadow of a dream.
> *Ham.* A dream itself is but a shadow.
> *Ros.* Truly, and I hold ambition of so airy and light a quality that it is but a shadow's shadow.[104]

Other works that T. may also have had in mind include *Endymion* i 853–57: 'No, no, I'm sure, / My restless spirit never could endure / To brood so long upon one luxury, / Unless it did, though fearfully, espy / A hope beyond the shadow of a dream.'; Shelley's *Ode to Heaven* (1820) 33–36: 'Where a world of new delights / Will make thy best glories seem / But a dim and noonday gleam / From the shadow of a dream!'; and Hemans's *The Peasant Girl of the Rhone* (1828) 41–42: 'and in his friend's clear eye / There dwelt no shadow of a dream gone by'.

i *31*. 'While life was yet in bud and blade'. For the latter phrase, cp. Robert Folkestone Williams's *The Young Napoleon* (1833) 16–20: 'Visionings of beauty — like the mists, / Which, clearing from the uplands as they fade, / Leave to the gaze all that the eye enlists / Of nature's loveliness, in bud and blade, / In hill and vale, in forest and in glade.'

i *242–43*. 'And then to bed, where half in doze I seemed / To float about a glimmering night'. For the latter phrase, cp. Shakespeare's *A Midsummer Night's Dream* II i 74–80 (Oberon speaking): 'How canst thou thus for shame, Titania, / Glance at my credit with Hippolyta, / Knowing I know thy love to Theseus? / Didst not thou lead him through the glimmering night / From Perigenia, whom he ravished? / And make him with fair [Aegles] break his faith, / With Ariadne, and Antiopa?' As George Steevens observes in his commentary on the play, 'The *glimmering night* is the night, *faintly illuminated* by stars.'

---

[104] The same passage of *Hamlet* is echoed in T.'s poem 468, *Balin and Balan*, lines 199–200: 'The crown is but the shadow of the King, / And this a shadow's shadow'.

Part II

ii 7–10. 'out we paced, / I first, and following through the porch that sang / All round with laurel, issued in a court / Compact of lucid marbles'. Instances of *lucid marble* singular occur in the Pope–Broome–Fenton *Odyssey* iii 520–21: 'With unguents smooth the lucid marble shone, / Where ancient *Neleus* sat, a rustic throne'; in Downman's *Ode, on reading Mr. Hole's Arthur, or The Northern Enchantment* (1790) viii 63–64: 'Ambrosial blossoms deck each spray, / The streams o'er lucid marble play.'; and in G. L. Newnham Collingwood's *Alfred the Great* (1836), Book I, p. 14: 'And motionless she seem'd a statue, framed / By Grecian artist, to adorn the fane / Of Dian or Minerva, where enshrined / In lucid marble, maiden dignity / Fresh with immortal youth and grace repose.' There seem not to have been any prior instances of *lucid marbles* plural.

ii 21–22. 'liker to the inhabitant / Of some clear planet close upon the Sun'. In his *Poems, by the Author of the Village Curate, and Adriano* (1790), cp. Rev. James Hurdis's *Elmer and Ophelia*, where a passage on p. 44 reads: 'The fainting stars withdraw, the moon grows pale, / And the clear planet, messenger of light, / Hides in the splendor of returning day.' Another *clear planet* occurs in lines 57–58 of a poem *To the Memory of H. K. White*, 'By A Lady', included in the 1808 edition of *The Remains of Henry Kirke White*, vol. 1, p. 286: 'Like some clear planet, shadow'd from our sight, / Leaving behind long tracks of lucid light'.

ii 28–29. '["]not without redound / Of use and glory to yourselves ye come["]'. Cp. Davenant's *Gondibert* VIII 3–4: 'Ambition is of use, / And Glory in the Good needs no excuse.'

ii 71–74. 'Dwell with these, and lose / Convention, since to look on noble forms / Makes noble through the sensuous organism / That which is higher.' For *sensuous organism*—a phrase traceable to Kant's *Critique of Pure Reason* (1781)—cp. *The Literary Remains of Samuel Taylor Coleridge*, vol. 3 (1838), p. 408, which quotes from Coleridge's *Notes on Irving's Ben-Ezra*: 'It flashes on every reader whose imagination supplies an unpreoccupied, unrefracting, *medium* to the Apostolic assertion, that corruption in this passage [1 *Corinthians* xv] is a descriptive synonyme of the material sensuous organism common to saint and sinner'.[105]

ii *87–88*. 'like morning doves / That sun their milky bosoms on the thatch'. Among pre-T. instances of *milky bosom* singular or plural, cp. Phineas Fletcher's *Piscatory Eclogues* (new edition, Edinburgh, 1771), with, on p. 45, a previously unpublished stanza reading: 'And, if you dare such matchless charms to brave, / Fly round her lips, and hover o'er her breast: / Kiss those red lips; and on the rolling wave / Of her smooth milky bosom trembling rest.'; Campbell's *Stanzas, Written on Leaving a Scene in Bavaria* (1801) viii 1–4: 'Unheeded spreads thy blossom'd bud / Its milky bosom to the bee, / Unheeded falls along the flood / Thy desolate and aged tree!';[106] and William Henry Ireland, *The Sailor-Boy* (1809), Canto II ('Ship under Weigh') 5–8: 'The war-ship thus from hempen bondage free, / In lordly motion rides towards main sea, / While sails expand their milky bosoms wide, / Which, kiss'd by Boreas, swell in graceful pride.'

ii *292–96*. 'and betwixt them blossomed up / From out a common vein of memory / Sweet household talk, and phrases of the hearth, / And far allusion, till the gracious dews / Began to glisten and to fall'. Line 295's *gracious dews* may itself be a far allusion, to the earliest of several instances, with *dew* plural or singular, in secular and religious verse: Sonnet 85 of Barnabe Barnes's *Parthenophil and Parthenophe* (1591) 1–5: 'From East's bed rosy, whence Aurora riseth; / Be thy cheeks figured, which their beams display / In smiles! whose sight mine heart with joy surpriseth; / And which my Fancy's flowers do fair array, / Cleared with the gracious dews of her regard.' Other, later instances of the phrase occur in Pope's *Epilogue to the Satires* (1738), Dialogue I, 69–70: 'The gracious dew of pulpit Eloquence, / And all the well-whipt cream of

---

105 Coleridge's title refers to the translation by his friend Edward Irving, a minister of the Church of Scotland, of an 1810 work entitled *La venida del Mesias en gloria y majestad*—in Irving's translation (1827) *The Coming of Messiah in Glory and Majesty*—by the Jesuit priest Manuel Lacunza writing under the pseudonym 'Rabbi Juan Josafat Ben-Ezra'.

106 Campbell's poem seems to have appeared first in *The Lady's Magazine*, vol. 32 (Oct. 1801), 548–49; next in the March 1802 issue of *The Edinburgh Magazine: or Literary Miscellany*, vol. 19 (Mar. 1802), 213–15; next in *The Poetical Register, and Repository of Fugitive Poetry, for 1805*, vol. 5 (1807), pp. 219–24.

courtly Sense'; Charles Wesley's hymn *None Is Like Jeshurun's God* (1742) 38: 'Gracious dew his heavens distill'; Cowper's *Truth* (1782) 179–80: 'What purpose has the King of saints in view? / Why falls the Gospel like a gracious dew?';[107] and, in Cary's 1814 translation of the *Paradiso*, iii 88–90: 'Then saw I clearly how each spot in heav'n / Is Paradise, though with like gracious dew / The supreme virtue show'r not over all.'

Part III

iii 79–80. 'and light, / As flies the shadow of a bird, she fled.' Cp. Hart Simonds, *The Arguments of Faith* (1822), p. 4: 'Therefore, should every reflecting man call himself to account for the sins he has committed, and endeavour to expiate them during his existence — since all our days pass as a shadow, not as the shadow of a tree, but as the shadow of a bird flying in the air, are our days on the earth'.

Part IV

iv 166. 'The weight of all the hopes of half the world'. Cp. Charlotte Smith, *Lydia* (1800), ending (lines 61–64): '["]Tho' with her wane, thy visions fade, / "Yet hopest thou, till again she shine?" / —The hopes of half the World, poor Maid! / Are not more rational than thine!'

iv 169. 'To drench his dark locks in the gurgling wave'. Instances of the latter phrase occur in Charlotte Elizabeth (née Browne) Tonna — publishing as Charlotte Elizabeth — *Izram, a Mexican Tale* (1826) iv 637–38: 'He marvelled how the gurgling wave / Forced entrance to their costly cave'; from his *Juvenilia, or a Collection of Poems: Written between the Ages of Twelve and Sixteen* (1801), in Leigh Hunt's *Pastoral II. Season, Summer. — Time, Noon.* 41–42: 'And told me, bending o'er the gurgling wave / Not morn herself such lovely blushes gave'; and, from his *Emmett, the Irish Patriot, and Other Poems* (Canterbury, 1832), in Henry Playsted Archer's *The Sailor's Grave* vi 1–2: 'Oh, smooth grades the deep, for the gurgling wave / Hath ceased on its surface to bend'.

---

107 In vol. 1 of the 1808 Johnson edn of Cowper's *Poems* (see note 16), and (the missing) vol. 1 of the 1830–31 Pickering edn of his *Poetical Works* (see note 38).

iv 246–48. 'at mine ear / Bubbled the nightingale and heeded not, / And secret laughter tickled all my soul.' For the *bubbling nightingale* cp., in Crashaw's *Music's Duel* (1646), *The Nightingale's Song* 21–27: 'Then starts she suddenly into a throng / Of short thick sobs, whose thundering volleys float, / And roll themselves over her lubric throat / In panting murmurs, stilled out of her breast; / That ever-bubbling spring, the sugared nest / Of her delicious soul, that there does lie / Bathing in streams of liquid melody'.

For *secret laughter*, cp. Goldsmith's *The Deserted Village* (1770) 27–28: 'The swain mistrustless of his smutted face, / While secret laughter titter'd round the place'.[108]

iv 272. 'but Lady Blanche erect / Stood up and spake, an affluent orator.' Cp. Francis Gentleman, in *The Dramatic Censor: or, Critical Companion* (1770), speaking of Addison's *Cato*: 'a very culpable manner; so far that we will be hardy enough to assert, to a nice ear he proved himself more of the methodical spouter, than the affluent orator.' The phrase may be traceable to *suave et affluens* [smooth and flowing] in Cicero's *Orator*, section xxiv: '*Unum aderit, quod quartum numerat Theophrastus in orationis laudibus, ornatum illud, suave et affluens: acutae crebraeque sententiae ponentur, et nescio unde ex abdito erutae, atque in hoc oratore dominabuntur*'; or, as translated by Edward Jones (1776): 'There is one thing, however, which must never be omitted, and which is reckoned by Theophrastus to be one of the chief beauties of composition;—I mean that sweet and flowing ornament, a plentiful intermixture of lively sentiments, which seem to result from a natural fund of good sense, and are peculiarly graceful in the Orator we are now describing.'[109]

iv 435–36. 'I cannot cease to follow you, as they say / The seal does music'. Cp. Scott's *Lord of the Isles* I ii 9–10: 'Rude Heiskar's seal through surges dark / Will long pursue the Minstrel's bark'. Scott adds in a note to the line: 'The seal displays a taste for music, which could scarcely be expected from his habits and local predilections. They will long follow a

---

[108] Goldsmith's poem was among those in the 1836 Daly edn of his *Poetical Works*, which, as noted above (note 36), T. owned and on the fly-leaf of which he wrote 'A. Tennyson March 1847'.

[109] For edns of Cicero owned by George Clayton Tennyson and signed by T., see note 52.

boat in which any musical instrument is played, and even a tune simply whistled has attractions for them.'

iv 495. 'Full of weak poison, turnspits for the clown'. Cp. Francis Hodgson, *Statius to his Wife Claudia. The Fifth of the Sylvae—Book the Third* (1809) 5–6: 'Let threat'ning Vengeance hear! thy spotless heart / Braves the weak poison of seductive art.'

iv 502–3. 'then with a smile, that looked / A stroke of cruel sunshine on the cliff'. Cp. John Armstrong's *The Art of Preserving Health* (1744) iv 291–93: 'Riches are oft by guilt and baseness earn'd; / Or dealt by chance, to shield a lucky knave, / Or throw a cruel sun-shine on a fool.'; and—apparently alluding to Armstrong's poem—Polwhele's *An Epistle from an Under-Graduate at Oxford to his Friend in the Country, written in 1780* (1792) 301–4: 'Yet, in the rear, a reverend train / Demand a tributary strain; / Since Fortune whimsically sheds / "A cruel sunshine" round their heads.'

iv 531–32. 'But on my shoulder hung their heavy hands, / The weight of destiny'. Cp. Mary Shelley's post-apocalyptic novel *The Last Man* (1826), chap. 9, speaking of Lord Raymond (a character thought to be based on Byron): 'His passions, always his masters, acquired fresh strength, from the long sleep in which love had cradled them, the clinging weight of destiny bent him down; he was goaded, tortured, fiercely impatient of that worst of miseries, the sense of remorse.'

Ovid twice employs phrases translatable, and sometimes translated, as *weight of destiny*: once in *Fasti* I, 518: '*quis tantum fati credat habere locum?*' [who could believe the place held such weight of destiny?]; and again, referring to the ship in which Romulus and Remus were exposed, in *Fasti* II, 408: '*heu quantum fati parva tabella vehit!*' [Ah, what weight of destiny does this little plank carry!][110]

iv 546–47. 'and on my spirits / Settled a gentle cloud of melancholy'. Cp. Keats, *Ode on Melancholy* (1820) 11–12, where the cloud falls far less gently than in T.'s poem: 'But when the melancholy fit shall fall / Sudden from heaven like a weeping cloud'; and *Private Correspondence*

---

110 For edns of Ovid owned and/or read by T., see note 31.

of William Cowper, Esq. with several of his most intimate friends, ed. by John Johnson (Colburn, 1824), in which, on p. 174 of vol. 1, a letter to the Rev. John Newton dated 27 November 1781 begins: 'First Mr. Wilson, then Mr. Teedon, and lastly Mr. Whitford, each with a cloud of melancholy on his brow, and with a mouth wide open, have just announced to us this unwelcome intelligence from America.'[111]

Part V

v 253–54. 'shone / Their morions, washed with morning, as they came.' Collins (*Illustrations*, p. 85) called *washed with morning* 'a beautiful expression in which Tennyson had been anticipated by Browning', line 7 of whose *Old Pictures in Florence* (1855) reads (correcting Collins's misquotation of the line, as of the poem's title): 'Washed by the morning's water-gold'. In fact, the publication of T.'s poem, in 1847, pre-dates that of Browning's by eight years, and its composition by at least two more. But T.'s line does contain echoes of two other, prior works: *Taming of the Shrew* II i 172–73 (Petruchio speaking): 'Say that she frown, I'll say she looks as clear / As morning roses newly wash'd with dew'; and Scott's *Lady of the Lake* IV i 3, 'The rose is sweetest washed with morning dew'.

v 513. 'As comes a pillar of electric cloud'. Cp. *Exodus* xiv 19, 'And the angel of God, which went before the camp of Israel, removed and went behind them; and the pillar of the cloud went from before their face, and stood behind them'; and xiv 24, 'And it came to pass, that in the morning watch the LORD looked unto the host of the Egyptians through the pillar of fire and of the cloud, and troubled the host of the Egyptians'. Another instance of *electric cloud* occurs in Wiffen's *Jerusalem Delivered* XII xliv 4–6: 'They bound abroad, and all concealment shun: / As from the' [sic] electric cloud or levelled gun, / At the same instant comes the flash, the thunder'. As noted by Thomas T. Biddulph in *The Theology of the Early Patriarchs*, vol. 1 (1825), pp. 417–18, 'An electric cloud […] was the usual symbol of the Divine Presence'.

---

111 T.'s copy of this two-volume work (Item 790 in *Lincoln*) has 'A. Tennyson' on the title page of vol. 1.

Part VI

vi 3. 'Seeing I saw not, hearing not I heard'. Cp. *Matthew* xiii 13: 'Therefore speak I to them in parables: because they seeing see not; and hearing they hear not, neither do they understand.'

vi 47. 'Blanched in our annals, and perpetual feast'. For the latter phrase, cp. *Comus* 476–80: 'How charming is divine Philosophy! / Not harsh, and crabbed, as dull fools suppose, / But musical as is Apollo's lute, / And a perpetual feast of nectar'd sweets, / Where no crude surfeit raigns.' Cp. also Watts, *O how I love Thy holy law!* (1719), stanza iv: 'Am I a stranger or at home, / 'Tis my perpetual feast; / Not honey dropping from the comb / So much allures the taste.'; and the Pope–Broome–Fenton *Odyssey* ix 3–6: 'How sweet the products of a peaceful reign! / The heaven-taught Poet, and enchanting strain; / The well-fill'd palace, the perpetual feast, / A land rejoicing, and a people blest!'

vi 62–63. 'by them went / The enamoured air sighing'. Cp. Shelley's *Epipsychidion* 205: 'Breathed but of *her* to the enamoured air'; his *The Triumph of Life* (1824) 39: 'Sweet talk in music through the enamoured air.'; and the several prior instances of the phrase including in Drayton's *The Owle* (1604) 707–10: 'His Ashie coate that bore a glosse so faire, / So often kiss'd of th' enamored aire; / Worne all to ragges and fretted so with rust, / That with his feete he troad it in the dust'; Charlotte Smith's *Flora* (1807) 43–44: 'Some wandering tresses of her radiant hair / Luxuriant floated on the enamour'd air'; and George Grenville's *Portugal, a Poem, in two Parts* (1812), p. 54: 'For sure some nobler influence than the power / Which waits on Beauty in her Myrtle bower, / Which gilds her smile and woos the enamoured air / To fan with gentlest breath her auburn hair'.

vi 65. 'And over them the tremulous isles of light'. For the latter phrase Ricks cites Gisborne's *Walks in a Forest* (1794), which has, in *Walk the Third. Summer. — Moonlight.* 40–41: 'Ye sparkling isles of light that stud the sea / Of empyréan ether!', and the seventh (1808) Cadell and Davies edition of which (as Ricks notes, and as noted above) was at Somersby. But the same phrase also occurs in Byron's *The Siege of Corinth* (1816) 201–2, 'Bespangled with those isles of light, / So wildly, spiritually bright'; in Moore's *Lalla Rookh*, Part III ('The Fire-Worshippers'), p. 249: 'And her fair islets, small and bright, / With their green shores reflected there, / Look like those Peri isles of light, / That hang by spell-work in the air'; as well as in line 8 of the song beginning 'Thou art not dead — thou art not dead!' in Moore's *Evenings in Greece. Second Evening* (1832): 'Through isles of light, where heroes tread'.

vi ∧ vii

1. 'Ask me no more: the moon may draw the sea'. Cp. Donne's *A Valediction of Weeping* (1633) 19–20: 'O more than Moone, / Draw not up seas to drowne me in thy spheare'.

2–3. 'The cloud may stoop from heaven and take the shape / With fold to fold, of mountain or of cape'. Cp. Cowper, *Truth* 77–78: 'But Christ as soon would abdicate his own, / As stoop from heav'n to sell the proud a throne.'; and Keats, *To Hope* (1817) 41–42: 'But let me see thee stoop from heaven on wings / That fill the skies with silver glitterings!'

7. 'I love not hollow cheek or faded eye'. Cp. J. B. Taylor's 1804 translation of Petrarch's *Canzoniere*, poem 35 ('*Solo e pensoso i più deserti campi*') 7–8: 'While in my hollow cheek and haggard eye, / Appears the fire that burns my inmost heart'; and Hemans's *Song. Founded on an Arabian Anecdote* (1839) 17–18: 'This wither'd cheek, this faded eye, / Are seals of thee—behold! and fly!' All three passages may ultimately point to *Purgatorio* xxiii 22–3: '*Ne li occhi era ciascuna oscura e cava, / palida ne la faccia, e tanto scema*', reading, in Boyd's translation, 'With hollow cheek, and ghastly features wan, / Each shew'd the semblance of a famish'd Man'.[112]

Part VII

vii 24. 'And suck the blinding splendour from the sand'. Cp. *Revolt of Islam* I lii 3–5: 'and now poured it thro' the woof / Of spell-inwoven clouds hung there to screen / Its blinding splendour'.

vii 180–81. 'But cease to move so near the Heavens, and cease / To glide a sunbeam by the blasted Pine'. Ricks notes that J. McCue compares T.'s 'to glide a sunbeam' to *Paradise Lost* iv 555–56: 'Thither came *Uriel,*

---

112 Somersby had the 1802 Cadell edn of Boyd's translation (Item 52 in *Lincoln*).

gliding through the Eeven / On a Sun beam, swift as a shooting starr'. But cp. also *Romeo and Juliet* II v 4–5 (Juliet speaking): 'Love's heralds should be thoughts, / Which ten times faster glide than the sun's beams'; as well as Wilson's *Isle of Palms* iii 87–90: 'And where are the birds that cheer'd thine eyes / With wings and crests of rainbow dyes, / That wont for aye to glide / Like sun-beams through the shady bowers'.

vii 235–37. 'and a bird, / That early woke to feed her little ones, / Sent from a dewy breast a cry for light'. Cp., among other instances of *dewy breast*, Crashaw's *The Tear* (1646) 18–20: 'Such a Pearle as this is, / (Slipt from *Aurora's* dewy Brest) / The Rose buds sweet lip kisses'; and, from stanza x of Clare's *The Approach of Spring* (1822): 'Sweet shalt thou feel the morning sun / To warm the dewy breast, / And chase the chill mist's purple dun / That lingers in the west.'

vii 277. 'Then comes the statelier Eden back to men'. Cp. Wordsworth's *Song at the Feast of Brougham Castle* (1807) 46–47: 'And she that keepeth watch and ward / Her statelier Eden's course to guard'.

vii 297. 'Or keeps his winged affections clipt with crime'. Cp. Fanshawe's translation of Guarini's *Il Pastor Fido* (1590) as *The Faithfull Shepherd* (1647) III iii, 'To those lov'd beauties (as unto her sole) / With all her wing'd affections flyes my soul.'; and Charles Hopkins's *Boadicea, Queen of Britain* (1697) II ii (Decius speaking): 'To such a pitch my wing'd Affections soar, / I love not now my Fame or Honour more'. The phrase recurs, more appositely to T.'s use of it, in *The Fall of Man*, the poem with which the Scottish churchman Ralph Erskine's *Gospel Sonnets* (1726) begins; its first quatrain—'Old Adam once, a heav'n of pleasure found, / While he with perfect innocence was crown'd; / His wing'd affections to his God could move / In raptures of desire, and strains of love'—followed by eleven more documenting man's descent into sin and death.

289 To — , After Reading a Life and Letters (*wr* c. 1848–49)

6. 'A life that moves to gracious ends'. While Ricks cites Pope's *Essay on Man*, Epistle I, line 141, 'But errs not Nature from this gracious end', cp. also, in Thomson's *Liberty: A Poem* (1735), Part IV ('Britain') 1040, 'High heaven to gracious ends directs the storm'; Young's *The Complaint,*

Night Seventh, 1290–92: 'Not man alone, all rationals, Heaven arms / With an illustrious, but tremendous, power / To counteract its own most gracious ends'; his Night Eighth ('Virtue's Apology') 134–35: 'O Thou, who dost permit these ills to fall / For gracious ends, and wouldst that man should mourn!'; and Wordsworth's *Peter Bell* III vii: 'Yet, potent Spirits! well I know, / How ye, that play with soul and sense, / Are not unused to trouble friends / Of goodness, for most gracious ends — / And this I speak in reverence!'

9–10. 'And you have missed the irreverent doom / Of those that wear the Poet's crown'. For *irreverent doom*, cp. Richard Monckton Milnes, Lord Houghton, *On the Church of the Madeleine, at Paris* (1838) 1–5: 'The Attic temple whose majestic room / Contained the presence of the Olympian Jove, / With smooth Hymettus round it and above, / Softening the splendour by a sober bloom, / Is yielding fast to Time's irreverent doom'. Ricks writes in his headnote that T.'s poem was at least partly prompted by his negative reaction to Lord Houghton's *Letters and Literary Remains of Keats*; that 'Since Houghton (Richard Monckton Milnes) was a friend of his, T. wished to veil the poem'; but that 'it seems very likely that Houghton's publication (Aug. 1848) precipitated [it]'. T.'s use of a phrase from Houghton's *On the Church of the Madeleine, at Paris* further suggests that Ricks is right.

29–32. 'Who make it seem more sweet to be / The little life of bank and brier, / The bird that pipes his lone desire / And dies unheard within his tree'. For *bank and brier*, cp., in his *Wild Flowers; or, Pastoral and Local Poetry* (1806), Robert Bloomfield's *The Broken Crutch. A Tale.*, p. 63: 'O'er clover-field and fallow, bank and brier, / Pursu'd the nearest cut, and fann'd the fire / That burnt within him.'

For *lone desire*, cp. Arthur Hallam's poem for Emily Tennyson, *To the Loved One* (1834) 28–31, 'Sometimes thy pensive form is seen / On the dear seat beside the fire; / There plainest thou with Madeline / Or Isabella's lone desire.'

For the voice that *dies unheard*, cp. Byron, *Childe Harold* III xcvii 8: 'But as it is, I live and die unheard'; Keats, *Ode on a Grecian Urn* (1820) 11–12: 'Heard melodies are sweet, but those unheard / Are sweeter; therefore, ye soft pipes, play on'; and, writing as 'Ellis Bell', Emily Brontë, *Honour's Martyr* (1846) stanza vii: 'Bleak, bleak the east wind sobs and sighs, /

And drowns the turret bell, / Whose sad note, undistinguished, dies / Unheard, like my farewell!'[113]

290 The Losing of the Child (*wr* 1849)

8–9. 'O the child so meek and wise, / Who made us wise and mild!' Echoing the title and opening lines of Charles Wesley's 1742 hymn beginning and known as 'Gentle Jesus, meek and mild, / Look upon a little child'.[114] Line 20 of T.'s poem, 'The child was lost and found again', echoes another familiar hymn, John Newton's *Amazing Grace* (1779): 'Amazing grace! (how sweet the sound) / That sav'd a wretch like me! / I once was lost, but now am found, / Was blind, but now I see.'—based in turn on the Parable of the Prodigal Son in Luke 15, where verse 24 reads: 'For this my son was dead, and is alive again; he was lost, and is found.'

291 The Sailor Boy (*wr* 1849)

1. 'He rose at dawn and, fired with hope'. For the latter phrase, cp., among other instances, Lewis's *Thebaid* vi 665–67, in a passage describing a chariot race: 'On great *Æmonius Thoas*' Car runs foul, / While, fir'd with Hope, he gathers all his Soul / To pass *Admetus*'; Cowper's *Iliad* xii 371–73: 'So high his courage to the assault impell'd / Godlike Sarpedon, and him fired with hope / To break the barrier'; Mason's *Caractacus: A Dramatic Poem: Written on the Model of the Ancient Greek Tragedy* (1759), p. 33: 'When fir'd with hope of conquest, oft I saw / A sigh unbidden heave the younger's breast'; and Barry Cornwall's *Gyges* (1820) iii 8: 'Some fired with hope, and plenty plagued with fears'.

2. 'Shot o'er the seething harbour-bar'. Cp. Coleridge's *Rime of the Ancient Mariner* (1834 text) 469–72: 'We drifted o'er the harbour-bar, / And I with sobs did pray– / O let me be awake, my God! / Or let me sleep alway.'

---

[113] Published by Smith, Elder & Co. in *Poems by Currer, Ellis, and Acton Bell*—Charlotte, Emily, and Anne Brontë—pp. 140–43.

[114] Wesley's hymn is also echoed in T.'s *Lancelot and Elaine* (poem 470), lines 850–53: 'but the meek maid / Sweetly forbore him ever, being to him / Meeker than any child to a rough nurse, / Milder than any mother to a sick child'.

9. 'The sands and yeasty surges mix'. As Ricks notes, 'yeasty waves', from *Macbeth* IV i 53, occurs in line 15 of T.'s *Timbuctoo*, and 'yeasty wave' in *The Devil and the Lady* I i 73. Instances, all singular, of the phrase *yeasty* (or *yesty*) *surge* itself occur in Robert Fergusson's *A Saturday's Expedition. In Mock Heroics.* (1773) 35–38: 'Now o'er the convex surface of the flood / Precipitate we fly. Our foaming prow / Divides the saline stream. On either side / Ridges of yesty surge dilate apace'; in *The Shipwreck*, by 'the late B. Thompson, Esq.', published in full in (and apparently only in) *The Mirror of Literature, Amusement and Instruction* vol. 2, no. 62 (20 Dec. 1823), 502, lines 5–6: 'See yonder wretches, 'mid the tempest dark, / Upon the yeasty surge at random tost'; and in a passage from Aeschylus's *Prometheus Bound* as translated by 'Mr. [Matthew James] Chapman' in *Blackwood's Edinburgh Magazine* vol. 40, no. 254 (Dec. 1836), 735: 'When the stream is crost, / That is the boundary of continents, / Direct thy steps towards the burning east, / The path o' the sun. Then cross the yeasty surge / Of roaring ocean, till thou shalt arrive / At far Cisthene's Gorgonean plains'.

296* In Memoriam A. H. H. (*wr* 1833–49)

[Prologue] *1–3*. 'Strong Son of God, immortal Love, / Whom we, that have not seen thy face, / By faith, and faith alone, embrace'. On line 2, Ricks as well as Shatto and Shaw[115] cite *1 Peter* i 8, 'Whom having not seen, ye love; in whom, though now ye see him not, yet believing, ye rejoice with joy unspeakable and full of glory'; but cp. also *Exodus* xxxiii 23: 'And I will take away mine hand, and thou shalt see my back parts: but my face shall not be seen.'

[Prologue] *12*. 'And thou has made him: thou art just.' As Ricks notes in his *Selected Edition*, Collins (in *Illustrations*, p. 97) compares the line with George Herbert's *The Discharge* (1633) 55: 'My God hath promis'd; he is just'. But cp. also, in the *Apocrypha*, *Tobit* iii 2: 'O Lord, thou art just, and all thy works and all thy ways are mercy and truth, and thou judgest truly and justly for ever.' The phrase *Thou art just* also occurs in the lyrics of many hymns.

---

115 Tennyson, *In Memoriam*, ed. by Susan Shatto and Marion Shaw (Oxford: Clarendon, 1982)—hereinafter 'S & S'—p. 160.

[Prologue] 33–36. 'Forgive what seemed my sin in me; / What seemed my worth since I began; / For merit lives from man to man, / And not from man, O Lord, to thee.'; and [Prologue] 40, 'I find him worthier to be loved.' Although T.'s prologue begins, and is addressed to, 'Strong Son of God, immortal Love', this four-line passage also evokes the opening lines of Shakespeare's *Sonnet 72*, addressed to another, secular love, the so-called Fair Friend: 'O Least the world should taske you to recite, / What merit liu'd in me that you should loue / After my death (deare loue) for get me quite, / For you in me can nothing worthy proue.'; as well as its final line, 'And so should you, to loue things nothing worth.'

[Prologue] 41. 'Forgive these wild and wandering cries'. For *wild and wandering* Ricks cites Shakespeare's *Troilus and Cressida* I i 102: 'Let it be call'd the wild and wand'ring flood'. Later instances of the same phrase include, from *Poly-Olbion, The Fifth Song* 107–9, 'Next, *Loghor* leads the way, who with a lusty crew / (Her wild and wand'ring steps that ceaselessly pursue) / Still forward is inforc'd'; Aphra Behn's *A Thousand Martyrs* (1688) 5–6, with 'The untam'd Heart to hand I brought, / And fixt the wild and wandring Thought'; Watts's *Grace Shining, and Nature Fainting* (1709) 12–14, with 'Why should I appear like one / Wild and wand'ring all alone, / Unbeloved and unknown?'; Scott's *Lord of the Isles* II xxx 6–7, 'And from his pale blue eyes were cast / Strange rays of wild and wandering light'; Hemans's *Forest Sanctuary* I lxxxix 8–9: 'turn / My wild and wandering thoughts back from their starless bourne!'; and, from Canto I, p. 13, of Sotheby's *Rome* (1825), 'The lowings of the wild and wandering herd'.

[Prologue] 42. 'Confusions of a wasted youth'. Cp. Landon's *Success Alone Seen* (1832) 11: 'The long privations of a wasted youth'—the phrase perhaps borrowed from Canto I of her friend and mentor Felicia Hemans's *The Abencerrage* i 285–88: 'And yet not hers in bitterness to prove / The sleepless pangs of unrequited love; / Pangs, which the rose of wasted youth consume, / And make the heart of all delight the tomb'; or from her lyric *The Palmer* (1830) 13–14: 'Say what hast thou brought from the distant shore, / For thy wasted youth to pay?' Any or all of T., Hemans, and Landon may also have had in mind that embodiment of wasted youth, Sir John Falstaff, who says in *1 Henry IV* II iv 399–402: 'for though the camomile, the more it is trodden on, the faster it grows, [yet] youth, the more it is wasted, the sooner it wears.'

i 1–4. 'I held it truth, with him who sings / To one clear harp in divers tones, / That men may rise on stepping-stones / Of their dead selves to higher things.' In *Memoir*, vol. 2, p. 391, Hallam Tennyson printed his father's reply, dated 3 November 1891, to an American correspondent who had asked him to explain the allusions in these lines of the poem. T. wrote: 'I believe I alluded to Goethe. Among his last words were these: "Von Aenderungen zu höheren Aenderungen," "from changes to higher changes." Yours sincerely, TENNYSON.' According to S & S (p. 162): 'These words have not been found among all the reported "last words" of Goethe in the final months of his life, nor in his letters of this time'. But the *Goethe-Jahrbuch* for 1891, edited by Ludwig Geiger (Frankfurt, 1891), p. 187, did in fact report the existence of a letter from Jenny von Pappenheim (1811–90) in the possession of her granddaughter, Lily von Kretschmann, in which von Pappenheim says that among Goethe's last words, to her, clear and distinct—words later slightly misquoted by T.—were 'Nun kommt die Wandelung zu höheren Wandelungen' [Now comes the change to higher changes]. Goethe died on 22 March 1832. Ricks reports, in vol. 2 of *The Poems of Tennyson*, p. 305n, as does Tennyson biographer Robert Bernard Martin,[116] that T. and Arthur Hallam spent July 1832 on a tour of the Rhine country. Perhaps—if T. did not belatedly learn of Goethe's words from the *Goethe-Jahrbuch* in 1891 or from some other, prior source, and retroactively apply them to his poem—he and Arthur Hallam met von Pappenheim during their 1832 trip and were told of Goethe's words by her directly, or met and were told of them by someone else with whom she had shared them.

i 10. 'Let darkness keep her raven gloss'. Ricks and S & S cite *Comus* 251–52: 'smoothing the Raven doune / Of darknes till it smil'd'. But cp. also, from his *Fables, Ancient and Modern* (1700), Dryden's *Cymon and Iphigenia. From Boccace.*, 151–53: 'The snowy Skin, and Raven-glossy Hair, / The dimpled Cheek, the Forehead rising fair, / And ev'n in Sleep it self a smiling Air.'; and Barbauld, *Ovid to His Wife: Imitated from different*

---

116 Martin, *Tennyson: The Unquiet Heart* (Oxford: Clarendon, 1980), pp. 145–60.

Parts of his Tristia (1773) 1–4: 'My aged head now stoops its honours low, / Bow'd with the load of fifty winters' snow; / And for the raven's glossy black assumes / The downy whiteness of the cygnet's plumes'.

ii 7–8. 'And in the dusk of thee, the clock / Beats out the little lives of men.' Cp. Philips's *Cyder* ii 175–76, speaking of birds: 'they leave their little lives / Above the clouds, precipitant to earth'; and Pope's *Windsor Forest* (1713) 132–33: 'Oft, as the mounting Larks their Notes prepare, / They fall, and leave their little lives in Air.' In his 1791 edition of the work now spelled *Cider*, Charles Dunster notes that Philips's lines are:

> From the following passage in Virgil's third Georgic, V. 546:
>
> > Ipsis est aer avibus non æquus, et illæ
> > Præcipites alta vital sub nube relinquunt.
>
> > Ev'n their own skies to birds unfaithful prove,
> > Headlong they fall and leave their lives above.
> >   Warton

Joseph Warton's translation of Virgil's *Georgic III*, including its lines 546–47 as quoted above, appeared in vol. 1 of Warton's *The Works of Virgil, in Latin and English*, published in 1753.

iii 12. '["]A hollow form with empty hands."' As Ricks notes, the previous line (11), 'A hollow echo of my own', echoes Spenser's *Shepherd's Calendar: August* (1579) 160: 'The hollow Echo of my carefull cryes'. Line 12's *hollow form* points in turn to two other works: Cowper's *Expostulation* (1782) 121–22: 'Happy to fill religion's vacant place / With hollow form and gesture and grimace.';[117] and Thomas Carlyle's translation of the first part of Goethe's *Faust*, published in 1822 as *Faust's Curse*, lines 11–12: "Each hollow form so lovely seeming / That shines our senses to deceive!'

iv 1. 'To Sleep I give my powers away'. Cp. Rev. Philip Doddridge's hymn beginning 'Interval of grateful shade', first published in his

---

117 In vol. 1 of the 1808 Johnson edn of Cowper's *Poems* (Item 90 in *Lincoln*). As stated above (see note 38), T.'s library as catalogued in *Lincoln* had only vol. 2 of the three-volume Pickering edn of Cowper's *Poetical Works*. *Expostulation* appeared in vol. 1.

posthumous *Hymns founded on various texts in the Holy Scriptures* (Salop, 1755), pp. 315–16, stanza ii: 'My great master still allows / Needful periods of repose: / By my heav'nly father blest, / Thus I give my pow'rs to rest'.

iv 3. 'I sit within a helmless bark'. Cp. *'barca [...] senza governo'* in Petrarch's *Canzoniere*, poem 132 (beginning *'S' amor non è, che dunque è quel ch'io sento?'*), lines 9–11 of which read *'Et s'io 'l consento, a gran torto mi doglio. / Fra sí contrari vènti in frale barca / mi trovo in alto mar senza governo'* [And if I consent, I do myself great wrong. Amid winds so contrary in a frail bark, I find myself rudderless in a high sea].

Pre-T. instances of *helmless bark* itself include Moir (as 'Δ'), *Future Prospects of the World*, in *Blackwood's Edinburgh Magazine* vol. 16, no. 92 (Sept. 1824), 278–84,[118] lines 95–96: 'And wavering Fancy wanders to explore, / In helmless bark, a sea without a shore'; and, by the American poet Henry Wadsworth Longfellow, his early poem *The Sea-Diver* (1825) 17–20: 'At night upon my storm-drench'd wing, / I poised above a helmless bark, / And soon I saw the shattered thing / Had passed away and left no mark.'

iv 11. 'Break, thou deep vase of chilling tears'. The phrase *chilling tears* may be traced to such classical sources as *Iliad* xxiv 524, 'οὐ γάρ τις πρῆξις πέλεται κρυεροῖο γόοιο' [for nothing comes of chill lament]; and *Odyssey* iv 103, 'παύομαι: αἰψηρὸς δὲ κόρος κρυεροῖο γόοιο' [I cease, for men soon have excess of chill lament], where κρυεροῖο γόοιο may be and has been translated as *chilling tears*. Among several pre-T. poets employing the phrase itself, Robinson does so twice, first in her *Ode to the Nightingale* (1791) 66–67, 'And, as her chilling tears diffuse / O'er the white thorn their silv'ry dews'; and again in her *Ode to Night* (1793) 35–36, 'The wild winds shake the distant spheres, / And Nature hides her face, bedew'd with chilling tears!' As noted a century ago by A. C. Bradley,[119] the image though not the phrase also occurs in line 11 of Byron's 1815 lyric *There's Not a Joy*: 'That heavy chill has frozen o'er the fountain of our tears'.

---

[118] Subsequently republished in Moir (as 'Delta'), *The Legend of Genevieve: With Other Tales and Poems* (Edinburgh and London, 1825), pp. 290–303.

[119] In his *Commentary on Tennyson's In Memoriam*, second edn (Macmillan, 1907), p. 88.

v 5–6. 'But, for the unquiet heart and brain, / A use in measured language lies'. Cp. Wordsworth, *Descriptive Sketches* (1820 version) 162–65: 'Yet arts are thine that soothe the unquiet heart, / And smiles to Solitude and Want impart. / I lov'd, 'mid thy most desert woods astray, / With pensive step to measure my slow way'.

vi 4. 'And vacant chaff well meant for grain.' Cp. Thomson's *Autumn* 331–32: 'Or whirl'd in air, or into vacant chaff / Shook waste'; and lines 405–6 of William Mills's translation (1780) of Virgil's *Georgic I*: 'The wintry storm has blown: and wide dispers'd / The flying stubble and the vacant chaff.'

vi 16. 'Drops in his vast and wandering grave.' While Ricks and S & S cite (as does Collins, though misnumbering the scene) the doomed Clarence's dream of drowning in *Richard III* I iv 39—'To find [or, in some editions, *seek*] the empty, vast, and wand'ring air'—see also Parnell's *Jonah* (1758) 139–42: 'Then to the midst brought down, the seas abide / Beneath my feet, the seas on ev'ry side; / In storms the billow, and in calms the wave, / Are moving cov'rings to my wand'ring grave'.

vi 25. 'O somewhere, meek, unconscious dove'. Cp. Landor, *Gebir* (1798) xvi ('To My Watch') 19–22: '["]So, to some distant ile, the unconscious dove / Bears at her breast the billet dear to love, / But drops, while viewless lies the happier scene, / On some hard rock or desert beach between."'

ix 1–2. 'Fair ship, that from the Italian shore / Sailest the placid ocean-plains'. Ricks and S & S cite *Queen Mab* viii 65: 'Ruffle the placid ocean-deep'; Mustard, Ricks, and S & S also citing *Aeneid* x 103: *'placida aequora'* [in calm seas]. But cp. also Wilson's *Isle of Palms* i 61–64: 'Oh! whither, in this holy hour, / Have those fair creatures fled, / To whom the ocean-plains are given / As clouds possess their native heaven?' Line 57 of the same passage, itself echoing Virgil's *placida aequora*, speaks of the night-time ocean's 'placid face'.

ix 3–4. 'With my lost Arthur's loved remains, / Spread thy full wings, and waft him o'er.' Notwithstanding J. Sendry's note, as reported by Ricks, that 'waft' occurs in *Lycidas* 164, the phrase *waft him o'er* itself occurs in several poems, among them Thomas Creech's partial translation of Virgil's *Fourth Georgick* (1685) 106, 'In vain; for *Charon* wou'd not waft him o'er'; James Scott's *Ode to the Muse* (1775) III i 1–3, 'Haste then! – for soft Etesian gales / Supply the pilot's welcome sails, / And waft him o'er the main'; and Cowper's *Iliad* xxiv 430–34: 'He spake, nor the embassador of heaven / The Argicide delay'd, but bound in haste / His undecaying sandals to his feet, / Golden, divine, which waft him o'er the floods / Swift as the wind, and o'er the boundless earth.'

ix 7–8. 'and lead / Through prosperous floods his holy urn.' For *prosperous floods*, cp. Anne Finch, Countess of Winchilsea, *The Change* (1713) 7–8: 'And *Fish*, that in thy Bosom lay, / Chuse in more prosp'rous Floods to play.'; and, by T.'s Cambridge friend Richard Chevenix Trench, *Orpheus and the Sirens*, stanza x: 'And force and fraud o'ercome, and peril past, / Its hard-won trophy raised in open view, / Through prosperous floods was bringing home at last / Its high heroic crew'. Ricks notes that T. probably wrote section ix around 1833, so it is possible that Trench heard or read it before publishing his poem in 1842.

ix 9–10. 'All night no ruder air perplex / Thy sliding keel'. Among prior instances of *ruder air*, cp. Armstrong's *Art of Preserving Health* ii 336–37: 'Earth's vaunted progeny: in ruder air / Too coy to flourish, even too proud to live'; the American John Trumbull's mock-epic *M'Fingal* (1782), Canto IV ('The Vision') 887–88: 'His tatter'd robe expos'd him bare, / To ev'ry blast of ruder air'; and Landon's *Portrait of a Lady. By Sir Thomas Lawrence.* (1825) 23–24: 'Cheek unused to ruder air / Than what hot-house rose might bear'.

For *sliding keel*, cp. Charles Cotton's *Winter* (1689) stanza xiii: 'With massy trident high, he heaves / Her sliding keel above the Waves, / Opening his Liquid Arms to take / The bold invader in his wrack.'

x 11–14. 'O to us, / The fools of habit, sweeter seems / To rest beneath the clover sod, / That takes the sunshine and the rains'. For *fools of habit*, cp. Sophia Lee's six-volume epistolary novel *The Life of a Lover: In a Series of Letters*, vol. 5 (1804), p. 99: 'More men are the fools of habit than passion; and, after being slaves all their youth from supposing themselves to be free, they continue so all their age from the painful though secret conviction that the band is too strong to be broken.'

xi 6. 'And on these dews that drench the furze'. Cp. Rogers, *The Pleasures of Memory* 303–4: 'When not a distant taper's twinkling ray / Gleam'd o'er the furze to light him on his way'; followed in lines 321–26 by 'And see, the master but returns to die! / Yet who shall bid the watchful servant fly? / The blasts of heav'n, the drenching dews of earth, / The wanton insults of unfeeling mirth, / These, when to guard Misfortune's sacred grave, / Will firm Fidelity exult to brave.'

xi 11–12. 'And crowded farms and lessening towers, / To mingle with the bounding main'. Instances of *lessening towers* occur in Boyse's *Gamelyn: or The Cook's Tale* (1741): 'The Courser mounts, and agile as the Wind, / Soon leaves the lessening Tow'rs obscur'd behind'; Lady Mary Wortley Montagu's *Julia to Ovid. Written at Twelve Years of Age, in Imitation of Ovid's Epistles* (1803) 39–40: 'When back to Rome your wishing eyes are cast, / And on the lessening towers you gaze your last'; and Robert Bradstreet's *The Sabine Farm* (1810) i 13–14: 'But, as we leave Rome's lessening towers behind, / How the past ages croud upon the mind!'

Pre-T. instances of *bounding main* include Ogilvie's *The Day of Judgment* (1753) 315–16: 'One foot stood firmly on th' extended plain, / Secure, and one repell'd the bounding main'; and Byron's *Lara* I ii 1–2: 'The chief of Lara is return'd again: / And why had Lara cross'd the bounding main?'

xi 15–16. 'And in my heart, if calm at all, / If any calm, a calm despair'; also xvi 2–3, 'Can calm despair and wild unrest / Be tenants of a single breast'. For *calm despair*, cp. Ann Yearsley's *A Poem on the Inhumanity of the Slave-Trade* (1788) 222–25: 'Time inures the youth, / His limbs grow nervous, strain'd by willing toil; / And resignation, or a calm despair, / (Most useful either) lulls him to repose.'; James Montgomery's *The Wanderer of Switzerland* (1806) II xvi: 'Then to heaven, in calm despair, / As they turn'd the tearless eye, / By their country's wrongs they sware / With their country's rights to die'; and Hemans's *The Abencerrage* iii 79–80: 'Who leads th' invaders on?—his features bear / The deep-worn traces of a calm despair'.

xi 17. 'Calm on the seas, and silver sleep'. For the latter phrase, cp. lines 8–9 of *Faerie Queene* VI ix st. 22: 'But all the night in silver sleepe I spend, / And all the day to what I list I doe attend'; also Polwhele, *The Minstrel*:

a Poem, in Five Books (1814) III xxxiii 8–9: 'And, the moon hung above the bridge's sweep, / The silent waters seem'd all hush'd in silver sleep.'[120]

xi *19–20*. 'And dead calm in that noble breast / Which heaves but with the heaving deep.' For the latter line Ricks and others cite Byron's *The Bride of Abydos* (1813) 1088: 'His head heaves with the heaving billow'; but cp. also the American George D. Prentice's *The Dead Mariner* (1829) 3–4: 'The wave is round thee—and thy breast / Heaves with the heaving deep'.

xv *16–18*. 'on yonder cloud / That rises upward always higher, / And onward drags a labouring breast'. Collins (in *Illustrations*, p. 100) cites Marlowe's *Doctor Faustus* (1604 text) V ii 92: 'Into the entrails of yon labouring cloud'; while Ricks cites (among other antecedents) Milton's *L'Allegro* 73–74: 'Mountains on whose barren breast / The labouring clouds do often rest.' But cp. also the several instances of *labouring breast* itself, among them Dryden's *Æneis* vi 74–75, 'Her Hair stood up; convulsive Rage possess'd / Her trembling Limbs, and heav'd her lab'ring Breast.', and vi 150–51: 'Th'ambiguous God, who rul'd her lab'ring Breast, / In these mysterious Words his Mind exprest'; Pope's *Iliad* x 23–24: 'A thousand Cares his lab'ring Breast revolves; / To seek sage *Nestor* now the Chief resolves'; Gay's *Dione: A Pastoral Tragedy* (1719) I i: 'I'll speak; though sorrow rend my lab'ring breast.'; Scott's *Lord of the Isles* V xxx 11–13: 'And once, when scarce he could resist / The Chieftain's care to loose the vest, / Drawn tightly o'er his labouring breast.'; as well as Barbauld's *Ode to Remorse* (1825) 78–79: 'Lives there a man whose labouring breast / Is with some dark and guilty secret prest'.

xvi *9–10*. 'That holds the shadow of a lark / Hung in the shadow of a heaven?' Cp. Bunyan, *Upon the Lark and the Fowler* (1686) 33: 'This simple Lark's a shadow of a Saint'.[121]

---

120 Following the death in 1803 of James Beattie, author of Books I and II of *The Minstrel, or, The progress of genius* (published in 1771 and 1774, respectively), Richard Polwhele took over and completed it, writing three more books and publishing the entire work in 1814.

121 The only copy of Bunyan reported in *Lincoln* postdates T.'s poem: the three-volume edn (Glasgow: Blackie, 1859) of *The Works of John Bunyan* (Item 663).

xvi 20. 'And mingles all without a plan?' Anticipating and implicitly answering the question posed by T.'s poem is Pope's *Essay on Man* i 6: 'A mighty Maze! but not without a Plan'.

xvii 1–6. The opening lines, particularly the sixth, of this section,

> Thou comest, much wept for: such a breeze
>   Compelled thy canvas, and my prayer
>   Was as the whisper of an air
> To breathe thee over lonely seas.
>
> For I in spirit saw thee move
>   Through circles of the bounding sky

echo four lines (77–80), particularly the fourth, of Dialogue VIII ('Fishing for Pike with Lay-hooks') in Thomas Scott's piscatory eclogue *The Anglers. Eight Dialogues in Verse* (1758):

> Come, and with me our northern landskips share,
> Our mountains climb, and look thro' purer air:
> Seas, rivers, rocks and vales in prospect ly,
> In the vast circle of the bounding sky.

Either or both T. and Scott may have had in mind the first-century Roman poet and astrologer Marcus Manilius, whose astrological treatise *Astronomica*, 'done into English verse' by Thomas Creech and published in 1700 under the title *The Five Books of M. Manilius*, has *bounding Sky* on page 23 of the first Book,

> But since the *Earth* hangs midst the spacious All,
> The *Solid* Centre of the *Liquid* Ball,
> Therefore as far as e'er our Eyes can pass
> Upward, or downward, could they pierce the Mass,
> Till bounding Sky the wearied Sight confines,
> Is equal to the distance of *two* Signs.
> And *six* such spaces the vast Round complete
> Where All the Signs their constant Whirls repeat,
> And each lies distant in an equal Seat.

followed a few lines later by 'Thus far advanc't my towring Muse must rise, / And sing the *Circles* that confine the Skies'.

xviii 5–7. ''Tis little; but it looks in truth / As if the quiet bones were blest / Among familiar names to rest'. S & S, p. 181, note that *quiet bones* was a classical commonplace, occurring, for example, in Ovid, *Amores* III ix 67: '*ossa quieta, precor, tuta requiescite in urna*' [O bones, rest quiet in protecting urns, I pray]. Pre-T. instances of the phrase *quiet bones* itself include Thomas Randolph's *The Jealous Lovers* (staged for King Charles I in 1632 by Randolph's fellow students at Trinity College, Cambridge) IV iii, in a speech by Asotus, Simo's prodigal son: 'For heaven's sake, sexton, lay my quiet bones / By some precise religious officer, / One that will keep the peace.'; and, by John Boys, *Æneas his descent into Hell as it is inimitably described by the prince of poets in the sixth of his Æneis* (1661) 370–71: 'None may be ferri'd o're this *Deep*, / Till in the Earth their quiet bones doe sleep.'

xix 12. 'I brim with sorrow drowning song.' In Dowland's *Second Book of Songs or Ayres* (1600), no. 22 ('Humor say what makst thou heere'), the First Voice sings: 'Mirth then is drown'd in Sorrow's brim, / O, in sorrow all things sleep.' Cp. also, in Fletcher's *Rollo, Duke of Normandy* (1639) Act II, scene ii, stanza i of the Drinking Song: 'Drink to-day, and drown all sorrow, / You shall perhaps not do it to-morrow: / Best, while you have it, use your breath; / There is no drinking after death.'

xx 1–2. 'The lesser griefs that may be said, / That breathe a thousand tender vows'. For *lesser griefs*, cp. Wordsworth's *The Emigrant Mother* (1807) 3: 'The big and lesser griefs with which she mourned'; for *tender vows*, his *Female Vagrant* 76: 'What tender vows our last sad kiss delayed!' Other instances of *lesser griefs* occur in Burton's *Anatomy of Melancholy*: 'Intollerable paine and anguish, long sicknes, captivity, misery, losse of goods, losse of friends, and those lesser griefes, doe sometimes effect it, or such dismall accidents.'; in Thomas Flatman's *On the Death of the Right Honourable Thomas Earl of Ossory. Pindariq' Ode.* (1682) ii 21: 'Those lesser Griefs with pain she thus exprest'; and in John Kenyon's *Recalling* (1738) 3: 'When lesser griefs this mind annoy'.

For *tender vows*, cp. also Thomas Yalden's translation of *Ovid's Art of Love*, Book II (1709) 191–92: 'With tender Vows the yielding Maid endear, / And let her only Sighs and Wishes hear.'; Langhorne's *Verses in Memory of a Lady* 5–6: 'My Verse the God of tender Vows inspires, / Dwells on my Soul, and wakens all her Fires.'; and Samuel Jackson's *Sympathy: or, a sketch of the social passion.* (1781) Book I, 173–74: 'That plighted pairs, amidst the hazel boughs, / To me unseen, impart their tender vows'.

xx 3–4. 'Are but as servants in a house / Where lies the master newly dead'. Cp. Rogers, *The Pleasures of Memory* 321–22: 'And see, the master but returns to die! / Yet who shall bid the watchful servant fly?'[122]

xx 16. 'Or like to noiseless phantoms flit'. Cp. John Walker Ord, *Queen Victoria at Windsor* (1841) xviii 1–4: 'Gaze reverently, fair Queen! a thousand years / Gather their memories o'er thy youthful head, / Dim visions of the past—of hopes and fears— / Crowd from these noiseless phantoms of the dead'.

xx 19–20. 'To see the vacant chair, and think, / "How good! how kind! and he is gone."' Cp., among other *vacant chair* poems, Longfellow's *Footsteps of Angels* (1839), on the early death of his first wife, vii 1–4: 'With a slow and noiseless footstep / Comes that messenger divine, / Takes the vacant chair beside me, / Lays her gentle hand in mine'; and (as 'Currer Bell') Charlotte Brontë's *The Teacher's Monologue* (1846) 45–50: 'And, if I should return and see / The hearth-fire quenched, the vacant chair; / And hear it whispered mournfully, / That farewells have been spoken there, / What shall I do, and whither turn? / Where look for peace? When cease to mourn?'

xxi 7–8. '"This fellow would make weakness weak, / And melt the waxen hearts of men."' For *waxen hearts*, cp. lines 29–30 of the speech by Viola in *Twelfth Night* with which Act II, scene ii, ends: 'How easy is it for the proper-false / In women's waxen hearts to set their forms!'; and Donne's *To M[r]. I[zaak]. W[alton].* (1719) 17–20: 'O, how I greeve that late-borne modestie / Hath gott such roote in easie waxen harts, / That men maye not themselves their owne good parts / Extoll, without suspect of surquedrie.'

xxi 13–16. 'A third is wroth: "Is this an hour / For private sorrow's barren song, / When more and more the people throng / The chairs and thrones of civil power?["]' For *barren song* cp., in Frederick William Faber's *The Styrian Lake, and Other Poems* (1842), the closing lines (165–70) of *An Epistle to a Young M.P.*: 'To thee, still in the lap of our old dream, / This

---

122 *The Pleasures of Memory* was included in the 1812 Cadell and Davies edn of Rogers's *Poems*, which, as previously stated (note 12), was at Somersby. From around the time he began writing *In Memoriam*, T. himself owned the 1834 Cadell edn of Rogers (Item 1895 in *Lincoln*), which also contained *The Pleasures of Memory*.

uncouth teaching for awhile must seem / A cold philosophy, a barren song; / But it will not seem so unto thee long. / Thou too wilt one day learn—it is not cold / To speak of boyhood as a thing grown old.'

xxi 17–20. '"A time to sicken and to swoon, / When Science reaches forth her arms / To feel from world to world, and charms / Her secret from the latest moon?"' Prior instances of *from world to world* include *Purgatorio* v 61–63: '["]voi dite, e io farò per quella pace / che, dietro a' piedi di sì fatta guida, / di mondo in mondo cercar mi si face."', reading, in Cary's translation: '["]Speak; and I will perform it, by that peace, / Which on the steps of guide so excellent / Following from world to world intent I seek."'; Thomson's *Hymn on the Seasons* 69–72: 'Great source of day! best image here below / Of thy creator, ever darting wide, / From world to world, the vital ocean round, / On nature write with every beam his praise,'; and Mary Darwall's *The Pleasures of Contemplation* (1764) 52–55: 'Now tow'ring Fancy takes her airy Flight / Without Restraint, and leaves this Earth behind; / From Pole to Pole, from World to World, she flies; / Rocks, Seas, nor Skies, can interrupt her Course.'

xxii 9–12. 'But where the path we walked began / To slant the fifth autumnal slope, / As we descended following Hope, / There sat the Shadow feared of man'. In his *Poems on Serious and Sacred Subjects* (Chichester, 1818), cp. William Hayley's *Epistle to Mrs. Hannah More*, lines 37–42: 'O that, while glowing with celestial hope, / Gently we haste down life's autumnal slope, / Each well convinc'd, and with a mind serene, / From long experience of our chequer'd scene, / Convinc'd no blessings of this earth transcend / The countless value of a Christian friend'. Cp. also, in his *The Baptistery, or The Way of Eternal Life,* Part IV (1844), Isaac Williams's *The Spiritual Husbandman*, p. 67, speaking of 'Recompense': 'This sends the ploughman on the autumnal slope, / This calls the daily herdsman to the stall; / Through the long year the husbandman's sole hope; / The circle binding each in less or ampler scope.'

xxii 13. 'Who broke our fair companionship, / And spread his mantle dark and cold'. Cp. the closing lines of Henry Spicer's *The Night-Voices* (1844): 'O, for such fair companionship—to trace / Beyond the sounds of grief, or sense of guile, / Those heavenward footsteps. Hold! a chilling cloud / Enwraps my soaring soul; around me rise / The moonlight, and the woodlands, and the shore— / I have been dreaming. To the world again.'

xxiv 3–4. 'The very source and fount of Day / Is dashed with wandering isles of night.' For *wandering isles* Ricks cites Shelley's *Prologue to Hellas* 17–18, 'The fairest of those wandering isles that gem / The sapphire space of interstellar air', and his *Witch of Atlas* 474, 'Upon those wandering isles of aëry dew'. But cp. also W[illiam]. Preston's translation of *The Argonautics of Apollonius Rhodius* (1803) iv 1262–63, '"Their vessel thro' the wandering isles I bore, / Where, charg'd with fire tremendous tempests roar["]'; and iv 1488–90: 'When to those wandering isles the vessel came, / Above her snowy knees each sea-born dame / With eager haste her floating garments drew'. And also *Faerie Queene* II xii st. 11: '"That may not be, said then the Ferryman, / Least we vnweeting hap to be fordonne; / For those same Islands, seeming now and than, / Are not firme lande, nor any certein wonne, / But straggling plots, which to and fro do ronne / In the wide waters: therefore are they hight / The Wandring Islands. Therefore doe them shonne'.

xxiv 9–10. 'And is it that the haze of grief / Makes former gladness loom so great?' For *haze of grief,* cp. lines 93–96 of Mrs. Acton Tindal's *The Lament of Joanna of Spain,* first published in *Douglas Jerrold's Shilling Magazine,* vol. 6, no. 31 (July 1847), 32–34: 'Mother! Cassandra-like, I see / Our long line's mournful destiny— / And, in a haze of grief and shame, / The barren ending of our name!' The poem was reprinted in *Littell's Living Age,* vol. 14, no. 170 (14 Aug. 1847), then collected in Mrs. Tindal's *Lines and Leaves* (1848).

xxvi 5–7. 'And if that eye which watches guilt / And goodness, and hath power to see / Within the green the mouldered tree'. Cp. Wordsworth's *Excursion,* Book VI ('The Church-yard Among the Mountains') 503–4: 'So, where the mouldered Tree had stood, was raised / Yon Structure'; and his *White Doe of Rylstone* vii 79–82: 'And so—beneath a mouldered tree, / A self-surviving leafless Oak, / By unregarded age from stroke / Of ravage saved—sate Emily.'

xxvii 2. 'The captive void of noble rage'. For the latter phrase Ricks cites Gray's *Elegy* 51: 'Chill Penury repress'd their noble rage'. Other instances include Blackmore's *King Arthur* ii 316–17: 'In Heavenly plains fir'd with a noble rage / Our Troops did all the Allmighty's Host engage.'; Pope's *Iliad* v 188–89, 'Those slain he left; and sprung with noble rage / Abas and Polyïdus to engage', and vii 205–6: 'All these, alike inspired with noble rage, / Demand the fight'; Wiffen's *Jerusalem Delivered* XX lviii 8–9, 'Rinaldo so, thus unopposed, lays by / Much of his noble rage, and calms his angry eye.'; and Thomson's *Castle of Indolence* xxxii 8–9: 'The Sage's Calm, the Patriot's noble Rage, / Dashing Corruption down through every worthless Age.'

xxvii 10–11. 'The heart that never plighted troth / But stagnates in the weeds of sloth'. For the latter phrase, cp. *Achilles in Scyros* (1800)—John Hoole's translation from the Italian of Metastasio's libretto for the opera *Achille in Sciro* (1737)—I iii, in which Achilles speaks, then Nearchus:

> *Ach.* O! did yon splendid helmet deck my brows,
> Yon falchion grace my side—no more, Nearchus,
> I'm weary of disguise—this sex's weeds
> Of sloth inglorious—time demands—
>
> *Near.* What time?
> O! Heaven! remember that this sex's weeds
> Have won and still preserv'd the fair-one thine.

Cp. also *Lord Byron and Some of his Contemporaries* (1828), p. 384, in which Leigh Hunt says of Benjamin Franklin: 'I feel grateful to him, for one, inasmuch as he extended the sphere of liberty, and helped to clear the earth of the weeds of sloth and ignorance, and the wild beasts of superstition'. The commonplace association of weeds and sloth is scriptural in origin, *Proverbs* xxiv 30–31 reading: 'I went by the field of the slothful, and by the vineyard of the man void of understanding; And, lo, it was all grown over with thorns, and nettles had covered the face thereof, and the stone wall thereof was broken down.'

xxix 11. 'Make one wreath more for Use and Wont'. As Ricks notes, Alfred Gatty cites the motto to chap. 14 of Scott's *The Pirate* (1822), which includes it, but T.'s capitalization of the common phrase *use and wont*—meaning established practice—may point to another poem in which it was similarly and repeatedly capitalized: *An Elegy on Auld Use and Wont* in Alexander Nicol's *The Rural Muse* (Edinburgh, 1753), pp. 12–15. That poem begins with a four-line *Epitaph*, 'Here lies Auld honest Use and Wont, / Which loss we never will surmount; / As lang as time remains, her death / Will to all ranks be meikle skaith.', followed by a first stanza reading: 'Oh Scotland, Scotland! hae ye not, / Tho' ye have stupidly forgot, / Ye have avow'dly cut the throat / Of Use and Wont; / And brought upo' you sic a blot / Ye'll ne're surmount?'; and twenty-one more containing another four instances of the same capitalized phrase.

xxx 19. '"They rest," we said, "their sleep is sweet"'. S & S, p. 192, cite the portion of the Burial Service based on *Revelation* xiv 13: 'blessed are the dead which die in the LORD [...] for they rest from their labours', and *Proverbs* iii 24, reading in part: 'Yea, thou shalt lie down, and thy sleep shall be sweet'. But cp. also Robert Lowth's *The Judgment of Hercules* (Glasgow, 1743)—also known as *The Choice of Hercules*, and translating a fable of Prodicus of Ceos—section xxii of which begins: 'Nor need my friends the various costly feast; / Hunger to them th' effect of art supplies; / Labor prepares their weary limbs to rest; / Sweet is their sleep; light, chearful, strong, they rise'. Like others quoted in this study, Lowth's lines gained wide exposure through their inclusion in Vicesimus Knox's *Elegant Extracts: or, Useful and Entertaining Pieces of Poetry*, at least ten new editions of which were published between 1789 and 1826.

xxx 22–23. 'Once more we sang: "They do not die / Nor lose their mortal sympathy["]'. S & S note Hallam's essay *On Sympathy* (1830), which he defines as 'assumed similarity' between two people leading to understanding and compassion. The phrase *mortal sympathy* itself occurs in Wordsworth's *Sympathy* (1827) 11–12: 'Sun, moon, and stars, all struggle in the toils / Of mortal sympathy'; and, from his *The Dacoit, and Other Poems* [1840], in Samuel Sloper's *The Heart's Bitterness* 37–39: 'The deadlier from concealment which doth prey / Intensely on the spirit,—nor will seek / Relief from aught of mortal sympathy'.

xxx 27. 'Pierces the keen seraphic flame'. Ricks cites *Revolt of Islam* xii 45: 'Pierce like reposing flames the tremulous atmosphere', but *seraphic flame(s)* itself occurs in several hymns and poems, among them Watts's *Come, Lord Jesus* (from his *Horae Lyricae*, 1706 and later editions) stanza xi: 'Jesus, the God of Might and Love, / New moulds our Limbs of Cumbrous Clay, / Quick as Seraphick Flames we move, / Active and Young and Fair as they.' Cp. also, in his *Odes and Epistles* (1739), Robert Craggs, Lord Nugent's *An Epistle to the Right Honourable the Earl of*

Chesterfield, p. 76: 'And Thou, seraphic Flame! who couldst inspire / The *Prophet*'s Voice, and wrap his Soul in Fire'; Thomson's *Castle of Indolence* lxxiv 4–5: 'Sweet Love their Looks a gentle Radiance lends, / And with seraphic Flame Compassion blends.'; William Stevenson's *Vertumnus; or, The Progress of Spring* (1765) iv 137–38: 'Faith's beatific views, Ambition's aim, / Devotion's raptures, Love's seraphic flame'; and, in a supplement to the 1805 and subsequent editions of Watts's *Horae Lyricae*, his *To Sir John Hartopp, Baronet. The Wish.* xv 1–2: 'Cupid, avaunt with all thy fires! / Seraphic flame my soul inspires'.

xxxi 11–12. 'A solemn gladness even crowned / The purple brows of Olivet.' For *purple brow* singular, cp. Ogilvie's *Ode to Evening* (1762) 79–80: 'Now from the green hill's purple brow / Let me mark the scene below'; and Radcliffe's *Sun-set* (1816) 1–2: 'Soft o'er the mountain's purple brow / Meek twilight draws her shadows grey'. For *purple brows* plural, as in T.'s poem, cp. *A Scene on Windermere*, signed 'G.R.C.', in *The Mirror of Literature, Amusement, and Instruction* vol. 20, no. 575 (10 Nov. 1832) 308, lines 24–26: 'Afar the lovely panorama glow'd, / Until the mountains, on whose purple brows / The clouds were pillow'd, closed it from our view.' (Ricks notes that xxxi, 'one of the earliest sections', was written in 1833–34.)

xxxiii 8. 'A life that leads melodious days.' As Ricks and S & S note, T. himself compared Statius, *Silvae* I iii 22–23: *'ceu placidi veritus turbare Vopisci / Pieriosque dies et habentes carmina somnos'* [as if afraid to disturb the Pierian days and music-haunted slumbers of tranquil Vopiscus] to his line. But cp. also Langhorne's *Proemium, Written in MDCCLXVI* (1766), lines 17–20: 'Yet, if resolv'd, secure of future praise, / To tune sweet songs, and live melodious days, / Let not the hand, that decks my holy shrine, / Round Folly's head the blasted laurel twine.' Note that Langhorne's rhyme pair is *praise* and *days*, T.'s, *prays* and *days*.

xxxiv 4. 'And dust and ashes all that is'. Cp. *Job* xlii 6: 'Wherefore I abhor myself, and repent in dust and ashes'. As noted below (p. 194), the same scriptural verse is evoked in T.'s *Maud, a Monodrama* (1854–55) i 32: 'Cheat and be cheated, and die: who knows? we are ashes and dust.'

xxxiv 13–16. ''Twere best at once to sink to peace, / Like birds the charming serpent draws, / To drop head-foremost in the jaws / Of vacant darkness and to cease.' Ricks compares line 14 to *Revolt of Islam* ii 414: 'as the charmed bird that haunts the serpent's den'; S & S, to a passage on the charming of squirrels and birds on p. 479 of T.'s copy of Sir Richard Phillips's *The Hundred Wonders of the World* (1821).[123] But cp. also *Zara: or, The Black Death. A Poem of the Sea.* (1827) 'by the Author of "Naufragus."' (elsewhere identified as M[offat]. J[ames]. Horne) Canto XXX, lines 6–8: 'She feared not war—its horrors—nor the dead, / But shrunk beneath the STRANGER's basilical eye, / As bird 'neath serpent's gaze will twitter, droop and die.'

xxxv 1–2. 'Yet if some voice that man could trust / Should murmur from the narrow house'. A common euphemism for the grave, *narrow house* was previously employed by, among others, Burns in *Lament of Mary, Queen of Scots* (1791) 53–54, 'And, in the narrow house of death, / Let Winter round me rave'; the American William Cullen Bryant in *Thanatopsis* (1821) 12, 'And breathless darkness, and the narrow house'; Hemans in line 5—'Dust, to its narrow house beneath!'—of the dirge beginning 'Calm on the bosom of thy God' in her *Siege of Valencia*; and Wordsworth in *The Earl of Breadalbane's Ruined Mansion, and Family Burial-Place, Near Killin* (1831) 1–2, 'Well sang the Bard who called the grave, in strains / Thoughtful and sad, the "narrow house."' The 'Bard' was James Macpherson's fictive Ossian, in whose purported collected works, published in 1765, the phrase occurs eleven times.

xxxv 9. 'The moanings of the homeless sea'. Ricks cites Shelley's *The Cyclops* (1824) 709: 'By wandering long over the homeless sea'; but cp. also Wilson's *Isle of Palms* ii 454–55: 'So careless doth she seem to be / Thus left by herself on the homeless sea'. For T.'s dismissive response to Collins's suggestion, in the Jan. 1880 issue of *The Cornhill Magazine*, that T.'s line was partly based on Horace's *Odes* II xx, *Visam gementis litora Bospori*, see the Preface, p. 5.

xxxv 14. '"The sound of that forgetful shore["]'. As does Collins (*Illustrations*, pp. 102–3), Ricks compares T.'s line to *Paradise Lost* ii 74: 'that forgetful Lake'. But cp. also *oblivia ripae* [the forgetful shore] in Lucan's *Pharsalia* iii 28–30: 'me non Lethaeae, coniunx, oblivia ripae / inmemorem fecere tui, regesque silentum / permisere sequi.' [Not even the

---

123 Not noted in *Lincoln*.

forgetful shore of Lethe has banished my husband from my memory, and I am permitted by the rulers of the dead to haunt you too.]¹²⁴

xxxv 24. 'And basked and battened in the woods.' S & S cite *Hamlet* III iv 66–67: 'Could you on this fair mountain leave to feed, / And batten on this moor?' But cp. also, in the widely read, reviewed, and excerpted *Sermons By the Late Rev. Walter Blake Kirwan, Dean of Killala* (1814), his Sermon XII (on *Psalm* xviii 16–19), p. 362: 'But how many others, with concience [sic] equally tranquil, would seem to imagine themselves placed upon this earth, not for the happiness of others temporal or everlasting, but to bask and batten in indolence like the pampered animal of the field?' The phase *bask and batten* had previously occurred in the anonymous (though most likely by Richard Alsop or Theodore Dwight) *Symptoms of the Millennium, in the Year 1801,* in *The Echo: With Other Poems* (New York, 1807)—an anthology of poems by the so-called Hartford Wits—p. 291: 'If the MILLENNIUM were not near, / Would *Duane* bask and batten here? / Would *Dallas*, insect of an hour, / Roll round in splendour, wealth and power?'

xxxviii 8. 'A doubtful gleam of solace lives.' Cp. Sotheby's 1798 translation from the German of Christoph Martin Wieland's *Oberon* (1780), VII xlvi 3–4: 'At last a ray that seems to sooth[e] his grief, / A gleam of solace, steals upon his heart'.

xxxix 3. 'With fruitful cloud and living smoke'. For *fruitful cloud*, cp. Jeremy Taylor's *Life of Christ, or The Great Exemplar of Sanctity and Holy Life* (1649), Part 1, section 3, 'The Nativity of our blessed Saviour *JESUS*', which begins (p. 26): 'The holy Maid long'd to be a glad Mother, and she who carried a burden, whose proper commensuration is the dayes of Eternity counted the tedious minutes, expecting when the Sun of Righteousnesse should break forth from his bed where nine moneths he hid himself as behinde a fruitful cloud.'¹²⁵

---

124 The 1818 Dove edn of Lucan's *De Bello Civili* (the *Pharsalia*), with 'A. Tennyson' on the fly-leaf, was at Somersby (Item 205 in *Lincoln*).

125 A modernized version of 'The Nativity of our Blessed Saviour Jesus' was included in (among other later collections of Taylor's works) vol. 2 of the fifteen-volume *The Whole Works of The Right Rev. Jeremy Taylor, D.D.* (1822); the quoted passage (with which it begins) on p. 19 of that volume. T. owned the five-volume (1831) Valpy edn

Cp. also, in his *Carolina, or, Loyal Poems* (1683), Thomas Shipman's *New Libanus. 1679.* — dedicated 'To the Right Honourable *Catherine* Countess of *Rutland;* Vpon the Blessings brought to that (well-near-extinguisht) Family by Her self and Honourable Issue.'—lines 45–48: 'By friendly *Fate,* your happy *Lord's* allow'd / To meet a *Iuno* in a fruitful *Cloud.* / Fruitful as those i' th' Spring when blessings pours, / Upon the Earth, and *Silver* melts in show'rs.'; and Sir Aubrey De Vere's *Mary Tudor, an Historical Drama* (1847) III vii (Mary speaking): 'I ask but prayer: I seek no miracle. / Though holy prayer availed to part the sea— / Though prayer brought manna from the fruitful cloud'.

As explained in John Swan's *Speculum Mundi, or, a Glass Representing the Face of the World* (1670), p. 104: 'A fertil or fruitful cloud affordeth rain; but a barren cloud doth not, because it is at length by the blasts of wind, and vertue of the heavenly bodies, turned into thin air.'

xl 1. 'Could we forget the widowed hour'. Prior instances of the latter phrase, singular or plural, include the Pope–Broome–Fenton *Odyssey* iv 147–48: 'And the chaste partner of his bed and throne, / Wastes all her widow'd hours in tender moan'; in her *Moral Tales* (1801), Maria Edgeworth's *The Knapsack* II i, stanza i of Catherine's song: 'Turn swift my wheel, my busy wheel, / And leave my heart no time to feel; / Companion of my widow'd hour, / My only friend, my only dow'r'; and, in *Poems, by Mrs. G.* [Mary Young] *Sewell* (Egham and Chertsey, 1803), *An Elegy, To the Memory of a Dear Mother, Lady Young, of Chertsey Abbey. Sept. 1801*, lines 5–6: 'Alas! how lately in the widow'd hour, / She came—a messenger of Mercy's power!'

xliii 5. 'Unconscious of the sliding hour'. Ricks notes that *sliding* is 'a traditional epithet, as in Dryden's "the sliding Sun" [in] *Palamon and Arcite* iii 131; and "the sliding year" [in] Virgil's *Pastorals* iii 62.' Instances of *the sliding hour* itself occur in Thomas Harrison's *Thoughts under Affliction*—from his *Poems on Divine Subjects* (1719)—stanza i: 'I will not, cannot dote on Life, / Or dread the Thoughts of being summon'd hence: / Here various Ills each sliding Hour commence; / Here I am held in chains of Sorrow, Care, and Strife'; in William Giles (ed.), *Serious Thoughts on a*

---

of Taylor's *Works* (Item 2175 in *Lincoln*), which did not, however, include Taylor's *Life of Christ*.

Late Coronation (1775) 9–10, 'No trampling sound swims o'er the silent floor, / But the slow clock, that counts the sliding hour'; and in Ogilvie's *Human Life, a Poem, in Five Parts.* (1806), p. 105: 'Here, with his friend, his loved companion near, / Sophronius wore the sliding hour away; / Light shone serene on every rolling year, / To gild the cloud of life's declining day.'

xliv 1. 'How fares it with the happy dead?' As S & S point out (p. 208), 'That the dead are happy is a commonplace of classical and Christian poetry' (as, for example, in the Elysian Fields of Hades in *Odyssey* iv and *Aeneid* vi). With regard to the phrase itself, they and Ricks note that, as first reported by John Sparrow in 'Tennyson and Thomson's Shorter Poems', *London Mercury* xxi (1930), 429, *the happy dead* previously occurred in James Thomson's *Song* (c. 1740), which begins: 'Tell me, thou soul of her I love, / Ah! tell me, whither art thou fled; / To what delightful world above, / Appointed for the happy dead?'; to which may be added Crabbe's *The Village* (1783) i 323–24: 'There lie the happy dead, from trouble free, / And the glad parish pays the frugal fee'.[126]

xlvi 1–4. 'We ranging down this lower track, / The path we came by, thorn and flower, / Is shadowed by the growing hour, / Lest life should fail in looking back.' For *the growing hour*, cp. William King's *The Art of Love* (1709), his 'imitation' of Ovid, Book XIV, lines 2100–3: 'Resist at first: for help in vain we pray, / When ills have gain'd full strength by long delay. / Be speedy; lest perhaps the growing hour / Put what is now within, beyond our power.'

xlvi 10. 'The fruitful hours of still increase'. Cp. Hood, *The Irish Schoolmaster* (1826) 253–55: 'And so he wisely spends the fruitful hours, / Link'd each to each by labour, like a bee; / Or rules in Learning's hall, or trims her bow'rs;— / Would there were many more such wights as he'.

lii 15. 'Abide: thy wealth is gathered in'. Cp. *Zechariah* xiv 14: 'And Judah also shall fight at Jerusalem; and the wealth of all the heathen round about shall be gathered together, gold, and silver, and apparel, in great abundance.' Also Cowper's *Adam* V iv ('The World'): 'Ah labour as thou wilt! and sigh, or sweat / In this pursuit of gold, / Thy cares and woes shall gather in proportion / To all thy gather'd wealth.'

---

126 In Crabbe's *Poetical Works* (see note 35), *The Village* was in vol. 2.

lviii 6–7. 'Of hearts that beat from day to day, / Half-conscious of their dying clay'. For the latter phrase, cp., in Watts's *Horae Lyricae* (all editions), *Death and Eternity*, stanza iv: 'But where the Souls, those deathless things, / That left this dying Clay? / My Thoughts, now stretch out all your Wings, / And trace Eternity.' The phrase also occurs in poems by Matthew Prior, William Barnes, and several others.

lviii 9–10. 'The high Muse answered: "Wherefore grieve / Thy brethren with a fruitless tear?["]' Cp. *Inferno* xxix 4–6, *'Ma Virgilio mi disse: "Che pur guate? / perché la vista tua pur si soffolge / là giù tra l'ombre triste smozzicate?"'*, reading, in Boyd's translation: 'At length, the Mantuan Bard exclaim'd, "Forbear! / Why ever thus distil the fruitless tear, / And mourn in vain the sentenc'd bands of night?"' As does Boyd's 'Mantuan Bard', T.'s 'high Muse' denotes Virgil, to whom Dante refers by name.

lxi 9. 'Yet turn thee to the doubtful shore'. Cp. *litus dubium* in Lucan's *Pharsalia* i 409–10: *'quaque iacet litus dubium, quod terra, fretumque / vindicat alternis vicibus'* [and others left the doubtful shore, which land and sea alternately claim]. The phrase also occurs in James Howell's *A Poem Heroique, Presented to his late Majesty for a New Year's Gift* (1663) 23–24: 'No *Arras* or rich *Carpets*, freighted ore / The Surging Seas from *Asia*'s doubtful shore.'; and in John Harvey's *The Bruciad* (1769) Book V, p. 133: '"I know thou dar'st," he said, "but hast thou pow'r / "To match yon captain on the doubtful shore.["]'

lxii 12. 'Is matter for a flying smile.' Cp. Landor, *Acon and Rhodope; or, Inconstancy* (1847) 40–47: '"May never we / Love as they loved!" said Acon. She at this / Smiled, for he said not what he meant to say, / And thought not of its bliss, but of its end. / He caught the flying smile, and blusht, and vow'd / Nor time nor other power, whereto the might / Of love hath yielded and may yield again, / Should alter his.'

lxiv 23–24. 'He played at counsellors and kings, / With one that was his earliest mate'. Cp. *Job* iii 13–14: 'For now should I have lain still and been quiet, I should have slept: then had I been at rest / With kings and counsellors of the earth, which build desolate places for themselves'. Also, in his *Barbadoes, and other Poems* (1833), M[atthew]. J[ames]. Chapman's *From Job, Chap. III.*, 17–20: 'Then had I been still, quiet and at rest, / With counsellors and kings, who once possessed / Silver and gold, and beauty-haunted bowers— / Sweet homes of pleasure, and embattled towers.'; and, among other works containing the scriptural phrase *kings and counsellors* itself, Robert Fergusson's *Job, Chap. III, Paraphrased* (1779) 25–26: 'For now my soul with quiet had been blest, / With kings and counsellors of earth at rest'.

lxx 5. 'Cloud-towers by ghostly masons wrought'. Ricks compares the 'nightmare scene' in this and the lines immediately following to a passage in Carlyle's *The French Revolution* (1837) iii V iii on the taking of Fort L'Eguillette. The phrase *ghostly masons* occurs not there, however, but in another nightmare scene, by Charles Henry Knox in *The Devil's Road* vii, from his volume *Day Dreams* (1843): 'Unearthly shrieks and fiendish clatter, / The lion's roar, and monkey's chatter, / With goblin laugh and elfish cry, / Their task the ghostly masons ply.'

lxxii 15. 'A chequer-work of beam and shade'. Ricks cites Milton's *L'Allegro* 96: 'Chequer'd shade'. But cp. also the phrase *beam and shade* itself in Hunt's *Story of Rimini* ii 227–28: 'So ride they in delight through beam and shade;— / Till many a rill now passed, and many a glade'.

lxxvi 1. 'Take wings of fancy, and ascend'. As Ricks notes, alongside Collins's assertion, in the Jan. 1880 issue of *The Cornhill Magazine*, that these words are 'from Petrarch, *Sonnet* lxxxii.: ["]Volo con l' ali de' pensieri al cielo["]', T. in his copy wrote '!!! nonsense'. But the suggestion of an affinity between T.'s line and Petrarch's was not unreasonable, the latter line, literally translated, reading: 'Fly with the wings of thoughts to the sky'.

Cp. also Cowper's *On the Receipt of My Mother's Picture Out of Norfolk* (1798), in the closing lines of which (118–21) the phrase *wings of fancy* itself occurs: 'And, while the wings of fancy still are free, / And I can view this mimic shew of thee, / Time has but half succeeded in his theft— / Thyself removed, thy power to soothe me left.'[127]

lxxvii 5. 'These mortal lullabies of pain'. Cp. Hood, *Hero and Leander* (1827) xxxvii 1–4: 'They say there be such maidens in the deep, /

---

[127] Petrarch's sonnet, which begins with the quoted line, was incorporated into the *Canzoniere* as poem 362. Cowper's *On the Receipt* appeared in vol. 2 of both the 1808 Johnson edn (see note 16) and the 1830–31 Pickering edn (see note 38) of Cowper's poems.

Charming poor mariners, that all too near / By mortal lullabies fall dead asleep, / As drowsy men are poison'd through the ear'.

lxxvii 13–14. 'But what of that? My darkened ways / Shall ring with music all the same'. For *darkened ways*, cp. *Endymion* i 6–11: 'Therefore, on every morrow, are we wreathing / A flowery band to bind us to the earth, / Spite of despondence, of the inhuman dearth / Of noble natures, of the gloomy days, / Of all the unhealthy and o'er-darkened ways / Made for our searching'.

lxxxii 1–4. 'I wage not any feud with Death / For changes wrought on form and face; / No lower life that earth's embrace / May breed with him, can fright my faith.' Before T.'s use of it, the phrase *earth's embrace* occurred in Byron's *Lines inscribed upon a Cup formed from a Skull* (1814), stanza v: 'Quaff while thou canst—another race, / When thou and thine like me are sped, / May rescue thee from earth's embrace, / And rhyme and revel with the dead'; and in Shelley's *Julian and Maddalo* (1824) 5–6: 'Matted with thistles and amphibious weeds, / Such as from earth's embrace the salt ooze breeds'. A greater textual and thematic affinity with T.'s lines may be found, however, in Hemans's *Forest Sanctuary* II lvii, where the phrase also occurs:

> But the true parting came!—I look'd my last
> On the sad beauty of that slumbering face;
> How could I think the lovely spirit pass'd,
> Which there had left so tenderly its trace?
> Yet a dim awfulness was on the brow—
> No! not like sleep to look upon art Thou,
> Death, death!—She lay, a thing for earth's embrace,
> To cover with spring-wreaths.—For earth's?—the wave
> That gives the bier no flowers—makes moan above her grave!

lxxxiii 3. 'Thou doest expectant nature wrong'. Cp. *Snow: Afternoon* in William Mackenzie's *The Rustic Bower; or, Sketches From Nature* (Edinburgh, 1844), p. 227: 'The murky canopy of continuous clouds, descending on fearful and expectant nature, prepares to wrap the earth in a mantle of snow.'

lxxxv 25. 'And led him through the blissful climes'. S & S call T.'s line 'a reminiscence' of *Paradise Lost* xi 707–8: 'to walk with God / High in salvation and the climes of bliss'. But cp. also Eusden's translation of Pluto's speech to Proserpine from Book II of Claudian's unfinished, late-fourth-century epic *De raptu Proserpinae*, as first published in *The Guardian* no. 164 (18 Sept. 1713), 212–14, as reprinted in *The British Essayists*, ed. by L. T. Berguer, vol. 18 (1823), pp. 189–90, and reading in part: 'The blissful climes no change of ages knew, / The golden first began, and still is new.'; as well as Samuel Johnson's *Friendship, An Ode* 21–24: 'Nor shall thine ardour cease to glow, / When souls to blissful climes remove: / What rais'd our virtue here below, / Shall aid our happiness above.'[128]

lxxxvi 1–2. 'Sweet after showers, ambrosial air, / That rollest from the gorgeous gloom'. T. may have owed the latter phrase to Hemans, in whose poems it occurs four times: in *The Indian City* (1825) i 31–32, 'He turn'd where birds through the gorgeous gloom / Of the woods went glancing on starry plume'; *Juana* (1827) 1–2, 'The night-wind shook the tapestry round an ancient palace-room, / And torches, as it rose and fell, waved thro' the gorgeous gloom'; *The Coronation of Inez de Castro* (1828) 21–22, 'Loading the marble pavement old / With a weight of gorgeous gloom'; and *The Minster* (1830) 11–12, 'Flushing proud shrines, or by some warrior's tomb / Dying away in clouds of gorgeous gloom'. It also occurs in Lady Emmeline Stuart-Wortley's *Greece* 29–32, 'The sceptered leader's tomb / A glory wears, / Brightening eve's gorgeous gloom, / But not like their's!'; and in her *Lines on Martin the Painter* 54–55, '(For, still the immortal day-spring seems to bloom / And break through all the intense, the gorgeous gloom[)]', both in her *Poems* (1833).

lxxxvi 11. 'Throughout my frame, till Doubt and Death, / Ill brethren, let the fancy fly'. As with the capitalized 'Use and Wont' in line 11 of section xxix, the capitalized 'Doubt and Death' here may point to a particular earlier poem, though one in which the pair are not brothers but parents: *Childe Harold* II iii 9: 'Poor child of Doubt and Death, whose hope is built on reeds.'

---

128 First published in the July 1743 issue of *The Gentleman's Magazine*, then in James Boswell's *The Life of Samuel Johnson, LL.D.* (1791), the four-volume 1826 Talboys and Wheeler edn of which, with Johnson's poem on pp. 112–13 of vol. 1 and 'Alfred Tennyson' on that volume's front board, was at Somersby (Item 54 in *Lincoln*).

lxxxvi 13. 'From belt to belt of crimson seas'. In Young's *The Love of Fame, the Universal Passion* (1728), cp. *Satire VII. To the Right Honourable Sir Robert Walpole.* 41–42: 'What slaughter'd *hosts!* what *cities* in a blaze! / What wasted *countries!* and what crimson *seas!*'; and, also by Young, *The Foreign Address, or The Best Argument for Peace* (1734) xxvi 3–6: 'If scenes of blood avenging Fates decree, / For thee the sword brave Britons wield; / For thee charge o'er the' [*sic*] embattled field, / Or plunge through seas, through crimson seas, for thee.'

lxxxvii 7–8. 'And thunder-music, rolling, shake / The prophet blazoned on the panes'. Cp. Robert Montgomery's *Messiah*, Book VI, p. 236: 'He whose spirit oft has heard / The thunder-music of thy tempest roll'.

lxxxvii 39–40. 'And over those ethereal eyes / The bar of Michael Angelo.' Cp. Richard Savage, *The Volunteer Laureat. A Poem on Her Majesty's Birth-Day, 1734–5* (1735) 35–36: 'Behold, sweet-beaming, her ethereal eyes! / Soft as the Pleiads o'er the dewy skies'; and *Queen Mab* iii 1–4: 'Fairy! the Spirit said, / And on the Queen of Spells / Fixed her ethereal eyes, / I thank thee.'

lxxxviii 4. 'O tell me where the passions meet'. Poems where *passions meet* include Aphra Behn's *On the Honourable Sir Francis Fane, on his Play called the Sacrifice* (1697) 61–62: 'In your *Despina* all those passions meet, / Which womans frailties perfectly compleat.'; Richard Brinsley Sheridan's *Monody on Garrick* (1780) 51–52: 'Whate'er the theme, through every age and clime, / Congenial passions meet the according rhyme'; Akenside's *Ode IX. To Curio, 1744.* (1781) 48–49: 'While he whom virtue in his blest retreat / Bad social ease and publick passions meet'; and Bowles's sonnet beginning 'O Harmony! thou tenderest nurse of pain' (1797) 9–11: 'For when thou leadest all thy soothing strains / More smooth along, the silent passions meet / In one suspended transport, sad and sweet'.

lxxxix 17. 'O sound to rout the brood of cares'. Cp. Thomas Noble's *A Monody, Occasioned by the Death of the Right Hon. Charles James Fox* (1806)—reprinted in his *Poems* (Liverpool, 1821)—177–79: 'rent the breast / Where Peculation, with its brood of cares, / Tormenting lay'.

lxxxix 27–28. 'Or here she brought the harp and flung / A ballad to the brightening moon'. For the latter phrase, cp. lines 4–5 of *Ode Written in a Picture-Gallery. 1786.*, signed 'P.', in a volume entitled *Poems, Chiefly by Gentlemen of Devonshire and Cornwall* (Bath, 1792) and edited by Richard Polwhele: 'His tresses gray / To the brightening moon he shook'; Southey's *Thalaba the Destroyer* III xxii 17–18: 'Then, if the brightening Moon that lit his face, / In darkness favour'd hers'; from his *Juvenilia*, Leigh Hunt's *Remembered Friendship* 76: 'The bright'ning moon with broad effulgent ray'; and Allan Cunningham's *The Bride of Allanbay* (1825) 22–26: 'For ere yon bright'ning moon / Lift her wondrous lamp above the wave / Amid night's lonely noon / There shall be shriekings heard at sea, / Lamentings heard ashore'.[129]

lxxxix 29–30. 'Nor less it pleased in livelier moods, / Beyond the bounding hill to stray'. For *bounding hill*, cp., in William Browne of Tavistock's *Britannia's Pastorals. The Second Booke* (1616), *The First Song* 332–34: 'by thickets which aray'd / The high Sea-bounding hill, so neare she went, / She saw what wight made such lowd dreriment.'; Elton's *The Brothers. A Monody.* (1820) 35–37: 'The scene behind look'd sylvan; higher rose / The bounding hill, where turfy paths were track'd / Up the bare herbage, gnarl'd with scatter'd crags'; and John Hogan's *Blarney; A Descriptive Poem* (1842), p. 63: 'Our way now turns, and rises higher still, / As doubling off, it takes the bounding hill'.

lxxxix 36. 'Or threaded some Socratic dream'. Cp. Hunt's *A Thought of the Nile* (1818) 1–2: 'It flows through old hushed Egypt and its sands, / Like some grave mighty thought threading a dream'.

lxxxix 37. 'But if I praised the busy town'. For the latter phrase, cp. Gay's *Trivia; or, the Art of Walking the Streets of London* (1716) ii 25: 'If cloath'd in Black, you tread the busy Town'; his *Epistle II. To the Right Honourable the Earl of Burlington. A Journey to Exeter. 1716.* (1729) 117–18: 'Behind us soon the busy town we leave, / Where finest lace industrious lasses weave.'; Lyttelton's *Verses written at Mr. Pope's House at Twickenham, which he had lent to Mrs. Greville, In August 1735.* (1788) stanza i: 'Go, Thames! and tell the busy Town / Not all its wealth or pride / Could tempt me from the

---

129 T. owned the four-volume 1825 Taylor edn of Cunningham's *The Songs of Scotland, Ancient and Modern; with an introduction and notes, historical and critical, and characters of the lyric poets* (Item 810 in *Lincoln*), with Cunningham's own poem in vol. 3.

charms that crown / Thy rural flow'ry side'; and Fergusson's *The Town and Country Contrasted* (1799) 1–2: 'From noisy bustle, from contention free, / Far from the busy town I careless loll'.

xc 7–8. 'They would but find in child and wife / An iron welcome when they rise'. For *iron welcome,* cp. Landon, *Admiral Benbow* (1837) 16–20: 'Our Admiral he gave the word— / Up rose the gallant crew; / And far across the sounding seas / Their iron welcome threw.' The phrase also occurs in Edward Henry Bickersteth's *Caesar's Invasion of Britain*—which won the Chancellor's Gold Medal at Cambridge in 1846, eighteen years after T.'s *Timbuctoo* did so—in a line reading: 'Such iron welcome to her freeborn hills'.

xciv 1–4. 'How pure at heart and sound in head, / With what divine affections bold / Should be the man whose thought would hold / An hour's communion with the dead.' Cp., by the American poet Henry Theodore Tuckerman, *The Holy Land* (1840) 45–48: 'How dear were one repentant night / Where Mary's tears of love were shed! / How blest beside the Saviour's tomb, / One hour's communion with the dead!'

xcv *15–16* and *51–52*. 'The white kine glimmered, and the trees / Laid their dark arms about the field.' Cp. Wordsworth, *Lines Left upon a Seat in a Yew-tree* (1827 version) 8–12: 'Who he was / That piled these stones, and with the mossy sod / First covered o'er, and taught this aged Tree / With its dark arms to form a circling bower, / I well remember.'

xcv *49–50*. 'Till now the doubtful dusk revealed / The knolls once more'. For *doubtful dusk,* cp. Fitchett and Roscoe's *King Alfred,* vol. 3, p. 116, lines 333–36: 'Thus as amidst the gloom I trembling stood, / Sudden methought, that through the doubtful dusk / The shadow of a human figure crept / Startled away before my wondering gaze.' Ricks notes that this section was 'possibly written 1841–42'; if so, its composition coincided with publication of the first complete, commercial edition of Fitchett's epic poem.[130]

---

[130] As stated above (note 78), Fitchett's epic, unfinished at his death in 1838, was completed by Robert Roscoe and published in 1841–42.

xcv 64. 'To broaden into boundless day.' Instances of the latter phrase occur in Cowper's *On the Death of the Bishop of Ely* (1748) 33–34: 'To call encumber'd souls away / From fleshly bonds to boundless day';[131] Ogilvie's *Solitude* 802: 'When from the courts of bright and boundless day'; Shelley's *With a Guitar—To Jane* (1824) 74–77: 'and it knew / That seldom-heard mysterious sound, / Which, driven on its diurnal round, / As it floats through boundless day, / Our world enkindles on its way'; Robert Montgomery's *Woman, the Angel of Life*, Canto III, p. 129: 'Like air-wing'd hopes they glide away, / Commingling with the boundless day!'; and Thomas Oldham's *The Muse's Triumph* (1840) 41–43: 'Say! will the Captive of tyrannic sway, / Restored to genial air, and boundless day, / Turn to his dungeon's suffocating night?'

xcvi 2–3. 'Sweet-hearted, you, whose light-blue eyes / Are tender over drowning flies'. For the latter phrase, cp. Barbauld's mock-heroic *Washing-Day* (1797) 3–6: 'Come, then, domestic Muse, / In slip-shod measure loosely prattling on / Of farm or orchard, pleasant curds and cream, / Or drowning flies, or shoe lost in the mire'.

xcvii 2–3. 'He finds on misty mountain-ground / His own vast shadow glory-crowned'. For *misty mountain-ground*, cp. Pope's *Thebais* 498: 'Now smoaks with show'rs the misty mountain-ground'.

For *vast shadow*, cp. the opening lines of Vaughan's *The World* (1650): 'I saw Eternity the other night / Like a great *Ring* of pure and endless light, / All calm, as it was bright, / And round beneath it, Time in hours, days, years / Driv'n by the spheres / Like a vast shadow mov'd, In which the world / And all her train were hurl'd'; Dryden's translation of *The Tenth Satire of Juvenal* (1693) 21–22, 'Would look like little dolphins, when they sail / In the vast shadow of the British whale.'; and, referring to the Fiend, Darwin's *Botanic Garden* I iv 304: 'And his vast shadow darkens all the land.'

xcvii 19. 'Though rapt in matters dark and deep'. For the latter phrase, cp. Thomas Warton's *Ode XVII. For His Majesty's Birth-Day, June 4th, 1786.*, 32: 'And Pan's own umbrage, dark and deep'. A note on Warton's

---

131 As stated above (note 38), T.'s library as catalogued in *Lincoln* had only vol. 2 of the Pickering edn of Cowper's *Poetical Works. On the Death of the Bishop of Ely* was in vol. 3.

line by Richard Mant in Warton's *Poetical Works*, vol. 2 (1802), p. 101, cites as its literary antecedents[132] Theocritus's *Idylls* viii 49: 'βάθος ὕλας μυρίον';[133] Drayton's *Poly-Olbion, The Ninth Song*, 91–92: 'When else the hanging rocks, and valleys dark and deep, / The summer's longest day would us from meeting keep'; Joseph Warton's translation of *Georgic III* 333–34 *('aut sicubi nigrum / Ilicibus crebris sacra nemus adcubet umbra')*: 'Or where the ilex-forest dark and deep / Sheds holy horrors o'er the hanging steep'; and *Paradise Lost* iii 11: 'The rising world of waters dark and deep'. It also occurs in poems by Swift, Scott, and Shelley.

xcvii 34–36. 'She darkly feels him great and wise, / She dwells on him with faithful eyes, / "I cannot understand: I love."' Ricks notes line 34's echo of Pope's *Essay on Man* ii 4: 'A being darkly wise, and rudely great'; but cp. also *Troilus and Cressida* I iii 68–69 (Ulysses speaking): 'yet let it please both, / Thou great, and wise, to hear Ulysses speak.'; Matthew Prior's *Alma: or, The Progress of the Mind* (1718) iii 478–79: 'Thy pride of being great and wise / I do but mention, to despise';[134] and—combining *great and wise* with the inability to *understand*—Ralph Waldo Emerson's paraphrase, in his essay *History* (1841), of a remark by Socrates at 22b–c of Plato's *Apology*: 'Poets utter great and wise things which they do not themselves understand'.

xcviii 12–14. 'rather dream that there, / A treble darkness, Evil haunts / The birth, the bridal'. Cp. Ogilvie's *Providence* iii 1024–26: '"What tho' my ways, / "Remote from Thought's bewilder'd search, are wrapt / "In triple darkness?["]' Also Alexander Dyce's *Select Translations from the Greek of Quintus Smyrnaeus* (Oxford, 1821), p. 65: 'And ancient Night, to please her daughter dear, / Shed treble darkness o'er the starless sky.'

xcviii 30–32. 'and breaks / The rocket molten into flakes / Of crimson or in emerald rain.' For *flakes of crimson*, cp. Shelley's *The Sensitive Plant*

---

132 In addition to conforming Mant's citations to those employed in the present study, I have corrected his handful of misquotations.
133 George Clayton Tennyson's library had a 1765 edn of Theocritus in Greek and Latin, on the fly-leaf of which was written: 'G. C. Tennyson, Somersby, Lincolnshire. Alfred Tennyson.' (Item 344 in *Lincoln*) T. himself owned an 1819 edn, also in Greek and Latin, in which he wrote his name on the inside front board (Item 2202 in *Lincoln*).
134 The two-volume 1779 Strahan edn of *The Poetical Works of Matthew Prior*, with *Alma: or, The Progress of the Mind* in vol. 1, was at Somersby (Item 273 in *Lincoln*).

200–1, where *crimson* is not noun but adjective: 'The rose-leaves, like flakes of crimson snow, / Paved the turf and the moss below.' The same phrase also occurs in vol. 1 of an anonymous work 'By a Graduate of Oxford'—later revealed to be John Ruskin—called *Modern Painters: their Superiority in the Art of Landscape Painting to the Ancient Masters*, published in 1843 and reviewed later that year in (among other journals) *The Gentlemen's Magazine*.[135] A passage from the book speaking of the later work of J. M. W. Turner and quoted in the review (on pp. 461–62) reads in part:

> They do not rise everywhere, but three or four together in wild groups, fitfully and furiously, as the under strength of the swell compels or permits them; leaving between them treacherous spaces of level and whirling water—now lighted with green and lamp-like fire—now flashing back the gold of the declining sun—now fearfully dyed from above with the indistinguishable images of the burning clouds, which fall upon them in flakes of crimson and scarlet, and give to the reckless waves the added motion of their own fiery flying.[136]

cii *21–24*. 'I turn to go: my feet are set / To leave the pleasant fields and farms; / They mix in one another's arms / To one pure image of regret.' While evoking the expulsion of Adam and Eve from Eden in the closing moments of *Paradise Lost* xii, T.'s lines—especially 23, 'They mix in one another's arms'—also point to *PL* iv 502–8, especially 506:

>   aside the Devil turnd
> For envie, yet with jealous leer maligne
> Ey'd them askance, and to himself thus plaind.
>
> Sight hateful, sight tormenting! thus these two
> Imparadis't in one another's arms
> The happier *Eden*, shall enjoy their fill
> Of bliss on bliss, while I to Hell am thrust[.]

ciii *53–54*. 'And while the wind began to sweep / A music out of sheet and shroud'. Cp. Imlah, *To Sea* (1841) 11–12: 'Now hark! the glad wind harps aloud / Its fitful strain on sheet and shroud'.

---

135 *The Gentlemen's Magazine*, n.s., vol. 20 (Nov. 1843), 451–69. T.'s library as catalogued in *Lincoln* had *Modern Painters* (Item 1915) along with other of Ruskin's works, but only vol. 5 and only the 1860 (Smith, Elder) edn.

136 The painting under discussion is Turner's *Slave Ship (Slavers Throwing Overboard the Dead and Dying—Typhoon Coming In)* (1840).

cv 1–2. 'Tonight ungathered let us leave / This laurel, let this holly stand'. Cp. Wordsworth, *Epitaphs Translated from Chiabrera* (1810) vi 11–14: 'With Archimedes also he conversed / As with a chosen Friend, nor did he leave / Those laureat wreaths ungathered which the Nymphs / Twine on the top of Pindus.'

cv 23–24. 'No dance, no motion, save alone / What lightens in the lucid east'. As discussed above (p. 126) in connection with line 154 of *Locksley Hall*, T.'s command of Italian would have enabled him easily to derive *the lucid east* from *lucido oriente* in poem 337 of Petrarch's *Canzoniere*, which begins *'Quel, che d'odore et di color vincea / l'odorifero et lucido oriente'*. Other pre-T. instances of *lucid east* itself that he may have had in mind include George Woodley's *Britain's Bulwarks; or, The British Seaman* (Plymouth-Dock, 1811), Book VII, p. 183: 'No ruddy glances from the lucid east / Foretold a coming day of peace and rest'; and, by James Mills, *The Universe* (1821), p. 33: 'Still, from his lucid East, the Sun goes forth, / With unabated fire'.

cvii 13–14. 'Together, in the drifts that pass / To darken on the rolling brine'. Instances of the latter phrase occur in Bowles, *St. Michael's Mount* (1803) 29–30: 'Or think on those, who, in yon dreary mine, / Sunk fathoms deep beneath the rolling brine'; and in William Stewart Rose's translation (1823) of Ariosto's *Orlando Furioso* VI xxiii 7–8: 'And to a myrtle, nigh the rolling brine, / Made fast, between a bay-tree and a pine.'[137]

cviii 2. 'And, lest I stiffen into stone'. Cp. Charles Cotton's translation (1685) of Montaigne's essay *De la Tristesse* as *Of Sorrow*, in which he renders a Latin epigraph, *'Diriguisse malis'*—from *Metamorphoses* vi 303 and translatable as 'petrified with misfortunes'—as 'Whom Grief alone / Had Pow'r to stiffen into stone'.[138] Cp. also Elton's *Specimens of the Classic Poets [...] translated into English verse* (1814), vol. 2, p. 266, where his translation of Propertius's *Elegiae* III xvii as *On His Jealousy of a Rival* has, in line 13, 'At Gorgon's visage stiffen into stone'.

---

137 T. himself owned a 1577 Venetian edn of Ariosto's *Orlando Furioso*, on the inside front board of which he wrote 'A. Tennyson, 1833, Feb. 23' (Item 435 in *Lincoln*).

138 In the sentence immediately preceding the epigraph Montaigne has *transmuée en rocher*, which Cotton translates as 'transform'd into a Rock'.

cviii 4. 'Nor feed with sighs a passing wind'. Instances of *passing wind* in conjunction with *sighs* include Cowper's *Expostulation* 29–30: 'Or only what in cottages confin'd, / Sighs unregarded to the passing wind'; Hogg's *The Queen's Wake: A Legendary Poem* (Edinburgh, 1813), Night Three, p. 280: 'When fancy moulds upon the mind / Light visions on the passing wind, / And wooes, with faultering tongue and sigh, / The shades o'er memory's wilds that fly'; and, its final line a near-perfect match with T.'s, stanza xxvii of Rev. John Bethune's *Hymns of the Churchyard—II* (1840): 'By stranger hands, her beauteous clay / Was to the dust consign'd; / No friend was there her name to say, / Or load with sighs the passing wind.'

cviii 5. 'What profit lies in barren faith'. Cp. *James* ii 14: 'What doth it profit, my brethren, though a man say he hath faith, and have not works? can faith save him?' In a chapter on 'The Doctrine of the Apostle *James*, concerning Faith and Works' in his *The Doctrine of Justification by Faith, through the Imputation of the Righteousness of Christ* (1667; new edition, 1816), the English theologian John Owen wrote (on p. 573 of the original edition, p. 360 of the new): 'He doth not at all enquire or determine how a sinner is justified before God, but how Professors of the Gospel can prove or demonstrate that they are so, and that they do not deceive themselves by trusting unto a lifeless and barren Faith.'

cix 1. 'Heart-affluence in discursive talk'. Cp. the third quatrain of the sonnet *Largess* (1848) by the Irish-American poet Anne C[harlotte]. Lynch (later Lynch Botta): 'But thy heart's affluence lavish uncontrolled; / The largess of thy love give full and free, / As monarchs in their progress scatter gold; / And be thy heart like the exhaustless sea'.[139]

cix 9. 'High nature amorous of the good'. Cp. Theophilus Gale, *The Anatomie of Infidelitie, Or, An Explication of the Nature, Causes, Aggravations, and Punishment of Unbelief* (1672), p. 204, speaking of 'the true Believer': 'He is so *amorous* of the good things that belong unto his peace, that he can part with althings for them; yea his wil is carried with a violent propension towards them, as the *Iron* to the *Load-stone*.'

---

[139] The collection in which *Largess* first appeared, *Poems by Anne C. Lynch* (1849), was published in New York by George P. Putnam, a firm represented in London (as stated on the book's title page) by Putnam's American Agency.

cix 10. 'But touched with no ascetic gloom'. Cp. Scott's novel *The Talisman* (1825), chap. 4: 'the former [the Saracen] with an austere expression of ascetic gloom, the latter [Sir Kenneth] with anxious curiosity deeply impressed on his manly features';[140] and, in Robert Montgomery's poem *Luther* (1842), [section 24] *A Landscape of Domestic Life*, p. 220: 'Yes! beautiful behind the scenes to gaze, / And there no mock attempt, whose aping pride / Would play the hero in ascetic gloom / To witness'.

cxii 15–16. 'And world-wide fluctuation swayed / In vassal tides that followed thought.' Instances of *vassal tide* singular or plural occur in lines 13–14 of Cowper's 1791 translation from the Italian of an ode by Antonio Francini in praise of Milton: 'In Ocean's blazing flood enshrin'd / Whose vassal tide around her swells'; and in Drummond's *Battle of Trafalgar* 375–76: 'In awe-commanding power Britannia rides / With red-cross banner o'er her vassal tides'.

cxiii 12. 'A pillar steadfast in the storm'. Cp. Dryden, *Absalom and Achitophel* (1681) 888–89: 'Hushai, the friend of David in distress; / In public storms, of manly steadfastness'.

cxviii 7–9. 'They say, / The solid earth whereon we tread / In tracts of fluent heat began'. Cp. Good's *The Nature of Things* iii 130–34, where *fluent heat* applies to animate life: 'Hence may'st thou judge that not in every part / Dwells the same portion of percipient power, / Nor health from each flows equal; but that those / Chief nurture life, and check its flight abrupt, / Rear'd from aërial seeds, or fluent heat.' Also Philip James Bailey's *Festus* (second, expanded Pickering edition, 1845),[141] where, in 'Scene — The Centre', Lucifer tells Festus: 'Nature, the delegate of God, brings forth / Her everlasting elements, and breathes / Around that fluent heat of life which clothes / Itself in lightnings, wandering through the air, / And pierces to the last and loftiest pore / Of Earth's snow-mantled mountains.'

---

140 T.'s library had copies of the Cadell edns of twenty-five Scott novels including this one, and of Scott's *Poetical Works* (Items 1853 through 1980, except 1866, in *Lincoln*), all published between 1841 and 1847.
141 T. owned this edn (Item 481 in *Lincoln*).

cxviii 21. 'But iron dug from central gloom'. Pre-T. instances of the latter phrase include, among others, Helen Maria Williams's *Part of an Irregular Fragment, Found in a Dark Passage of the Tower* (1786) 10–11: 'I shudd'ring pass that fatal room / For ages wrapt in central gloom'; Wordsworth's *An Evening Walk* (1793) 181, 'Far in the level forest's central gloom'; and Polwhele's *Ode to the Spirit of Freshness* (1798) 28–31: 'I see thee not — But lo! a vapory shape / That oft belies thy form, emerging slow, / From that deep central gloom, / Rests on the moontipt wood'. The sense closest to T.'s may be that in *Prometheus Unbound* III iii 84–87, where The Earth says: 'I hear, I feel; / Thy lips are on me, and thy touch runs down / Even to the adamantine central gloom / Along these marble nerves'.

cxix 3. 'the city sleeps'. Cp. Hemans, *The Last Constantine* (1823), with two instances of the same phrase: in lxxviii 3–5, 'and in the very lap of war, / As if young Hope with Twilight's ray were born, / Awhile the city sleeps!'; and lxxix 1: 'The city sleeps! — aye! on the combat's eve'.

cxxii 1–4. 'Oh, wast thou with me, dearest, then, / While I rose up against my doom, / And yearned to burst the folded gloom, / To bare the eternal Heavens again'. Cp. Bowles, *The Spirit of Discovery: or, the Conquest of Ocean* (1804) iv 116–17: 'To burst the gloom, though dragons guard the shore, / Or beings more than mortal pace the sands'; and (commemorating Poland's then-recent anti-Russian uprising) Campbell's *Lines on Poland* (1831) 138–39: 'Though Poland (Lazarus-like) has burst the gloom, / She rises not a beggar from the tomb'. But T.'s lines more strongly suggest the last stanza (lines 41–44) of Mary Tighe's poem THE LILY. May, 1809 — first published in *Psyche: with other poems by the late Mrs. Henry Tighe* (1811) — where Faith bids Sorrow 'bear the long, cold, wintry night, / And bear her own degraded doom, / And wait till Heaven's reviving light, / Eternal Spring! shall burst the gloom.'

cxxii 15–16. 'As in the former flash of joy, / I slip the thoughts of life and death'. Cp. Coleridge's *Rime of the Ancient Mariner*, where 'A flash of joy' is the sidenote alongside Part III, lines 162–66, 'With throats unslaked, with black lips baked, / Agape they heard me call: / Gramercy! they for joy did grin, / And all at once their breath drew in, / As they were drinking all.' — lines followed immediately by the appearance of the skeleton ship.

cxxii 17. 'And all the breeze of Fancy blows'. Cp. Hazlitt's essay on William Godwin in his *Spirit of the Age*: 'so Mr. Godwin has rendered an essential service to moral science, by attempting (in vain) to pass the Arctic Circle and Frozen Regions, where the understanding is no longer warmed by the affections, nor fanned by the breeze of fancy!'[142]

cxxiii 5–6. 'The hills are shadows, and they flow / From form to form, and nothing stands'. As Ricks notes, S & S cite *Isaiah* lxiv 1 ('The mountains flowed down at thy presence') and *Judges* v 5 ('The mountains melted from before the LORD'), both of which T. himself quoted in a note to line 31 of his *Babylon* (poem 46), 'And the mountains shall flow at my presence'. As to the phrase *and nothing stands*, cp. also Shakespeare's *Sonnet 60* ('Like as the waues make towards the pibled shore') 9–12: 'Time doth transfixe the florish set on youth, / And delues the paralels in beauties brow, / Feedes on the rarities of natures truth, / And nothing stands but for his sieth to mow.'; and, as noted earlier,[143] the view of Heracleitus, as quoted by Socrates in Plato's *Cratylus* at 402a, that all things move and nothing stands still.

cxxv 14. 'To seek thee on the mystic deeps'. In his 1829 essay *Signs of the Times*, Carlyle bemoans the impact of industrialization on Christianity, which, he says, 'arose in the mystic deeps of man's soul'.

cxxv 15–16. 'And this electric force, that keeps / A thousand pulses dancing'. S & S note that the lines allude 'to the contemporary physiological theory that electricity is associated with the phenomena of life.' But cp. also, more specifically, Sir Aubrey De Vere's *Julian the Apostate, A Dramatic Poem* (1822), p. 199, where, moments before his death, Julian says: 'I tell ye I am strong. A lightning rushes / Through my hot veins would swell a thousand pulses.'

cxxviii 8–9. 'Yet O ye mysteries of good, / Wild Hours that fly with Hope and Fear'. Cp. *Epipsychidion* 379–81: 'as the star of Death / And Birth is worshipped by those sisters wild / Called Hope and Fear'.

---

142 On p. 47 of George Clayton Tennyson's first (1825) Colburn edn (see note 59).
143 See, on p. 127, the commentary on line 22 of T.'s *The Golden Year*.

cxxviii 13. 'To draw, to sheathe a useless sword'. For the latter phrase, cp. *Aeneid* ii 510–11, speaking of Priam at the fall of Troy: *'et inutile ferrum / cingitur'* [and is girded with a useless sword]. Later instances of the same phrase include, among others, Pye's *Alfred* i 527: 'My powers no more the useless sword retain'; and W. E. Meredith's *Llewelyn ap Jorwerth* (1818) I xxvii 9: 'To the victorious prince he gave his useless sword.'

cxxviii 14. 'To fool the crowd with glorious lies'. For the latter phrase Ricks cites Horace's *splendide mendax* in *Odes* III xi 35; but cp. also the phrase itself in Crashaw's *To the Same Party* [*A Young Gentlewoman*]: *Counsel Concerning Her Choice* (1652): 'Gilded dunghills, glorious lies'.

cxxx 6–7. 'But though I seem in star and flower / To feel thee some diffusive power'. For *star and flower*, cp. Elton's *Roses, From the Latin of Ausonius* (1824) 19–20: 'In dew, in tint the same, the star and flower; / For both confess the queen of beauty's power.', translating lines 17–18 of the fourth-century poet's *De rosis nascentibus* [On budding roses]: *'ros unus, color unus et unum mane duorum, / sideris et floris nam domina una Venus.'*

cxxx 14. 'I have thee still, and I rejoice'. Echoing but inverting *Macbeth* II i 35 (Macbeth speaking): 'I have thee not, and yet I see thee still.'

[Epilogue] 62. 'The joy to every wandering breeze'. Echoing, though not verbatim, line 7 of Shakespeare's *Sonnet 116* ('Let me not to the marriage of true mindes'): 'It is the star to euery wandring barke'. But cp. also Falconer's *The Shipwreck* i 827–28: 'While all to court the wandering breeze are plac'd; / With yards now thwarting, now obliquely brac'd.'; and *caretque / ripa vagis taciturna ventis* [untroubled by the wandering breeze] in Horace, *Odes* III xxix 23–24.

[Epilogue] 79–80. 'My drooping memory will not shun / The foaming grape of eastern France.' For *drooping memory*, cp. Fulke Greville's *Life of the Renowned Sr. Philip Sidney* (1652), chap. 1: 'So that although with *Socrates*, I professe to know nothing for the present; yet with *Nestor* I am delighted in repeating old newes of the ages past; and will therefore stir up my drooping memory touching this man's worth, powers, wayes, and designes'. Another pre-T. instance of the phrase occurs in Cicero's letter to Atticus, Book XII, Epistle 1, as translated by William Guthrie (1752): "But, as you jeer me, that my Morning Vigour begins to droop; let me tell you, there is no greater Symptom of old Age than a drooping Memory.'—Cicero's *memoriola vacillare.*

[Epilogue] *117–18*. 'And touch with shade the bridal doors, / With tender gloom the roof, the wall'. For *tender gloom*, Collins, S & S, and Ricks cite Thomson's *Castle of Indolence* i 507: 'A certain tender Gloom o'erspred his Face'. But cp. also Barbauld's *To Mr. S. T. Coleridge. 1797.*, line 29: 'And loves the softened light and tender gloom'; Byron's *Oh! Snatch'd Away* (1815) 5: 'And the wild cypress wave in tender gloom'; Wilson's *The Scholar's Funeral* (1816) viii 4–5: 'Nor is it hard a tender gloom to trace / On the young chorister's sunshiny face'; and Hemans's *Forest Sanctuary* II xxxiv 4–5: 'And the soft darkness of her serious eyes, / Misty with tender gloom'.

297 To the Vicar of Shiplake (*wr* 13 June 1850)

18–19. 'I shall come through her, I trust, / Into fuller-orbed completeness'. Cp. Lucan's *Pharsalia* as translated by Nicholas Rowe (1718) iii 69–70: 'Such seems the Moon, while, growing yet, she shines, / Or waining from her fuller Orb declines'.

20. 'Though but made of erring dust.' For the latter phrase, cp. Samuel Howell's *Village Rambles* (1810), Canto I ('The Church Yard'), p. 17: 'The Heav'nly congress guards our erring dust, / Reclaims the wand'rer, or confirms the just'; Ebenezer Elliott's *Love* (1823) iii, p. 117: '"But Heaven is not forgetful. God is just; / God weighs in Mercy's scale our erring dust.["]';[144] and John Edmund Reade's *The Drama of a Life* (1840), scene vi, p. 63: 'I, too, believed it was no Vision, no / Tale to be scoffed at, that a God was born / From woman [...] thus allying / Our erring dust to immortality!'

299* To the Queen (*wr* Mar. 1851)

8. 'Of him that uttered nothing base'. While, as Ricks notes, T. here refers to Wordsworth, the line also echoes a passage in James Endell Tyler's *Meditations from the Fathers of the First Five Centuries* (1849) — specifically, Tyler's translation of a homily by the fourth-century bishop John Chrysostom on *Romans* xii 1 that includes, on p. 73 of vol. 2: 'How (one

---

144 Retitled *Withered Wild Flowers* in later edns. As noted above (see note 63 on p. 102), T. owned the three-volume (1844) Steill edn of Elliott's poems.

will say) can the body become a sacrifice? Let the eye look on nothing evil, and it becomes a sacrifice; let the tongue utter nothing base and shameful, and it becomes an offering'.[145]

12. 'If aught of ancient worth be there'. Cp. Wordsworth's *The Prelude*, 1798 version, xiv 388–89; 1805 version, xiii 386–87: 'Whether to me shall be allotted life, / And, with life, power to accomplish aught of worth'; either or both poets perhaps also having in mind lines 5–6 of Shakespeare's *Sonnet 38* ('How can my Muse want subiect to inuent'): 'Oh giue thy selfe the thankes if ought in me, / Worthy perusal stand against thy sight'.

300 'Little bosom not yet cold' (*wr* 1851)

3. 'Little hands of mighty mould'. The latter phrase occurs in several pre-T. poems, one of which, Schiller's *Lied von der Glocke* translated by Lord Francis Leveson Gower as *Song of the Bell* (1823), reads in part: 'Break me down the mighty mould, / It has reach'd its master's aim; / Let the longing eye behold / The created child of flame.' Cp. also Hazlitt's essay *On the Qualifications Necessary to Success in Life*, in his *The Plain Speaker: Opinions on Books, Men, and Things* (1826), vol. 2, p. 8: 'I do not think (to give an instance or two of what I mean) that Milton's mind was (so to speak) greater than the Paradise Lost; it was just big enough to fill that mighty mould; the shrine contained the Godhead.'

301* To E. L., on His Travels in Greece (*wr* 1851–52)

5. 'Tomohrit, Athos, all things fair'. Among other instances of the latter phrase, cp. Spenser's *Hymne in Honour of Beautie* 57–58: 'That is the thing which giveth pleasant grace / To all things faire, that kindleth lively fyre'; *Paradise Lost* ix 602–5: 'Thenceforth to Speculations high or deep / I turnd my thoughts, and with capacious mind / Considerd all things visible in Heav'n, / Or Earth, or Middle, all things fair and good'; and *Endymion* iii 189–90: 'For as he lifted up his eyes to swear / How his own goddess was past all things fair'.

---

145 See also, on pp. 106–7, the commentary on the echo of Hood's *Ode to Melancholy* in line 4 of T.'s *On a Mourner*.

21–22. 'From him that on the mountain lea / By dancing rivulets fed his flocks'. For *dancing rivulets,* cp.—in the third (1715) and subsequent editions of Watts's *Horae Lyricae—Divine Judgments,* stanza ii: 'Old *Boreas* with his freezing Pow'rs / Turns the Earth Iron, makes the Ocean Glass, / Arrests the dancing Riv'lets as they pass'. The third of these lines recurs verbatim, other than the standardized spelling of *Riv'lets* as *rivulets,* in Thomson's *On a Country Life* 23–24: 'Keen frost then turns the liquid lakes to glass, / Arrests the dancing rivulets as they pass.'

306 The Third of February, 1852 (*wr* Dec. 1851–Feb. 1852)

8. 'Wild War, who breaks the converse of the wise'. Pre-T. instances of the latter phrase occur in Thomson, *A Poem to the Memory of the Right Honourable The Lord Talbot. Addressed to His Son.* (1737) 209, 'As free the converse of the wise and good'; and, first published in *Idler* no. 101 for 22 March 1760, in Samuel Johnson's essay *Omar's Plan of Life,* in which, says Johnson, Omar 'gave back to the calif the keys of trust and the seals of secrecy; and sought no other pleasure for the remains of life than the converse of the wise, and the gratitude of the good.'

307 Hands All Round! [1852] (*wr* late 1851–early 1852)

7–8. 'That man's the true Conservative, / Who lops the mouldered branch away.' Cp. Macpherson's purported translation of 'Fragment VII' in his *Fragments of Ancient Poetry* (Edinburgh, 1760), p. 24: 'I, like an ancient oak on Morven, I moulder alone in my place. The blast hath lopped my branches away; and I tremble at the wings of the north.'

308 Suggested by Reading an Article in a Newspaper (*wr* Feb. 1852)

41–42. 'There hang within the heavens a dark disgrace, / Some vast Assyrian doom to burst upon our race.' Cp. Bulwer-Lytton's *King Arthur* (1849) I lxiii: '"O thou, the Almighty Lord of earth and heaven, / Without whose will not ev'n a sparrow falls, / If to my sight the fearful truth was given, / If thy dread hand hath graven on these walls / The Assyrian's doom, and to the stranger's sway / My kingdom and my crown shall pass away, —[″]'.

310* Will (*wr* c. 1852)

15–17. 'He seems as one whose footsteps halt, / Toiling in immeasurable sand, / And o'er a weary sultry land'. For line 16 Ricks cites *Queen Mab* viii 70: 'Those deserts of immeasurable sand'. For the *weary sultry land* of line 17, cp. *Isaiah* xxxii 2: 'And a man shall be as an hiding place from the wind, and a covert from the tempest; as rivers of water in a dry place, as the shadow of a great rock in a weary land.' The verse from Isaiah is evoked in language even closer to T.'s in a passage from *Carne's Eastern Letters* (1826) as reprinted in *Extracts from The Works of Travellers, Illustrative of Various Passages in Holy Scripture*, ed. by M. F. Maude (1841), p. 204:

> The same gentleman, going towards Jericho, says, 'We entered on a tract of soft sand; ascending a sand-hill that overlooked the plain, we saw Jericho, contrary to our hopes, at a great distance, and the level tract we must pass to arrive at it, was exposed to a sultry sun, without a single tree to afford us a temporary shade. The simile of the shadow of a great rock in a weary land, was never more strongly felt.'

18. 'Far beneath a blazing vault'. Cp. Maurice, *An Elegiac and Historical Poem, sacred to the Memory and Virtues of the Honourable Sir William Jones* (1795), the eighty-fifth of whose hundred and twenty quatrains reads: 'Majestic, lo! on Tigris' hallow'd shore, / A second Babel seems the skies to threat; / Whence Bagdad's seers yon blazing vault explore, / And trace the mystic characters of fate.'; and, also by Maurice, *The Fall of the Mogul, a Tragedy* (1806) IV iv 37ff.: 'And let the dread example show mankind, / That high above yon vast and blazing vault, / [...] / Eternal JUSTICE sits, and rules the globe!' Cp. also Atherstone's *A Midsummer Day's Dream*, p. 83, from the opening lines of 'Dream Continued': 'We shot / Rapidly down, immeasurably deep; / Then burst at length into a blazing vault, / Bright as the sun'.

19. 'Sown in a wrinkle of the monstrous hill'. Instances of the latter phrase occur in Thomas Watson's *Hekatompathia* (1582), *Sonnet LVIII* 1–2: 'There is a monstrous hill in Sicil soil, / Where works that limping

God, which Vulcan hight'; George Chapman's *Iliad* (1611) ii 695–96: 'In Arime, men say, the grave is still, / Where thunder tomb'd Typhœius, and is a monstrous hill'; *Poly-Olbion, The Tenth Song* 318–19: 'vntill the monstrous hill / At length shewes like a cloud'; and, also from *Poly-Olbion, The Fourteenth Song* 122: 'When as those monstrous Hills so much that vs despise'.

311* The Daisy (*wr* 1853)

106. 'Perchance, to charm a vacant brain'. Among other instances of the latter phrase, cp. *Rape of the Lock* i 83: 'Then gay ideas crowd the vacant brain'; and *Alastor* 189–91: 'sleep, / Like a dark flood suspended in its course, / Rolled back its impulse on his vacant brain'.

312* To the Rev. F. D. Maurice (*wr* 1854)

1. 'Come, when no graver cares employ'. Among other instances of *graver cares*, cp. line 30 of Scott's introduction to Canto IV of his *Marmion*: 'When leisure graver cares denied'; Rose's translation of *Orlando Furioso*, I iv 7–8: 'So thou thy graver cares some little time / Postponing, lend thy leisure to my rhyme.'; and William Peach's *Cwm Dhu; or, The Black Dingle* (1853) I viii 4–5: 'Where, should no graver cares demand / His tendance, would he pensive stand'.

13. 'Where, far from noise and smoke of town'. In vol. 1 of his *Euphrosyne: or, Amusements on the Road of Life* (1776), cp. Richard Graves's *The Rural Retreat* 1–4: 'Sick of the noise and smoke of Town, / Old Simon, fat and wealthy grown, / Resolv'd to seek some snug Retreat, / And buy, or build a country Seat.'

21–22. 'For groves of pine on either hand, / To break the blast of winter, stand'. Instances of *the blast of winter* occur in Dryden's *Second Miscellany* (1668) 45, translating a line from Horace's *Second Epode*: 'But when the blast of Winter blows'; and in Byron's *Giaour* 626–27: 'While eddying whirl, and breaking wave, / Rous'd by the blast of winter, rave'.

41–42. 'Come, Maurice, come: the lawn as yet / Is hoar with rime, or spongy-wet'. For *hoar with rime*, cp. Polwhele's *The Minstrel: a Poem in Five Books* (1814) III xxii 1–2: 'There, as he nearer drew, he saw that speck / Into a bridge expand, all hoar with rime'; and R[ichard]. H[engist]. Horne's *Orion: An Epic Poem in Three Books* (1843) III i 267–68: 'The Cyclops hoar with rime, / His coarse hair flying, through the wet woods ran'.

For *spongy-wet*, cp., from her *Poems and Fancies* (1653), Margaret Cavendish, *The Foure Principall* Figur'd Atomes *make the foure* Elements, *as* Square, Round, Long, *and* Sharpe 11–14: 'As *Waters are round drops, though nere so small, / Which shew that water is all sphæricall, / That Figure makes it spungy,* spungy, wet, / For being hollow, softnesse doth beget.' Cp. also Horace Smith's *A Tour to the Lakes* (1830) 89–93: 'For then th' impending clouds were spied, / Like monstrous udders—spongy, wet, / Flapping and flagging, / Lagging and dragging / Against the mountain sides'.

313 The Brook (*wr* 1854?)

3. 'One whom the strong sons of the world despise'. For *sons of the world*, cp. Spenser's *Prosopopoia: or Mother Hubberds Tale* (1591) 135–36: 'And as we be Sons of the World so wide, / Let us our Fathers Heritage divide'; Shakespeare's *Sonnet 33* ('Full many a glorious morning haue I seene') 14: 'Suns of the world may staine, whe[n] heauens sun stain[eth]'; and Matthew Arnold's *Stanzas from the Grande Chartreuse* (written c. 1851–52, first published Apr. 1855) 161–62: 'Sons of the world, oh, haste those years; / But, till they rise, allow our tears!' Also first published in 1855, T.'s poem may or may not reflect a reading of Arnold's.

7–8. 'yet himself could make / The thing that is not as the thing that is.' The impossibility of thinking or saying *the thing that is not* is a recurring theme in Plato's dialogues, including his *Sophist, Cratylus*, and *Theaetetus*. Cp. also Swift's *Gulliver's Travels* (1726), Part IV, chap. 4, where the Houyhnhnms, having no word for *lie*, instead employ the phrase 'to say a thing which is not'.[146]

---

146 As catalogued in *Tennyson in Lincoln* (Item 333), George Clayton Tennyson's library had vol. 2 only of the two-volume 1726 Motte edn of Swift's *Travels into Several Remote Nations of the World. By Captain Lemuel Gulliver*, in which volume T. wrote 'A. Tennyson' on the inside front board and on the remains of a fly-leaf. T. himself

59–62. 'And here and there a foamy flake / Upon me, as I travel / With many a silvery waterbreak / Above the golden gravel'. For the latter phrase, cp. Sylvester's translation of a motto by Du Bartas ('Pauvre Ver, travaille, tracasse' etc.) that, as translated, begins: 'Goe, silly Worm, drudge, trudge, and travell, / Despising Pain; / So thou maist gain / Some Honour, or some Golden Gravell'. Cp. also Wyatt's *Tagus Farewell*—or as published in the first edition of *Tottel's Miscellany* (1557), *Of his returne from Spain*—which, reflecting an ancient belief that Spain's river Tagus flowed over golden gravel, begins: 'Tagus, fare well, that westward with thy stremis, / Torns up the grayns of gold alredy tryd : / With spurr and sayle for I go seke the Temis, / Gaynward the sonne that showth her welthi pryd'; Swift's *The Fable of Midas* (1712) 37–38: 'Fame spreads the News, and People travel / From far, to gather *golden* Gravel'; and, in an Appendix to Robert Bradstreet's *The Sabine Farm* (1810), Bradstreet's translation of Statius's *Villa Tiburtina Manlii Vopisci* [The Tiburtine Villa of Vopiscus], which ends: '*Et limo splendente Tagus! Sic docta frequenta / Otia, sic omni detectus pectora nube / Finem Nestoreae precor egrediare senectae*'; or, as translated in lines 138–41: 'And Tagus' golden gravel heap the coast!— / Oft may these scenes your learned pleasure boast! / And you, while health your cloudless bosom cheers, / Outlive the period of a Nestor's years!'

63–64. 'And draw them all along, and flow / To join the brimming river'. Cp. Caroline Anne (née Bowles) Southey, *The River* (1829) stanza iii: 'River! River! brimming River! / Broad and deep and *still* as Time, / Seeming *still*—yet still in motion, / Tending onward to the ocean, / Just like mortal prime.'

96–97. '"She told me. She and James had quarrelled. Why? / What cause of quarrel? None, she said, no cause["]'. Cp. *Othello* V ii 299 (Cassio speaking): 'Dear general, I never gave you cause.';[147] and the couplet of Shakespeare's *Sonnet 49* ['Against that time (if euer that time come)']: 'To leaue poore me, thou hast the strength of lawes, / Since why to loue, I can alledge no cause.'

---

owned the 1864 Cassell edn of *Gulliver's Travels into several remote regions of the world* (Item 2136 in *Lincoln*).

147 As discussed below (p. 222), Cassio's speech is also echoed in T.'s *Lancelot and Elaine* 1288–89.

135. 'Then, seated on a serpent-rooted beech'. In William George Clark's *A Score of Lyrics* (1849), cp. stanza iii of his *Gwentavon Ghyll*, reading in part: 'On either side to gaunt grey rock / Cling serpent-rooted birch and oak'.

168–69. 'and found the sun of sweet content / Re-risen in Katie's eyes, and all things well.' Cp. Dekker's twenty-line lyric *O Sweet Content* (1603), in which that title phrase recurs six times.

174–75. 'I slip, I slide, I gloom, I glance, / Among my skimming swallows'. In Tonson's *Miscellany* (1684) and some later poetry collections, cp. *Epistle From Mr. Otway to Mr. Duke* 15–16: 'Sometimes upon a River's Bank we lye, / Where skimming Swallows o'er the Surface fly'; and Baillie's *Hymn on the Seasons* (1823) 35–37: 'When panting heat lists to the cooling gush / Of gelid springs, or marks the sportive band / Of skimming swallows o'er the gray lake rush'.

316* Maud, A Monodrama (*wr* 1854–55)

Part I

i 1. 'I hate the dreadful hollow behind the little wood'. In her edition of T.'s poem,[148] Susan Shatto, on pp. 162–63, compares its opening lines to the murder of Montague Tigg in Dickens's *Martin Chuzzlewit* (1844), chap. 47. But *the dreadful hollow* (Dickens has *a hollow place*) may also owe something to Samuel Sharp's *Letters from Italy. Describing the Customs and Manners of that Country, in the Years 1765, and 1766. To which is Annexed, an Admonition to Gentlemen who Pass the Alps, in Their Tour Through Italy* (1766), pp. 147–48: 'Perhaps, could we know what a dreadful hollow we tread upon, and what a quantity of combustible matter there is within it, we should rejoice that we are on the point of leaving such treacherous ground.'[149] Or to *The Siege of Bhurtpoor, A Poem in Five Cantos* (Calcutta, 1828) 'By a Subaltern of the Field Army', iii 173–74: 'Suppose the plain

---

148 Susan Shatto, *Tennyson's Maud: A Definitive Edition* (London: Athlone, 1986).
149 The quoted text occurs in Letter XXXIV, dated 3 Mar. 1766, on pp. 144–53 of Sharp's book, three edns of which were published in 1766–67. It is also part of the long excerpt from Sharp published in *The London Magazine*, vol. 36, [no. 1] (Jan. 1767), 17–20.

were passed, how shall they cross / The dreadful hollow of the yawning fosse'.[150]

i 2. 'Its lips in the field above are dabbled with blood-red heath'. Cp. the opening lines of Shelley's long-suppressed—and (until 2006) long thought lost—*Poetical Essay on The Existing State of Things* (1811), which begins: 'DESTRUCTION marks thee! o'er the blood-stain'd heath / Is faintly borne the stifled wail of death'.

i 3. 'The red-ribbed ledges drip with a silent horror of blood'. In John Edmund Reade's *Sacred Poems, from Subjects in the Old Testament* (1843), p. 23, cp. *Abraham's Offering of Sacrifice* vi 5–7: 'Dark, as in silent horror, stood / The solemn trees, o'ershadowing round / That sacrifice of human blood'.

i 5. 'For there in the ghastly pit long since a body was found'. Cp. Wilson's *City of the Plague* I ii: 'Things past, or yet to come? give me one look, / That I may see his face so beautiful, / Where'er it be; or in that ghastly pit, / Or smiling 'mid his comrades on the deck'. Also Browning's *Pippa Passes* (1841) 273–74: 'A hurrying-down within me, as of waters / Loosened to smother up some ghastly pit'.[151]

i 9. 'Did he fling himself down? who knows? for a vast speculation had failed'. Shatto (p. 164) notes that the line is usually taken as referring to Matthew Allen's failed wood-carving venture, in which T. and his family a decade earlier had lost a fortune. But for *vast speculation*, cp. also Isaac D'Israeli, *An Essay on the Manners and Genius of the Literary Character* (1795), chap. 9 ('Some Observations respecting the Infirmities and Defects of Men of Genius'), p. 104:

> The occupation of making a great name, is, perhaps, more anxious and precarious than that of making a great fortune. We sympathise with the merchant when he communicates melancholy to the social circle in consequence of a bankruptcy, or when he feels the elation of prosperity

---

[150] The siege of the title, occurring in the Indian princely state so-named between Dec. 1825 and Jan. 1826, had ended with the capture of its fortress by British troops under Lord Combermere.

[151] *Pippa Passes* was first published in 1841 as the first of eight parts of Browning's *Bells and Pomegranates*. As catalogued in Item 632 of *Lincoln*, T. owned only parts seven and eight.

at the success of a vast speculation. The author is not less immersed in cares, or agitated by success, for literature has it's [sic] bankruptcies and it's [sic] speculations.

i 11. 'And out he walked when the wind like a broken worldling wailed'. For *broken worldling* cp., in *Heath's Book of Beauty* (1843), Alexander Baillie Cochrane's *Stanzas to* —, stanza iv: 'Ofttimes the broken worldling here / Has calmed his troubled gaze, / And found in pensive solitude / The hope of brighter days; / Caught inspiration from the soil / Of deep religious lore, / And learned to gaze with confidence / On life's receding shore.' A similar phrase had previously occurred in a long, unsigned article on the works of Thomas Carlyle in *The Quarterly Review*, vol. 66, no. 132 (Sept. 1840), reading in part (p. 497):

> Has Mr. Carlyle never heard of a body of men, who, for 1800 years, have been preaching this annihilation of self; this indifference to the world; this renunciation of its pleasures and its pains, as idle vanities; who have not waited to preach this to the jaded, haggard, wretched, heart-broken worldling, but have declared these truths to the child on its mother's lap, that it might never fall into that depth of misery, by ceasing to remember them?

i 32. 'Cheat and be cheated, and die: who knows? we are ashes and dust.' As above (p. 164) in connection with *In Memoriam* xxxiv 4 ('And dust and ashes all that is'), cp. *Job* xlii 6: 'Wherefore I abhor myself, and repent in dust and ashes.'

i 48. 'War with a thousand battles, and shaking a hundred thrones.' Cp. the Pope–Broome–Fenton *Odyssey* xi 683–84: 'With thee we fell; *Greece* wept thy hapless fates, / And shook astonish'd thro' her hundred states'. Also, in his *Poems, Chiefly Dramatic and Lyric* (Dublin, 1793), cp. Boyd's *The Temple of Vesta, a Dramatic Poem* II ii, p. 196: 'such was the scene / My father told, who pass'd the wond'rous vale / With Israel's squadrons, such were then the deeds / That scatter'd terrour thro' the nations round / And shook Arabia's hundred thrones, from Nile / To Jordan!'

i 57. 'Would there be sorrow for *me*? there was *love* in the passionate shriek'. T.'s *passionate shriek*—referring to 'the shrill-edged shriek of [the speaker's] mother' in *i* 16 when she learns of her husband's suicide—may have been been suggested by another, in Nathaniel Hawthorne's *The Blithdale Romance*, published in Boston and London in 1852, two or three years before T. wrote *Maud*. It occurs in chap. 28 ('Blithedale—Pasture'), and issues from the distraught Zenobia before her own suicide:

> Then the tears gushed into my eyes, and I forgave him. For I remembered the wild energy, the passionate shriek, with which Zenobia had spoken those words–"Tell him he has murdered me! Tell him that I'll haunt him!" and I knew what murderer he meant, and whose vindictive shadow dogged the side where Priscilla was not.

i 151. 'Where if I cannot be gay let a passionless peace be my lot'. Cp. Charlotte Brontë's *Villette* (1853), chap. 20, where Lucy Snowe says, of the ladies attending an evening recital, that 'for their depth of expressionless calm, of passionless peace, a polar snow-field could alone offer a type.' Brontë's own use of the phrase may reflect her reading of the posthumous memoirs (1852) of the American journalist, feminist, transcendentalist, and critic Margaret Fuller Ossoli, where her letter to Emerson of 23 February 1840 reads in part: 'the stars smiled upon him satirically from their passionless peace; and he knew they were like the sun, as unfeeling, only more distant.'[152]

i 363. 'A wounded thing with a rancorous cry'. Cp. Shelley's *Witch of Atlas*, where stanza 50 reads in part: 'And whilst the outer lake beneath the lash / Of the winds' scourge, foamed like a wounded thing'.

i 402–4. 'Then let come what come may, / What matter if I go mad, / I shall have had my day.' Shatto (p. 190) and Ricks cite *Macbeth* I iii 146–47 (Macbeth speaking): 'Come what come may, / Time and the hour runs through the roughest day.' But cp. also the conclusion of Edmund Burke's speech to the Electors of Bristol prior to the election of September 1780: 'Gentlemen, I have had my day. I can never sufficiently express my gratitude to you for having set me in a place, wherein I could lend the slightest help to great and laudable designs.',[153] reprinted in several editions of Knox's *Elegant Extracts: or, Useful and Entertaining Passages*

---

152 Margaret Fuller, *Memoirs of Margaret Fuller Ossoli* (Boston and London, 1852). In the two-volume American edn, the passage quoted appears in vol. 1, p. 290; in the three-volume English, in vol. 2, pp. 80–81.

153 T. owned some or all of the sixteen-volume—not eight-volume as stated in Item 667 of *Lincoln*—1801 edn of *The Works of the Right Honourable Edmund Burke*, in which Burke's speech to the Electors of Bristol occupies pp. 1 to 73 of vol. 4, with the quoted passage on p. 72.

in Prose from 1783 on. Cp. also the familiar expression 'Every dog has his day', echoed in, or echoing, *Hamlet* V i 291–92 (Hamlet speaking): 'Let Hercules himself do what he may, / The cat will mew, and dog will have his day.', as well as the Pope–Broome–Fenton *Odyssey* xxii 41–42: 'Dogs, ye have had your day; ye fear'd no more / *Ulysses* vengeful from the Trojan shore'.

i 516–18. 'I heard no sound where I stood / But the rivulet on from the lawn / Running down to my own dark wood'. Cp. *una selva oscura*, the *dark wood* in which Dante as narrator finds himself in the opening passage of the *Inferno*.[154]

i 533–34. 'Shall I not take care of all that I think, / Yea even of wretched meat and drink'. Cp. *Matthew* vi 31: 'Therefore take no thought, saying, What shall we eat? or, What shall we drink? or, Wherewithal shall we be clothed?'

i 686–87. 'My dream? do I dream of bliss? / I have walked awake with Truth.' Also ii *191*, 'And I wake, my dream is fled'. Cp. the final lines (79–80) of Keats's *Ode to a Nightingale*: 'Was it a vision, or a waking dream? / Fled is that music:—Do I wake or sleep?'

Part II

ii 172–74. 'And a dewy splendour falls / On the little flower that clings / To the turrets and the walls'. For *dewy splendour* Ricks cites *Witch of Atlas* 78: 'Since in that cave a dewy splendour hidden', the poem, he adds, going on to describe 'A lovely lady garmented in light'. But cp. also the opening lines of an early version of Robert Montgomery's *Omnipresence of the Deity* published in, and apparently only in, *The Inspector, and West of England Review*, vol. 1, no. 1 (May 1826), 374: 'It is the cooling hour when flowrets breathe / Their farewell fragrance ere their beauties wreath, / Ere yet parade of hue and perfume close / Their dewy splendour in the night's repose';[155] and Horace Smith's *Hymn to the Flowers* (1832), stanza

---

154 For edns of Dante owned by T. and his father, see note 24.
155 The two-page passage, on pp. 374–75, totals 104 lines, followed by '[to be continued]'. The complete poem as first published in 1828 preserves only a handful of these lines, nearly all of which were partially rewritten.

ix of which T. may also have had in mind: 'Floral Apostles! that, in dewy splendour, / "Weep without woe, and blush without a crime," / Oh! may I deeply learn, and ne'er surrender / Your lore sublime!'[156]

ii 213–14. 'And on my heavy eyelids / My anguish hangs like shame.' Shatto (p. 207) cites Hood's *The Dream of Eugene Aram, The Murderer* (1831) 145–48: 'All night I lay in agony, / In anguish dark and deep; / My fever'd eyes I dared not close / But stared aghast at Sleep.' But for *my heavy eyelids*, cp. the earliest (of many) and most familiar instance of the phrase, in the opening lines of Shakespeare's *Sonnet 61*: 'Is it thy wil, thy Image should keepe open / My heauy eielids to the weary night?'

ii 221–22. 'Would the happy spirit descend, / From the realms of light and song'. Cp. Robert Craggs, Lord Nugent's translation of Schiller's *Die Theilung der Erde* as *The Parting of the Earth* (1846), stanza viii: '"List, then," said Jove, "the Earth is others' fee, — / "The Pasture, Forest, Mart, no more are mine. / "But, in my Heaven would'st Thou abide with Me, / "Mount, son! — the realms of light and song are thine."'

317 The Letters (*wr* c. 1853–55)

2. 'A black yew gloomed the stagnant air'. For the latter phrase Ricks cites *Revolt of Islam* IX xxxii 7, 'Peopling with golden dreams the stagnant air'. But cp. also Blackmore's *King Arthur* I vi 466–67: 'So black the Shade, so thick the stagnant Air, / That no reviving Sunbeams enter'd there.'; and Byron's *Darkness* 80: 'The winds were wither'd in the stagnant air'.

28. 'But in my words were seeds of fire.' For the latter phrase, cp. Dryden's *Annus Mirabilis* ccxvii 1–2, on the Great Fire of London: 'In this deep quiet, from what scource [sic] unknown, / Those seeds of Fire their fatal Birth disclose'; Watts's *Hymn of Praise for three great Salvations* (1706), *1. From the Spanish Invasion, 1588*, stanza vii: 'Beneath the Senate and the Throne / Engines of Hellish Thunder lay, / There the dark Seeds of Fire were sown / To spring a Bright, but dismal Day.'; and Thompson's *Sickness* ii 496–98: 'As when the flinty seeds of fire embrace / Some fit materials, stubble, furze, or straw, / The crackling blaze ascends'.

---

156 First published in *The New Monthly Magazine* vol. 35, no. 143 (1 Nov. 1832), 421–22.

324* Tithonus (*wr* 1833)

2. 'The vapours weep their burthen to the ground'. See the commentary above (p. 109) on line 2 ('The vapours weep their substance to the ground') of T.'s poem *Tithon*, an earlier or alternate version of *Tithonus*.

55. 'Changed with thy mystic change'. Cp. Rev. Moses Browne's *Piscatory Eclogues* (1729), IV. *The Sea Swains*, 109–12: 'And thou, O Glaucus! now a God confess'd, / Ador'd, and of Divinity possess'd, / What wond'rous Herbs thy mystic Change began, / And form'd the dread Immortal of the Man!'; and, in Samuel Boyse's *Deity. A Poem.* (1739), subsection vi, *Omnipotence* 437–38: 'Yet juster thought the mystic change pursues, / And with delight Almighty Wisdom views!'

61–62. 'Whispering I knew not what of wild and sweet, / Like that strange song I heard Apollo sing'. Cp. *Childe Harold* III lxxix 1–2: 'This breathed itself to life in Julie, *this* / Invested her with all that's wild and sweet'; Keats, *I stood tip-toe* (1817) 155: 'And garlands woven of flowers wild, and sweet'; and *Prometheus Unbound* II i 185–87: 'While our music, wild and sweet, / Mocks thy gently falling feet, / Child of Ocean!'

66–67. 'Coldly thy rosy shadows bathe me, cold / Are all thy lights, and cold my wrinkled feet'. See the commentary above (p. 110) on lines 56–57 of *Tithon*, to which these lines are identical.

329 Ode Sung at the Opening of the International Exhibition (*wr* Oct.–Nov. 1861)

10. 'The world-compelling plan was thine, –'. In this paean to the late Prince Albert and the exhibition he had envisaged, T. may have borrowed *world-compelling* from another paean, by Lady Emmeline Stuart-Wortley on p. 15 of her *London at Night* (1834), to the great writers, philosophers, and scientists of England's past:

> To something far more precious and divine
> Than columned fane or jewel-fretted shrine—
> In wondrous Shakspeare's long-evanished frame,
> Shakspeare! –illustrious, universal name!
> In Chaucer, Spencer, and each laurelled sage,

> That rose the enlightener of his raptured age;
> In sightless Milton's venerable mould;
> In Locke and Verulam—sublimely bold;
> In world-compelling Newton's aspect old,
> Genius, appear!—and that last name might well
> Break blank Annihilation's deadliest spell!

16. 'Secrets of the sullen mine'. Cp.—by T.'s friend Walter White, signing himself 'W.', in *The Athenaeum* no. 993 (7 Nov. 1846), 1141—*Hope For All* 1–2: 'Hewer in the sullen mine, / Far from day's joy-teeming shine'.

330* Enoch Arden (*wr* Nov. 1861–Apr. 1862)

31–32. 'then would Philip, his blue eyes / All flooded with the helpless wrath of tears, / Shriek out "I hate you, Enoch[.]"' Cp. Chapman's *Iliad* xxiii 350–53: 'and then their Lord had turn'd / The race for him, or given it doubt, if Phœbus had not smit / The scourge out of his hands, and teares of helplesse wrath with it / From forth his eyes to see his horse for want of scourge made slow'.

37. 'But when the dawn of rosy childhood past'. Cp. the anonymous *Tales and Stories for the Young: Adorned with Pictures.* (1846), pp. 123–24, where a poem entitled *Rosy Childhood* begins: 'Joyous dawn of rosy childhood! / Thou art beautiful to see, / The green earth, with its wild-wood, / Hath no flower so sweet as thee'.

38. 'And the new warmth of life's ascending sun'. Cp. Coleridge, *Israel's Lament on the death of the Princess Charlotte of Wales. From the Hebrew of Hyman Hurwitz.*—first published as a pamphlet in 1817 and reprinted, minus five of its fourteen stanzas, in 1836—stanza ii of which in both versions reads: 'Mourn the young Mother, snatch'd away / From Light and Life's ascending Sun! / Mourn for the Babe, Death's voiceless prey, / Earn'd by long pangs and lost ere won.'

89–90. 'When two years after came a boy to be / The rosy idol of her solitudes'. Cp. Moore's *The Fall of Hebe. A Dithyrambic Ode.* (1806) 88–91: 'Or, as in temples of the Paphian shade, / The myrtled votaries of the queen behold / An image of their rosy idol, laid / Upon a diamond shrine!'

91. 'While Enoch was abroad on wrathful seas'. Cp. Horace's *Epode 2*, line 6, *'neque horret iratum mare'*, reading, in William Sewell's *Odes and Epodes of Horace* (1850), p. 152, 'Nor thrills with terror at the wrathful seas'. In *The World Encompass'd* (1628), a popular edition of which was issued by the Hakluyt Society in 1854, Sir Francis Drake speaks of 'the pleasure of God in the violent force of the winds, intollerable workeing of the wrathful seas', and other adverse conditions he encountered on his global voyage.

93. 'Enoch's white horse, and Enoch's ocean-spoil'. For *ocean-spoil*, cp. *Poly-Olbion, The Eighth Song* 229–30: 'The noblest naval crown, upon his palace pitch'd; / As with the *Ocean's* spoil his *Rome* who had enrich'd.'; and, in her *Abdul Medjid: A Lay of the Future. And Other Poems.* (Edinburgh, 1854), H. B. Macdonald's *The Greenlander*, final stanza: 'The winter came, and he pined away, / For his ocean spoil, and the feathery spray; / And with his dreamy eye / Gazing towards that constant star, / Which look'd on his northern home afar, / He laid him down to die.'[157]

101. 'Then came a change, as all things human change.' Cp. the opening lines of Dryden's *MacFlecknoe* (1684): 'All human things are subject to decay, / And, when Fate summons, monarchs must obey'.

128–30. 'So now that shadow of mischance appeared / No graver than as when some little cloud / Cuts off the fiery highway of the sun'. For *shadow of mischance*, cp. Wordsworth's *The Blind Highland Boy* (1803) stanza xix: 'Thus lived he by Loch-Leven's side / Still sounding with the sounding tide, / And heard the billows leap and dance, / Without a shadow of mischance, / Till he was ten years old.'

281–82. 'Cared not to look on any human face, / But turned her own toward the wall and wept.' Cp. *Isaiah* xxxviii 2: 'Then Hezekiah turned his face toward the wall, and prayed unto the LORD'; and xxxviii 4–5: 'Then came the word of the LORD to Isaiah, saying, Go and say to Hezekiah, Thus saith the LORD, the God of David thy father, I have

---

157 T. owned the first edn (Item 1475 in *Lincoln*), with 'From the author' on the fly-leaf. *The Greenlander* had previously been published in the annual miscellany *Friendship's Offering; and Winter's Wreath: A Christmas and New Year's Present for MDCCCXLII* (1842).

heard thy prayer, I have seen thy tears: behold, I will add unto thy days fifteen years.'

300–1. 'And if he come again, vext will he be / To find the precious morning hours were lost.' Cp. the English Puritan Richard Baxter's *A Christian Directory, or, A Body of Practical Divinity* (1673), chap. 17 ('Directions for each particular Member of the Family how to spend every ordinary day of the Week'), which counsels readers to 'Proportion the time of your sleep aright (if it be in your power) that you waste not your precious morning hours sluggishly in your bed'—advice echoed a century later in Lord Chesterfield's letter (no. 179) to his son dated 26 Dec. 1749 (1775): 'If, by chance, your business, or your pleasures, should keep you up till four or five o'clock in the morning, I would advise you, however, to rise exactly at your usual time, that you may not lose the precious morning hours; and that the want of sleep may force you to go to bed earlier the next night.'

538. 'Through many a fair sea-circle, day by day'. In his *The Sisters, Inisfail, and Other Poems* (1861), cp. Aubrey Thomas de Vere's *Semper Eadem* 1–4: 'The moon, freshly risen from the bosom of ocean, / Hangs o'er it suspended, all mournful yet bright; / And a yellow sea-circle with yearning emotion / Swells up as to meet it, and clings to its light.'[158]

556–58. 'So the three, / Set in this Eden of all plenteousness, / Dwelt with eternal summer, ill-content.' Cp. line 9 of Shakespeare's *Sonnet 18* ('Shall I compare thee to a Summers day?'): 'But thy eternall Sommer shall not fade'; and Milton's *Comus* 988–91: 'There eternal Summer dwells, / And West-Winds, with musky wing, / About the cedar'n alleys fling / Nard and Cassia's balmy smells.'

843–46. '["]Ay, ay, I mind him coming down the street; / Held his head high, and cared for no man, he." / Slowly and sadly Enoch answered her; / "His head is low, and no man cares for him."' Cp. *Genesis* xvi 11–12: 'And the angel of the LORD said unto [Hagar], Behold, thou

---

[158] T.'s library had the volume (Item 854 in *Lincoln*), inscribed on its fly-leaf to 'Alfred and Emily Tennyson from Aubrey de Vere Oct. 29/61'. Aubrey de Vere—also known as Aubrey Thomas de Vere—Irish poet and critic (1814–1902), was the son of Sir Aubrey De Vere (1788–1846), Anglo-Irish poet and landowner.

art with child and shalt bear a son, and shalt call his name Ishmael; because the LORD hath heard thy affliction. And he will be a wild man; his hand will be against every man, and every man's hand against him'; and, echoing *Genesis* but closer to home, Dickens, *A Tale of Two Cities* (1859), Book II, chap. 4, Sidney Carton speaking to Charles Darnay: 'Then you shall likewise know why [I have been drinking]. I am a disappointed drudge, sir. I care for no man on earth, and no man on earth cares for me.'

337 Aylmer's Field 1793 (*wr* July 1862–Dec. 1863)

1. 'Dust are our frames; and, gilded dust, our pride'. Cp. Shakespeare's *Richard II*, I i 179 (Thomas Mowbray speaking): 'Men are but gilded loam or painted clay'; and his *Troilus and Cressida* III iii 178–79 (Ulysses speaking): 'And [give] to dust, that is a little gilt, / More laud than gilt o'erdusted.' Also Edward Burnaby Greene's *Friendship: a Satire* (1763), with, on p. 21: 'Shall that fond harlot INT'REST spread her charms, / And win the soul a captive to her arms? / Bid us with transport gilded dust behold, / And pour devotions to the shrine of gold?'; and Browning's *Paracelsus* 827: 'Breath-bubbles, gilded dust!'

5. 'Which at a touch of light, an air of heaven'. Cp. Campbell, *Gertrude of Wyoming; a Pennsylvanian Tale.* (1809) II x 2–4: 'His arms the everlasting aloes threw: / Breath'd but an air of heav'n, and all the grove / As if with instinct living spirit grew'.[159]

16. 'Sprang from the midriff of a prostrate king'. Among other instances of the latter phrase, cp. Congreve's translation of a passage from Homer, *Priam's Lamentation and Petition to Achilles, for the Body of his Son Hector* (1693), 32–33: 'Divine *Achilles*, at your Feet behold / A prostrate King, in Wretchedness grown old'; Gibbon's *Decline and Fall*, vol. 9, chap. 51:

> "My brethren," said Tarik to his surviving companions, "the enemy is before you, the sea is behind; whither would ye fly? Follow your general:

---

[159] The quoted passage is from the third (1810) edn of Campbell's *Gertrude of Wyoming; and Other Poems*, which, with 'Alfred Tennyson' on the fly-leaf, was at Somersby (Item 72 in *Lincoln*).

I am resolved either to lose my life or to trample on the prostrate king of the Romans."

as well as Lynch's *On Seeing Mrs. Kean as Constance in King John* (1848) 13–14: 'And in his scarlet robes arrayed, the haughty legate strode, / As when above the prostrate King, in ancient days he trode.'

20–21. 'Whose eyes from under a pyramidal head / Saw from his windows nothing save his own'. Cp. the description of howling monkeys in Baron Cuvier's *The Animal Kingdom,* vol. 1 (1827) p. 221, where they are said to be 'distinguished by a pyramidal head, the upper jaw of which descend[s] much below the cranium.'[160]

30. 'Than his own shadow in a sickly sun.' For the latter phrase, Ricks cites Crabbe's *Delay Has Danger* (1812) 720: 'And slowly blackened in the sickly sun'.[161] But cp. also, among other instances, Barbauld's *The Invitation* (1773) 25–26: 'And gold and gems with artificial blaze, / Supply the sickly sun's declining rays'; Robinson's *The Lascar* (1800) 1–4: '"Another day, ah! me, a day / Of dreary sorrow is begun! / And still I loath[e] the temper'd ray, / And still I hate the sickly Sun!"; and, by John Struthers, *The Peasant's Death* 19: 'The sickly sun sinks gloomy in the west'.

69. 'Their best and brightest, when they dwelt on hers'. Cp. Shelley's *To Jane: The Invitation* (1822) 1: 'Best and brightest, come away!'; and Moore's air (1827) beginning: 'Oh say, thou best and brightest, / My first love and my last'.

102–3. 'as the music of the moon / Sleeps in the plain eggs of the nightingale.' T. may have had in mind some such work as H. L. Meyer's *Coloured Illustrations of British Birds and Their Eggs* (1844), where, in vol. 2, p. 231, a Rock Pipit's egg is said to be 'of an even tint of greenish grey, much resembling the colour of some of the plain specimens of the nightingale's eggs'.

---

160 T.'s library had the four-volume 1834 Henderson edn of Cuvier's work, translated by H. McMurtrie and with 'F. T. Palgrave, Sep. 1859' inscribed on the title page of vol. 1 (Item 812 in *Lincoln*).
161 In Crabbe's *Poetical Works* (see note 35), *Tales of the Hall. Book XIII. Delay Has Danger.* was in vol. 7.

158. 'A close-set robe of jasmine sown with stars'. Cp. Cowper's *Adam* III i: 'If the celestial tiller, / Who the fair face of Heaven / Has thickly sown with stars'.

159–60. 'This had a rosy sea of gillyflowers / About it'. Cp. Goethe's *Willkommen und Abschied* (1775) iii 5–6, 'Ein rosenfarbnes Frühlingswetter / Umgab das liebliche Gesicht';[162] or, as translated by Alfred Baskerville in *The Poetry of Germany* (1854) under the title *Welcome and Parting*: 'Round thy sweet face a rosy sea / Of vernal bloom shone bright and fair.'[163]

169–70. 'Queenly responsive when the loyal hand / Rose from the clay it worked in as she past'. Cp. Shakespeare's *Sonnet 111* ('O for my sake doe you with fortune chide') 6–7: 'And almost thence my nature is subdu'd / To what it workes in, like the Dyers hand'.

373–75. 'He believed / This filthy marriage-hindering Mammon made / The harlot of the cities'. For the latter phrase, cp. *Amos* vii 17, which begins: 'Therefore thus saith the Lord; Thy wife shall be an harlot in the city, and thy sons and thy daughters shall fall by the sword, and thy land shall be divided by line'.

573–74. 'found the girl / And flung her down upon a couch of fire'. Cp. Blake's *Milton: Book the First*, Plate 18, lines 39–40: 'So spoke Orc when Oothoon & Leutha hoverd over his Couch / Of fire'; and Byron's *A Sketch from Private Life* (1816) 93–94: 'Oh, may thy grave be sleepless as the bed, — / The widow'd couch of fire, that thou hast spread!'

769. 'Is this a time to madden madness then?' Cf. Melville's *The Whale* (London, Oct. 1851; and New York, Nov. 1851, the latter under the title *Moby-Dick; or, The Whale*), chap. 37 ('Sunset'), Ahab speaking: 'They think me mad — Starbuck does; but I'm demoniac, I am madness maddened!'

---

[162] T. owned the five-volume Tétot Frères edn of Goethe's *Sämmtliche Werke* (Paris, 1836) — mistranscribed as 'Sammliche Werke' in *Lincoln* Item 1014 — in which he wrote 'Alfred Tennyson' on the inside front board of vol. 1. *Willkommen und Abschied* is on pp. 11–12 of that volume.

[163] Baskerville's book, with 'Audrey [Hallam's wife] from Father, 1872' inscribed on the fly-leaf, is at *Lincoln* (Item 2646 in the Hallam Tennyson section).

782–83. 'Poor souls, and knew not what they did, but sat / Ignorant'. Cp. *Luke* xxiii 24: 'Then said Jesus, Father, forgive them; for they know not what they do.'

339 A Dedication (*wr* c. 1864)

7. 'As one who feels the immeasurable world'. Cp. Shelley's posthumous fragment *Marenghi* (1824) 142–44: 'Communed with the immeasurable world; / And felt his life beyond his limbs dilated, / Till his mind grew like that it contemplated.'; as well as Carlyle's essay *Jean Paul Friedrich Richter* (1830): 'And when I looked up to the immeasurable world for the Divine *Eye*, it glared on me with an empty, black, bottomless *Eye-socket*'.

8. 'Attain the wise indifference of the wise'. Cp. William Shenstone's *Verses to a Lady. Together With Some Colour'd Patterns of Flowers. October 7, 1736* (1737) 47–50: 'Let serious Triflers, fond of Wealth or Fame, / On Toils, like these, bestow too soft a Name; / Each gentler Art with wise Indiff'rence view, / And scorn one Trifle, millions to pursue'. Both poets express, as does Horace in his Book One, Sixth Epistle, and its Imitation by Pope (also 1737, and perhaps inspiring Shenstone's poem), a core value of Stoicism: indifference to, and equanimity before, the distractions and vicissitudes of the world.

353 The Higher Pantheism (*wr* Dec. 1867)

5. 'Earth, these solid stars, this weight of body and limb'. Cp. *Prometheus Unbound* III ii 2–3 (Apollo speaking): 'Aye, when the strife was ended which made dim / The orb I rule, and shook the solid stars'.

355 Lucretius (*wr* Oct. 1865–Jan. 1868)

225–32. 'To make a truth less harsh, I often grew / Tired of so much within our little life, / Or of so little in our little life – / Poor little life that toddles half an hour / Crowned with a flower or two, and there an end – / And since the noble pleasure seems to fade, / Why should I, beastlike as I find myself, / Not manlike end myself?' For the iterated *little life*, cp., in *The Tempest* IV i 156–58, Prospero's 'We are such stuff / As dreams are made on; and our little life / Is rounded with a sleep.' T.'s lines also less directly suggest passages in two other Shakespeare plays: *Hamlet* III i 55–59 (Hamlet speaking): 'To be, or not to be, that is the question: / Whether 'tis nobler in the mind to suffer / The slings and arrows of outrageous fortune, / Or to take arms against a sea of troubles, / And by opposing, end them.'; and *Macbeth* V v 23–26 (Macbeth speaking): 'Out, out, brief candle! / Life's but a walking shadow, a poor player, / That struts and frets his hour upon the stage, / And then is heard no more.'

251–53. 'and at that hour perhaps / Is not so far when momentary man / Shall seem no more a something to himself'. An early — perhaps the earliest — instance of *momentary man* may be found in Francis Quarles's emblem book *Enchyridion: containing Institutions Divine and Moral* (1640–41), the last of whose first *century* (hundred) of aphorisms ends with that phrase:

> The Birds of the air die to sustain thee; the Beasts of the field die to nourish thee, the Fishes of the sea die to feed thee. Our stomachs are their common Sepulcher. Good God with how many deaths are our poor lives patch't up! how full of death is the miserable life of momentary man!

A later instance of the same phrase occurs in Dryden's *Cleomenes, the Spartan heroe, a tragedy* (1692) IV i 226–28 (Cleomenes's son Cleonidas speaking): 'I wou'd have swopp'd / Youth for old Age, and all my Life behind, / To have been then a momentary Man.'

363 To the Rev. W. H. Brookfield (*wr* c. July 1874)

10. 'Dead of some inward agony — is it so?' As Ricks notes, *inward agony* previously appeared in T.'s *Claribel* (poem 199). But before that, it had done so in several poems by others, including Spenser's *Prosopopoia* 58: 'Hear then my Pain and inward Agony'; Barry Cornwall's *The Last Day of Tippoo Saib* (1820) 40–42: 'And glassy as with death: his lips compressed / Spoke inward agony, yet seem'd he resolute / To die a King.'; and Landon's *The Castilian Nuptials* — first published in *The Literary Gazette for Sept. 28, 1822*, and first collected in 1835 — lines 186–87: 'his face was black / With inward agony'.

367 Prefatory Sonnet to the 'Nineteenth Century' (*wr* c. Feb. 1877)

13–14. 'If any golden harbour be for men / In seas of Death and sunless gulfs of Doubt.' For *seas of Death,* cp. Matthew Arnold's *Tristram and Iseult* (1852), II ('Iseult of Ireland') 97–98: 'Now to sail the seas of Death I leave thee; / One last kiss upon the living shore!'[164]

As for *sunless gulfs of Doubt,* the phrase *sunless gulfs* occurs in many pre-T. poems, but *gulfs of doubt* apparently only once, in an anonymous translation of Alphonse de Lamartine's *Voyage en Orient* (1835) as *Travels in the East, including a Journey in the Holy Land* (Edinburgh, 1839), p. 82: 'Unless a new inspiration shall descend upon our gloomy times, the lyres will remain mute, and man will pass in silence between two gulfs of doubt, without having loved, or prayed, or sung!'

377* Prefatory Poem to My Brother's Sonnets (*wr* 30 June 1879)

2. 'The breakers lash the shores'. Cp. Campbell, *Lord Ullin's Daughter* (1804), which ends: "Twas vain : the loud waves lash'd the shore, / Return or aid preventing; / The waters wild went o'er his child, / And he was left lamenting.';[165] and, with diction more nearly matching T.'s, Charles Dibdin's *William and Jesse* (1808), which begins: 'The whitened breakers lashed the shore / When William did from Jesse part, / And, as the surge heaved more and more, / So swelled with grief her bursting heart.'

3–4. 'The cuckoo of a joyless June / Is calling out of doors'. Cp. John Burroughs's essay *Birds and Birds,* first published in *The Century Magazine* vol. 15 (Jan. 1878), 354–62, section II of which begins: 'Here comes the cuckoo, the solitary, the joyless, enamored of the privacy of his own thoughts'.

---

164 Arnold's *Tristram and Iseult* appeared on pp. 97–143 of *Poems by Matthew Arnold*, second edn (Brown, 1854), a copy of which T. owned (Item 450 in *Lincoln*).

165 T. owned the one-volume (1849) Moxon edn of Campbell's *Poetical Works*, which included *Lord Ullin's Daughter* and in which, on the half-title page, T. wrote 'A. Tennyson, Chapel House' (Item 706 in *Lincoln*).

383 De Profundis (begun 11 Aug. 1852, Hallam Tennyson's birth-date; completed *c.* 1880)

8. 'And nine long months of antenatal gloom'. In Horace Smith's *The Tin Trumpet; or, Heads and Tales, for the Wise and Waggish*, vol. 2 (1836), cp. *Stanzas* i 1–2: 'Life! thou bright flash between the infinitudes / Of posthumous and antenatal gloom'.

9–10. 'With this last moon, this crescent — her dark orb / Touched with earth's light'. Cp. Browning's *Paracelsus* 878: 'And the dark orb which borders the abyss'.

30–31. 'From that true world within the world we see, / Whereof our world is but the bounding shore'. Cp., in Browne of Tavistock's *Britannia's Pastorals. The Second Booke.*, lines 245–46 of *The Second Song*: 'Rapt with their melodie, a thousand more / Run to be wafted from the bounding shore'; and Mickle's *Lusiad* v 25–28: 'Far to the right the restless ocean roared, / Whose bounding surges never keel explored; / If bounding shore, as Reason deems, divide / The vast Atlantic from the Indian tide.'

33–34. 'With this ninth moon, that sends the hidden sun / Down yon dark sea, thou comest, darling boy.' Both *hidden sun* and *dark sea* occur in Byron, the former phrase in his *Siege of Corinth* vi 15–16: 'Whose clouds that day grew doubly dun, / Impervious to the hidden sun'; and the latter in *Don Juan* II (1819) xci 1–2: 'Now overhead a rainbow, bursting through / The scattering clouds, shone, spanning the dark sea'.

40–41. 'this fleshly sign / That thou art thou'. In Shakespeare's *Sonnet 84*, cp. lines 1–2: 'Who is it that sayes most, which can say more, / Then this rich praise, that you alone, are you'; and lines 7–8: 'But he that writes of you, if he can tell, / That you are you, so dignifies his story.'

386 Sir John Oldcastle, Lord Cobham (*pub* 1880)

3. 'I have broke their cage, no gilded one, I trow –'. Prior instances of *gilded cage* occur in Wordsworth's *The Contrast: The Parrot and the Wren* (1827), which begins: 'Within her gilded cage confined, / I saw a dazzling

Belle, / A Parrot of that famous kind / Whose name is NON-PAREIL.'; and in Christina Rossetti's *A Linnet in a Gilded Cage* (1872), which begins: 'A linnet in a gilded cage, — / A linnet on a bough, — / In frosty winter one might doubt / Which bird is luckier now.'

110. 'The Gospel, the Priest's pearl, flung down to swine –'. Cp. *Matthew* vii 6: 'Give not that which is holy unto the dogs, neither cast ye your pearls before swine, lest they trample them under their feet, and turn again and rend you'.[166]

390 Prologue to General Hamley [The Charge of the Heavy Brigade] (*wr* Nov. 1883)

31–32. 'and the stars in heaven / Paled, and the glory grew.' A coincidence, perhaps, but cp. Abram Lent Smith, *The Romaunt of Lady Helen Clyde* (New York, 1882), stanza xxiv of which ends: 'And the great, pure stars in heaven paled beneath her hopeless woe.'

392 Epilogue [The Charge of the Heavy Brigade] (*wr* after Sept. 1883)

73–76. 'The man remains, and whatsoe'er / He wrought of good or brave / Will mould him through the cycle-year / That dawns behind the grave.' Cp. Moir, *Stanzas to the Memory of David Macbeth Moir, Third Son of D. M. Moir, Esq.*, first published in *The Scottish Christian Herald*, vol. 2, no. 60 (22 Feb. 1840), 115–16; and reprinted as *Elegiac Stanzas. To the Memory of D. M. M.* in *The Poetical Works of David Macbeth Moir*, ed. by Thomas Aird (1852), pp. 31–35. The poem ends: 'Hope gives to faith the victory, / And glory dawns beyond the grave!'

394* To Virgil (*wr* c. July-Aug. 1882)

1–2. 'Roman Virgil, thou that singest / Ilion's lofty temples robed in fire'. In Virgil, see, for example, *Aeneid* II 624–25: '*Tum vero omne mihi*

---

166 As discussed below (p. 225), the scriptural phrase *pearls before swine* is also echoed in T.'s *The Last Tournament* 310: 'For I have flung thee pearls and find thee swine.'

visum considere in ignis / Ilium et ex imo verti Neptunia Troia', reading, in Dryden's 1697 translation, 'Troy sunk in flames I saw (nor could prevent), / And Ilium from its old foundations rent'. For *robed in fire*, cp. Shakespeare's *The Winter's Tale* IV iv 29–30 (Florizel speaking): 'the fire-robed god, / Golden Apollo'.

395 The Throstle (*wr* c. Feb. 1889)

1. '"Summer is coming, summer is coming.["]' Echoing the first line of the Middle English lyric that begins: 'Sumer is icumen in / Lhude sing cuccu'—although that line, in modern English, means 'Summer has arrived.'

398* To E. FitzGerald (*wr* June 1883)

3. 'Glance at the wheeling Orb of change'. Ricks notes that *the wheeling orb* previously occurred in the poem *On Golden Evenings* (1827) by T.'s brother Charles (in lines 7–8: 'But when the wheeling orb again / Breaks gorgeous on the view'). But cp. also the phrase's prior occurrence in *Mercury*, the first section of Thomas Carew's *The Masque: Coelum Britannicum* (1634), 44–46: 'In whose vacant rooms / First you succeed ; and of the wheeling Orb / In the most eminent and conspicuous point'.

399 Poets and their Bibliographies (*wr* c. 1883)

9–10. 'If, glancing downward on the kindly sphere / That once had rolled you round and round the Sun'. For *kindly sphere*, cp. stanza ii of Langhorne's *Fable II. The Evening Primrose* from his *Fables of Flora*: 'That far from Envy's lurid eye / The fairest fruits of Genius rear, / Content to see them bloom and die / In Friendship's small but kindly sphere.'

400* The Dead Prophet (*wr* 1882–84)

5–6. 'Dead! / "Is it *he* then brought so low?"' Cp. *Titus Andronicus* III ii 76–78 (Titus speaking): 'Yet I think we are not brought so low, / But that between us we can kill a fly / That comes in likeness of a coal-black

Moor.'; and *Julius Caesar* III i 148 (Antony speaking): 'O mighty Caesar! dost thou lie so low?' Cp. also Browning's *Sordello* (1840) ii 262–63: 'What must his future life be: was he brought / So low, who was so lofty this spring morn?'; and, from a sermon on *Psalm* xxii preached by John Keble and posthumously published in his *Sermons for the Christian Year* (Oxford, 1876), p. 388: 'Here the Almighty One says, "I am altogether dissolved through weakness, I am as water that runneth apace." And why is He brought so low? It is to atone for the many sins which we have committed in abuse of the strength which He has given'.

407 Freedom (*wr* c. 1884)

37–40. 'Men loud against all forms of power – / Unfurnished brows, tempestuous tongues – / Expecting all things in an hour – / Brass mouths and iron lungs!' Cp. William King's satirical and pseudonymous *The Toast, An Epic Poem in Four Books. Written in* Latin *by Frederick Scheffer, Done into* English *by Peregrine O Donald, Esq* (1736), Book 2 of which begins: 'Had I Mouths a whole Hundred, an Hundred loud Tongues, / Or the Voice of the *Warior*, or *Vol*'s Iron Lungs'.

410 The Fleet (*wr* c. April 1885)

7. 'Our own fair isle, the lord of every sea –'. Cp. William Thomas Fitzgerald's *Written for the Anniversary of the Literary Fund, at Freemasons'-Hall, May 2, 1811*,[167] reading, in its near-final lines: 'Thus shall Britannia's Monarch ever be / Renown'd on every Shore, and Lord of every Sea!'

413 Vastness (*wr* c. 1885)

12. 'Craft with a bunch of all-heal in her hand, followed up by her vassal legion of fools'. For the latter phrase, cp. George Etherege's *The Man of Mode; or, Sir Fopling Flutter* (1676) V ii 350 (Mrs. Loveit speaking): 'Legion of Fools, as many Devils take thee!'

---

[167] First published in *The Gentleman's Magazine* vol. 81 (May 1811), 468–69.

415 The Ancient Sage (*wr* 1885)

204. 'I hate the black negation of the bier'. Pre-T. instances of *black negation* occur in Robert Merry's four-hundred-page *The Laurel of Liberty* (1790), one of the several excerpts from which in the Jan. 1791 issue of *The Monthly Review* (Article X, on pp. 56–62) reads in part: '"O better were it ever to be lost / In black Negation's sea, than reach the coast / Where nought appears but prospects dull, and dire["]'; and in Charles Lamb's *Existence, Considered in Itself, No Blessing, From the Latin of Palingenius* (1832) 18–20: "tis the same / With life, which simply must be understood / A black negation, if it be not good.' The phrase also occurs from time to time in clerical literature as a metonym for death, as in William Henderson's *Christianity and Modern Thought: Twelve Lectures* (Ballaarat, 1861), p. 7: 'The grim time-shadows are just all that is hanging over the soul: bare, black negation yawns, a howling abyss, before it.'

417* Locksley Hall Sixty Years After (*wr* 1886)

201–2. 'What are men that He should heed us? cried the king of sacred song; / Insects of an hour, that hourly work their brother insect wrong'. Among other pre-T. instances of *insect(s) of an hour*, cp. William Holloway's *The Suicide. Occasioned by the providential Rescue of a Friend in the Commission of that horrible Act of Desperation.*, published in *European Magazine* 38 (Aug. 1800), 133, lines 39–40: "Tis not for man, the insect of an hour, / To question, or evade, Almighty Pow'r'; and Cottle's *Alfred* xxiii 235–39: '"Arraign the Deity! with critic eye / "Scan all his ways, here of improvements speak, / "There charge with folly.—Insects of an hour! / Before, thus impious, Heaven's eternal King / "You venture to instruct, say who you are!["]'.

420 Demeter and Persephone (*wr* c. May 1887)

45. 'Ascending, pierce the glad and songful air'. Cp. Harriett Stockall's *Malcolm* (1879), which begins: 'How glad and songful is the morning time! / Glad with the radiance of the rising sun, / Songful with birds rejoicing in the prime / Of new, delightful summer time begun.' T. would have been aware of Stockall's poem from having been sent, by its author, the book in which it appeared, her *Poems and Sonnets* (1879) — a volume that also contained a paean to T., entitled *Alfred Tennyson, D.C.L., Poet Laureate*, as, in line 15, 'Great Poet! greater Preacher! greatest Sage!'[168]

57–58. 'and forth again / Among the wail of midnight winds'. Instances of *midnight winds* include, among others, Ambrose Philips's 1709 translation of Virgil's Fourth Pastoral,[169] in which Argol's final speech reads in part: 'O Colinet, how sweet thy Grief to hear! / How does thy Verse subdue the list'ning Ear! / Not half so sweet the midnight Winds, that move / In drousie Murmurs o'er the waving Grove'; Baillie's *De Monfort: A Tragedy* (1806) V v (1st Monk speaking): 'Ay, who knows / What voices mix with the dark midnight winds?';[170] Byron's *Don Juan* IV (1821) xcix 7–8: 'The grass upon my grave will grow as long, / And sigh to midnight winds, but not to song'; and Wordsworth's *Presentiments. Written at Rydal Mount.* (1835) 37–42: 'But who can fathom your intents, / Number their signs or instruments? / A rainbow, a sunbeam, / A subtle smell that Spring unbinds, / Dead pause abrupt of midnight winds, / An echo, or a dream.'

73. 'And fled by many a waste, forlorn of man'. Prior instances of *waste forlorn*, with or without a medial comma, occur in Henry Brooke's *Tasso's Jerusalem, an Epic Poem* (1738) Book II, 628–29: '"Till *Macon* be no more, and waste, forlorn, / "Sad *Asia* like some widow'd Matron mourn["]'; Rev. Henry Rowe's *Sun* (1796) 1–5: 'ANGEL, king of streaming morn; / Cherub, call'd by Heav'n to shine; / T' orient tread the waste forlorn; / Guide aetherial, pow'r divine; / Thou, Lord of all within!'; Hood's *The Desert-Born* (1837) 212–13: 'Oh! slowly, slowly, slowly on, from starry night till morn, / Time flapp'd along, with leaden wings, across that waste forlorn!';[171] and White's initially untitled *The Hermit*

---

168 T. acknowledged its receipt in a note to Stockall dated 10 Sept. 1879: 'I thank you for your volume of Poems and Sonnets. The wreath you have sent me is too big for me to wear, but I thank you for that also none the less.' See Robert Douglas-Fairhurst, 'Introduction,' in *Tennyson Among the Poets*, p. 3n.
169 T. owned the 1748 Tonson and Draper edn of Philips's *Pastorals, Epistles, Odes; and Other Original Poems, with translations from Pindar, Anacreon and Sappho* (Item 1780 in *Lincoln*), in which this pastoral appears.
170 The [1808] Longman edn of Baillie's *De Monfort* 'with remarks by Mrs. Inchbald', was at Somersby (Item 20 in *Lincoln*).
171 *The Desert-Born* was reprinted in vol. 4 of the Moxon edn of Hood's *Works* (see note 69).

of the Dale (1811) 39–42: 'And, till usurp'd his long unquestioned sway, / The solitary bittern wing'd its way, / Indignant rose, on dismal pinions borne, / To find, untrod by man, some waste forlorn'.

424 Happy, The Leper's Bride (*wr* Feb.–Apr. 1888)

35. 'This wall of solid flesh that comes between your soul and mine'. Cp. *Hamlet* I ii 129–30 (Hamlet speaking): 'O that this too too solid flesh would melt, / Thaw, and resolve itself into a dew!'

425* To Mary Boyle (*wr* Spring 1888)

41–43. 'When this bare dome had not begun to gleam / Through youthful curls, / And you were then a lover's fairy dream'. Cp. Thomas Warton's *Verses on Reynolds's Painted Window at New-College* 36–38: 'Ah, spare the weakness of a lover's heart! / Chase not the phantoms of my fairy dream, / Phantoms that shrink at Reason's painful gleam!'

45–48. 'And you, that now are lonely, and with Grief / Sit face to face, / Might find a flickering glimmer of relief / In change of place.' Cp. Polwhele's *Sir Allan; or, The Knight of Expiring Chivalry* (1806) vol. 1, Canto IV, p. 123: 'Alas! how soon that glimmer of relief / From sickly fancy, was immerst in grief.'

59–60. 'So close are we, dear Mary, you and I / To that dim gate.' Cp. Leveson Gower's translation of Goethe's *Faust* (1823), p. 39: 'To view the dark abyss, and not to quake, / Where fancy dooms us to eternal woes, / Through the dim gate our venturous way to take, / Around whose narrow mouth hell's furnace glows'; and Emma Tatham, *The Mother's Vigil*, in the posthumous second edition of her *Dream of Pythagoras, and Other Poems* (1855), p. 39: 'Oh life! thou glad and throbbing heat— / Oh life! thou cup of heavenly sweet! / Past is the dim gate of death, / See, I draw immortal breath.'

65–68. 'To change our dark Queen-city, all her realm / Of sound and smoke, / For his clear heaven, and these few lanes of elm / And whispering oak.' Cp. Faust's speech to Margaret beginning '*Mißhör mich nicht, du holdes Angesicht!'* (in Abraham Hayward's 1833 translation, 'Mistake me not, thou lovely one!') from Goethe's *Faust, Part One* (1808), chap. 19: *'Name ist Schall und Rauch, / umnebelnd Himmelsglut'* (Hayward again: 'Name is sound and smoke, clouding heaven's glow').

426* Far — Far — Away (*wr* c. Aug.–Sept. 1888)

11 and 13. 'From some fair dawn beyond the doors of death' and 'from o'er the gates of Birth'. In Blake's *Jerusalem* (1804), cp. *To the Jews* 63–64: 'Entering thro' the Gates of Birth, / And passing thro' the Gates of Death'.

16–18. 'What charm in words, a charm no words could give? / O dying words, can Music make you live / Far — far — away?' Cp. Shakespeare's *Sonnet 16* ('But wherefore do not you a mightier waie') 9–12: 'So should the lines of life that life repaire / Which this (Times pensel or my pupill pen) / Neither in inward worth nor outward faire / Can make you liue your selfe in eies of men[.]'

427* To the Marquis of Dufferin and Ava (*wr* c. 1888–89)

1–2. 'At times our Britain cannot rest, / At times her steps are swift and rash'. See above (p. 96) the commentary on poem 194, *Hail Briton!* Lines 21–22 of that poem, 'For Britain had an hour of rest; / But now her steps are swift and rash', are an early or alternate version of lines 1–2 of this one.

10–12. 'Your viceregal days / Have added fulness to the phrase / Of "Gauntlet in the velvet glove."' A recognizable if somewhat garbled version of the expression 'iron hand (or fist) in a velvet glove', usually attributed (including by Carlyle) to Napoleon.

27. 'Had never swerved for craft or fear'. Cp. William Shippen's *Faction Display'd* (1704), lines 404–5: '"For how should he, that moves by Craft and Fear, / "Or ever greatly think, or ever greatly dare?["]'; and Algernon Charles Swinburne's late poem *The Armada* (finished July 1888, published in his *Poems and Ballads: Third Series* c. May 1889), VII ii

16–18: 'Greed and fraud, unabashed, unawed, may strive to sting thee at heel in vain: / Craft and fear and mistrust may leer and mourn and murmur and plead and plain: / Thou art thou: and thy sunbright brow is hers that blasted the strength of Spain.'

33. 'But ere he left your fatal shore'. For the latter phrase, cp. Chapman's *Iliad* vii 384–85, 'The bulwark batter'd, thou mayst quite devour it with thy waves, / And cover, with thy fruitless sands, this fatal shore of graves'; Dryden's *Æneis* xi 186–87, 'First for his friends he won the fatal shore, / And sent whole herds of slaughter'd foes before'; Campbell's *Lord Ullin's Daughter* 41–44, 'And still they rowed amidst the roar / Of waters fast prevailing; / Lord Ullin reach'd that fatal shore– / His wrath was chang'd to wailing'; Wordsworth's *Laodamia* (1815) 49–52: '"Supreme of Heroes—bravest, noblest, best! / Thy matchless courage I bewail no more, / That then, when tens of thousands were deprest / By doubt, propelled thee to the fatal shore["]; and *Don Juan* IV xlii 4–6: 'Stern as her sire: "On me," she cried, "let death / Descend — the fault is mine; this fatal shore / He found — but sought not.["]'

431 Merlin and the Gleam (*wr* Aug. 1889)

31. 'The landskip darkened'. Cp. *Paradise Lost* ii 488–91: 'As when from mountain tops the dusky clouds / Ascending, while the north-wind sleeps, o'er-spread / Heav'n's chearful face; the louring element / Scowls o'er the darken'd landskip snow, or shower'.

41–42. 'And dancing of Faeries / In desolate hollows'. Cp. Swinburne's *By the North Sea* (1880) i 9–12: 'Far flickers the flight of the swallows, / Far flutters the weft of the grass / Spun dense over desolate hollows / More pale than the clouds as they pass'.

44–45. 'And rolling of dragons / By warble of water'. Cp. Sir William Jones, *The Seven Fountains, An Eastern Allegory, written in the Year 1767* (1772) 501–6: 'But when he saw the foaming billows rave, / And dragons rolling o'er the fiery wave, / He stopp'd: his guardian caught his lingering hand, / And gently led him o'er the rocky strand; / Soon as he touch'd the bark, the ocean smil'd, / The dragons vanish'd, and the waves were mild.'

441 The Death of Œnone (*wr* Aug. 1889–July 1890)

73. 'There, like a creature frozen to the heart'. Cp. John S. Dwight's *Ride to the Hartz in Winter* (1839), translating Goethe's *Harzreise im Winter* (1789), and specifically lines 12–13, *'Wem aber Unglück / Das Herz zusammenzog'*: 'But whom misfortune / Hath frozen to the heart'.

443 St Telemachus (*wr* c. Aug. 1890)

5. 'The wrathful sunset glared against a cross'. The phrase *wrathful sunset* seems not to have occurred in any pre-T. poems, but does do so twice in Dickens: first in chap. 33 of his historical novel *Barnaby Rudge: A Tale of the Riots of Eighty* (1841):

> At this, the three turned their heads, and saw in the distance—straight in the direction whence they had come—a broad sheet of flame, casting a threatening light upon the clouds, which glimmered as though the conflagration were behind them, and showed like a wrathful sunset.

and again, in *Little Dorrit* (1857), in the first paragraph of Book I, chap. 11: 'The flat expanse of country about Chalons lay a long heavy streak, occasionally made a little ragged by a row of poplar trees, against the wrathful sunset.'

28–29. 'And called arose, and, slowly plunging down / Through that disastrous glory, set his face'. For *disastrous glory*, cp. Robert Montgomery's *The Gospel in Advance of the Age: being A Homily for the Times* (Edinburgh, 1844):

> But as long as the achievements of mere intellect, apart from the purity of heart and life, continue to awaken the ecstasies of literary admiration,— what can we expect but an increasing tendency in the public mind, to consider Talent, or Intellectual Greatness, the noblest adornment of our nature? Hence too, a voracious appetite for a disastrous glory is engendered; and the reading youth of our country are taught to aspire after those mental superiorities, which gain the enthusiastic homage of mankind, without the remotest deference to those qualities of the self-denying heart and the crucified will,—which the Lord of our souls hath Himself approved.[172]

---

172 Quoted from p. 344 of the third edn (1848).

454 Kapiolani (*wr* 1892)

12. 'Through blasted valley and flaring forest in blood-red cataracts down to the sea!' The phrase *blood-red cataracts* previously occurred in *The Mine, the Forest, and the Cordillera*, an unsigned piece in *Blackwood's Edinburgh Magazine* vol. 60, no. 370 (Aug. 1846), 179–93, translating a section of J[ohann]. J[akob]. von Tschudi's recently published *Peru. Reiseskizzen aus den Jahren 1838–1842* [*Peru. Travel Sketches from the Years 1838–1842*]: 'For hours together flash followed flash in uninterrupted succession, painting blood-red cataracts upon the naked precipices; the thunder crashed, the zigzag lightning ran along the ground, leaving long furrows in the scorched grass.'

462* Crossing the Bar (*wr* Oct. 1889)

6. 'Too full for sound and foam'. Cp., by the American poet John Greenleaf Whittier, *The Seeking of the Waterfall* (1878) 15–16: 'Along the rugged slope they clomb, / Their guide a thread of sound and foam.'

11–12. 'And may there be no sadness of farewell, / When I embark'. Cp. Charles Welsh Mason, *Zagala* (1863) — translating a poem by the seventeenth-century Spaniard Juan de Linares, *Chanzoneta No. 189* — stanza ii: '"Yet, before I pass away, / Dost thou share my sorrow, say?" / "Silent grief can deftly tell / All the sadness of Farewell."' — the last phrase, in the original, *el dolor de la partida*.

Idylls of the King

464* The Coming of Arthur (*wr* 1869)

378–80. 'Wave after wave, each mightier than the last, / Till last, a ninth one, gathering half the deep / And full of voices, slowly rose and plunged'. For *full of voices*, cp. Vaughan's *Distraction* (1650) 11–14: 'The world / Is full of voices; Man is call'd, and hurl'd / By each, he answers all, / Knows ev'ry note, and call'; and, two centuries later, Hemans's *To Wordsworth*— first published under the title *To the Author of the Excursion and the Lyrical Ballads*—(1826) 1-4: 'Thine is a strain to read among the hills, / The old and full of voices;–by the source / Of some free stream, whose gladdening presence fills / The solitude with sound'. It may also owe something to Caliban's speech in *The Tempest* III ii 135–40:

> Be not afeard, the isle is full of noises,
> Sounds, and sweet airs, that give delight and hurt not.
> Sometimes a thousand twangling instruments
> Will hum about mine ears; and sometime voices,
> That if I then had wak'd after long sleep,
> Will make me sleep again[.]

465* Gareth and Lynette (*wr* c. 1869–72)

13. 'Linger with vacillating obedience'. One prior instance of the latter phrase may be found on p. 424 of Sir Harford Jones Brydges's 1833 translation, from the Persian of the eighteenth-century poet-scholar Abd-al-Razzaq Beg Donboli, of *The Dynasty of the Kajars*: 'and at the same time orders were given to [Pir Kuly Khan] to send a body of troops, to bring by force, to this side of the Aras, a tribe of the Chabbiyanhu of Karachehdagh, who had passed over into Karabagh, and there pursued the reprehensible path of vacillating obedience.' And another, in E. B. Pusey's *A Course of Sermons on Solemn Subjects* (Oxford, 1845), p. 231:

> Contemplate we them in their contrast with ourselves, how they shewed forth their faith by their deeds, and by works was their faith made perfect, until we be ashamed of our great profession of the purity of our faith, with our laggard steps, our self-indulgence, penurious almsgiving, unsacrificing ease, vacillating obedience, the things of nought upon which we have at some time wasted our energies, the ashes which most of us have, at some time, eaten for bread![173]

130–32. 'And Gareth answered quickly, "Not an hour, / So that ye yield me — I will walk through fire, / Mother, to gain it — your full leave to go.["]' For *walk through fire*, cp. *Isaiah* xliii 2: 'When thou passest through the waters, I will be with thee; and through the rivers, they shall not

---

173 *Lincoln* (Item 1840) reports that T. owned Pusey's *Sermons Preached before the University of Oxford between A. D. 1859 and 1872* (Oxford, 1872), but this sermon was not among them.

overflow thee: when thou walkest through the fire, thou shalt not be burned; neither shall the flame kindle upon thee.'

466* The Marriage of Geraint (*wr* c. 1856–59)

803–4. 'And such a sense might make her long for court / And all its perilous glories'. For the latter phrase, cp. Thomas Noon Talfourd's *Final Memorials of Charles Lamb* (1848), vol. 2, 'Chapter the Last', p. 125:

> The former [circle] possessed the peculiar interest of directly bordering on the scene of political conflict—gathering together the most eloquent leaders of the Whig party, whose eager repose from energetic action spoke of the week's conflict, and in whom the moment's enjoyment derived a peculiar charm from the perilous glories of the struggle which the morrow was to renew'.[174]

Cp. also John Richard Green's *Stray Studies from England and Italy* (1876), where the essay entitled *The Winter Retreat* has, on p. 76: 'The first sign of eve is the signal for dispersion homeward, and it is only from the safe shelter of his own room that the winter patient ventures to gaze on the perilous glories of the sunset.'[175]

815–16. 'That never shadow of mistrust can cross / Between us.'[176] For *shadow of mistrust*, cp. Scott's historical novel *Woodstock, or The Cavalier. A Tale of the Year Sixteen Hundred and Fifty-one.* (1826), chap. 10:

> With manly frankness, and, at the same time, with princely condescension, he requested her, exhausted as she was, to accept of his arm on the way homeward, instead of that of Doctor Rochecliffe; and Alice accepted of his support with modest humility, but without a shadow of mistrust or fear.[177]

---

[174] As Ricks and others have noted, before T. amended it to read 'perilous glories' in the edn of 1873, line 804 had 'dangerous glories'—a phrase that had occurred in, among other works, Cowley's *Davideis* (1656) ii 178: 'That name alone does dangerous glories bring'.

[175] T. owned five of Green's books, including the 1876 Macmillan edn of *Stray Studies* (Item 1059 in *Lincoln*).

[176] The phrase *shadow of mistrust* recurs in T.'s *Geraint and Enid* (poem 467 below), lines 247–49 of that poem reading 'his own false doom, / That shadow of mistrust should never cross / Betwixt them, came upon him, and he sighed'.

[177] T. owned the 1842 Cadell edn of *Woodstock* (Item 1980 in *Lincoln*) and two dozen other Scott novels (see note 140).

467* Geraint and Enid (*wr* c. 1857)

928–29. 'As the south-west that blowing Bala lake / Fills all the sacred Dee.' Echoing the variously numbered Charles Wesley hymn beginning 'Jesus, thou say'st I shall receive' (1762) iii 7–8: 'While Father, Son, and Holy Ghost / Fills all the sacred void.'

468* Balin and Balan (*wr* 1872–74)

77–78. 'Thereafter, when Sir Balin entered hall, / The Lost one Found was greeted as in Heaven'. Cp. the parable of the prodigal son and—less familiarly but here more aptly—brother in *Luke* xv, where verse 32 reads: 'It was meet that we should make merry, and be glad: for this thy brother was dead, and is alive again; and was lost, and is found.'

188–89. 'Being so stately-gentle, would she make / My darkness blackness?' Cp. *Jude* i 13: 'Raging waves of the sea, foaming out their own shame; wandering stars, to whom is reserved the blackness of darkness for ever.' The scriptural phrase *blackness of darkness* recurs in *Moby-Dick* chap. 2 ('The Carpet-Bag'):

> It seemed the great Black Parliament sitting in Tophet. A hundred black faces turned round in their rows to peer; and beyond, a black Angel of Doom was beating a book in a pulpit. It was a negro church; and the preacher's text was about the blackness of darkness, and the weeping and wailing and teeth-gnashing there. Ha, Ishmael, muttered I, backing out, Wretched entertainment at the sign of 'The Trap!'

192. 'In lieu of this rough beast upon my shield'. Cp. *The Rape of Lucrece* 545–46: 'To the rough beast that knows no gentle right, / Nor aught obeys but his foul appetite.'

251–52. 'So loyal scarce is loyal to thyself, / Whom all men rate the king of courtesy.' Cp. *1 Henry IV*, II iv 9–11 (Prince Hal speaking): 'They take it already upon their salvation, that though I be but Prince of Wales, yet I am the king of courtesy'.

312–15. 'Whereout the Demon issued up from Hell. / He marked not this, but blind and deaf to all / Save that chained rage, which ever yelpt within, / Past eastward from the falling sun.' For *chained rage*, cp.

Sylvester's *Henrie the Great (The Fourth of that Name) Late King of France and Navarre; His Tropheis and Tragedy* (1612; repr. 1880 by A. B. Grosart) — translating Pierre Mathieu's panegyric of the French king assassinated two years earlier. Sylvester begins with a dedicatory poem addressed 'To the right honourable William Cecill, Earle of Salisbury', lines 6–10 of which read:

> The rather, sith we first receiv'd from you,
> The speedy Notice (no lesse quick then true)
> Of HENRY's Death through Hell's dis-chained Rage.
> You saw this Sunne, at his High-Noone-shine Set
> In suddaine Clowd of his owne Royall Bloud.

469* Merlin and Vivien (*wr* Feb.–Mar. 1856)

33. '"Here are snakes within the grass["]'. A common expression traceable to *latet anguis in herba* in Virgil's *Eclogues* iii 93.

253. '"And lo, I clothe myself with wisdom["]'. Cp. John Wesley's hymn beginning 'O God, what offering shall I give' (1831) stanza v: 'Send down thy likeness from above, / And let this my adorning be; / Clothe me with wisdom, patience, love, / With lowliness and purity, / Than gold and pearls more precious far, / And brighter than the morning-star.'

381–82. 'I think ye hardly know the tender rhyme / Of "trust me not at all or all in all."'; and 447, '["]So trust me not at all or all in all."' Cp. 1 *Corinthians* xv 28, 'And when all things shall be subdued unto him, then shall the Son also himself be subject unto him that put all things under him, that God may be all in all'. The sacrilegious scriptural echo, for those recognizing it, further conveys the evil of Vivien's efforts to subdue Merlin and subvert Arthur's court.

959. 'Till now the storm, its burst of passion spent'. Cp. Milton, *Samson Agonistes* (1671), line 1758: 'And calm of mind all passion spent'.

470* Lancelot and Elaine (*wr* July 1858–Feb. 1859)

1288–89. 'I swear by truth and knighthood that I gave / No cause, not willingly, for such a love'. Echoing Cassio's far more credible protestation of innocence in *Othello* V ii 299, 'Dear general, I never gave you cause.'[178]

471* The Holy Grail (*wr* Sept. 1868)

318–20. 'This chance of noble deeds will come and go / Unchallenged, while ye follow wandering fires / Lost in the quagmire!' Prior instances of *wandering fires*—usually signifying the planets—include *Paradise Lost* v 177–78, 'And ye five other wand'ring fires that move / In mystic dance not without song'; and Dryden's *The Hind and the Panther* (1687) i 72–75: 'My thoughtless youth was wing'd with vain desires, / My manhood, long misled by wandring fires, / Follow'd false lights; and when their glimps was gone, / My pride struck out new sparkles of her own.'

456. '"Thou hast not lost thyself to save thyself ["]'. Cp. *Matthew* xvi 25: 'For whosoever will save his life shall lose it: and whosoever will lose his life for my sake shall find it.'

901–3. 'Not easily, seeing that the King must guard / That which he rules, and is but as the hind / To whom a space of land is given to plow.' Cp. Pope's *Iliad* x 419–22: 'So distant they, and such the space between, / As when two Teams of Mules divide the green, / (To whom the Hind like shares of Land allows) / When now few furrows part th' approaching ploughs.'

472* Pelleas and Ettarre (*wr* 1869)

390. 'And marred his rest – "A worm within the rose."' Quoting, from Robert Calder Campbell's *Lays From the East* (1831), *There is Sadness in My Heart* iv 1–2: 'There is a worm within the rose though brightly it may shine, / And lightning lurks within the cloud, and earthquake in the mine'.

555–56. '"Yea, but thy name?" "I have many names," he cried: / "I am wrath and shame and hate and evil fame["]'. Cp. *Revelation* xvii 3: 'So he carried me away in the spirit into the wilderness: and I saw a woman sit

---

178 As discussed above (p. 191), Cassio's speech is also echoed in T.'s *The Brook* 96–97.

upon a scarlet coloured beast, full of names of blasphemy, having seven heads and ten horns.' Cp. also, among the many references to gods and devils with *many names* in classical and Christian literature, the *Letter of George Fox to Friends in Holland* (1674): 'And there are many names in the world by which there is no salvation; the beast hath many names, which all the world wondereth after, and receive the beast's mark'.

597. 'And Modred thought, "The time is hard at hand."' As Ricks notes, *Matthew* xxvi 18, 'My time is at hand', has been cited as a source of this line with which *Pelleas and Ettarre* ends. But closer to both T.'s language and the point of the passage is *Revelation* i 3, in the prologue with which the *Book of Revelation* begins: 'Blessed is he that readeth, and they that hear the words of this prophecy, and keep those things which are written therein: for the time is at hand.'

473* The Last Tournament (*wr* Nov. 1870–May 1871)

4 and 242. [Dagonet] 'Danced like a withered leaf before the hall.' Cp. Wordsworth's *Peter Bell* Part II (1819 version) 178, '—A dancing leaf is close behind', and (all versions) 181–85, 'When Peter spies the withered leaf, / It yields no cure to his distress, / "Where there is not a bush or tree, / The very leaves they follow me— / So huge hath been my wickedness!"' For readers recognizing it as such, T.'s echo of Wordsworth's dark poem further darkens the mood of his own.

86. '["]and say his hour is come["]'. As Ricks notes, John D. Rosenberg[179] cites *John* xii 23, 'And Jesus answered them, saying, The hour is come, that the Son of man should be glorified.'; but the Red Knight's grim warning also points to the second sentence of *Revelation* iii 3: 'If therefore thou shalt not watch, I will come on thee as a thief, and thou shalt not know what hour I will come upon thee.' Cp. also *Julius Caesar* V v 17–20 (Brutus speaking): 'The ghost of Caesar hath appear'd to me / Two several times by night; at Sardis once, / And this last night, here in Philippi fields. / I know my hour is come.'

---

179 Rosenberg, *The Fall of Camelot: A Study of Tennyson's "Idylls of the King"* (Cambridge, Mass.: Harvard University Press, 1973), p. 86.

151. 'The sudden trumpet sounded as in a dream'. Another of the idyll's several echoes of the *Book of Revelation*, this one pointing to *Revelation* viii 6–7: 'And the seven angels which had the seven trumpets prepared themselves to sound. The first angel sounded, and there followed hail and fire mingled with blood, and they were cast upon the earth: and the third part of trees was burnt up, and all green grass was burnt up.'

310. 'For I have flung thee pearls and find thee swine.' Cp. once again (as in poem 386, *Sir John Oldcastle, Lord Cobham,* line 110, as discussed on p. 209 above) *Matthew* vii 6: 'Give not that which is holy unto the dogs, neither cast ye your pearls before swine, lest they trample them under their feet, and turn again and rend you.'; also *Don Juan* X (1823) lxxv 6–8: 'and her infant brow / Was bent with grief that Mahomet should resign / A mosque so noble, flung like pearls to swine.'

343–45. 'and grew / So witty that ye played at ducks and drakes / With Arthur's vows on the great lake of fire.' Cp. *Revelation* xx 10: 'And the devil that deceived them was cast into the lake of fire and brimstone, where the beast and the false prophet are, and shall be tormented day and night for ever and ever.'

450–51. 'Sware by the scorpion-worm that twists in hell, / And stings itself to everlasting death'. J. M. Gray (as Ricks notes) cites *Revelation* ix 3, 'As the scorpions of the earth have power', and *Mark* ix 44, 'Where their worm dieth not'.[180] But both verbally and thematically, Eliza Cook's *Melaia* (1838) 202–10 is closer than either:

> Strip off the robes of purple dye,
> Throw all the peacock trappings by,
> And nothing more than man is found;
> And often *less*—some scorpion worm,
> That crawls and stings in human form;
> Some upright brute, whose ruthless might,
> In covert of a regal den,
> Lays waste all mercy, sense, and right;
> Defies a God, and tramples men.

---

180 Gray, *Thro' the Vision of the Night: A Study of Source, Evolution and Structure in Tennyson's Idylls of the King* (Montreal: McGill University Press, 1980), p. 55.

569. 'He [Lancelot] answered, "O my soul, be comforted!["]'. Although, as Ricks notes, Gray (p. 56) cites *Psalm* xvi 2, 'O my soul, thou has said unto the Lord, Thou art my Lord: my goodness extendeth not to thee', T.'s line also evokes *Psalm* lxxvii 2, 'In the day of my trouble I sought the Lord: my sore ran in the night, and ceased not: my soul refused to be comforted'. Both echoes suggest the depth of Lancelot's guilt, and the inadequacy of his prayer.

474* Guinevere (*wr* c. July 1857)

226–27. 'What canst thou know of Kings and Tables Round, / Or what of signs and wonders'. Cp. both *John* iv 48, 'Then said Jesus unto him, Except ye see signs and wonders, ye will not believe'; and *Hebrews* ii 4, 'God also bearing them witness, both with signs and wonders, and with divers miracles, and gifts of the Holy Ghost, according to his own will?'

475* The Passing of Arthur (*wr* 1869)

36. 'And I am blown along a wandering wind'. As Ricks notes, T. (in *Eversley* vol. 5, p. 507) 'compares *Aeneid* vi 740–41, on the fate of the dead: "*aliae panduntur inanes / suspensae ad ventos*"' [Some are hung stretched out to the empty winds]. Pre-T. instances of *wandering wind* itself include Shakespeare's *Pericles, Prince of Tyre* I i 96 (Pericles speaking): 'For vice repeated is like the wand'ring wind'; Shelley, *The Pine Forest of the Cascine Near Pisa* (1824) 109–10: 'Until a wandering wind crept by, / Like an unwelcome thought'; and Hemans, *The Wandering Wind* (1834), with its thrice-repeated line 'The Wind, the wandering Wind!'

265. 'The King is sick, and knows not what he does.' As with line 126 of poem 277, T.'s *The Vision of Sin*, cp. *Luke* xxiii 34: 'Then said Jesus, Father, forgive them; for they know not what they do.'

Alphabetical Index of Tennyson Poems Discussed

The following index lists in alphabetical order the titles of the Tennyson poems discussed in this study (italicized), the number assigned to each by Christopher Ricks in the three-volume second edition of Tennyson's poems (boldfaced), followed by the page of the present volume on which the discussion of each poem occurs or begins. If a poem's title begins with a definite or indefinite article (*The*, *A*) and no prior punctuation (such as *'The*), it is indexed based on the initial letter of its next word. Here as in the text proper, an asterisk immediately following a poem number indicates that the poem appears in both the selected (one-volume) and the complete (three-volume) Ricks editions; the absence of an asterisk, that it appears only in the latter.

Adeline **87**, p. 56
'Among some Nations Fate hath placed too far' **62**, p. 48
Amphion **270**, p. 124
Amy **124**, p. 65
Ancient Sage, The **415**, p. 212
Ante-Chamber, The **207**, p. 98
Anthony and Cleopatra **10**, p. 39
Armageddon **3**, p. 30
Aylmer's Field 1793 **337**, p. 202

Babylon **46**, p. 42
Balin and Balan **468***, p. 221
Blackbird, The **240**, p. 114

Brook, The **313**, p. 190
Burial of Love, The **79**, p. 53

Character, A **88***, p. 57
Chorus, in an Unpublished Drama, Written Very Early **101**, p. 60
Coach of Death, A Fragment, The **4**, p. 35
'Come hither, canst thou tell me if this skull' **50**, p. 44
Coming of Arthur, The **464***, p. 218
Crossing the Bar **462***, p. 218

Daisy, The **311***, p. 189
Day-Dream, The **241***, p. 115
Dead Prophet, The **400***, p. 210
Death of Œnone, The **441**, p. 217
Dedication, A **339**, p. 205
Dell of E—, The **9**, p. 37
Demeter and Persephone **420**, p. 212
De Profundis **383**, p. 208
Devil and the Lady, The **2**, p. 24
'Did not thy roseate lips outvie' **16**, p. 39
Dream of Fair Women, A **173***, p. 90
Dying Man to His Friend, The **51**, p. 45

Early Spring [1833] **200**, p. 97
Edwin Morris or, The Lake **275***, p. 126
Eleänore **161**, p. 78
Enoch Arden **330***, p. 199
Epic [Morte d'Arthur], The **225***, p. 112
Epilogue [The Charge of the Heavy Brigade] **392**, p. 209
Exhortation to the Greeks **48**, p. 44

'Fair is that cottage in its place' **233**, p. 114
Farewell, A **265***, p. 123
Far – Far – Away **426***, p. 215
Fatima **163***, p. 81
Fleet, The **410**, p. 211
Flight, The **259**, p. 122
Fragment [Where is the Giant of the Sun], A **143**, p. 71
Freedom **407**, p. 211

Gardener's Daughter; Or, The Pictures, The **208**, p. 98
Gareth and Lynette **465***, p. 219
Geraint and Enid **467***, p. 221
Golden Year, The **276***, p. 127
Grasshopper, The **99**, p. 60
Guinevere **474***, p. 226

'*Hail Briton!*' **194**, p. 96
Hands All Round! **307**, p. 187
Happy, The Leper's Bride **424**, p. 214
'*Hark! the dogs howl!*' **214**, p. 104
Hero to Leander **95**, p. 60
Hesperides, The **169**, p. 88
Higher Pantheism, The **353**, p. 205
Holy Grail, The **471***, p. 223
Home **61**, p. 48

'*If I were loved, as I desire to be*' **158**, p. 75
'*I loving Freedom for herself*' **238**, p. 114
'*In deep and solemn dreams*' **132**, p. 70
In Memoriam A. H. H. **296***, p. 148
Invasion of Russia by Napoleon Buonaparte, The **58A**, p. 46

Kapiolani **454**, p. 218
Kate **176**, p. 91

Lady Clara Vere de Vere **246**, p. 118
Lady of Shalott, The **159***, p. 75
Lancelot and Elaine **470***, p. 222
Lark, The **64**, p. 49
Last Tournament, The **473***, p. 224
Letters, The **317**, p. 197
Lines on Cambridge of 1830 **140**, p. 70
'*Little bosom not yet cold*' **300**, p. 186
Locksley Hall **271***, p. 124
Locksley Hall Sixty Years After **417***, p. 212
Losing of the Child, The **290**, p. 147
Lotos-Eaters, The **170***, p. 88
Love [Almighty Love!] **47**, p. 43

Love and Duty **279**, p. 132
Lover's Tale, The **153**, p. 73
Lucretius **355**, p. 205

Madeline **75**, p. 50
Margaret **175**, p. 91
Mariana **73***, p. 50
Mariana in the South **160***, p. 77
Marriage of Geraint, The **466***, p. 220
Maud, A Monodrama **316***, p. 192
Memory [Ay me!] **126**, p. 65
Memory [Memory! dear enchanter] **5**, p. 36
Merlin and the Gleam **431**, p. 216
Merlin and Vivien **469***, p. 222
Miller's Daughter, The **162**, p. 81
'My life is full of weary days' **155**, p. 75
'My Rosalind, my Rosalind' **172**, p. 89

Œnone **164***, p. 83
'O wake ere I grow jealous of sweet Sleep' **144**, p. 71
Ode: O Bosky Brook **127**, p. 66
Ode Sung at the Opening of the International Exhibition **329**, p. 198
Ode to Memory **84**, p. 53
'Oh! that 'twere possible' **227***, p. 113
'Oh! ye wild winds, that roar and rave' **45**, p. 42
On a Mourner **216***, p. 106
On Sublimity **26**, p. 39
Outcast, The **55**, p. 45

Palace of Art, The **167***, p. 86
Passing of Arthur, The **475***, p. 226
Pelleas and Ettarre **472***, p. 223
Perdidi Diem **128**, p. 68
'Pierced through with knotted thorns of barren pain' **190**, p. 94
Playfellow Winds **59**, p. 48
Poet, The **91**, p. 58
Poets and their Bibliographies **399**, p. 210
Prefatory Poem to My Brother's Sonnets **377***, p. 207
Prefatory Sonnet to the 'Nineteenth Century' **367**, p. 207

Princess, A Medley, The **286***, p. 133
Progress of Spring, The **193**, p. 95
Prologue to General Hamley [The Charge of the Heavy Brigade] **390**, p. 209

Recollections of the Arabian Nights **83**, p. 53
Remorse **8**, p. 37
Rosalind **171**, p. 89
Ruined Kiln, The **192**, p. 95

Sailor Boy, The **291**, p. 147
Semele **220**, p. 112
Sense and Conscience **130**, p. 69
Sir John Oldcastle, Lord Cobham **386**, p. 208
Song [Who can say] **174**, p. 91
Sonnet [Ah, fade not yet from out the green arcades] **250**, p. 118
Sonnet [Alas! how weary are my human eyes] **185**, p. 94
Sonnet [Could I outwear my present state of woe] **107**, p. 62
Sonnet [How thought you that this thing could captivate?] **255**, p. 119
Sonnet [Shall the hag Evil die with child of Good] **109**, p. 63
Sonnet [The pallid thunderstricken sigh for gain] **110**, p. 65
Sonnet [There are three things which fill my heart with sighs] **151**, p. 72
Sonnet [Though Night hath climbed her peak of highest noon] **108**, p. 63
Sonnet [When that rank heat of evil's tropic day] **146**, p. 72
St Agnes' Eve **212**, p. 104
St Simeon Stylites **210***, p. 104
St Telemachus **443**, p. 217
Suggested by Reading an Article in a Newspaper **308**, p. 187
Supposed Confessions of a Second-Rate Sensitive Mind **78***, p. 51

'*The constant spirit of the world exults*' **145**, p. 71
'*The musky air was mute*' **54A**, p. 45
'*The tenth of April! is it not?*' **263**, p. 123
Third of February, 1852, The **306**, p. 187
Three Sonnets to a Coquette **254**, p. 119
Three Translations of Horace **1A**, p. 17
Throstle, The **395**, p. 210
Timbuctoo **67**, p. 49
Time: An Ode **27**, p. 41
Tiresias **219**, p. 110

Tithon **218***, p. 109
Tithonus **324***, p. 198
To — *, After Reading a Life and Letters* **289**, p. 145
To — *[As when with downcast eyes]* **179**, p. 93
To — *. With the Following Poem [The Palace of Art]* **166***, p. 85
To a Lady Sleeping **106**, p. 61
To E. FitzGerald **398***, p. 210
To E. L., on His Travels in Greece **301***, p. 186
To Mary Boyle **425***, p. 214
To Poesy [O God, make this age great] **63**, p. 49
To Rosa **251**, p. 119
To the Marquis of Dufferin and Ava **427***, p. 215
To the Queen **299***, p. 185
To the Rev. F. D. Maurice **312***, p. 189
To the Rev. W. H. Brookfield **363**, p. 206
To the Vicar of Shiplake **297**, p. 185
To Virgil **394***, p. 209
Translation of Claudian's 'Rape of Proserpine' **1**, p. 18
Two Voices, The **209***, p. 99

Ulysses **217***, p. 107

Vastness **413**, p. 211
Vision of Sin, The **277***, p. 129
Voyage, The **257**, p. 119

Walk at Midnight, The **30**, p. 41
Wanderer, The **285B**, p. 132
'Wherefore, in these dark ages of the Press' **276A**, p. 128
Whispers **215**, p. 105
Will **310***, p. 188
Will Waterproof's Lyrical Monologue **267**, p. 123

Youth **223**, p. 112

Index of Antecedent Writers and Works Discussed

The antecedent works listed below, along with their authors' names (where known) and their dates of first publication, each contain one or more phrases or short passages of two or three to as many as several words that are similar or identical to phrases or passages in one or more Tennyson poems. The latter are identified here, as in the main text, by their Ricks-assigned poem numbers (boldfaced), section numbers if any (in roman numerals), and line numbers (italicized). So, for example, in the first entry, A. B.'s poem *The Seeker*—published or first published in London (since no other place of publication is indicated) in 1822—has been found to contain a phrase or short passage similar or identical to a phrase or short passage in Tennyson's poem number **9** (*The Dell of E—*), line *12* ('And glistening 'neath each lone entangled glade'), a textual parallel discussed, as the entry indicates, on pages 37–38.

'A. B.'
    The Seeker (1822): **9** *12*, pp. 37–38
Acton, Eliza
    Cards of Fortune (1826): **217** *31*, pp. 108–9
Addison, Joseph
    Cato (1712): **277** *151–52*, p. 131; mentioned, **286** iv *272*, p. 140
    Hymn ('How are Thy servants blest, O Lord!') (1712): **214** *15*, p. 105
Aeschylus
    Agamemnon: **159** *96–98*, p. 76
    Prometheus Bound as tr. by M. J. Chapman (1836): **291** *9*, p. 148
Aikin, Anna Lætitia
    see Barbauld, Anna Lætitia

Aikin, John (as 'J. B. A.')
On Approaching My Home After Long Absence (1808): **263** 2, p. 123
Aird, Thomas
The Captive of Fez (1830): **219** 93–95, p. 111
as editor of The Poetical Works of David Macbeth Moir (1852): **392** 73–76, p. 209
Akenside, Mark
Ode IX. To Curio, 1744. (1781): **296** lxxxviii 4, p. 173
Ode XVIII. To the Right Honourable Francis Earl of Huntingdon from his Hymn to the Naiads (1746): **1A** iii 80, p. 18, note 5
Song ('The shape alone let others prize') (1745): **241**, Prologue 3, p. 115
The Pleasures of Imagination (1744): **276A** 11–13, pp. 128–29
To the Cuckoo (1745): **238** 7–8, p. 114
Allnatt, Charles A.
Poverty: A Poem from his Poverty: A Poem. With several others, on various subjects, chiefly Religious and Moral (Shrewsbury, 1801): **67** 103–4, p. 49
Ambrose, Rev. Isaac
Ultima, The Last Things (1650): **3** i 125, p. 33
Ammianus Marcellinus
Res Gestae (fourth century AD) quoted and as tr. by J. C. Rolfe (1940): **4** 121–28, p. 35
Anderson of Carlisle, Robert
Sonnet XIX. To Eliza. from his Poems On Various Subjects (Carlisle, 1798): **26** 8, p. 40
Anonymous
A Scene on Windermere, by 'G. R. C.', in The Mirror of Literature, Amusement, and Instruction (1832): **296** xxxi 11–12, p. 164
A Song Setting Forth the Good Effects of the Spring (wr early fourteenth century; collected by J. Ritson in his Ancient Songs and Ballads, 1829): **179** 5–6, p. 93
All is Vanity. Eccles. i.2, by 'H. G.' (1748): **109** 5, p. 64
Broomeholme Priory, or The Loves of Albert and Agnes. A Poem, In Four Books. (1801): **87** 31–32, pp. 56–57
Fergusson and Burns; or the Poet's Reverie. Part II. (1822), by 'C. B.': **54A** 3–4, p. 45
Ode Written in a Picture-Gallery. 1786., signed 'P.', in R. Polwhele's edn of Poems, Chiefly by Gentlemen of Devonshire and Cornwall (Bath, 1792): **296** lxxxix 27–28, pp. 173–74
Rosy Childhood from Tales and Stories for the Young: Adorned with Pictures. (1846): **330** 37, p. 199
Stanzas to the Lady Jane Grey, at Bradgate from an article signed 'E. H.' (1822): **259** 13, p. 122
'Sumer is icumen in' (first line of the anonymous Middle English lyric): **395** 1, p. 210

The Blasted Swain, from the Dryden–Tonson *Miscellany Poems* (1702): **241**, The Sleeping Palace *1–2*, p. 116

The Mine, the Forest, and the Cordillera (1846): **454** *12*, p. 218

The Modern Gyges. A Tale of Trials. (1829): **161** *49–50*, p. 79

The Noble and Renowned History of Guy Earl of Warwick, by 'G. L.' (Chiswick, 1821): **2** I v *163–64*, p. 29

The Seasons, by 'an American Lady' (1821): **173** *69–70*, pp. 90–91

The Siege of Bhurtpoor, A Poem in Five Cantos, 'By a Subaltern of the Field Army' (Calcutta, 1828): **316** I *1*, p. 192

The Tower and the Ivy, a Tale. Addressed to the Admirers of Shakespeare. (1773): **257** *43–44*, pp. 120–21

The Universal Hallelujah, by 'H. E.', in *The Evangelical Magazine and Missionary Chronicle*, vol. 4 (1826): **51** *5–6*, p. 45

To the Memory of H. K. White, 'By A Lady', in *The Remains of Henry Kirke White* (1808): **286** ii *21–22*, p. 137

To the Morning, not to make Haste, tr. of Ovid's *Elegy XIII* 'By an unknown Hand' (1729): **127** *56*, p. 67

Travels in the East, including a Journey in the Holy Land (Edinburgh, 1839), tr. of A. de Lamartine's *Voyage en Orient* (1835): **367** *13–14*, p. 207

tr. of Pindar's *Ode I* in *Miscellany Poems and Translations By Oxford Hands* (1685): **160** *3*, p. 77

Anster, John
The Times: A Reverie (Edinburgh, 1819): **127** *78*, pp. 67–68

Apollonius Rhodius
see Fawkes, Francis

Aquinas, Thomas
Summa Theologica (1485): **216** *1–2*, p. 106

Archer, Henry Playsted
The Sailor's Grave from his *Emmett, the Irish Patriot, and Other Poems* (Canterbury, 1832): **286** iv *169*, p. 139

Ariosto, Ludovico
see Rose, William Stewart

Aristophanes
see Hickie, William James

Aristotle
praised by Cicero: **164** *66–68*, pp. 83–84
Nicomachean Ethics, tr. by Thomas Taylor (1811): **164** *119–20*, p. 84

Armstrong, John
The Art of Preserving Health (1744): **286** iv *502–3*, p. 141; **296** ix *9–10*, p. 154

Arnold, Matthew
Stanzas from the Grande Chartreuse (1855): **313** *3*, p. 190
Tristram and Iseult (1852): **367** *13–14*, p. 207

Ashmole, Elias
　　The Way to Bliss (1658): **194** 21–22, pp. 96–97
Aston, James and Edward
　　To the Evening Star in their *Pompeii, and Other Poems* (1828): **193** 48–49, p. 95
Atherstone, Edwin
　　A Midsummer Day's Dream (1824): **140** 8–9, p. 70; **310** 18, p. 188
Ausonius
　　see Elton, Sir Charles Abraham
Austin, William
　　Atlas Under Olympus, an heroick poem (1664): **277** 135, p. 131

Bailey, Philip James
　　Festus (second edn, 1845): **296** cxviii 7–9, p. 181
Bailey, Thomas
　　Ireton (1827): **241** 15–16, pp. 116–17
Baillie, Joanna
　　Christopher Columbus (1821): **2** III ii 78, p. 29
　　De Monfort: A Tragedy (1806): **420** 57–58, p. 213
　　Evening (1823): **271** 9, p. 124
　　Hymn on the Seasons (1823): **313** 174–75, p. 192
　　The Legend of Lady Griseld Baillie from her *Metrical Legends of Exalted Character* (1821): **78** 49, p. 52
Bannerman, Anne
　　The Spirit of the Air (1800): **277** 31, pp. 129–30
Barbauld, Anna Lætitia (née Aikin)
　　mentioned: *Preface*, p. 13
　　A Summer Evening's Meditation (1773): **207** 51, p. 98; **257** 83, pp. 121–22
　　Epistle to William Wilberforce, Esq. On the Rejection of the Bill for Abolishing the Slave Trade (1791): **209** 10, p. 99
　　Ode to Remorse (1825): **296** xv 16–18, p. 156
　　Ovid to His Wife: Imitated from different Parts of his Tristia (1773): **296** i 10, pp. 150–51
　　The Invitation (1773): **337** 30, p. 203
　　To Mr. C—ge, first published anonymously in 1799, later signed, renamed, and republished as *To Mr. S. T. Coleridge. 1797.* (1825): **257** 54, p. 121; **296** [Epilogue] 117–18, p. 185
　　To Mrs. P——, With some Drawings of Birds and Insects (1773): **16** 25, p. 39
　　Washing-Day (1797): **296** xcvi 2–3, p. 176
Barnes, Barnabe
　　Sonnet 85 of his *Parthenophil and Parthenophe* (1591): **286** ii 292–96, p. 138
Barnes, William
　　mentioned: **296** lviii 6–7, p. 169

Baskerville, Alfred
tr. of Goethe's *Willkommen und Abschied* as *Welcome and Parting*, from his *The Poetry of Germany* (1854): **337** 159–60, p. 204

Baxter, Richard
A Christian Directory, or, A Body of Practical Divinity (1673): **330** 300–1, p. 201

Bayly, Thomas H.
The Last Green Leaf from his *Miniature Lyrics* (Dublin, 1824): **227** 23, p. 113

Beattie, James, and later also Richard Polwhele
The Minstrel; or, the Progress of Genius (1771): **47** 35, p. 44; **190** 32, p. 94; **296** xi 17, pp. 155–56; **312** 41–42, pp. 189–90

Beaumont, Francis
and John Fletcher, *A King and No King* (1619): **209** 219, p. 102
and Philip Massinger, *The Elder Brother* (1637): **176** 18, pp. 92–93

Beaumont, Rev. Joseph
Psyche, or, Loves mysterie in XX. canto's: displaying the intercourse betwixt Christ and the soule. (1648): **1** 1, p. 18; **110** 4–6, p. 65; **216** 26, p. 107; **286** [Prologue] 36, p. 133

Beckford of Somerley, William
A Descriptive Account of the Island of Jamaica (1790): **84** 65–66, pp. 55–56

Behn, Aphra
A Thousand Martyrs (1688): **296** [Prologue] 41, p. 149
On the Honourable Sir Francis Fane, on his Play called the Sacrifice (1697): **296** lxxxviii 4, p. 173

Betham, Mary Matilda
Translation [from Metastasio's *Cantata Dello Stesso*] from her *Elegies and Other Small Poems* (Ipswich, 1797): **167** 69, p. 87

Bethune, Rev. John
Hymns of the Church-yard—II (1840): **296** cviii 4, p. 180

Betterton, Thomas
'character' of *The Wife of Bath* from a 'modernis'd' version, by several hands, of *The Canterbury Tales* (Dublin, 1742): **159** 56, p. 75

Bickerstaff, Isaac, *pseud.*
see Swift, Jonathan

Bickersteth, Edward Henry
Caesar's Invasion of Britain (1846): **296** xc 7–8, p. 175
Hymn 304 from his edn of *Christian Psalmody, A Collection of Above 700 Psalms, Hymns, and Spiritual Songs* (1833): **276** 57, pp. 127–28

Bingham, Rev. Peregrine
The Pains of Memory (1811): **10** 5, p. 39; **277** 43, p. 130

Blackmore, Sir Richard
mentioned: *Preface*, p. 13
A Paraphrase On The Book of Job (1700): **3** i 39, p. 32

Creation: A Philosophical Poem (1712): **271** 153, p. 126

King Arthur: An Heroick Poem in Twelve Books (1697): **1** 64, p. 22; **296** xxvii 2, p. 161; **317** 2, p. 197

Prince Arthur (1695): **1** 60, p. 22; **3** i 2–4, p. 30; **3** i 83–84, p. 32; **62** 11–12, p. 48

Blair, Robert

The Grave (1743): **160** 44, p. 77; **241**, Prologue 3, p. 115

Blake, William

mentioned: *Preface*, p. 12

A Poison Tree from *Songs of Experience* (1794): **164** 230, p. 85

Ah! Sun-flower from *Songs of Experience*: **91** 1–2, pp. 58–59

All Religions Are One (1788): **3** i 1, p. 30; **185** 11–12, p. 94

Jerusalem, The Emanation of the Giant Albion (1804–20): **1** 74, p. 23

Milton (1808): **3** i 1, p. 30; **107** 1, p. 62; **337** 573–74, p. 204

The [First]Book of Urizen (1794): **161** 29–30, p. 79

The Keys of the Gates from *The Gates of Paradise* (c. 1810): **209** 10, p. 99

To the Jews from *Jerusalem*: **426** 11 and 13, p. 215

Visions of the Daughters of Albion (1793): **171** 32, p. 89

Bloomfield, Robert

mentioned: **143** 10, p. 71

The Broken Crutch. A Tale. from his *Wild Flowers; or, Pastoral and Local Poetry* (1806): **289** 29–32, p. 146

Booker, Rev. Luke

The Snowdrop (1789): **124** 18, p. 65

Boswell, Sir Alexander

The Soldier-Laddie: **286** [Prologue] 85–86, p. 133

Boswell, James

mentioned: **296** lxxxv 25, pp. 171–72, note 128

Botta, Anne Charlotte Lynch

see Lynch, Anne C[harlotte].

Bowles, William Lisle

Bereavement (1789): **173** 13–16, p. 90

Hope (1789): **132** 43, p. 70

Sonnet ('O Harmony! thou tenderest nurse of pain') (1797): **296** lxxxviii 4, p. 173

St. Michael's Mount (1803): **296** cvii 13–14, p. 179

The Spirit of Discovery: or, the Conquest of Ocean (1804): **296** cxxii 1–4, p. 182

Bowring, Sir John

Fourth Week. Winter. Sunday Morning. from his *Matins and Vespers with Hymns and Occasional Devotional Pieces* (1823): **130** 79, pp. 69–70

Boyd, Rev. Henry

The Temple of Vesta, a Dramatic Poem from his *Poems, Chiefly Dramatic and Lyric* (Dublin, 1793): **316** i 48, p. 194

tr. of Dante's *Inferno* xxix (1802): **296** lviii *9–10*, p. 169
tr. of Dante's *Purgatorio* xxiii (1802): **286** vi ∧ vii *7*, p. 144
tr. of Dante's *Paradiso* xxvi (1802): **161** *130–31*, p. 80
tr. of *Petrarch's Trionfi* as *The Triumph of Chastity* (1806): **130** *79*, pp. 69–70

Boys, John
Æneas his descent into Hell as it is inimitably described by the prince of poets in the sixth of his Æneis (1661): **296** xviii *5–7*, pp. 157–58

Boyse, Samuel
Cambuscan, or the Squire's Tale (1741), completed by Joseph Sterling: **87** *31–32*, pp. 56–57
Deity. A Poem. (1739): **324** *55*, p. 198
Gamelyn: or The Cook's Tale (1741), after Chaucer: **296** xi *11–12*, p. 155

Bradstreet, Robert
The Sabine Farm (1810): **296** xi *11–12*, p. 155
tr. of Statius's *Villa Tiburtina Manlii Vopisci* (1810): **313** *59–62*, p. 191

Bree, John
Saint Herbert's Isle: A Legendary Poem (1832): **164** *205–8*, p. 84

Bright, John
Palmyra (1822): **153** i *58*, p. 73

Brontë, Charlotte (as 'Currer Bell')
The Teacher's Monologue (1846): **296** xx *19–20*, p. 159
Villette (1853): **316** i *151*, p. 195

Brontë, Emily (as 'Ellis Bell')
Honour's Martyr (1846): **289** *29–32*, pp. 146–47

Brooke, Henry
Tasso's Jerusalem, an Epic Poem (1738): **420** *73*, p. 213

Broome, William
To Belinda at the Bath from *A Collection of Select Epigrams* […] *by the most eminent hands*, ed. John. Hackett (1757): **169** *75*, p. 88
see also Alexander Pope for instances of the Pope–Broome–Fenton *Odyssey*

Brown, Charles Brockden
Wieland; or The Transformation: An American Tale (New York, 1798; London, 1822): **3** ii *52–54*, p. 34

Browne, Mary Ann
I Speak Not of Beauty from her *Mont Blanc, and Other Poems* (1827): **78** (title), p. 51

Browne, Rev. Moses
Piscatory Eclogues (1729): **64** *4*, p. 49; **324** *55*, p. 198

Browne of Tavistock, William
The First Song from his *Britannia's Pastorals. The Second Booke* (1616): **296** lxxxix *29–30*, p. 174; **383** *30–31*, p. 208

Browning, Robert
    his comment on T. quoted: *Preface*, p. 10
    Old Pictures in Florence (1855), mis-quoted and mis-cited by Collins: **286** v 253–54, p. 142
    Paracelsus (1835): **259** 11, p. 122; **337** 1, p. 202; **383** 9–10, p. 208
    Pippa Passes (1841): **316** i 5, p. 193
    Sordello (1840): **400** 5–6, pp. 210–11

Bruni, Leonardo
    see Scott, James

Bryant, William Cullen
    Thanatopsis (1821): **296** xxxv 1–2, p. 165

Brydges, Sir Harford Jones
    tr. from the Persian of *The Dynasty of the Kajars* (1833): **465** 13, p. 219

Bulwer-Lytton, Edward
    disparages T. and his poetry in *The New Timon. A Romance of London* (Colburn, 1846): *Preface*, p. 2
    King Arthur (1849): **308** 41–42, pp. 187–88

Bunyan, John
    Upon the Lark and the Fowler (1686): **296** xvi 9–10, p. 156

Burke, Edmund
    misquoted by Robert Carruthers: **87** 26–27, p. 56
    Speech to the Electors of Bristol (1780) from *The Works of the Right Honourable Edmund Burke* (1801), which edn T. owned; also repr. in Vicesimus Knox's *Elegant Extracts: or, Useful and Entertaining Passages in Prose* (1783 and later edns): **316** i 402–4, pp. 195–96

Burns, Robert
    Lament of Mary, Queen of Scots (1791): **296** xxxv 1–2, p. 165
    Liberty.—A Fragment (1816): **217** 31, p. 108
    Song V. Again rejoicing nature sees, also known as *Composed in Spring* (1786): **170** 6, p. 88
    Song—My Peggy's Charms (1787): **47** 31, p. 43

Burroughs, John
    Birds and Birds (1878): **377** 3–4, p. 207

Burton, Robert
    The Anatomy of Melancholy (1621): **1** 49, p. 21; **296** xx 1–2, p. 158

Bury, Catherine Maria (née Dawson), Countess of Charleville
    La Pucelle; or, The Maid of Orleans (1796): **217** 1, p. 107

Byron, George Gordon, Lord
    mentioned by T.: *Preface*, p. 5; as canonical author, *Preface*, p. 12; **3** i 2–4, p. 30; **3** i 87–88, p. 33; **286** iv 531–32, p. 141
    A Sketch from Private Life (1816): **337** 573–74, p. 204
    A Very Mournful Ballad on the Siege and Conquest of Alhama (1818): **1A** iii 80, p. 18, note 5

Childe Harold's Pilgrimage (1812 to 1818): **1A** iii *83–85*, p. 18; **10** *5*, p. 39; **62** *11–12*, p. 48; cited by Ricks, **67** *140–42*, pp. 49–50; **153** i *6*, p. 73; **161** *11–12*, p. 78; **170** *6*, p. 88; **271** *106*, p. 125; **289** *29–32*, p. 145; **296** lxxxvi *11*, p. 172; **324** *61–62*, p. 198

Darkness (1816): **170** *62*, p. 88; **317** *2*, p. 197

Don Juan (1819 to 1824): **383** *33–34*, p. 208; **420** *57–58*, p. 212; **427** *33*, p. 216; **473** *310*, p. 225

Heaven and Earth: A Mystery (1823): **2** I i *7–8*, p. 24

Lara, A Tale (1814): **58A** *75*, pp. 47–48; **296** xi *11–12*, p. 155

Lines inscribed upon a Cup formed from a Skull (1814): **296** lxxxii *1–4*, p. 171

Mazeppa (1819): **132** *43*, p. 70; **170** *128*, p. 89

Oh! Snatch'd Away (1815): **296** [Epilogue] *117–18*, p. 185

Sardanapalus, A Tragedy (1821): **218** *56–57*, p. 110

The Bride of Abydos (1813): cited by Ricks and others, **296** xi *19–20*, p. 156

The Corsair (1814): **209** *266*, p. 102

The Giaour (1813): **84** *1–4*, pp. 53–54; **312** *21–22*, p. 189

The Prisoner of Chillon (1816): **286** [Prologue] *9*, p. 133

The Siege of Corinth (1816): **286** vi *65*, p. 143; **383** *33–34*, p. 208

There's Not a Joy (1815): cited by A. C. Bradley, **296** iv *11*, p. 152

Translation From Horace from *Hours of Idleness* (1807): **1A** iii *5*, pp. 17–18

Cameron, David
Friendship. Written in Autumn from his *Poems* (Glasgow, 1815): **218** *2*, p. 109

Cameron, William
Lyric Odes II.2 from his *Poems on Various Subjects* (Edinburgh, 1780): **51** *5–6*, p. 45

Camões, Luís Vaz de
see Fanshawe, Sir Richard *and* Mickle, William Julius

Campbell, Robert Calder
There is Sadness in My Heart from his *Lays From the East* (1831): **472** *390*, p. 223

Campbell, Thomas
mentioned: *Preface*, p. 12
Gertrude of Wyoming; a Pennsylvanian Tale (1809): **337** *5*, p. 202
Hymn ('When Jordan hushed his waters still') (1795): **58A** *36*, p. 47
Lines on Poland (1831): **296** cxxii *1–4*, p. 182
Lord Ullin's Daughter (1804): **377** *2*, p. 207; **427** *33*, p. 216
Stanzas, Written on Leaving a Scene in Bavaria (1801): **286** ii *87–88*, p. 138
The Pleasures of Hope (1799): **58A** *36*, p. 47; **215** *3*, p. 106; **277** *61*, p. 130

Campion, Thomas
The Lords' Masque (1613): **4** *31–32*, p. 35

Carew, Thomas
Mercury from *The Masque: Coelum Britannicum* (1634): **398** *3*, p. 210

Carey, David
    To the Aurora Borealis (1807): **67** 140–42, pp. 49–50

Carlyle, Thomas
    mentioned: **427** 10–12, p. 215
    subject of an anonymous essay in *The Quarterly Review* (1840): **316** i 11, p. 194
    Jean Paul Friedrich Richter (1830): **339** 7, p. 205
    Signs of the Times (1829): **296** cxxv 14, p. 183
    The French Revolution (1837): cited by Ricks, **296** lxx 5, p. 170
    tr. of Part I of Goethe's *Faust* as *Faust's Curse* (1822): **296** iii 12, p. 151\

Carne, John
    Carne's Eastern Letters (1826) as repr. in *Extracts from The Works of Travellers, Illustrative of Various Passages in Holy Scripture*, ed. by M. F. Maude (1841): **310** 15–17, p. 188

Carrington, N[icholas]. T[oms].
    The Gamester (1827): **257** 51–52, p. 121
    Written on the Last Night of the Year 1819 (1820): **286** i 9–10, p. 135

Carruthers, Robert
    misquotes Edmund Burke in his edn of *The Poetry of Milton's Prose* (1827): **87** 26–27, p. 56

Cary, Rev. H[enry]. F[rancis].
    The Vision; or, Hell, Purgatory, and Paradise, of Dante Alighieri (1814): **9** 45, p. 38, note 24
    tr. of *Paradiso*: **286** ii 292–96, pp. 138–39
    tr. of *Purgatorio*: **241**, Prologue 6, p. 115; **296** xxi 17–20, p. 160

Catullus, Gaius Valerius
    Carmina 58b: **124** 5, p. 65

Cavendish, Margaret
    'The Foure Principall Figur'd Atomes *make the foure* Elements, *as* Square, Round, Long, *and* Sharpe', from her *Poems and Fancies* (1653): **312** 41–42, pp. 189–90

Chapman, George
    tr. of *Batrachomyomachia* (1624): **73** 63–64, p. 50
    tr. of the *Iliad* (1611): **310** 19, pp. 188–89; **330** 31–32, p. 199; **427** 33, p. 216

Chapman, M[atthew]. J[ames].
    From Job, Chap. III from *Barbadoes, and other Poems* (1833): **296** lxiv 23–24, p. 169
    tr. of Aeschylus, *Prometheus Bound*: **291** 9, p. 148

Chatfield, Paul, M.D.
    see Smith, Horace

Chatterton, Thomas
    Elinoure and Juga (1777), excerpted and anonymously 'modernized' in *The Gentleman's Magazine* (1778): **257** 42, p. 120

The Death of Nicou. An African Eclogue. (1770): **3** i *83–84*, pp. 32–33

see also Samuel Taylor Coleridge's *Monody on the Death of Chatterton* (1790); Thomas Dermody's lines on Chatterton in *The Life of Thomas Dermody* (1806); and Anna Seward's *Chatterton's Poem Charity, Modernised from its Obsolete English* (1803), cited under the names of those authors.

Chaucer, Geoffrey

General Prologue, The Canterbury Tales (1387): **173** *5–8*, p. 90

see also Chaucer as the subject or source of poems by Samuel Boyse, Samuel Daniel, and Richard Wharton, cited under those names.

Chesterfield, Lord

Letter no. 179 to his son (1775): **330** *300–1*, p. 201

Recipient of verse epistle by Robert Craggs, Lord Nugent (1739): **296** xxx *27*, pp. 163–64

Chrysostom, John

Homily 8 on *1 Corinthians* iii 1–3: **88** *1–4*, p. 57

Homily on *Romans* xii 1, as tr. by James Endell Tyler (1849): **299** *8*, pp. 185–86

Cicero, Marcus Tullius

Academica: **164** *66–68*, p. 83

Letter to Atticus quoted: **277** *151–52*, pp. 131–32; as tr. by William Guthrie (1752): **296** [Epilogue] *79–80*, p. 184

Orator section xxiv, quoted and as tr. by Edward Jones (1776): **286** iv *272*, p. 140

Clare, John

March from *The Shepherd's Calendar* (1827): **127** *15*, p. 66

The Approach of Spring (1822): **286** vii *235–37*, p. 145

see also Jacob Jones, Jun., *Sonnet to Clare, the Northamptonshire Peasant-Poet* (1824)

Clark, William George

Gwentavon Ghyll from *A Score of Lyrics* (1849): **313** *135*, p. 192

Claudian (Claudius Claudianus)

see translations cited under Laurence Eusden, J. J. Howard, and Jacob George Strutt

Cochrane, Alexander Baillie

Stanzas to —, in *Heath's Book of Beauty* (1843): **316** i *11*, p. 194

Cole, B[enjamin]. T[homas]. H[olcott].

The Holy Wars. Seatonian Prize Poem (1808): **241**, The Sleeping Palace *15–16*, p. 116

Coleridge, Samuel Taylor

mentioned: *Preface*, p. 12

Dura Navis (1787): **1** *70*, p. 23

Fears in Solitude (1798): **215** *3*, p. 106; **277** *61*, p. 130

France: An Ode (1798): **166** *4*, pp. 85–86

Israel's Lament on the death of the Princess Charlotte of Wales. From the Hebrew of Hyman Hurwitz (1817; rev. 1836): **330** 38, p. 199
   Love (1799): **286** i 12–13, p. 135
   Monody on the Death of Chatterton (1790): **47** 32, p. 43
   Notes on Irving's Ben-Ezra from *The Literary Remains of Samuel Taylor Coleridge*, vol. 3 (1838): **286** ii 71–74, pp. 137–38
   On Receiving an Account that his Only Sister's Death was Inevitable (1791): **84** 30, p. 55
   Reflections on having Left a Place of Retirement (1796): **3** ii 24, p. 34
   Sonnet on La Fayette ('Within his cage the imprison'd Matin Bird') (1794): **132** 43, p. 70
   The Destiny of Nations. A Vision (1817): **3** i 125, p. 33; **246** 47–48, p. 118
   The Rime of the Ancient Mariner (1834 text): **1** 2, p. 19; **257** 51–52, p. 121; **291** 2, p. 147; **296** cxxii 15–16, p. 182
   The Silver Thimble (1796): **161** 11–12, p. 78
   addressed in a poem by Barbauld: **257** 54, p. 121; and **296** [Epilogue] 117–18, p. 185

Collingwood, G[eorge]. L[ewes]. Newnham
   Alfred the Great (1836): **286** ii 7–10, p. 137

Collins, John
   To-Morrow (1804): **159** 56, p. 75

Collins, William
   Ode on the Poetical Character (1746): **1** 27–28, p. 19

Congreve, William
   The Judgment of Paris (1701): **78** 1–2, p. 51
   tr. of the passage in *Iliad* xxiv on *Priam's Lamentation and Petition to Achilles, for the Body of his Son Hector* (1693): **337** 16, p. 202
   tr. of the passage in *Metamorphoses* x on *Orpheus and Euridice* (1717): **193** 90–91, p. 95

Cook, Eliza
   Melaia (1838): **473** 450–51, p. 225

Cornwall, Barry (pen name of Bryan Waller Procter)
   Address to the Ocean (1820): **271** 143, p. 125
   Dramatic Fragment 22 ('Loss of Strength') from his *English Songs: and Other Small Poems* (1832): **159** 102–3, p. 76
   Gyges (1820): **291** 1, p. 147
   Song CLXV. ('Sister, I Cannot Read To-day') from *English Songs*: **286** [Prologue] 222, p. 133
   Stanzas no. 10 ('For not alone with Alpine heights my soul') from *Dramatic Scenes and Other Poems* (1819): **218** 2, p. 109
   The Last Day of Tippoo Saib (1820): **363** 10, p. 206

Corry, John
   Elegy to Maria M. (1797): **64** 4, p. 49

Cottle, Joseph
　Alfred, an Epic Poem (1800): **101** 9–10, 19–20, and 29–30, pp. 60–61; **417** 201–2, p. 212

Cotton, Charles
　Winter (1689): **296** ix 9–10, p. 154
　tr. of Montaigne's *De la Tristesse* as *Of Sorrow* (1685): **296** cviii 2, p. 179

Cowley, Abraham
　Davideis, A Sacred Poem of the Troubles of David (1656): **1** 60, p. 22; **466** 803–4, p. 220, note 174
　Lilium Candidum (1668), Latin poem tr. by Nahum Tate as *White-LILY* (1689): **130** 79, p. 69
　Pyramus and Thisbe (1628): **209** 219, p. 102
　The Plagues of Egypt (1656): cited by Ricks, **219** 93–95, p. 110

Cowper, William
　mentioned: *Preface*, p. 12
　A Fable (1780): **128** 24 and 33, p. 68
　Adam: a sacred drama (1810): **83** 90, p. 53; **296** lii 15, p. 168; **337** 158, p. 204
　Contentment (1779): **217** 11, p. 108
　Expostulation (1782): **296** iii 12, p. 151; **296** cviii 4, p. 180
　On the Death of the Bishop of Ely (1748): **296** xcv 64, p. 176
　On the Receipt of My Mother's Picture Out of Norfolk (1798): **296** lxxvi 1, p. 170
　Private Correspondence of William Cowper, Esq. (Colburn, 1824): **286** iv 546–47, pp. 141–42
　Table Talk (1782): **26** 23, p. 40
　The Nativity (1801): **62** 11–12, p. 48
　The Poet, The Oyster, and Sensitive Plant (1782): **2** I ii 26, p. 26
　The Progress of Error (1782): **246** 47–48, p. 118
　The Task (1785): **176** 18, p. 92; **214** 15, p. 105
　To Mary (1803): **87** 11–13, p. 56
　Truth (1782): **286** ii 292–96, pp. 138–39; **286** vi ∧ vii 2–3, p. 144
　tr. of Antonio Francini's ode on Milton (1791): **296** cxii 15–16, p. 181
　tr. of *Batrachomyomachia* (1791): **73** 63–64, p. 50
　tr. of the *Iliad* (1791): **153** ii 135–37, pp. 74–75; **291** 1, p. 147; **296** ix 3–4, pp. 153–54

Crabbe, Rev. George
　Delay Has Danger (1812): cited by Ricks, **337** 30, p. 203
　Inebriety (1775): **83** 90, p. 53
　Letter X. Clubs and Social Meetings from *The Borough* (1810): **275** 86–88, p. 127
　Sir Eustace Grey (1807): **217** 45, p. 109
　Tale X. The Lover's Journey from *Tales in Verse* (1812): **1** 49, p. 21
　The Village (1783): **296** xliv 1, p. 168

Crashaw, Richard
　The Nightingale's Song from *Music's Duel* (1646): **286** iv 246–48, p. 140

The Tear (1646): **286** vii 235–37, p. 145

To the Same Party [*A Young Gentlewoman*]: *Counsel Concerning Her Choice* (1652): **296** cxxviii 14, p. 184

Creech, Thomas
tr. of Lucretius's *De Rerum Natura* (1682) cited: **214** 10, pp. 104–5, note 67
tr. of Marcus Manilius's *Astronomica* as *The Five Books of M. Manilius* (1700): **296** xvii 1–6, p. 157
tr. (partial) of Virgil's *Fourth Georgick* (1685): **296** ix 3–4, pp. 153–54

Croly, George
Castor and Pollux (1822): **209** 11–12, p. 99
Salathiel: A Story of the Past, the Present, and the Future (1828): **218** 51, pp. 109–10

Cumberland, Richard
Prologue to *The Princess of Parma* (1778): **75** 28–29, p. 51

Cunningham, Allan
The Bride of Allanbay (1825): **296** lxxxix 27–28, p. 174

Cunningham, John
The Contemplatist: A Night Piece (1762): **208** 67, p. 98

Cuvier, Georges, Baron Cuvier
The Animal Kingdom (1827): **337** 20–21, p. 203

Dacre, Charlotte
The Vanity of Hope in *Hours of Solitude: A Collection of Original Poems* (1805): **78** (title), p. 51

Daniel, Samuel
Musophilus (1599): **2** III ii 78, p. 29

Dante Alighieri
mentioned: *Preface*, p. 12
Inferno: **9** 45, p. 38; **107** 13–14, pp. 62–63; **164** 66–68, pp. 83–84; **296** lviii 9–10, p. 169; **316** i 516–18, p. 196
Purgatorio: **209** 67–69, p. 100; **241** 6, p. 115; **286** vi ∧ vii 7, p. 144; **296** xxi 17–20, p. 160
Paradiso: **161** 130–31, p. 80; **286** ii 292–96, pp. 138–39

Dart, John
tr. of Tibullus's *Book III, Elegy III* (1720): **1** 31, p. 20

Darwall, Mary
The Pleasures of Contemplation (1764): **296** xxi 17–20, p. 160

Darwin, Erasmus
mentioned: *Preface*, p. 13
The Botanic Garden (1791): **1** 2, p. 19; **2** I ii 26, pp. 26–27; **30** 29–30, p. 42; **78** 1–2, p. 51; **101** 28, p. 61; **241**, Prologue 3, p. 115; **271** 10, p. 124; **296** xcvii 2–3, p. 176

d'Aulnoy, Madame (Marie-Catherine)
  The history of the Earl of Warwick, sirnam'd the King-maker (1708): **286** i 2, p. 134
Davenant, William
  Gondibert (1651): **164** 230, p. 85; **286** ii 28–29, p. 137
Davenport, Richard Alfred
  Sonnet to Ianthe (1800): **2** I iv 7–8, p. 27
Davenport, Selina
  An Angel's Form and a Devil's Heart (1818): **255** 12, p. 119
Dekker, Thomas
  O Sweet Content (1603): **313** 168–69, p. 192
  The Honest Whore (1630): **166** 5, p. 86
Dermody, Thomas
  A Fragment of Petronius Arbiter, Imitated from *Poems on Various Subjects* (1802): **270** 95, p. 124
  Carrol's Complaint (1800): **233** 5, p. 114
  Ode to Terror (1789): **1** 55, p. 21
  previously unpublished poem on Chatterton excerpted in Raymond's *Life of Thomas Dermody* (1806): **84** 35–36, p. 55
de Vere, Aubrey Thomas
  Semper Eadem from *The Sisters, Inisfail, and Other Poems* (1861): **330** 538, p. 201
De Vere, Sir Aubrey
  Julian the Apostate, A Dramatic Poem (1822): **296** cxxv 15–16, p. 183
  Mary Tudor, an Historical Drama (1847): **296** xxxix 3, pp. 166–67
Diaper, Rev. William
  Eclogue II from *Nereides: or Sea-Eclogues* (1712): **167** 69, p. 87
  Eclogue XIII from the same: **277** 31, p. 129
Dibdin, Charles
  William and Jesse (1808): **377** 2, p. 207
Dickens, Charles
  A Tale of Two Cities (1859): **330** 843–46, pp. 201–2
  Barnaby Rudge: A Tale of the Riots of Eighty (1841): **443** 5, p. 217
  Little Dorrit (1857): **443** 5, p. 217
  Martin Chuzzlewit (1844): cited by Shatto, **316** i 1, p. 192
D'Israeli, Isaac
  An Essay on the Manners and Genius of the Literary Character (1795): **316** i 9, p. 193
  Mejnoun and Leila, The Arabian Petrarch and Laura (1799): **169** 75, p. 88
Doddridge, Rev. Philip
  Hymn ('Interval of grateful shade') from his posthumous *Hymns founded on various texts in the Holy Scriptures* (Salop, 1755): **296** iv 1, pp. 151–52

Dodsley, Robert
  Public Virtue: A Poem in Three Books (Dublin, 1754): **3** i *33–34*, p. 32
Donne, John
  A Funerall Elegie (1611): **190** *32*, pp. 94–95
  A Sermon Preached at the Temple (1661): **210** *7*, p. 104
  A Valediction of Weeping (1633): **286** vi ∧ vii *1*, p. 144
  To M[r]. I[zaak]. W[alton]. (1719): **296** xxi *7–8*, p. 159
Dorset, Mrs. [Catherine Ann Turner]
  To a Friend, Who Asserted that Life Had No Pleasure After Early Youth from *The Peacock at Home; and Other Poems* (1809): **271** *132*, p. 125
Dowland, John
  Eyes and Hearts from his *Second Book of Songs or Ayres* (1600): **4** *31–32*, p. 35
  Humor say what makst thou heere from the same: **296** xix *12*, p. 158
Downey, Thomas
  Pleasures of the Naval Life (1813): **167** *69*, p. 87
Downman, Hugh, M.D.
  Ode, on reading Mr. Hole's Arthur, or The Northern Enchantment (1790): **286** ii *7–10*, p. 137
  Poem LXI ('Let others covet wealth or power') from his *Poems, Sacred to Love and Beauty* (Exeter, 1808): **277** *135*, p. 131
Drake, Sir Francis
  The World Encompass'd (1628), repr. by the Hakluyt Society (1854): **330** *91*, p. 200
Drayton, Michael
  mentioned: *Preface*, p. 13
  Ideas Mirrour (1594), sonnet 53 ('Cleere *Ankor*, on whose siluer-sanded shore'): cited by Collins and by Ricks, **84** *13–14*, p. 54
  Pastoral I: The First Eglogue from his *Pastorals* (1619): **1** *48*, p. 20
  Poly-Olbion (1612): *The Fifth Song*: **296** [Prologue] *41*, p. 149; *The Eighth Song*: **330** *93*, p. 200; *The Ninth Song*: **296** xcvii *19*, p. 177; *The Tenth Song* and *The Fourteenth Song*: **310** *19*, p. 189; *The Fifteenth Song*: **110** *4–6*, p. 65; *The Sixteenth Song*: **2** III ii *78*, p. 29; *The Nineteenth Song*: **257** *45–46*, p. 121
  The Owle (1604): **286** vi *62–63*, p. 143
  To the Virginian Voyage (1606): **161** *11–12*, p. 78
Drummond, William Hamilton
  Bruce's Invasion of Ireland (Dublin, 1826): **219** *93–95*, pp. 110–11
  The Battle of Trafalgar, a Heroic Poem (Belfast, 1806): **3** i *32*, p. 31; **296** cxii *15–16*, p. 181
Dryden, John
  mentioned: *Preface*, p. 12
  Absalom and Achitophel (1681): **296** cxiii *12*, p. 181
  Annus Mirabilis: The Year of Wonders, 1666 (1667): **227** *47–48*, p. 113; **317** *28*, p. 197

Cleomenes, the Spartan heroe, a tragedy (1692): **355** *251–53*, p. 206
Cymon and Iphigenia from his *Fables, Ancient and Modern* (1700): cited by Ricks, **1** *54*, p. 21; **296** i *10*, p. 150
MacFlecknoe (1684): **330** *101*, p. 200
Of the Pythagorean Philosophy. From Ovid's Metamorphoses, Book XV (1700): **170** *116*, pp. 88–89
Palamon and Arcite (1700): cited by Ricks, **241**, The Departure *13*, p. 117; cited by Ricks, **296** xliii *5*, p. 167
The Fire of London from *Annus Mirabilis: The Year of Wonders, 1666* (1667): **227** *47–48*, pp. 113–14; **317** *28*, p. 197
The Hind and the Panther (1687): **471** *318–20*, p. 223
tr. of Horace's *Second Epode* from *Second Miscellany* (1668): **312** *21–22*, p. 189
tr. of Juvenal's *Tenth Satire* (1693): **296** xcvii *2–3*, p. 176
tr. of Virgil's *Æneis* (1697): **1** *27–28*, pp. 19–20, and **1** *54*, p. 21; **27** *67*, p. 41; **91** *1–2*, pp. 58–59; **109** *8–9*, p. 64; **194** *50*, p. 97; **277** *151–52*, p. 131; **296** xv *16–18*, p. 156; **394** *1–2*, pp. 209–10; **427** *33*, p. 216
tr. of Virgil's *Fourth Eclogue* (1716): **240** *3*, pp. 114–15
tr. of Virgil's *Georgic II* (1697): **91** *1–2*, pp. 58–59; **194** *50*, p. 97

du Bartas, Guillaume de Salluste
see Sylvester, Josuah

Duck, Stephen
The Thresher's Labour (1730; rev. 1736): **1** *49*, p. 21

Duckett, William
Grecian Liberty: An Ode (1822): **101** *27*, p. 61

Dunkin, William
tr. of Swift's *Carberiæ Rupes* (1723) as *Carbery Rocks* (1735): **78** *96–97*, p. 52

Dwight, John S.
tr. of Goethe's *Harzreise im Winter* (1789) as *Ride to the Hartz in Winter* (1839): **441** *73*, p. 217

Dwight, Theodore and/or Richard Alsop [presumed author(s)]
Symptoms of the Millennium, in the Year 1801 from *The Echo: With Other Poems* (New York, 1807): **296** xxxv *24*, p. 166

Dyce, Alexander
Select Translations from the Greek of Quintus Smyrnæus (Oxford, 1821): **296** xcviii *12–14*, p. 177

Dyer, John
The Fleece (1757): **214** *15*, p. 105; **271** *37*, pp. 124–25
The Ruins of Rome (1740): **127** *64–65*, p. 67; **163** *34*, p. 83

Edgeworth, Maria
The Knapsack from her *Moral Tales* (1801): **296** xl *1*, p. 167

Edwards, Thomas
L'Envoy from *Narcissus* (1595): **108** *8*, p. 63

Egerton, F[rancis]. S[utherland]., first Earl of Ellesmere
  Boyle Farm. A Poem. (1827): **78** 22, p. 52
Egestorff, G[eorg]. H[einrich]. C.
  tr. from the German of Friedrich Gottlieb Klopstock's *Der Messias* as *Klopstock's Messiah, A Poem in Twenty Cantos*, vol. 1 (Hamburg, 1821; London, 1826): **50** 24, p. 44; **164** 3, p. 83
Elliott, Ebenezer
  Love (1823): **297** 20, p. 185
  To the Wood Anemone (1820): **209** 275–76, p. 102
Elton, Sir Charles Abraham
  mentioned: *Preface*, p. 13
  Elegy VIII (1810), after Propertius: **59** 4–5, p. 48
  Elegy XIV (1810), after Propertius: **1** 64, p. 22
  Roses, From the Latin of Ausonius (1824): **296** cxxx 6–7, p. 184
  The Brothers. A Monody. (1820): **296** lxxxix 29–30, p. 174
  The Duke's Feast (1810): **84** 85–86, p. 56
  tr. of Propertius's *Elegiae III* as *On His Jealousy of A Rival* in his *Specimens of the Classic Poets* [. . .] *translated into English verse* (1814): **296** cviii 2, p. 179.
Emerson, Ralph Waldo
  passage from Plato's *Apology* echoed in his essay *History* (1841): **296** xcvii 34–36, p. 177
  1840 letter to him from Margaret Fuller Ossoli: **316** i *151*, p. 195
Erskine, Ralph
  The Fall of Man from his *Gospel Sonnets* (1726): **286** vii *297*, p. 145
Etherege, George
  The Man of Mode; or, Sir Fopling Flutter (1676): **413** 12, p. 211
Euripides
  his *Hecuba* quoted and in 1697 tr. by John Potter: **106** 2, pp. 61–62
Eusden, Laurence
  Claudian's Court of Venus (1714): **265** 9, p. 123
  To Charles Lord Halifax. Occasioned by Translating into Latin Two Poems by His Lordship and Mr. Stepney (1709): **164** 205–8, p. 84
  tr. of *Alcithöe and her Sisters transform'd to Bats* from Book IV of Ovid's *Metamorphoses* (1717): **193** 90–91, p. 95
  tr. of Pluto's speech to Proserpine from Claudian's *De raptu Proserpinae* (1713): **296** lxxxv 25, p. 172
Evans, Lewis
  The Pleasures of Benevolence (1830): **91** 11–12, p. 59
Everaerts, Jan (as 'Johannes Secundus')
  his *Liber Basiorum* (1541) tr. by Elijah Fenton as *Basium* (1717): **164** 198–201, p. 84

Faber, Frederick William
An Epistle to a Young M. P. from *The Styrian Lake, and Other Poems* (1842): **296** xxi *13–16*, p. 159

Fairfax, Edward
tr. of Tasso's *Gerusalemme Liberata* as *Godfrey of Bulloigne, or, Jerusalem Delivered* (1600): **127** 52, p. 66, and **127** 81, p. 68; **176** 17, p. 92; **241**, The Departure *13*, p. 117

Falconer, William
The Shipwreck (1762): **27** 67, p. 41; **61** 4, p. 48; **241**, The Sleeping Palace *1–2*, p. 116; **296** [Epilogue] *62*, p. 184

Fanshawe, Sir Richard
tr. of Luís Vaz de Camões's *Os Lusiadas* as *The Lusiad, or, Portugals Historicall Poem* (1655): **153** i *298*, p. 74

tr. of Guarini's *Il Pastor Fido* as *The Faithfull Shepherd* (1590): **286** vii *297*, p. 145

Fawcett, Joseph
Change (1798): **285B** *1*, p. 132

Fawkes, Francis
tr. of Grammaticus Musæus's *De Herone et Leandro* as *The Loves of Hero and Leander* (1760): **1** *124*, p. 24

Fenton, Elijah
Basium I (1717): **164** *198–201*, p. 84

see also Jan Everaerts for *Liber Basiorum* and Alexander Pope for instances of the Pope–Broome–Fenton *Odyssey*

Fergusson, Robert
A Saturday's Expedition. In Mock Heroics (1773): **291** *9*, p. 148

Job, Chap. III, Paraphrased (1779): **296** lxiv *23–24*, pp. 169–70

The Town and Country Contrasted (1799): **296** lxxxix *37*, pp. 174–75

see also, by the otherwise anonymous 'C. B.', *Fergusson and Burns; or the Poet's Reverie. Part II.*

Finch, Anne, Countess of Winchilsea
Clarinda's Indifference at Parting with Her Beauty (1713): **151** *14*, p. 72

The Change (1713): **296** ix *7–8*, p. 154

Fitchett, John
Alfred, A Poem, vol. 1 (1808): **227** *40*, p. 113; and, continued and completed by Robert Roscoe, *King Alfred: A Poem* (1841–42): **227** *40*, p. 113; **296** xcv *49–50*, p. 175

Fitzgerald, William Thomas
Written for the Anniversary of the Literary Fund, at Freemasons'-Hall, May 2, 1811 (1811): **410** *7*, p. 211

Flatman, Thomas
On the Death of the Right Honourable Thomas Earl of Ossory. Pindariq' Ode. (1682): **296** xx *1–2*, p. 158

Fletcher, Giles
    Christ's Victorie and Triumph, in Heaven, in Earth, over and after Death (1610): **193** *57–58*, p. 95

Fletcher, John
    Rollo, Duke of Normandy (1639): **296** xix *12*, p. 158
    The Faithful Shepherdess (1609): **286** i *9–10*, p. 135
    and Francis Beaumont, *A King and No King* (1619), **209** *219*, p. 102
    and Philip Massinger, *The Custom of the Country* (1647): **166** *5*, p. 86
    and Philip Massinger, *The False One* (1647): **2** I v *119–20*, p. 28
    and Nathan Field and Philip Massinger, *The Queen of Corinth* (1647): **106** *2*, p. 61

Fletcher, Phineas
    Piscatory Eclogues (new edition, Edinburgh, 1771): **286** ii *87–88*, p. 138
    The Purple Island (1633): **163** *33*, p. 82

Ford, John
    Love's Sacrifice (1633): **159** *96–98*, p. 76

Fox, George
    Letter of George Fox to Friends in Holland: **472** *555–56*, pp. 223–24

Francini, Antonio
    see Cowper, William

Francis, Eliza S.
    Sir Wilibert de Waverley; or, the Bridal Eve (1815): **218** *56–57*, p. 110

Gale, Theophilus
    The Anatomie of Infidelitie, Or, An Explication of the Nature, Causes, Aggravations, and Punishment of Unbelief (1672): **296** cix *9*, p. 180

Garrick, David
    The Lying Valet (1821): **2** I v *119–20*, p. 28

Gay, John
    Dione: A Pastoral Tragedy (1719): **296** xv *16–18*, p. 156
    Epistle II. To the Right Honourable the Earl of Burlington. A Journey to Exeter. 1716. (1729): **296** lxxxix *37*, pp. 174–75
    Trivia; or, the Art of Walking the Streets of London (1716): **296** lxxxix *37*, pp. 174–75
    partial tr. of Ovid's *Metamorphoses* (1717; repr. 1813): **170** *17*, p. 88

Gentleman, Francis
    The Dramatic Censor: or, Critical Companion (1770): **286** iv *272*, p. 140

Gibbon, Edward
    History of the Decline and Fall of the Roman Empire (1776): **277** *151–52*, p. 131; **337** *16*, pp. 202–3
    see also Hayley, William

Gibson, William
    Conscience (1772): **162** *51–52*, p. 81
Giles, William, ed.
    Serious Thoughts on a Late Coronation (1775): **296** xliii *5*, pp. 167–68
Gisborne, Thomas
    mentioned: *Preface*, p. 13
    Conscience (1798): **190** *32*, p. 94
    Consolation: A Lyric Poem (1798): **246** *47–48*, p. 118
    Rothley Temple (1815): **214** *15*, p. 105
    To F. G. On His Birthday. Supposed to be Spoken by Himself. (1813): **193** *98*, p. 96
    Walk the Third. Summer.—Moonlight from *Walks in a Forest, and Other Poems* (1794) **9** *45*, p. 38; cited by Ricks, **286** vi *65*, p. 143
Glover, Richard
    The Atheniad (1787): **250** *1*, p. 118
    The Story of Teribazus and Ariana from *Leonidas* (sixth edn, 1770): **267** *29–30*, p. 123
Goethe, Johann Wolfgang von
    confirmation of T.'s report to a correspondent that Goethe's dying words are echoed in the opening lines of *In Memoriam*: **296** i *1–4*, p. 150
    Faust, Part One: **425** *65–68*, pp. 214–15; tr. by Carlyle as *Faust's Curse* (1822): **296** iii *12*, p. 151
    Harzreise im Winter (1789) tr. by John S. Dwight as *Ride to the Hartz in Winter* (1839): **441** *73*, p. 217
    Willkommen und Abschied (1775) tr. by Alfred Baskerville as *Welcome and Parting* in *The Poetry of Germany* (1854): **337** *159–60*, p. 204
    see also Gower, Lord Francis Leveson (1823) *and* Hayward, Abraham (1833)
Goldsmith, Oliver
    The Deserted Village (1770): **286** iv *246–48*, p. 140
    The Traveller. Or, a Prospect of Society (1764): **84** *1–4*, pp. 53–54; **209** *146*, p. 101
Good, John Mason
    tr. of Lucretius's *De Rerum Natura* as *The Nature of Things: A Didactic Poem* (1805): **214** *10*, p. 104
    tr. of *The Song of Songs* (1803): **241**, The Sleeping Beauty *19*, p. 117
Gower, Lord Francis Leveson
    tr. of Goethe's *Faust* (1823): **425** *59–60*, p. 214
    tr. of Schiller's *Lied von der Glocke* as *Song of the Bell* (1823): **300** *3*, p. 186
Grahame, James
    The Sabbath (Edinburgh, 1804): **73** *43–44*, p. 50
Graves, Richard
    The Rural Retreat from vol. 1 of his *Euphrosyne: or, Amusements on the Road of Life* (1776): **312** *13*, p. 189

Gray, Thomas
    Collins associates T. with Virgil, Tasso, and Gray: *Preface*, p. 7
    Couplet about Birds (1814): cited by Ricks, **16** 25, p. 39
    Elegy Written in a Country Churchyard (1751): cited by Thomas Warton in his 1785 edn of Milton's poems, **78** 83–86, p. 52; cited by Ricks, **296** xxvii 2, pp. 161–62
    Ode on the Pleasure Arising from Vicissitude (1775): **26** 1, p. 39
    The Bard (1757): **217** 1, p. 107
    The Descent of Odin: An Ode (1768): **277** 40, p. 130
    tr. of Statius's *Thebaid* (1775): **219** 93–95, pp. 110–11
    tr. of Tasso's *Gerusalemme Liberata* as *From Tasso* (1814): **1** 124, p. 24

Green, John Richard
    The Winter Retreat from *Stray Studies from England and Italy* (1876): **466** 803–4, p. 220

Greene, Edward Burnaby
    Friendship: a Satire (1763): **337** 1, p. 202

Grenville, George
    Portugal, a Poem, in two Parts (1812): **286** vi 62–63, p. 143

Greville, Fulke
    Life of the Renowned Sr. Philip Sidney (1652): **296** [Epilogue] 79–80, p. 184

Griffin, Bartholomew
    Sonnet 1 ('Fidessa fair! long live a happy maiden!') from *Sonnets to Fidessa* (1596): **145** 9, p. 71

Grinfield, Rev. Thomas
    Jesus Christ, the Comforter of Disquietude from *The Omnipresence of God: with Other Sacred Poems* (Bristol, 1824): **8** 17, p. 37
    Monitory Recollections on a New Year's Day (1824): **215** 3, p. 106
    tr. of *Aeneid vi* (1815): **1** 27–28, p. 19

Guarini, Giovanni Battista
    see Fanshawe, Sir Richard

Guthrie, William
    tr. of Cicero's letter to Atticus, Book XII, Epistle 1 (1752): **296** [Epilogue] 79–80, p. 184

Hall, Joseph
    Elegy on Dr. Whitaker (1596): **108** 8, p. 63

Hallam, Arthur
    On Sympathy (1830) cited by Shatto & Shaw: **296** xxx 22–23, p. 163
    To the Loved One (1834): **289** 29–32, pp. 146–47

Harington, John (as 'I. H.')
    The History of Polindor and Flostella (1657): **241**, The Sleeping Beauty 19, p. 117

Harley, G[eorge]. D[avies].
A Legacy of Love (1796): **209** *143*, p. 101
Harrison, Thomas
Thoughts under Affliction from his *Poems on Divine Subjects* (1719): **296** xliii *5*, p. 167
Harvey, Christopher
Ode 29 (*'The watering of the Heart'*) in his *Schola cordis* (1647): **163** *6*, p. 81
Harvey, John
The Bruciad (1769): **296** lxi *9*, p. 169
Hawthorne, Nathaniel
The Blithedale Romance (1852): **316** i *57*, pp. 194–95
Hayley, William
Epistle II from *An Essay on History; in Three Epistles to Edward Gibbon, Esq.* (1780): **3** i *33–34*, p. 32
Epistle to Mrs. Hannah More from his *Poems on Serious and Sacred Subjects* (Chichester, 1818): **296** xxii *9–12*, p. 160
The Triumphs of Temper (1781): **217** *31*, p. 108; **271** *153*, p. 126
Hayward, Abraham
Goethe's *Faust, Part One* (1808) as tr. by Hayward (1833): **425** *65–68*, pp. 214–15
Hazlitt, William
Essay on Jeremy Bentham from *The Spirit of the Age* (cited below): **176** *18*, pp. 92–93
Essay on William Godwin from *The Spirit of the Age* (cited below): **296** cxxii *17*, p. 183
Lectures on the English Poets (1818): **3** i *2–4*, pp. 30–31
On a Sun-Dial (1827): **143** *10*, p. 71; **212** *7–8*, p. 104
On the Past and Future from *Table-Talk* (1821): **277** *31*, pp. 129–30
On the Qualifications Necessary to Success in Life from *The Plain Speaker: Opinions on Books, Men, and Things* (1826): **300** *3*, p. 186
The Spirit of the Age: or Contemporary Portraits (1825): **176** *18*, pp. 92–93; **194** *167*, p. 97
Heber, Sir Reginald
Morte d'Arthur: A Fragment (1830): **108** *14*, p. 63
Hemans, Felicia Dorothea (née Browne)
mentioned: *Preface*, p. 13
Greek Funeral Chant or Myriologue (1825): **3** i *69–70*, p. 32
Imelda (1825): **164** *215*, pp. 84–85
Italian Girl's Hymn to the Virgin (1829): **259** *11*, p. 122
Juana (1827): **296** lxxxvi *1–2*, p. 172
Modern Greece (1817): **250** *1*, p. 118
Morning (1808): **130** *79*, pp. 69–70

Night-Blowing Flowers (1827): **193** *57–58*, p. 95
Owen Glyndwr's War-Song (1822): **10** *5*, p. 39
Song. Founded on an Arabian Anecdote (1839): **286** vi ∧ vii *7*, p. 144
The Abencerrage (1819): **26** *15*, p. 40; **241**, L'Envoi *41–42*, pp. 117–18; **257** *54*, p. 121; **296** [Prologue] *42*, p. 149; **296** xi *15–16*, p. 155
The Brigand Leader and his Wife (1827): **209** *266*, p. 102
The Bride of the Greek Isle (1825): **259** *11*, p. 122
The Captive Knight (1824): **176** *3*, pp. 91–92
The Charmed Picture (1829): **275** *86–88*, p. 127
The Coronation of Inez de Castro (1828): **296** lxxxvi *1–2*, p. 172
The Forest Sanctuary (1825): **2** III ii *78*, pp. 29–30; **296** [Prologue] *41*, p. 149; **296** lxxxii *1–4*, p. 171; **296** [Epilogue] *117–18*, p. 185
The Indian City (1825): **296** lxxxvi *1–2*, p. 172
The Last Constantine (1823): **296** cxix *3*, p. 182
The Last Song of Sappho (1831): **279** *85–87*, p. 132
The Meeting of the Bards (1822): **277** *32*, p. 130
The Minster (1830): **296** lxxxvi *1–2*, p. 172
The Olive Tree (1834): **241**, The Sleeping Palace *15–16*, p. 116
The Palmer (1830): **296** [Prologue] *42*, p. 149
The Palm-Tree (1827): **193** *57–58*, p. 95
The Peasant Girl of the Rhone (1828): **286** i *18*, p. 136
The Sicilian Captive (1825): **9** *8–9*, p. 37; **153** i *734*, p. 74
The Siege of Valencia (1823): **3** i *69–70*, p. 32; **241**, L'Envoi *41–42*, pp. 117–18; **296** xxxv *1–2*, p. 165
The Sunbeam (1826): **250** *1*, p. 118
The Voice of Spring (1823): **9** *8–9*, p. 37
The Wandering Wind (1834): **475** *36*, p. 226
To My Brother and Sister, in the Country. Written in London. (1808): **160** *44*, p. 77
To the Author of the Excursion and the Lyrical Ballads, later renamed *To Wordsworth* (1826): **464** *378–80*, pp. 218–19

Henderson, William
Christianity and Modern Thought: Twelve Lectures (Ballaarat, 1861): **415** *204*, p. 212

Heracleitus
see Plato, *Cratylus*

Herbert, George
Repentance from *The Temple* (1633): **58A** *47*, p. 47
The Discharge from the same: cited by Collins, **296** [Prologue] *12*, p. 148
The Flower from the same: **146** *8*, p. 72

Herbert, Rev. William
Ode to Despair (1804): **55** *7*, pp. 45–46

Herbert, William, third Earl of Pembroke
  Sonnet ('Dear, when I think upon my first sad fall') (1660): **47** 32, p. 43
Hetherington, William Maxwell
  The Ewe-Bughts from his Twelve Dramatic Sketches Founded on the Pastoral Poetry of Scotland (1829): **267** 29–30, p. 123
Heywood, John
  If you know not me, You know no bodie: Or The troubles of Queene Elizabeth (1605); and The Second Part of, If you know not me, you know no bodie (1606): **217** 5, p. 108
  The Play of the Weather (1533): **5** 49–50, pp. 36–37
Heywood, Thomas
  The Fair Maid of the West (1631): **2** I v 163–64, p. 29
  The Golden Age. Or The liues of Iupiter and Saturne, with the deifying of the heathen gods (1611): **3** i 5–9, p. 31
Hickie, William James
  tr. of Aristophanes's The Wasps (1820): **241** 17, p. 117
Hill, Aaron
  Advice to the Poets (1731): **124** 5, p. 65
  An Ode; on Occasion of Mr. Handel's great Te Deum (1733): **161** 130–31, p. 80
  The Fanciad. An heroic poem. In six cantos. To His Grace the Duke of Marlborough, on the turn of his genius to arms. (1743): **163** 33, p. 82
  To Clio (1753): **143** 10, p. 71
Hodgson, Francis
  Statius to his Wife Claudia. The Fifth of the Sylvae—Book the Third (1809): **286** iv 495, p. 141
  The Friends (1818): **1** 124, p. 24
Hodson, Margaret
  Margaret of Anjou, a Poem in Ten Cantos (1816): **286** i 4, p. 135
Hogan, John
  Blarney; A Descriptive Poem (1842): **296** lxxxix 29–30, p. 174
Hogg, James
  Mador of the Moor (Edinburgh, 1816): **58A** 36, p. 47; **109** 8–9, p. 64
  The Queen's Wake: A Legendary Poem (Edinburgh, 1813): **296** cviii 4, p. 180
  Wat o' the Cleugh (1817): **176** 23–24, p. 93
Hole, Rev. Richard
  Arthur; or, the Northern Enchantment (1789): **209** 343–45, p. 103
  Ode to Terror (1792): **163** 17, p. 82
  see also Hugh Downman, Ode, on reading Mr. Hole's Arthur, or The Northern Enchantment (1790)
Holford, Margaret
  Wallace; or, The Fight of Falkirk; A Metrical Romance (1809): **1** 61–62, p. 22

Hollingsworth, Rev. A[rthur]. G[eorge]. H[arper].
Rebecca; or, the Times of Primitive Christianity (1832): **190** 22, p. 94

Holloway, William
The Suicide. Occasioned by the providential Rescue of a Friend in the Commission of that horrible Act of Desperation. (1800): **417** 201–2, p. 212

Homer
mentioned: *Preface*, pp. 1, 4, 5, 7, 8, 12

Iliad: **1** 54, p. 21; **1** 74, p. 23; **30** 29–30, p. 42; **153** ii 135–37, pp. 74–75; **163** 34, p. 83; **173** 45–47, p. 90; **194** 54, p. 97; **219** 93–95, pp. 110–11; **291** 1, p. 147; **296** iv 11, p. 152; **296** ix 3–4, pp. 153–54; **296** xv 16–18, p. 156; **296** xxvii 2, pp. 161–62; **310** 19, pp. 188–89; **330** 31–32, p. 199; **427** 33, p. 216; **471** 901–3, p. 223

Odyssey: **1** 48, pp. 20–21; **3** i 2–4, pp. 30–31; **30** 29–30, p. 42; **127** 81, p. 68; **214** 10, pp. 104–5; **219** 131–32, p. 111; **241**, L'Envoi 41–42, pp. 117–18; **286** ii 7–10, p. 137; **286** vi 47, p. 143; **296** iv 11, p. 152; **296** xl 1, p. 167; **296** xliv 1, p. 168; **316** i 48, p. 194; **316** i 402–4, pp. 195–96

for translators and translations of some or all of the Iliad *see* George Chapman, William Congreve, William Cowper, and Alexander Pope; *for the* Pope–Broome–Fenton Odyssey, *see* Alexander Pope

Homer, Philip Bracebridge
Observations On a Short Tour Made in the Summer of 1803, to the Western Highlands of Scotland (1804): **127** 72, p. 67

Hood, Thomas
Hero and Leander (1827): **296** lxxvii 5, pp. 170–71

Ode to Melancholy (1827): **216** 4, pp. 106–7

The Desert-Born (1837): **420** 73, pp. 213–14

The Dream of Eugene Aram, The Murderer (1831): cited by Shatto, **296** ii 213–14, p. 197

The Irish Schoolmaster (1826): **296** xlvi 10, p. 168

The Plea of the Midsummer Fairies (1827): **250** 1, pp. 118–19

Hoole, John
tr. of Metastasio's libretto for the opera *Achille in Sciro* as *Achilles in Scyros* (1800): **296** xxvii 10–11, p. 162

tr. of Tasso's *Gerusalemme Liberata* as *Jerusalem Delivered* (1763): **30** 29–30, p. 42; **91** 11–12, p. 59

Hope, John Thomas
The Arch of Titus (1824): **84** 85–86, p. 56

Hopkins, Charles
Boadicea, Queen of Britain (1697): **286** vii 297, p. 145

tr. of *The Passion of Scylla for Minos, From the Eighth Book of Ovid's Metamorphoses.* from his *The History of Love. A Poem: In a letter to a Lady.* (1695): **219** 93–95, pp. 110–11

Horace (Quintus Horatius Flaccus)
mentioned: *Preface*, pp. 1, 4, 5, 8, 12; **339** *8*, p. 205
Epode ii as tr. by Dryden: **312** *21–22*, p. 189
Epode ii 6 quoted and as tr. by William Sewell in his *Odes and Epodes of Horace* (1850): **330** *91*, p. 200
Epode v quoted: **1A** i *8*, p. 17
Epode xiv quoted and as tr. by Christopher Smart in *The Works of Horace* (1767): **241**, The Sleeping Palace *1–2*, p. 116
Odes I xii 'freely imitated' by Sydney Owenson, Lady Morgan (1822): **9** *12*, pp. 37–38
Odes II ix 3 quoted: **208** *67*, pp. 98–99
Odes II xx, Collins's citation of dismissed by T.: *Preface*, p. 5, and **296** xxxv *9*, p. 165
Odes III iii, tr. by Byron in his *Hours of Idleness* (1807): **1A** iii *5*, pp. 17–18
Odes III xi 35 cited by Ricks: **296** cxxviii *14*, p. 184
Odes III xxix 23–24 quoted: **296** [Epilogue] *62*, p. 184
Odes IV xiii (*Ode to Lyce*) quoted: **277** *31*, pp. 129–30
Pope, *First Satire of the Second Book of Horace, Imitated*: **30** *29–30*, p. 42

Horne, M[offat]. J[ames].
Zara: or, The Black Death. A Poem of the Sea. (1827): **296** xxxiv *13–16*, pp. 164–65

Horne, R[ichard]. H[engist].
Orion: an Epic Poem in Three Books (1843): **312** *41–42*, pp. 189–90

Houghton, Lord
see Milnes, Richard Monckton

Howard, Henry, Earl of Surrey
The meanes to attain happy life from *Tottel's Miscellany* (1557): **240** *3*, pp. 114–15

Howard, Rev. Henry
tr. of Claudian's *De Nuptiis Honorii et Mariæ* as *Epithalamium on the Marriage of Honorius and Maria* from his *Translations From Claudian* (1823): **161** *9–10*, p. 78

Howard, J. J.
tr. of Ovid's *Metamorphoses* (1807), including Book II: **26** *32*, p. 41, and **176** *23–24*, p. 93;
Book VII: **1** *119–20*, pp. 23–24; and Book XV: **4** *155*, p. 36

Howell, James
A Poem Heroique, Presented to his late Majesty for a New Year's Gift (1663): **296** lxi *9*, p. 169
'To the knowing Reader touching Familiar Letters', the introductory poem in his *Epistolæ Ho-Elianæ: Familiar Letters Domestick and Foreign* (1650): **208** *18*, p. 98

Howell, Samuel
   Village Rambles (1810): **297** 20, p. 185
Hoyland, Francis
   Rural Happiness, An Elegy (1763): **1** 55, pp. 21–22
Hudson, Henry
   Idyll I (Morning) from *The Hours* (1817): **192** 3, p. 95
Hunt, Leigh
   A Thought of the Nile (1818): **296** lxxxix 36, p. 174
   Lord Byron and Some of his Contemporaries (1828): **296** xxvii 10–11, p. 162
   Pastoral II. Season, Summer. — Time, Noon. (1801): **286** iv 169, p. 139
   Remembered Friendship from his *Juvenilia* (1801): **296** lxxxix 27–28, pp. 173–74
   The Story of Rimini (1816): **241** 15–16, pp. 115–16; **296** lxxii 15, p. 170
Hurdis, Rev. James
   Elmer and Ophelia from his *Poems, by the Author of the Village Curate, and Adriano* (1790): **286** ii 21–22, p. 137

Imlah, John
   To ...., from his May Flowers. Poems and Songs: Some in the Scottish Dialect (1827): **130** 40–41, p. 69
   To Sea (1841): **296** ciii 53–54, p. 178
Ingram, Henry
   Matilda, A Tale of the Crusades (1830): **160** 77–78, p. 77
   The Flower of Wye (1815): **4** 173, p. 36; **47** 31, p. 43
Ireland, William Henry
   The Sailor-Boy (1809): **286** ii 87–88, p. 138

Jackson, Samuel
   Sympathy: or, a sketch of the social passion. (1781): **296** xx 1–2, p. 158
James VI, King, of Scotland (attributed)
   Ane Poeme of Tyme from *Chronicle of Scottish Poetry: From the Thirteenth Century, to the Union of the Crowns*, ed. by James Sibbald (Edinburgh, 1802): **163** 13–14, p. 82
Johnson, C[harles]. H[enry].
   John the Baptist, A Prize Poem Recited in the Theatre, Oxford, in the year 1809, repr. in *The Poetical Register, and Repository of Fugitive Poetry, for 1810–1811* (1814): **209** 56–57, p. 99
Johnson, Samuel
   Essay from *The Rambler* No. 99 (1751): **217** 41, p. 109
   Essay from *The Rambler* No. 128 (1751): **217** 2, p. 108
   Friendship; An Ode (1743): **296** lxxxv 25, pp. 171–72
   Irene, A Tragedy (1749): **48** 19–20, p. 44
   Omar's Plan of Life from *The Idler* (1760): **306** 8, p. 187

Jones, Jacob, Jun.
  Sonnet to Clare, the Northamptonshire Peasant-Poet (1824): **164** 205–8, p. 84
Jones, James Athearn
  Bonaparte (New York, 1820): **8** 17, p. 37
Jones, Sir William
  The Seven Fountains, An Eastern Allegory, written in the Year 1767 (1772): **431** 44–45, p. 216
  see also Thomas Maurice, *An Elegiac and Historical Poem, sacred to the Memory and Virtues of the Honourable Sir William Jones* (1795)
Jonson, Ben
  Every Man Out of His Humour (1616): **209** 115, pp. 100–1
  Volpone; or, The Foxe (1607): **109** 4, pp. 63–64
Juvenal (Decimus Iunius Iuvenalis)
  Satire X quoted: **109** 4, pp. 63–64; tr. by Dryden (1693), **296** xcvii 2–3, p. 176

Keats, John
  mentioned: *Preface*, p. 12; **289** 9–10, p. 146
  Endymion (1818): cited by Ricks, **3** i 88–90, p. 33; cited by Ricks, **91** 1–2, pp. 58–59; **91** 9–10, p. 59; **155** 1, p. 75; **161** 6, p. 78; **209** 146, p. 101; **216** 4, pp. 106–7; **286** i 18, p. 136; **296** lxxvii 13–14, p. 171; **301** 5, p. 186
  Hyperion (abandoned epic, published, unfinished, in 1820): cited by Collins and by Ricks, **160** 90–92, pp. 77–78
  Imitation of Spenser (1817): **109** 8–9, p. 64
  I stood tip-toe (1817): **324** 61–62, p. 198
  Lamia (1820): cited by Ricks, **126** 3–4, pp. 65–66; **145** 9, pp. 71–72
  Ode on a Grecian Urn (1820): **289** 29–32, pp. 146–47
  Ode on Melancholy (1820): **286** iv 546–47, pp. 141–42
  Ode to a Nightingale (1819): cited by Ricks, **91** 11–12, p. 59; **316** i 686–87, p. 196
  Otho the Great: A Tragedy in Five Acts (1819): **3** ii 24, p. 34
  The Fall of Hyperion: A Dream (unfinished epic, first published as such 1856): cited by Ricks, **132** 59–60, p. 70
  To George Felton Mathew, **241**, L'Envoi 41–42, pp. 117–18
  To Hope (1817): **286** vi ∧ vii 2–3, p. 144
Keble, John
  Poem 53, *Third Sunday After Trinity* in *The Christian Year* (1827): cited by Ricks, **108** 8, p. 63
  Sermon on *Psalm* xxii posthumously published in *Sermons for the Christian Year* (1876): **400** 5–6, pp. 210–11
Kenyon, John
  Recalling (1738): **296** xx 1–2, p. 158

Killigrew, Henry
> *Book III, Epigram 5. To his Book.* from his *Epigrams of Martial, Englished with some other pieces, ancient and modern* (1695): **279** *10–11*, p. 132

King James Bible
> *Acts* ii 1–3: **173** *29–30*, p. 90
> *Amos* vii 17: **337** *373–75*, p. 204
> *Daniel* v 6: **46** *26*, pp. 42–43
> *Daniel* vii 9–10: **4** *121–28*, pp. 35–36
> *Deuteronomy* xxvi 9: **153** i *327–28*, p. 74
> *Ecclesiastes* iv 4: **209** *115*, pp. 100–1
> *Exodus* x 21: **3** i *125*, pp. 33–34
> *Exodus* xiii 21: **257** *17–20*, pp. 119–20
> *Exodus* xiv 19 and xiv 24: **286** v *513*, p. 142
> *Exodus* xix 5: **153** i *437–38*, p. 74
> *Exodus* xxxiii 23: **296** [Prologue] *1–3*, p. 148
> *Genesis* iii 17 and v 29: **209** *229*, p. 102
> *Genesis* xvi 11–12: **330** *843–46*, pp. 201–2
> *Isaiah* xxxii 2: **310** *15–17*, p. 188
> *Isaiah* xxxviii 2 and xxxviii 4–5: **330** *281–82*, pp. 200–1
> *Isaiah* xliii 2: **465** *130–32*, pp. 219–20
> *Isaiah* xlvi 1–2: **153** i *298*, p. 74
> *Isaiah* xlix 23: **2** I v *93–94*, p. 28
> *Isaiah* lxiv 1 and *Judges* v 5 cited (as Ricks notes) by Shatto & Shaw: **296** cxxiii *5–6*, p. 183
> *James* ii 14: **296** cviii *5*, p. 180
> *Jeremiah* ix 3: **217** *5*, p. 108
> *Job* iii 13–14: **296** lxiv *23–24*, pp. 169–70
> *Job* xiv 1: **209** *330*, p. 103
> *Job* xlii 6: **296** xxxiv *4*, p. 164; and **316** i *32*, p. 194
> *John* iv 48 and *Hebrews* ii 4: **474** *226–27*, p. 226
> *John* xii 23 cited (as Ricks notes) by John D. Rosenberg: **473** *86*, p. 224
> *Jude* i 13: **468** *188–89*, p. 221
> *Judges* xi 12 and *2 Kings* ix 19: **99** *34 and 40*, p. 60
> *Luke* xv 24: **290** *8–9*, p. 147
> *Luke* xv 32: **468** *77–78*, p. 221
> *Luke* xxiii 24: **337** *782–83*, p. 205
> *Luke* xxiii 34: **277** *123–26*, p. 131; and **475** *265*, p. 226
> *Mark* ix 44 cited (as Ricks notes) by J. M. Gray: **473** *450–51*, p. 225
> *Matthew* vi 31: **316** i *533–34*, p. 196
> *Matthew* vii 6: **386** *110*, p. 209; and **473** *310*, p. 225
> *Matthew* viii 29: **99** *34 and 40*, p. 60
> *Matthew* ix 1–8 and *Mark* ii 1–12: **209** *56–57*, p. 99
> *Matthew* xii 9–14, *Mark* iii 1–6, and *Luke* vi 6–11: **209** *56–57*, p. 99

Matthew xiii 13: **286** vi *3*, p. 143
Matthew xvi 25: **471** *456*, p. 223
Matthew xxiv 20: **210** *7*, p. 104
Matthew xxvi 18 cited by Ricks: **472** *597*, p. 224
Matthew xxvii 51: **209** *10*, p. 99
Numbers xx 11: **276** *59–60*, p. 128
Proverbs iii 24 cited by Shatto & Shaw: **296** xxx *19*, p. 163
Proverbs xiv 13: **78** *49*, p. 52
Proverbs xvi 24: **275** *25–27*, p. 126
Proverbs xxiv 30–31: **296** xxvii *10–11*, p. 162
Psalm vi 6: **164** *230*, p. 85
Psalm xvi 2 cited (as Ricks notes) by J. M. Gray: **473** *569*, p. 226
Psalm xviii 16–19: sermon on, by Rev. Walter Blake Kirwan, **296** xxxv *24*, p. 166
Psalm xxii: sermon on, by John Keble, **400** *5–6*, pp. 210–11
Psalm lxxvii 2: **473** *569*, p. 226
Psalm civ 3: **2** I i *84–85*, p. 25
Revelation i 3: **472** *597*, p. 224
Revelation iii 3: **473** *86*, p. 224
Revelation viii 6–7: **473** *151*, p. 225
Revelation ix 3 cited (as Ricks notes) by J. M. Gray: **473** *450–51*, p. 225
Revelation xiv 13 cited by Shatto & Shaw: **296** xxx *19*, p. 163
Revelation xvii 3: **472** *555–56*, pp. 223–24
Revelation xix 10: **3** i *1*, p. 30
Revelation xx 10: **473** *343–45*, p. 225
Revelation xxi 5: **200** *1–2*, p. 97
Romans xii 1: homily by John Chrysostom on, tr. by James Endell Tyler in *Meditations from the Fathers of the First Five Centuries* (1849): **299** *8*, pp. 185–86
Tobit iii 2 (*Apocrypha*): **296** [Prologue] *12*, p. 148
Zechariah xiv 14: **296** lii *15*, p. 168
1 Corinthians iii 1–3: **88** *1–4*, p. 57
1 Corinthians xv: **286** ii *71–74*, pp. 137–38
1 Corinthians xv 28: **469** *381–82*, p. 222
1 Kings xvii 1: **146** *8*, p. 72
2 Kings ix 19: **99** *34* and *40*, p. 60
1 Peter i 8 cited by Ricks and by Shatto & Shaw: **296** [Prologue] *1–3*, p. 148

King, Henry
 St. Valentine's Day (1657): **27** *67*, p. 41

King, James
 A Poem on Leigh Park, The Seat of Sir George Thos. Staunton, Bart. (1829): **194** *21–22*, pp. 96–97

King, William
  The Art of Love (1709), after Ovid: **296** xlvi 1–4, p. 168
  The Toast, An Epic Poem in Four Books. Written in Latin *by Frederick Scheffer, Done into* English *by Peregrine O Donald, Esq* (1736): **407** 37–40, p. 211
Kirwan, Rev. Walter Blake
  Sermon XII from *Sermons By the Late Rev. Walter Blake Kirwan, Dean of Killala* (1814): **296** xxxv 24, p. 166
Klopstock, Friedrich Gottlieb
  see Egestorff, G[eorg]. H[einrich]. C. *and* Raffles, Rev. Thomas
Knox, Charles Henry
  The Devil's Road from *Day Dreams* (1843): **296** lxx 5, p. 170
Knox, Vicesimus
  Elegant Extracts: or, Useful and Entertaining Pieces of Poetry, selected for the improvement of Youth, ed. by Knox (*pub* 1789–1826): **75** 5, pp. 50–51, note 33; **296** xxx 19, p. 163

Lamartine, Alphonse de
  Voyage en Orient (1835), tr. (anonymously) as *Travels in the East, including a Journey in the Holy Land* (Edinburgh, 1839): **367** 13–14, p. 207
Lamb, Charles
  Existence, Considered in Itself, No Blessing, From the Latin of Palingenius (1832): **415** 204, p. 212
  The Adventures of Ulysses (1808): **153** i 298, p. 74
  see also Thomas Noon Talfourd's *Final Memorials of Charles Lamb* (1848)
Landon, Letitia Elizabeth ('L.E.L.')
  mentioned: *Preface*, p. 13
  Admiral Benbow (1837): **296** xc 7–8, p. 175
  Fragment ('A solitude / Of green and silent beauty') (1823): **2** I iv 123–24, p. 27
  Portrait of a Lady. By Sir Thomas Lawrence. (1825): **296** ix 9–10, p. 154
  Sir Thomas Lawrence (1833): **241**, The Sleeping Beauty 19, p. 117
  Success Alone Seen (1832): **296** [Prologue] 42, p. 149
  The Castilian Nuptials (1822): **363** 10, p. 206
  The Fairy of the Fountains (1834): **257** 54, p. 121
  The Fate of Adelaide, A Swiss Romantic Tale (1821): **190** 22, p. 94
Landor, Walter Savage
  Acon and Rhodope; or, Inconstancy (1847): **296** lxii 12, p. 169
  Gebir (1798): **296** vi 25, p. 153
Langhorne, John
  mentioned: *Preface*, p. 13
  Elegy III from *The Visions of Fancy. In Four Elegies.* (1762): **109** 14, p. 64; **161** 11–12, pp. 78–79

Fable II. The Evening Primrose from *The Fables of Flora* (1771): **91** *9–10*, p. 59; **399** *9–10*, p. 210

Proemium, Written in MDCCLXVI. (1766): **296** xxxiii *8*, p. 164

The Correspondence of Theodosius and Constantia (1796): **2** III ii *78*, pp. 29–30

Verses in Memory of a Lady. Written at Sandgate Castle, MDCCLXVIII. (1768): **3** i *69–70*, p. 32; **296** xx *1–2*, p. 158

Law, William
A Serious Call to a Devout and Holy Life (1729): **1** *49*, p. 21

Leapor, Mary
The Enquiry (1748): **5** *15–16*, p. 36

Lee, Sophia
The Life of a Lover: In a Series of Letters, vol. 5 (1804): **296** x *11–14*, p. 154

Leigh, Edward and Henry
Select and Choyce Observations, Containing All the Romane Emperours (1657): **88** *20–22*, p. 58

Lewis, M[atthew]. G[regory]. 'Monk'
The Castle Spectre, a Drama in Five Acts (1798): **2** I v *119–20*, p. 28; **153** i *53–54*, p. 73

The Cloud-King from his *Tales of Wonder* (1801): **48** *19–20*, p. 44

Lewis, W[illiam]. L[illington].
tr. of Statius's *Thebaid* (1767): **1** *119–20*, pp. 23–24; **291** *1*, p. 147

Leyden, Dr. John
The Mermaid (1803): **170** *152*, p. 89

Sonnet Written at Woodhouselee in 1802 from *The Poetical Remains of the Late Dr. John Leyden* (1819): **286** [Prologue] *236–38*, p. 134

Linen, James Alexander
The Aged Mourner Comforted from his *Poems, in the Scots and English Dialect, on Various Occasions* (1815): **3** i *133*, p. 34

Lloyd, Charles
Stanzas, written 10th, 11th, and 12th November 1819 (1821): **87** *26–27*, p. 56

Lloyd, Robert
The First Book of the Henriade. Translated from the French of M. De Voltaire. (1762): **271** *37*, pp. 124–25

The Poet. An Epistle to C. Churchill. (1774): **217** *47–48*, p. 109

Lofft the Younger, Capel
Ernest; or Political Regeneration (1839): **279** *10–11*, p. 132

Longfellow, Henry Wadsworth
Footsteps of Angels from his *Voices of the Night* (Cambridge, Mass., 1839; London, 1843)

The Sea-Diver (1825): **296** iv *3*, p. 152

Lovibond, Edward
To the Thames (1785): **58A** *47*, p. 47

Lowth, Robert
  The Judgment of Hercules, also known as *The Choice of Hercules* (1743): **296** xxx 19, p. 163

Lucan (Marcus Annæus Lucanus)
  De Bello Civili, more commonly known as the *Pharsalia*: tr. by Thomas May (1631), **143** 10, p. 71; partly tr. by George Lord Lyttelton in *Cato's Speech to Labienus. In the Ninth Book of Lucan.* (1775), **219** 131–32, p. 111; quoted, **296** xxxv 14, pp. 165–66; quoted, **296** lxi 9, p. 169; tr. by Nicholas Rowe (1718), **297** 18–19, p. 185

Lucretius (Titus Lucretius Carus)
  De Rerum Natura (*wr* first century BC): tr. by John Mason Good as *The Nature of Things: A Didactic Poem* (1805), **214** 10, pp. 104–5; as origin of the phrase 'jaundiced eye', **271** 132, p. 125

Lynch, Anne C[harlotte]. (later Botta, Mrs. Anne Charlotte Lynch)
  Largess (1848): **296** cix 1, p. 180
  On Seeing Mrs. Kean as Constance in King John (1848): **337** 16, pp. 202–3

Lyttelton, George Lord
  Cato's Speech to Labienus. In the Ninth Book of Lucan. (1775): **219** 131–32, p. 111
  Verses written at Mr. Pope's House at Twickenham, which he had lent to Mrs. Greville, In August 1735. (1788): **296** lxxxix 37, pp. 174–75

Macaulay, Thomas Babbington, Lord Macaulay
  Dies Iræ (1826): **271** 153, p. 126
  Evening (1821): **153** i 58, p. 73; cited by Ricks, **215** 2, p. 105
  Pompeii (1819): **47** 31, p. 43

Macdonald, H. B.
  The Greenlander from her *Abdul Medjid: A Lay of the Future. And Other Poems.* (Edinburgh, 1854): **330** 93, p. 200

MacKay, Charles
  The Alder Tree from his *Songs and Poems* (1834): **265** 9, p. 123

Mackenzie, William
  Snow: Afternoon from *The Rustic Bower; or, Sketches From Nature* (Edinburgh, 1844): **296** lxxxiii 3, p. 171

Macpherson, James (and his fabricated 'Ossian')
  mentioned: *Preface*, p. 12; **296** xxxv 1–2, p. 165
  Carthon (1762 version): **193** 99, p. 96
  Cath-Loda (1763 version): **84** 15–17, p. 54
  Dar-Thula (1762 version): **193** 99, p. 96; (1820 version): **208** 67, pp. 98–99
  Death, A Poem (1805 version): **61** 4, p. 48
  Fingal (1761 version): **58A** 7, p. 46; **127** 61–62, p. 67; (1762 version): **158** 13, p. 75; **215** 3, p. 106
  'Fragment VII' in *Fragments of Ancient Poetry* (Edinburgh, 1760): **307** 7–8, p. 187

Sul-Malla of Lumon (1817 version): **257** *29–32*, p. 120
Temora (1773 version): **164** *215*, pp. 84–85
The Songs of Selma (1817 version): **1** *27–28*, pp. 19–20
Mallet, David
  The Excursion. A Poem. In Two Books. (1728): **215** *2*, p. 105; **223** *1*, p. 112
Mallock, David
  The Well of Bethlehem (1832): **207** *51*, p. 98
Marcus Manilius
  see Creech, Thomas
Marlowe, Christopher
  Doctor Faustus (1604 text) cited by Collins: **296** xv *16–18*, p. 156
Marston, John
  Parasitaster; or, The Fawn (1606; repr. 1814): **161** *29–30*, p. 79
  Satire II (1598): **3** i *125*, p. 33
Martial
  Ad Flaccum [To Flaccus] from his *Epigrams* IV: **84** *15–17*, pp. 54–55
  Carmina Priapea (anon. but sometimes attributed to Martial): **99** *34 and 40*, p. 60
  see also Killigrew, Henry
Marvell, Andrew
  Upon Appleton House (1651): **210** *7*, p. 104
Mary, Lady Chudleigh
  The Song of the Three Children Paraphras'd (1703): **208** *18*, p. 98
Mason, Charles Welsh
  Zagala (1863), tr. of a poem (*Chanzoneta No. 189*) by Juan de Linares: **462** *11–12*, p. 218
Mason, Rev. William
  Caractacus: A Dramatic Poem: Written on the Model of the Ancient Greek Tragedy (1759): **291** *1*, p. 147
  Elfrida, A Dramatic Poem. Written on the Model of the Ancient Greek Tragedy (1752): **84** *13–14*, p. 54; **277** *22*, p. 129
  Il Pacifico (1748): **171** *29*, p. 89
  Ode I. On Leaving St. John's College, Cambridge, 1746 (1797): **110** *2*, p. 65
Massinger, Philip
  The Duke of Milan (1623): **286** [Prologue] *36*, p. 133
  see also Beaumont, Francis *and* Fletcher, John
Maurice, Rev. Thomas
  An Elegiac and Historical Poem, sacred to the Memory and Virtues of the Honourable Sir William Jones (1795): **310** *18*, p. 188
  Hagley: a Descriptive Poem (Oxford, 1776): **167** *53–56*, pp. 86–87
  The Fall of the Mogul, a Tragedy (1806): **310** *18*, p. 188
  The Lotos of Egypt (1805): **83** *81*, p. 53

May, Thomas
  see Lucan (Marcus Annæus Lucanus)
Melville, Herman
  The Whale or *Moby-Dick* (1851): **337** *769*, p. 204; **468** *188–89*, p. 221
Meredith, W. E.
  Llewelyn ap Jorwerth (1818): **296** cxxviii *13*, p. 184
Merry, Robert
  The Laurel of Liberty (1790): **415** *204*, p. 212
Meyer, H[enry]. L[eonard].
  Coloured Illustrations of British Birds and Their Eggs (1844): **337** *102–3*, p. 203
M'Henry, James
  The Bard of Erin (Belfast, 1808): **161** *16*, p. 79
  The Pleasures of Friendship (Pittsburgh, 1822; Philadelphia, 1825): **91** *9–10*, p. 59
Mickle, William Julius
  tr. of Camões, *Os Lusiadas* (1572) as *The Lusiad; or, The Discovery of India. An Epic Poem.* (Oxford, 1776): **3** i *87–88*, p. 33; **128** *11*, p. 68; **190** *23*, p. 94; **277** *40*, p. 130; **383** *30–31*, p. 208
Middleton, Thomas
  A Yorkshire Tragedy (1606): **209** *115*, pp. 100–1
Mill, John Stuart
  The Spirit of the Age (1831): **194** *167*, p. 97
Miller, James
  The Lost Drave of Dunbar; or, the Witch of Keith from *St Baldred of the Bass, A Pictish Legend [...] with other Poems and Ballads* (Edinburgh, 1824): **153** i *7–9*, p. 73
Mills, James
  The Universe (1821): **296** cv *23–24*, p. 179
Mills, William
  tr. of Virgil's *Georgic I* (1780): **296** vi *4*, p. 153
Milman, Rev. H[enry]. H[art].
  Belshazzar: A Dramatic Poem, **219** *93–95*, pp. 110–11
Milnes, Richard Monckton, Lord Houghton
  mentioned: **257** *17–20*, pp. 119–20
  On the Church of the Madaleine, at Paris (1838): **289** *9–10*, p. 146
  role as editor of *Letters and Literary Remains of Keats* discussed by Ricks: **289** *9–10*, p. 146
Milton, John
  mentioned: *Preface*, p. 12; **2** I v *224–26*, p. 29; by Edmund Burke and, in turn, Robert Carruthers, **87** *26–27*, p. 56; in an ode by Antonio Francini, **296** cxii *15–16*, p. 181; in a poem by Lady Emmeline Stuart-Wortley, **324** *10*, pp. 198–99; by Blake, **337** *573–74*, p. 204
  Arcades (1634): discussed by Thomas Warton, **78** *83–86*, p. 52

Comus (1634): **2** I i *87*, p. 25; cited by Ricks, **30** *29–30*, p. 42; cited by Ricks, **84** *48*, p. 55; cited by Collins and by Ricks, **84** *85–86*, p. 56; cited by Ricks, **99** *34* and *40*, p. 60; **286** vi *47*, p. 143; cited by Ricks and by Shatto & Shaw, **296** i *10*, p. 150; **330** *556–58*, p. 201

Il Penseroso (1645): **2** I i *84–85*, p. 25; cited by Ricks, **26** *23*, p. 40; cited by Collins and by Ricks, **84** *85–86*, p. 56

L'Allegro (1645): cited by Ricks, **153** *53–54*, p. 73; cited by Ricks, **296** xv *16–18*, p. 156, and **296** lxxii *15*, p. 170

Lycidas (1638): cited by Ricks, **26** *8*, p. 40; cited by J. Sendry, **296** ix *3–4*, p. 153

Paradise Lost (1674 version): cited by Pollard, **1A** iii *5*, p. 17; cited by Ricks, plus another instance: **1A** iii *80*, p. 18; **1** *2*, p. 19; cited by Ricks: **1** *64*, p. 22; cited by Ricks **2** I i *3–5*, p. 24; cited by Ricks **2** I v *93–94*, p. 28; **3** i *2–4*, p. 30; cited by Ricks, **3** i *125*, p. 33; **3** ii *24*, p. 34; cited by Ricks, **4** *121–28*, p. 35; cited by Ricks, **4** *155*, p. 36; cited by Ricks, **4** *173*, p. 36; cited by Ricks, **9** *45*, p. 38; **26** *31*, p. 40; cited by Ricks, **45** *7*, p. 42; cited by Thomas Warton, **78** *83–86*, p. 52; **107** *1*, p. 62; **127** *56*, p. 67; cited by Ricks, **130** *79*, p. 69; **132** *59–60*, p. 70; cited by Ricks, **153** i *58*, p. 73; **170** *116*, pp. 88–89; cited (via Ricks) by J. McCue, **286** vii *180–81*, pp. 144–45; cited by Collins and by Ricks, **296** xxxv *14*, p. 165; cited by Shatto & Shaw, **296** lxxxv *25*, pp. 171–72; **296** xcvii *19*, p. 177; **296** cii *21–24*, p. 178; mentioned by Hazlitt (1826), **300** *3*, p. 186; **301** *5*, p. 186; **431** *31*, p. 216; **471** *318–20*, p. 223

Samson Agonistes (1671): **469** *959*, p. 222

Mitford, Mary Russell

The Wedding-Ring. A Dramatic Scene. from *Dramatic Scenes, Sonnets, and Other Poems* (1827): **286** i *9–10*, p. 135

Weston Grove, from the same: **200** *27*, pp. 97–98

Moir, David Macbeth (often as 'Δ' or 'Delta')

Future Prospects of the World (1824): **296** iv *3*, p. 152

Mary's Mount from *The Legend of Genevieve: With Other Tales and Poems* (1825): **166** *6–7*, p. 86

Stanzas to the Memory of David Macbeth Moir, Third Son of D. M. Moir, Esq. (1840): **392** *73–76*, p. 209

Sunset Thoughts (1823): **170** *6*, p. 88

Montagu, Lady Mary Wortley

Julia to Ovid. Written at Twelve Years of Age, in Imitation of Ovid's Epistles (1803): **296** xi *11–12*, p. 155

Montaigne, Michel de

see Cotton, Charles

Montgomery, James

mentioned: *Preface*, p. 12

Greenland (1819): **83** *81*, p. 53; **130** *79*, pp. 69–70; **215** *2*, p. 105

Instruction (1819): **146** *8*, p. 72

Sow in the Morn Thy Seed (1832): **240** *3*, pp. 114–15

The Pelican Island (1827): **233** *5*, p. 114

The Wanderer of Switzerland (1806): **296** xi 15–16, p. 155

The West-Indies. A Poem, in Four Parts. Written in Honour of the Abolition of the African Slave Trade, by the British Legislature, in 1807. (1809): **47** 32, pp. 43–44; **271** 168, p. 126

The World Before the Flood (1813): **241**, The Sleeping Palace 15–16, pp. 116–17; **275** 86–88, p. 127

Youth Renewed (1826): **174** 4–7, p. 91

Montgomery, Robert

mentioned: *Preface*, p. 12

Luther: A Poem (1842): **296** cix 10, p. 181

The Gospel in Advance of the Age: being A Homily for the Times (Edinburgh, 1844): **443** 28–29, p. 217

The Messiah (1832): **209** 151–53, p. 101; **271** 132, p. 125; **296** lxxxvii 7–8, p. 173

The Omnipresence of the Deity, final version (1828): **209** 379–81, p. 103; early version (1826): **316** ii 172–74, pp. 196–97

Satan. A Poem. (1830): **251** 1, p. 119

Woman, The Angel of Life (1833): **220** 12–13, p. 112; **296** xcv 64, p. 176

Moore, Dugald

The Bridal Night (Glasgow, 1831): **279** 8–9, p. 132

Moore, George

Ocean from *The Minstrel's Tale: And Other Poems* (1826): **2** I iv 75–76, p. 27

Moore, Thomas

mentioned: *Preface*, p. 12

Air ('Oh say thou best and brightest') (1827): **337** 69, p. 203

As Down in the Sunless Retreats (1816): **217** 11, p. 108

Evenings in Greece. Second Evening (1832): **286** vi 65, pp. 143–44

Fragment of a Mythological Hymn to Love (1806): **159** 127, p. 76

Lalla Rookh: An Oriental Tale (1817): **1A** ii 27, p. 17; **1** 48, pp. 20–21; **286** vi 65, pp. 143–44

Love's Young Dream (1811): **106** 2, pp. 61–62

Remonstrance (1820): **145** 9, pp. 71–72

Shall the Harp Then Be Silent, also known as *Grattan's Lamentation* (1815): **145** 9, pp. 71–72

Sublime Was the Warning (1808): **10** 5, p. 39

The Fall of Hebe. A Dithyrambic Ode. (1806): **330** 89–90, p. 199

tr. of *Ode XIII* from his *Odes of Anacreon* (1800): **163** 17, p. 82

Morgan, Sydney Owenson, Lady

see Horace (Quintus Horatius Flaccus)

Moxon, Edward

The Prospect from *The Prospect, and Other Poems* (1826): **47** 32, pp. 43–44

Musaeus, Grammaticus

see Fawkes, Francis

Newman, John Henry, Cardinal
Death from his *Lyra Apostolica* (Derby, 1836): **271** *143*, p. 125
Sermon delivered at St. Clement's, Oxford, on Sunday, January 2, 1825: **3** i *2–4*, pp. 30–31

Newton, Charles
Regular Lyric Ode from his *Poems* (Cambridge, 1797): **161** *73–74*, pp. 79–80

Newton, Rev. John
Amazing Grace (1779): **290** *8–9*, p. 147
Letter to him, from William Cowper, quoted (1781): **286** iv *546–47*, pp. 141–42

Nicol, Alexander
An Elegy on Auld Use and Wont from *The Rural Muse* (Edinburgh, 1753): **296** xxix *11*, pp. 162–63

Noble, Thomas
A Monody, Occasioned by the Death of the Right Hon. Charles James Fox (1806): **296** lxxxix *17*, p. 173
tr. of the *Argonautica* of Gaius Valerius Flaccus (1808): **1** *3*, p. 19

Norris, John
Reason and Religion, or the Grounds and Measures of Devotion, consider'd from the nature of God (1698): **216** *1–2*, p. 106

North, Christopher
see Wilson, John

Northcote, James
Memoirs of Sir Joshua Reynolds (1813): **2** I v *224–26*, p. 29

Norton, Caroline
I Would the World Were Mine (1829): **257** *54*, p. 121
The Sorrows of Rosalie. A Tale. (1829): **257** *54*, p. 121

Nugent, Robert Craggs, Lord Nugent
An Epistle to the Right Honourable the Earl of Chesterfield from his *Odes and Epistles* (1739): **296** xxx *27*, pp. 163–64
tr. from the German of Schiller's *Die Theilung der Erde* as *The Parting of the Earth* (1846): **316** ii *221–22*, p. 197

Odiorne, Thomas
Ethic Strains, On Subjects Sublime and Beautiful (Boston, 1821): **3** i *88–90*, p. 33

Ogilvie, Rev. John
mentioned: *Preface*, p. 13
Human Life, a Poem, in Five Parts. (1806): **296** xliii *5*, pp. 167–68
Ode to Evening (1762): **296** xxxi *11–12*, p. 164
Providence: An Allegorical Poem in Three Books (1764): **16** *25*, p. 39; **296** xcviii *12–14*, p. 177

Rona, A Poem, in Seven Books (1777): **3** i 32, p. 31; **227** 23, p. 113

Solitude: or, the Elysium of the Poets, a Vision (1765): **16** 25, p. 39; **296** xcv 64, p. 176

The Day of Judgment (1753): **296** xi 11–12, p. 155

Oldham, John

An Ode of Anacreon, Paraphras'd. The Cup (1683): **3** i 2–4, p. 30

Oldham, Thomas

The Muse's Triumph (1840): **296** xcv 64, p. 176

Ord, John Walker

Queen Victoria at Windsor (1841): **296** xx 16, p. 159

The Wandering Bard from *The Wandering Bard: and Other Poems* (Edinburgh, 1833): **208** 67, pp. 98–99

'Ossian'

see Macpherson, James

Ossoli, Margaret Fuller

Letter to R. W. Emerson quoted in her posthumous memoirs (1852): **316** i 151, p. 195

Otway, Thomas

Alcibiades, A Tragedy (1675): **1** 7–8, p. 19

Epistle From Mr. Otway to Mr. Duke from *Tonson's Miscellany* (1684): **313** 174–75, p. 192

The Atheist: or, The Second Part of the Souldiers Fortune (1684): **209** 388–90, p. 103

Ovid (Publius Ovidius Naso)

mentioned: *Preface*, p. 12

Amores III quoted: **296** xviii 5–7, pp. 157–58

Elegy XIII, anonymously tr. as *To the Morning, not to make Haste* in *Ovid's Epistles: with his Amours* (1729): **127** 56, p. 67

Epistulae 2.118 quoted and translated: **30** 8, p. 41

Fasti I, 518, and *Fasti* II, 408, quoted and translated: **286** iv 531–32, p. 141

Hero Leandro [Hero to Leander], Epistle XIX of *Epistulae Heroidum*, quoted and translated: **173** 69–70, pp. 90–91

Metamorphoses v 248–49 discussed: **58A** 26, p. 46; *Metamorphoses* ix 280 discussed: **209** 143, p. 101

see also translations and 'imitations' cited under Anna Lætitia Barbauld, William Congreve, John Dryden, Laurence Eusden, John Gay, Charles Hopkins, J. J. Howard, William King, Lady Mary Wortley Montagu, and Thomas Yalden

Owen, John

The Doctrine of Justification by Faith, through the Imputation of the Righteousness of Christ (1667; new edition, 1816): **296** cviii 5, p. 180

Two sermons: *The Everlasting Covenant, The Believer's Support Under Distress* (1756) and *The Branch of the Lord, the Beauty of Zion* (1650): **88** 7–9, pp. 57–58

Index of Antecedent Writers and Works Discussed 273

Parnell, Thomas
    Epigram beginning 'The greatest gifts that Nature does bestow' (1780): **161** 130–31, p. 80
    Jonah (1758): **296** vi 16, p. 153
    Piety; or, The Vision (1721): **83** 81, p. 53
    tr. of *Batrachomyomachia* (1717): **73** 63–64, p. 50

Pattison, Samuel
    To Peace (1792): **161** 73–74, pp. 79–80

Pattison, William
    Abelard to Eloisa (1728) **2** I iv 7–8, p. 27

Peach, William
    Cwm Dhu; or, The Black Dingle (1853): **312** 1, p. 189

Peacock, Thomas Love
    Rhododaphne, or The Thessalian Spell (1818): **2** III ii 78, pp. 29–30

Pearson, Susanna
    Sonnet, to Peter Pindar, Esq. (1790): **175** 11–12, p. 91

Peers, Charles
    The Siege of Jerusalem (1823): **48** 19–20, p. 44

Percy, Thomas
    Cynthia: an Elegiac Poem (1758): **233** 5, p. 114

Perry, James
    Mimosa: or, the Sensitive Plant (1779): **2** I ii 26, p. 26

Petrarch (Francesco Petrarca)
    mentioned: *Preface*, p. 12
    from the *Canzoniere* (1327):
        Poem 17 ('Piovonmi amare lagrime dal viso'): **271** 27–28, p. 124
        Poem 35 ('Solo e pensoso i più deserti campi'), tr. by J. B. Taylor (1804): **286** vi ∧ vii 7, p. 144
        Poem 128 ('Italia mia, benché 'l parlar sia indarno'): **193** 94–95, p. 96; **209** 106–8, p. 100
        Poem 132 ('S'amor non è, che dunque è quel ch'io sento?'): **296** iv 3, p. 152
        Poem 182 ('Amor, che 'ncende 'l cor d'ardente zelo'), tr. by Francis Wrangham (1817): **163** 17, p. 82
        Poem 337 ('Quel, che d'odore et di color vincea'): **271** 154, p. 126; **296** cv 23–24, p. 179
        Poem 362 ('Volo con l'ali de' pensieri al cielo'), claimed by Collins to have been a T. source, and T.'s dismissive response: **296** lxxvi 1, p. 170
    see also Rev. Henry Boyd's tr. of Petrarch's *Trionfi* as *The Triumph of Chastity* (1806)

Philips, Ambrose
    tr. of Virgil's *Fourth Pastoral* (1709): **420** 57–58, p. 213

Philips, John
    Cyder, A Poem in Two Books (1708), the main title after 1791 spelled *Cider*: **1A** iii *80*, p. 18, note 5; **5** *15–16*, p. 36; **296** ii *7–8*, p. 151

Phillips, Charles
    The Emerald Isle, sixth edn (1818): **58A** *45–46*, p. 47; **159** *82–84*, p. 75

Phillips, Sir Richard
    The Hundred Wonders of the World (1821) cited by Shatto & Shaw: **296** xxxiv *13–16*, pp. 164–65

Pinkerton, John
    Ode VI. The Prophecy of Tweed from his *Rimes* (1781): **162** *51–52*, p. 81

Pittis, William
    An epistolary poem to N. Tate, Esquire, and the poet laureat to His Majesty, occasioned by the taking of Namur (1696): **190** *23*, p. 94

Plato
    Apology of Socrates: passage at *Apology* 18d quoted, **286** i *9–10*, p. 135; remark of Socrates at *Apology* 22b–c paraphrased by Emerson in his essay *History* (1841): **296** xcvii *34–36*, p. 177
    Cratylus at 402a quoted: **276** *22*, p. 127; **296** cxxiii *5–6*, p. 183
    Republic Book IX at 588c quoted: **219** *15*, p. 110
    Symposium, tr. by Shelley as *The Banquet* (1818): **55** *7*, pp. 45–46
    Timaeus at 75d paraphrased: **164** *66–68*, pp. 83–84
    on thinking the thing that is not, in Plato's *Sophist*, *Cratylus*, and *Theaetetus*: **313** *7–8*, p. 190

Pollok, Robert
    The Course of Time (1827): **3** i *2–4*, pp. 30–31, and **3** i *87–88*, p. 33; **101** *9–10, 19–20,* and *29–30*, pp. 60–61

Polwhele, Richard
    mentioned: *Preface*, p. 13
    An Epistle from an Under-Graduate at Oxford to his Friend in the Country, written in 1780 (1792): **286** iv *502–3*, p. 141
    Ode to the Spirit of Freshness (1798): **296** cxviii *21*, p. 182
    Sir Allan; or, The Knight of Expiring Chivalry (1806): **425** *45–48*, p. 214
    The English Orator. A Didactic Poem. (1786): **193** *94–95*, p. 96
    The Fall of Constantinople (1822): **215** *1*, p. 105
    The Minstrel: a Poem, in Five Books (1814), taken over and completed after the death of James Beattie: **296** xi *17*, pp. 155–56; **312** *41–42*, pp. 189–90
    as editor, *Poems, Chiefly by Gentlemen of Devonshire and Cornwall* (Bath, 1792): **296** lxxxix *27–28*, pp. 173–74

Poole, Edward Richard
    Byzantium: A Dramatic Poem (1823): **1** *36*, p. 20

Pooley, Rev. William
    Untitled poem beginning 'Hence Melancholy, pensive maid' (1761): **84** *13–14*, p. 54

Pope, Alexander
mentioned: *Preface*, pp. 1, 5, 12; in a poem by Lyttelton, **296** lxxxix 37, pp. 174–75
An Essay on Criticism (1711): **271** 132, p. 125
An Essay on Man (1734): **4** 31–32, p. 35; **271** 153, p. 126; **277** 40, p. 130; cited by Ricks, **289** 6, pp. 145–46; **296** xvi 20, p. 157; cited by Ricks, **296** xcvii 34–36, p. 177
Elegy to the Memory of an Unfortunate Lady (1717): **84** 1–4, pp. 53–54
Epilogue to the Satires (1738): **286** ii 292–96, pp. 138–38
First Satire of the Second Book of Horace, Imitated (1733): **30** 29–30, p. 42
Imitation of Horace, Book One, Sixth Epistle (1737): **339** 8, p. 205
The Dunciad (1742 version): **1** 2, p. 19; **3** i 125, p. 33
The Rape of the Lock (1714): **1** 54, p. 21; **311** 106, p. 189
Windsor Forest (1713): **296** ii 7–8, p. 151
tr. of Homer's *Iliad* (1715–20): **1** 54, p. 21, and **1** 74, p. 23; **30** 29–30, p. 42; **163** 34, p. 83; **173** 45–47, p. 90; **194** 54, p. 97; **219** 93–95, pp. 110–11; **296** xv 16–18, p. 156, and xxvii 2, pp. 161–62; **471** 901–3, p. 223
with William Broome and Elijah Fenton, tr. of Homer's *Odyssey* (1726): **1** 48, pp. 20–21; **3** i 2–4, pp. 30–31; **30** 29–30, p. 42; **127** 81, p. 68; **214** 10, pp. 104–5; **219** 131–32, p. 111; **241**, L'Envoi 41–42, pp. 117–18; **286** ii 7–10, p. 137, and vi 47, p. 143; **296** xl 1, p. 167; **316** i 48, p. 194, and i 402–4, pp. 195–96
tr. of passages in Statius's *Thebaid*, Book I (1712): **1** 31, p. 20; **296** xcvii 2–3, p. 176

Porden, Eleanor Anne
mentioned: *Preface*, p. 13
The Arctic Expeditions (1818): **257** 45–46, p. 121
The Veils; or the Triumph of Constancy. A Poem, in Six Books (1815): **1A** iii 80, p. 18, note 5; **1** 61–62, p. 22; **83** 81, p. 53; **167** 69, p. 87; **241**, L'Envoi 41–42, pp. 117–18

Potter, John
Euripides's *Hecuba* tr. by Potter in his *Archæologia Græca, or The antiquities of Greece* (1697 and all later editions): **106** 2, pp. 61–62

Potter, R[obert].
tr. of Aeschylus's *The Seven Chiefs Against Thebes* in his *The Tragedies of Æschylus Translated* (Norwich, 1777): **26** 15, p. 40
tr. of Euripides's *The Bacchae* in vol. 1 of his *Tragedies of Euripides* (Oxford, 1823): **176** 7, p. 92

Prentice, George D.
The Dead Mariner (1829): **296** xi 19–20, p. 156

Preston, W[illiam].
tr. of *The Argonautics of Apollonius Rhodius* (1803): **296** xxiv 3–4, p. 161

Pringle, Thomas
The Emigrants (1824): **161** 16, p. 79

Prior, Matthew
  mentioned: **296** lviii 6–7, p. 169
  Alma: or, The Progress of the Mind (1718): **296** xcvii 34–36, p. 177
Procter, Bryan Waller
  see Cornwall, Barry
Propertius, Sextus
  see Elton, Sir Charles Abraham
Prudentius (Aurelius Prudentius Clemens)
  Psychomachia (early fifth century AD) quoted: **193** 94–95, p. 96; **209** 106–8, p. 100
Purchas, Samuel
  Purchas His Pilgrimage (1613): **161** 11–12, pp. 78–79
Pusey, E[dward]. B[ouverie].
  A Course of Sermons on Solemn Subjects (Oxford, 1845): **465** 13, p. 219
Pye, Henry James
  Alfred: An Epic Poem (1801): **1** 61–62, p. 22; **75** 28–29, p. 51; **159** 127, p. 76; **296** cxxviii 13, p. 184

Quarles, Francis
  Enchyridion: containing Institutions Divine and Moral (1640–41): **355** 251–53, p. 206
  mentioned as a co-author, along with Benedictus van Haeften, of Christopher Harvey's *Schola cordis* (1647): **163** 6, p. 81, note 50
  Sions Elegies (1625): **276A** 11–13, pp. 128–29

Radcliffe, Ann Ward
  The Romance of the Forest; interspersed with some pieces of poetry (Dublin, 1791; repr. Chiswick, 1823): **286** [Prologue] 236–38, p. 134
  Night from *The Romance of the Forest*: **47** 35, p. 44
  Sun-set (1816): **296** xxxi 11–12, p. 164
  The Fairie Court. A Summer's Night in Windsor Park, part two of *Edwy. A Poem in Three Parts* (1833): **223** 14, p. 112
Raffles, Rev. Thomas
  tr. from the German of Klopstock's *Der Messias* (1748–73) as *The Messiah* (1814): **1** 7–8, p. 19
Rafinesque, Constantine Samuel
  The World, or Instability. A Poem. In Twenty Parts. (1836): **257** 43–44, pp. 120–21
Rainsford, Marcus
  The Revolution, Or, Britain Delivered. A Poem, in Ten Cantos (1800): **26** 8, p. 40
Raleigh, Sir Walter
  Instructions to His Sonne And to Posterity (1632): **176** 7, p. 92

Index of Antecedent Writers and Works Discussed 277

Ramsay, Allan
Health, a Poem (Edinburgh, 1724): **143** *10*, p. 71; **159** *56*, p. 75
The Miser and Minos (1760): **1** *119–20*, pp. 23–24

Ramsay, John
Lines to Eliza from his *Poems* (Edinburgh, 1836): **271** *9*, p. 124

Randolph, Thomas
The Jealous Lovers (1632): **296** xviii *5–7*, pp. 157–58

Reade, John Edmund
Abraham's Offering of Sacrifice from Reade's *Sacred Poems, from Subjects in the Old Testament* (1843): **316** i *3*, p. 193
The Drama of a Life (1840): **297** *20*, p. 185

Robertson, T.
The Fallen Oaks from *The Poetical Register, and Repository of Fugitive Poetry, for 1804* (Rivington, 1806): **163** *1*, p. 81

Robinson, Mary
mentioned: *Preface*, p. 13
Ode on Adversity (1791): **3** i *83–84*, pp. 32–33
Ode to Night (1793): **296** iv *11*, p. 152
Ode to the Nightingale (1791): **296** iv *11*, p. 152
Sight. Inscribed to John Taylor, Esq. Oculist to His Majesty (1793): **1A** i *8*, p. 17
Sonnet Introductory from her *Sappho and Phaon* (1796): **84** *1–4*, pp. 53–54
Sonnet to Amicus (1791): **47** *32*, pp. 43–44
The Lascar (1800): **337** *30*, p. 203

Rogers, Samuel
The Pleasures of Memory (1792): **91** *1–2*, pp. 58–59; **296** xi *6*, p. 155, and xx *3–4*, p. 159
The Voyage of Columbus (1810): **1** *113–14*, p. 23
To an Old Oak (1812): **209** *61–63*, pp. 99–100

Rolls, Mrs. Henry
Ninth Day from her *Legends of the North, or the Feudal Christmas* (1825): **176** *3*, pp. 91–92

Rose, William Stewart
tr. of Ariosto's *Orlando Furioso* (1823): **296** cvii *13–14*, p. 179; **312** *1*, p. 189

Rossetti, Christina
A Linnet in a Gilded Cage (1872): **386** *3*, pp. 208–9

Rous the Elder, Francis
Thule, or Vertues Historie (1598): **108** *8*, p. 63

Rowe, Mrs. Elizabeth Singer
A Pastoral Elegy (1696): **241**, The Sleeping Palace *1–2*, p. 116
Friendship in Death: in Twenty Letters from the Dead to the Living (1728): **127** *78*, pp. 67–68

Rowe, Rev. Henry
  Reflections on the Ruins of a Monastery (1796): **271** *9*, p. 124
  Sun (1796): **420** *73*, pp. 213–14
Rowe, Nicholas
  tr. of Lucan's *Pharsalia* (1718): **297** *18–19*, p. 185
Ruskin, John
  Modern Painters: their Superiority in the Art of Landscape Painting to the Ancient Masters (1843): **296** xcviii *30–32*, pp. 177–78
Ryves, Mrs. F.
  Cumbrian Legends; or, Tales of Other Times (Edinburgh, 1812), with its prefatory *Address*: **2** I i *3–5*, p. 24; and **45** *7*, p. 42; and its *Music of the Chase*: **84** *15–17*, pp. 54–55

Sappho
  mentioned by Collins: *Preface*, pp. 7–8, note 20
  Fragment 2 (now generally known as *Fragment 31*) as an acknowledged source of T.'s *Eleänore* (1832): **161** *130–31*, p. 80
Savage, Richard
  The Genius of Liberty (1738): **127** *81*, p. 68
  The Volunteer Laureat. A Poem on Her Majesty's Birth-Day, 1734–5 (1735): **296** lxxxvii *39–40*, p. 173
Schiller, Friedrich
  see Gower, Lord Francis Leveson
Scott, James
  Ode to the Muse (1775): **296** ix *3–4*, pp. 153–54
Scott, Thomas
  The Anglers. Eight Dialogues in Verse. (1758): **296** xvii *1–6*, p. 157
Scott, Sir Walter
  mentioned: *Preface*, p. 12; **296** xcvii *19*, pp. 176–77
  Marmion: A Tale of Flodden Field (Edinburgh, 1808): **9** *45*, p. 38; **312** *1*, p. 189
  Rob Roy (1817): **2** I iv *133*, p. 28
  Rokeby (1813): **1** *60*, p. 22
  The Bride of Triermain (1813): **176** *17*, p. 92
  The Lady of the Lake (1810): **127** *9*, p. 66; **277** *61*, pp. 130–31; **286** v *253–54*, p. 142
  The Lay of the Last Minstrel (1805): **167** *5–6*, p. 86; **176** *3*, pp. 91–92
  The Lord of the Isles (1815): **163** *34*, p. 83; **286** iv *435–36*, pp. 140–41; **296** [Prologue] *41*, p. 149; and **296** xv *16–18*, p. 156
  The Monks of Bangor's March (1817): **176** *3*, pp. 91–92
  The Pirate (1822): **127** *54*, pp. 66–67; cited by Alfred Gatty, **296** xxix *11*, pp. 162–63
  The Talisman (1825): **296** cix *10*, p. 181

The Vision of Don Roderick (1811) cited by Ricks: **27** *67*, p. 41

Woodstock, or The Cavalier. A Tale of the Year Sixteen Hundred and Fifty-one. (1826): **466** *815–16*, p. 220

Seward, Anna

Chatterton's Poem Charity, Modernised from its Obsolete English By Anna Seward, from the *Poetical Register, and Repository of Poetry, for 1802* (1803): **219** *93–95*, pp. 110–11

Louisa (1784): **167** *53–56*, pp. 86–87

Sewell, Mrs. G. (Mary Young)

An Elegy, To the Memory of a Dear Mother, Lady Young, of Chertsey Abbey. Sept. 1801 from *Poems, by Mrs. G. Sewell* (Egham and Chertsey, 1803): **296** xl *1*, p. 167

Sewell, William

tr. of *Epode 2* from his *Odes and Epodes of Horace* (1850): **330** *91*, p. 200

Shackleton, Rev. John

see Macpherson, James

Shakespeare, William

mentioned: *Preface*, pp. 1, 8, 12; by *Ogilvie* in his *Providence*: **16** *25*, p. 39; **127** *54*, pp. 66–67; by Lewis Theobald in *The Cave of Poverty, a Poem. Writen in imitation of Shakespeare.* (1715), **241** *6*, p. 115; in the anonymous poem *The Tower and the Ivy, a Tale. Addressed to the Admirers of Shakespeare.* (1773): **257** *43–44*, pp. 120–21

A Lover's Complaint: **172** *13–14*, p. 89

A Midsummer Night's Dream: **286** i *242–43*, p. 136

Antony and Cleopatra: cited by Ricks, **10** *5*, p. 39; **185** *11–12*, p. 94; **220** *4–5*, p. 112

As You Like It: **212** *7–8*, p. 104

Hamlet: cited by Ricks, **3** i *39*, p. 32; **67** *36*, p. 49; **78** *180–82*, p. 53; **166** *4*, pp. 85–86; **209** *151–53*, p. 101; cited by Ricks, **217** *5*, p. 108; **275** *86–88*, p. 127; **279** *25–26*, p. 132; mentioned, **286** [Prologue] *222*, pp. 133–34; **286** i *18*, p. 136; cited by Shatto & Shaw, **296** xxxv *24*, p. 166; **316** i *402–4*, pp. 195–96; **355** *225–32*, pp. 205–6; **424** *35*, p. 214

1 Henry IV: **296** [Prologue] *42*, pp. 149–50; **468** *251–52*, p. 221

Henry V: **172** *32–33*, p. 89

Julius Caesar: **400** *5–6*, pp. 210–11; **473** *86*, p. 224

King John: **209** *115*, pp. 100–1

King Lear: mentioned, **127** *54*, pp. 66–67; **176** *18*, pp. 92–93

Macbeth: **2** I i *87*, p. 25; cited (via Ricks) by J. McCue, **2** I iv *133*, p. 28; cited by Collins and by Ricks, **91** *9–10*, p. 59; mentioned, **127** *54*, pp. 66–67; cited by Ricks, **291** *9*, p. 148; **296** cxxx *14*, p. 184; cited by Shatto and by Ricks, **316** i *402–4*, pp. 195–96; **355** *225–32*, pp. 205–6

Othello: **254** *2*, p. 119; **313** *96–97*, p. 191; **470** *1288–89*, pp. 222–23

Pericles, Prince of Tyre: **475** *36*, p. 226

Richard II: **337** *1*, p. 202

Richard III: cited by Collins, Ricks, and Shatto & Shaw, **296** vi *16*, p. 153
   Romeo and Juliet: cited by Collins and by Ricks, **73** *13–14*, p. 50; **164** *230*, p. 85; **286** vii *180–81*, pp. 144–45
   Sonnet 2 ('When fortie Winters shall beseige thy brow'): **2** I v *207–8*, p. 29
   Sonnet 16 ('But wherefore do not you a mightier waie'): **426** *16–18*, p. 215
   Sonnet 18 ('Shall I compare thee to a Summers day?'): **330** *556–58*, p. 201
   Sonnet 33 ('Full many a glorious morning haue I seene'): **313** *3*, p. 190
   Sonnet 38 ('How can my Muse want subiect to inuent'): **299** *12*, p. 186
   Sonnet 49 ('Against that time (if euer that time come)'): **313** *96–97*, p. 191
   Sonnet 60 ('Like as the waues make towards the pibled shore'): **296** cxxiii *5–6*, p. 183
   Sonnet 61 ('Is it thy wil thy Image should keepe open'): **227** *47–48*, pp. 113–14; **316** ii *213–14*, p. 197
   Sonnet 72 ('O least the world should taske you to recite'): **209** *331*, p. 103; **225** *38–39*, pp. 112–13; **271** *148*, p. 126; **296** [Prologue] *33–36*, p. 149
   Sonnet 84 ('Who is it that sayes most, which can say more'): **383** *40–41*, p. 208
   Sonnet 85 ('My toung-tide Muse in manners holds her still'): **276** *10*, p. 127
   Sonnet 111 ('O for my sake doe you wish fortune chide'): **337** *169–70*, p. 204
   Sonnet 116 ('Let me not to the marriage of true mindes'): **296** [Epilogue] *62*, p. 184
   Sonnet 126 ('O thou my louely Boy who in thy power'): **163** *1*, p. 81
   The Merchant of Venice: cited by Ricks, **200** *27*, pp. 97–98
   The Rape of Lucrece: **276** *67–68*, p. 128; **468** *192*, p. 221
   The Taming of the Shrew: **26** *31*, pp. 40–41; **286** v *253–54*, p. 142
   The Tempest: cited by Thomas Warton, **78** *83–86*, p. 52; **170** *116*, pp. 88–89; cited by Ricks, **176** *7*, p. 92; **276** *59–60*, p. 128; **355** *225–32*, pp. 205–6; **464** *378–80*, pp. 218–19
   The Winter's Tale: **394** *1–2*, pp. 209–10
   Titus Andronicus: **79** *2*, p. 53; **400** *5–6*, pp. 210–11
   Troilus and Cressida: cited by Ricks, **296** [Prologue] *41*, p. 149; **296** xcvii *34–36*, p. 177; **337** *1*, p. 202
   Twelfth Night: **216** *26*, p. 107; **241**, Prologue *3*, p. 115; **296** xxi *7–8*, p. 159
   Venus and Adonis: **164** *230*, p. 85

Sharp, Samuel
   Letters from Italy. Describing the Customs and Manners of that Country, in the Years 1765, and 1766. To which is Annexed, an Admonition to Gentlemen who Pass the Alps, in Their Tour Through Italy (1766): **316** i *1*, pp. 192–93

Sharpley, Charles Gregory
   The Coronation (1838): **271** *132*, p. 125

Shelley, Mary
   Frankenstein; or, The Modern Prometheus (1831 edn): **286** i *12–13*, p. 135
   The Last Man (1826): **286** iv *531–32*, p. 141

Shelley, Mary Wollstonecraft
  Letters Written During a Short Residence in Sweden, Norway, and Denmark (1796): **26** *23*, p. 40

Shelley, Percy Bysshe
  mentioned: by T., *Preface*, pp. 4 and 5, note 12; as a canonical author, *Preface*, p. 12; **296** xcvii *19*, pp. 176–77
  Adonais (1821): cited by Ricks, **127** *56*, p. 67; cited by Ricks, **130** *40–41*, p. 69; **166** *4*, pp. 85–86
  Alastor, or, The Spirit of Solitude (1816): **1** *2*, p. 19; **109** *14*, pp. 64–65; cited by Ricks, **160** *31–32*, p. 77; cited by Ricks, **161** *11–12*, pp. 78–79; **164** *215*, pp. 84–85; **311** *106*, p. 189
  Epipsychidion (1821): cited by Ricks, **3** ii *24*, p. 34; **286** vi *62–63*, p. 143; **296** cxxviii *8–9*, p. 183
  Ginevra (1824): cited by Ricks, **127** *56*, p. 67
  Hymn to Mercury (1824): **171** *32*, p. 89
  Julian and Maddalo (1824): **296** lxxxii *1–4*, p. 171
  Laon and Cythna (1817): **1** *2*, p. 19; revised and reissued as *The Revolt of Islam* (1818); subsequent citations under that title
  Letter to Maria Gisborne (1824): **91** *1–2*, pp. 58–59
  Lines Written among the Euganean Hills (1819): **209** *106–8*, p. 100
  Lines Written in the Bay of Lerici (1822): **159** *96–98*, p. 76
  Marenghi, fragment (1824): **339** *7*, p. 205
  Melody to a Scene of Former Times (1810): **2** I iv *7–9*, p. 27
  Ode to Heaven (1820): **286** i *18*, p. 136
  Ode to Naples. Epode 1.a (1820): **209** *85–87*, p. 100
  On Death (1816): cited by Ricks, **101** *9–10, 19–20*, and *29–30*, pp. 60–61
  Ozymandias (1818): mentioned, **286** [Prologue] *99*, p. 133
  Poetical Essay on The Existing State of Things (1811): **316** i *2*, p. 193
  Prologue to Hellas (1822): cited by Ricks, **1** *70*, p. 23; cited by Ricks, **296** xxiv *3–4*, p. 161
  Prometheus Unbound: **3** i *2–4*, pp. 30–31; **75** *5*, pp. 50–51; **88** *1–4*, p. 57; **106** *2*, pp. 61–62; cited by Ricks, **215** *2*, p. 105; **227** *40*, p. 113; **296** cxviii *21*, p. 182; **324** *61–62*, p. 198; **353** *5*, p. 205
  Queen Mab: A Philosophical Poem (1813): **3** ii *52–54*, pp. 34–35; cited by Ricks, **45** *7*, p. 42; **58A** *3*, p. 46; **63** *7–8*, p. 49; **73** *38*, p. 50; **176** *18*, pp. 92–93; cited by Ricks and by Shatto & Shaw, **296** ix *1–2*, p. 153; **296** lxxxvii *39–40*, p. 173; cited by Ricks, **310** *15–17*, p. 188
  Rosalind and Helen: A Modern Eclogue (1819): cited by Ricks, **127** *9*, p. 66
  Sonnet ('Lift not the Painted Veil') (1824): **55** *7*, pp. 45–46
  St. Irvyne; or, The Rosicrucian (1811): **127** *54*, pp. 66–67
  The Banquet (1818), tr. of Plato's *Symposium*: **55** *7*, pp. 45–46
  The Cyclops (1824): cited by Ricks, **296** xxxv *9*, p. 165
  The Indian Serenade (1822): cited by Ricks, **78** *1–2*, p. 51

The Pine Forest of the Cascine Near Pisa (1824): **475** *36*, p. 226

The Revolt of Islam, **1** *2*, p. 19; **1** *64*, pp. 22–23; cited by Ricks, **4** *101*, p. 35; **4** *159–60*, p. 36; **84** *15–17*, pp. 54–55; **84** *39*, p. 55; **91** *1–2*, pp. 58–59; **99** *34* and *40*, p. 60; cited by Ricks, **106** *9*, p. 62; **159** *127*, p. 76; **170** *62*, p. 88; **209** *10*, p. 99; **217** *11*, p. 108; **219** *131–32*, p. 111; **286** vii *24*, p. 144; cited by Ricks, **296** xxx *27*, pp. 163–64; cited by Ricks, **296** xxxiv *13–16*, pp. 164–65; cited by Ricks, **317** *2*, p. 197

The Sensitive Plant (1820): **2** I ii *26*, pp. 26–27; and **2** I iv *7–9*, p. 27; **296** xcviii *30–32*, pp. 177–78

The Triumph of Life (1824): **286** vi *62–63*, p. 143

The Witch of Atlas (1824): **106** *2*, pp. 61–62; **209** *85–87*, p. 100; cited by Ricks, **296** xxiv *3–4*, p. 161; **316** i *363*, p. 195; cited by Ricks, **316** ii *172–74*, pp. 196–97

The Woodman and the Nightingale (1824): cited by Ricks, **106** *9*, p. 62

To Jane: The Invitation (1822): **337** *69*, p. 203

With a Guitar — To Jane (1824): **296** xcv *64*, p. 176

Zastrozzi, a Romance (1810): **2** I i *7–8*, pp. 24–25; **127** *54*, pp. 66–67

Shenstone, William
Verses to a Lady. Together With Some Colour'd Patterns of Flowers. October 7, 1736 (1737): **339** *8*, p. 205

Sheridan, Richard Brinsley
Monody on Garrick (1780): **296** lxxxviii *4*, p. 173

Shipman, Thomas
New Libanus. 1679. in his *Carolina, or, Loyal Poems* (1683): **296** xxxix *3*, pp. 166–67

Shippen, William
Faction Display'd (1704): **427** *27*, pp. 215–16

Shirley, James
Song IX from *The Triumph of Peace* (1634): **124** *5*, p. 65

Sidney, Sir Philip
mentioned by T.: *Preface*, p. 4

An Apology for Poetry, also known as *The Defence of Poesy* (1595): **91** *9–10*, p. 59

see also Greville, Fulke

Simonds, Hart
The Arguments of Faith (1822): **286** iii *79–80*, p. 139

Sloper, Samuel
The Heart's Bitterness from *The Dacoit, and Other Poems* [1840]: **296** xxx *22–23*, p. 163

Smart, Christopher
On the Immensity of the Supreme Being: A Poetical Essay (1751): **2** I i *84–85*, p. 25

tr. of Horace's *Epode xiv* [elsewhere numbered *xvi*] in vol. 2 of his *Works of Horace* (1767): **241**, The Sleeping Palace *1–2*, p. 116

Smedley, Rev. Edward
  Prescience: or the Secrets of Divination (1816): **257** 17–20, pp. 119–20
Smith, Abram Lent
  The Romaunt of Lady Helen Clyde (New York, 1882): **390** 31–32, p. 209
Smith, Charlotte Turner
  mentioned: *Preface*, p. 13
  Apostrophe to an Old Yew Tree (1797): **30** 29–30, p. 42
  Flora (1807): **286** vi 62–63, p. 143
  Lydia (1800): **286** iv 166, p. 139
  Sonnet 45, *On leaving a part of Sussex* from *Elegiac Sonnets and Other Poems* (1784): **84** 30, p. 55
  Sonnet 75 (*'Where the wild woods and pathless forests frown'*) from the same: **58A** 75, pp. 47–48
  Sonnet 80, *To the Invisible Moon*, from the same: **106** 9, p. 62
  Studies by the Sea (1804): **128** 24 and 33, pp. 68–69
  The Gossamer (1800): **277** 61, pp. 130–31
Smith, Horace (as 'Paul Chapman, M.D.')
  A Tour to the Lakes (1830): **312** 41–42, pp. 189–90
  Hymn to the Flowers (1832): **316** ii 172–74, pp. 196–97
  Ozymandias (1818): **286** [Prologue] 99, p. 133
  The Tin Trumpet; or, Heads and Tales, for the Wise and Waggish, vol. 2 (1836): **383** 8, p. 208
Smollett, Tobias
  Ode to Independence, also known as *Independence: An Ode* (1773): **106** 8, p. 62; **209** 266, p. 102
  The History and Adventures of an Atom (1740): **219** 15, p. 110
Smyrnæus
  see Dyce, Alexander
Sophocles
  mentioned: *Preface*, p. 5
  Oedipus Rex: **88** 1–4, p. 57
Sotheby, William
  Genoa from *Farewell to Italy* (1818): **217** 2, p. 108
  Rome (1825): **296** [Prologue] 41, p. 149
  Virgil's Tomb (1818): **209** 10, p. 99
  tr. of Virgil's *Georgic III* (1800): **167** 53–56, pp. 86–87
  tr. (1798) from the German of Wieland's *Oberon*: **296** xxxviii 8, p. 166
Southey, Caroline Anne (née Bowles)
  The River (1829): **313** 63–64, p. 191
Southey, Robert
  mentioned: *Preface*, p. 12
  Chronicle of the Cid (1808): **241**, L'Envoi 41–42, pp. 117–18
  Hymn to the Penates (1796): **161** 89, p. 80

Joan of Arc, an Epic Poem (Bristol, 1796): **190** 22, p. 94

Madoc (1805; rev. 1812): **55** 7, pp. 45–46

Roderick, The Last of the Goths (1814): **215** 3, p. 106; **276** 57, pp. 127–28

Sonnet 1 ('Go Valentine and tell that lovely maid')(1794): **27** 67, p. 41

Sonnet ('A wrinkled crabbed Man they picture thee / Old Winter') (1800): **161** 130–31, p. 80

Thalaba the Destroyer (1801): **193** 71, p. 95; **296** lxxxix 27–28, pp. 173–74

The Curse of Kehama (1810): **2** I iv 133, p. 28; **3** i 32, p. 31

The Poet's Pilgrimage to Waterloo (1816): **161** 6, p. 78

The Spanish Armada (1798): **167** 69, p. 87

To a Brook near the Village of Corston (1794): **160** 44, p. 77

T.'s phrase 'in happy hour' in **241**, *L'Envoi* 41–42, pp. 117–18, occurs in Southey poems a total of twelve times

as editor, *The Remains of Henry Kirke White* (1807 and subsequent edns): **1** 74, p. 23

Spenser, Edmund

mentioned: by Collins, *Preface*, p. 8; as a canonical author, *Preface*, p. 12

An Hymne in Honour of Beautie (1596): **47** 32, pp. 43–44; **301** 5, p. 186

Muiopotmos: or The Fate of the Butterflie (1590): **240** 3, pp. 114–15

Prosopopoia: or Mother Hubberds Tale (1591): **313** 3, p. 190; **363** 10, p. 206

The Faerie Queene (1590): **108** 14, p. 63; **109** 8–9, p. 64; cited by Ricks, **126** 3–4, pp. 65–66; cited by Ricks, **159** 82–84, p. 75; **209** 219, p. 102, and **266**, p. 102; **296** xi 17, pp. 155–56, and xxiv 3–4, p. 161

The Ruines of Time (1591): **220** 4–5, p. 112

The Shepherd's Calender: August (1579): cited by Ricks, **296** iii 12, p. 151

Two Cantos of Mutabilitie (1609): **101** 9–10, 19–20 and 29–30, pp. 60–61

see also Keats, *Imitation of Spenser* (1817)

Spicer, Henry

The Night-Voices (1844): **296** xxii 13, pp. 160–61

Statius, Publius Papinius

Silvae I iii 22–23 cited by T. as a source of **296** xxxiii 8, p. 164

Thebaid: **1** 31, p. 20; **1** 119–20, pp. 23–24; **9** 45, p. 38; **26** 32, p. 41; **286** iv 495, p. 141

Villa Tiburtina Manlii Vopisci quoted: **313** 59–62, p. 191

see also translations by Robert Bradstreet, Francis Hodgson, W. L. Lewis, and Alexander Pope

Steele, Anne ('Theodosia')

A Dying Saviour from her *Poems on Subjects Chiefly Devotional* (1760): **127** 78, pp. 67–68

Steele, Richard

The Story of Inkle and Yarico (1767): **109** 5, p. 64

Stepney, George

The Nature of Dreams (c. 1700): **163** 34, p. 83

Sterling, Joseph
see Boyse, Samuel
Stevenson, William
Vertumnus; or, The Progress of Spring (1765): **296** xxx 27, pp. 163–64
Stewart, John
Ode (The Niliad) (1810): **161** 16, p. 79
The Pleasures of Love (1806): **9** 8–9, p. 37; **106** 8, p. 62
Stockall, Harriet
Malcolm from her *Poems and Sonnets* (1879): **420** 45, pp. 212–13
Stokes, Henry Sewell
The Lay of the Desert (1830): **257** 29–32, p. 120
Struthers, John
The Peasant's Death; or, A Visit to the House of Mourning (Glasgow, 1806): **159** 96–98, p. 76; **337** 30, p. 203
Strutt, Jacob George
tr. of Claudian's *Rape of Proserpine* (1814): **84** 48, p. 55
tr. of a Latin poem by Milton as *On the Fifth of November* (1814): **227** 47–48, pp. 113–14
Stuart-Wortley, Lady Emmeline
Greece from her *Poems* (1833): **296** lxxxvi 1–2, p. 172
Lines on Martin the Painter from the same: **296** lxxxvi 1–2, p. 172
London at Night (1834): **329** 10, pp. 198–99
Swan, Rev. Charles
The False One from his *Gaston; or, The Heir of Foiz: A Tragedy. With Other Poems* (1823): **3** i 39, p. 32
Swan, John
Speculum Mundi, or, a Glass Representing the Face of the World (1670), explains the meaning of *fruitful cloud*: **296** xxxix 3, pp. 166–67
Swift, Jonathan
mentioned: **296** xcvii 19, pp. 176–77
Carberiæ Rupes (1723): **78** 96–97, p. 52
Gulliver's Travels (1726): **313** 7–8, p. 190
The Fable of Midas (1712): **313** 59–62, p. 191
Swinburne, Algernon Charles
By the North Sea (1880): **431** 41–42, p. 216
The Armada from *Poems and Ballads: Third Series* (1889): **427** 27, pp. 215–16
Sylvester, Josuah
Henrie the Great (The Fourth of that Name) Late King of France and Navarre; His Tropheis and Tragedy (1612; repr. 1880): **468** 312–15, pp. 221–22
tr. of Du Bartas's *La Sepmaine; ou, Creation du Monde* (1578) as *Du Bartas His Diuine Weekes and Workes* (1604): **26** 31, pp. 40–41; **194** 21–22, pp. 96–97; **313** 59–62, p. 191

tr. of Odet de la Noue's *Paradoxe que les adversitez sont plus necessaires que les prosperités* as *A Paradox Against Libertie* (1594): **176** 17, p. 92

Symmons, Charles
tr. of *The Æneis of Virgil* (1817): **101** 21–22, p. 61

Tacitus
Annales v 2 quoted: **2** I i 58, p. 25

Talfourd, Thomas Noon
Final Memorials of Charles Lamb (1848): **466** 803–4, p. 220

Tasso, Torquato
mentioned by Collins: *Preface*, p. 7
see translations by Henry Brooke, Edward Fairfax, Thomas Gray, John Hoole, and J. H. Wiffen

Tate, Nahum
White-LILY (1689), tr. of Cowley's *Lilium Candidum*: **130** 79, pp. 69–70

Tatham, Emma
The Mother's Vigil from *Dream of Pythagoras, and Other Poems* (1855 edn): **425** 59–60, p. 214

Taylor, Rev. Jeremy
mentioned by Collins: *Preface*, p. 8, note 20
The Life of Christ, or The Great Exemplar of Sanctity and Holy Life (1649): **296** xxxix 3, p. 166

Taylor, J[ohn]. B.
tr. of Petrarch's poem 28 ('Solo e pensoso i più deserti campi') (1804): **286** vi ∧ vii 7, p. 144

Taylor, Thomas
tr. of Aristotle's *Nicomachean Ethics* (1811): **164** 119–20, p. 84

Theobald, Lewis
The Cave of Poverty, a Poem. Written in imitation of Shakespeare. (1715): **241** 6, p. 115

Theocritus
mentioned by Collins: *Preface*, p. 8, note 20
Idylls, cited by Richard Mant in his edn of Thomas Warton's *Poetical Works* (1802): **296** xcvii 19, pp. 176–77

'Theodosia'
see Steele, Anne

Thompson, B.
The Shipwreck (1823): **291** 9, p. 148

Thompson, Rev. William
An Hymn to May (1746): **215** 1, p. 105
Sickness. A Poem. In Three Books. (1745): **3** i 87–88, p. 33; **317** 28, p. 197

Thomson, James
mentioned: *Preface*, p. 12
A Hymn on the Seasons (1730): **160** *90–92*, pp. 77–78; **296** xxi *17–20*, p. 160
A Poem to the Memory of the Right Honourable The Lord Talbot. Addressed to His Son. (1737): **306** *8*, p. 187
Autumn (1730): cited by Ricks, **160** *90–92*, pp. 77–78; **296** vi *4*, p. 153
Edward and Eleanora. A Tragedy. (1739): **58A** *75*, p. 47
Liberty: A Poem (1735): **289** *6*, pp. 145–46
On a Country Life (1720): **3** i *33–34*, p. 32; **301** *21–22*, p. 187
Song ('Tell me, thou soul of her I love') (c. 1740): first cited (as noted by Shatto & Shaw and by Ricks) by John Sparrow (1930): **296** xliv *1*, p. 168
Spring (1728): **58A** *36*, p. 47
Summer (1727): **30** *25–26*, p. 42; **58A** *36*, p. 47
Tancred and Sigismunda, A Tragedy (1745): **8** *21–22*, p. 37
The Castle of Indolence (1748): cited by Ricks, **108** *14*, p. 63; **296** xxvii *2*, pp. 161–62, and xxx *27*, pp. 163–64; cited by Collins, Shatto & Shaw, and Ricks, **296** [Epilogue] *117–18*, p. 185
Winter (1726): cited by Ricks, **3** i *133*, p. 34; **5** *15–16*, p. 36; **47** *35*, p. 44; **83** *90*, p. 53; **106** *9*, p. 62; **128** *11*, p. 68; **160** *31–32*, p. 77

Thomson, Samuel
The Year in 12 Fits, ascribed to Damon. (1799): **276A** *50–53*, p. 129

Thurston, Joseph
The Fall; in Four Books (1732): **101** *27*, p. 61

Tibullus
see Dart, John

Tickell, Thomas
Lucy and Colin (1725), **241**, Prologue *3*, p. 115

Tighe, Mary
Good Friday, 1790 (1811): **8** *17*, p. 37
THE LILY. May, 1809. from *Psyche: with other poems by the late Mrs Henry Tighe* (1811): **296** cxxii *1–4*, p. 182

Tindal, Mrs. Acton
The Lament of Joanna of Spain (1847): **296** xxiv *9–10*, p. 161

Tonna, Charlotte Elizabeth (née Browne) (as 'Charlotte Elizabeth')
Izram, a Mexican Tale (1826): **286** iv *169*, p. 139

Trapp, John
Commentary or Exposition Upon All the Books of the New Testament (1656): **210** *7*, p. 104

Trench, Richard Chevenix
Orpheus and the Sirens (1842): **296** ix *7–8*, p. 154

Trevanion, Henry
The Influence of Apathy (1827): **144** *6*, p. 71

Trevelyan, Raleigh
    On the Ten Commandments (1820): **161** 73–74, pp. 79–80

Trumbull, John
    M'Fingal (1782): **296** ix 9–10, p. 154

Tschudi, J[ohann]. J[akob]. von
    Peru. Reiseskizzen aus den Jahren 1838–1842 [*Peru. Travel Sketches from the Years 1838–1842*], a section of which was tr. as *The Mine, the Forest, and the Cordillera* in Blackwood's Edinburgh Magazine (1846): **454** 12, p. 218

Tuckerman, Henry Theodore
    The Holy Land (1840): **296** xciv 1–4, p. 175

Tyler, James Endell
    Meditations from the Fathers of the First Five Centuries (1849): **299** 8, pp. 185–86

Urquhart, Sir Thomas
    tr. (1663) of Rabelais's *Pantagruel* (1532): **163** 6, pp. 81–82

Vaughan, Henry
    Distraction (1650): **464** 378–80, pp. 218–19
    The Night (1650): **62** 13–14, p. 49
    The World (1650): **296** xcvii 2–3, p. 176

Virgil (Publius Vergilius Maro)
    compared to T. by Collins: *Preface*, pp. 6, 7, 8, note 20
    mentioned, as canonical author: *Preface*, p. 12;
    as Dante's guide in the *Inferno*: **164** 66–68, pp. 83–84; **296** lviii 9–10, p. 169
    Aeneid quoted and/or cited: **101** 21–22, p. 61; by Mustard, Ricks, and Shatto & Shaw, **296** ix 1–2, p. 153; **296** cxxviii 13, p. 184; **394** 1–2, pp. 209–10; by T. himself: **475** 36, p. 226
    Eclogues quoted and/or cited: **240** 3, pp. 114–15; **469** 33, p. 222
    Georgics quoted and/or cited: **167** 53–56, pp. 86–87; **296** ii 7–8, p. 151; **296** vi 4, p. 153; **296** ix 3–4, pp. 153–54
    Pastorals quoted and/or cited: by Ricks, **296** xliii 5, pp. 167–68; **420** 57–58, p. 213
    see also translations of some or all of the *Aeneid* and other of Virgil's works by Thomas Creech, John Dryden, Thomas Grinfield, William Mills, Ambrose Philips, William Sotheby, Charles Symmons, Joseph Warton, and William Wordsworth

Voltaire
    see Lloyd, Robert

Waddington, George
    Columbus (1813): **163** 17, p. 82

Warton, Joseph
   Ode VI. Against Despair. in his *Odes on Various Subjects* (1746): **271** 143, p. 125
   Ode to Sleep (1748): **124** 5, p. 65
   tr. of Virgil's *Georgic III* in his *Works of Virgil, in Latin and English* (1753): **296** ii 7–8, p. 151; **296** xcvii 19, pp. 176–77

Warton, Thomas
   mentioned: *Preface*, p. 12
   comments also relevant to T. in his edn of Milton's *Poems upon Several Occasions* (1785): **78** 83–86, p. 52
   Ode XVII, For His Majesty's Birth-day, June 4th, 1786 (1786): **296** xcvii 19, pp. 176–77
   The Pleasures of Melancholy. Written in the Year 1745. (1747): **64** 4, p. 49; **106** 9, p. 62; **130** 52–53, p. 69
   Verses on Reynolds's Painted Window at New-College (1782): **275** 86–88, p. 127; **425** 41–43, p. 214

Watson, Thomas
   Sonnet LVIII of his *Hekatompathia* (1582): **310** 19, pp. 188–89

Watts, Isaac
   An Elegiac Ode On the Reverend Mr. T. Gouge (1706): **208** 18, p. 98
   Come, Lord Jesus from *Horae Lyricae* (1706): **296** xxx 27, pp. 163–64
   Death and Eternity (1706): **296** lviii 6–7, p. 169
   Divine Judgments (1715): **301** 21–22, p. 187
   God's Dominion over the Sea from the second, posthumous edn of his *Collection of Hymns and Sacred Poems* (1779): **215** 3, p. 106
   Grace Shining, and Nature Fainting (1709): **296** [Prologue] 41, p. 149
   Hymn of Praise for three great Salvations (1706): **317** 28, p. 197
   O how I love Thy holy law! (1719): **286** vi 47, p. 143
   Passion and Reason (1742): **190** 23, p. 94
   Stanzas to Lady Sunderland at Tunbridge-Wells, 1712 (1780): **75** 5, pp. 50–51
   The Hero's School of Morality (1709): **286** [Prologue] 99, p. 133
   The Incomprehensible (1706): **163** 33, p. 82
   To Her Majesty (1721): **1** 74, p. 23
   To Sir John Hartopp, Baronet. The Wish. (1805): **296** xxx 27, pp. 163–64
   To the Dear Memory of my Honoured Friend Thomas Gunston Esq. from *Horae Lyricae* (1706): **128** 11, p. 68
   Untitled poem beginning 'Let *Astrapé* forbear to blaze' in his *Reliquiae Juveniles. Miscellaneous Thoughts in Prose and Verse.* (1734): **128** 11, p. 68

Weever, John
   The Mirror of Martyrs, or, The life and death of that thrice valiant Capitaine, and most godly Martyre Sir John Old-castle knight, Lord Cobham (1601): **4** 155, p. 36

Wesley, Charles
   Hymn ('Gentle Jesus, Meek and Mild') (1742): **290** 8–9, p. 147

    Hymn ('Jesus, Lover of My Soul') (1740): **78** 1–2, p. 51
    Hymn ('Jesus, thou say'st I shall receive') (1762): **467** 928–29, p. 221
    Hymn ('None Is Like Jeshurun's God') (1742): **286** ii 292–96, pp. 138–39
Wesley, John
    Explanatory Notes on the Whole Bible (1754–65): **78** 49, p. 52
    Hymn ('O God, what offering shall I give') (1831): **469** 253, p. 222
Wesley, Samuel
    tr. of *Batrachomyomachia* (1726): **73** 63–64, p. 50
Wharton, Richard
    Cambuscan, An Heroic Poem, In Six Books Fables in vol. 2 of his *Fables* (1805): **1** 61–62, p. 22
White, Henry Kirke
    Sonnet ('What art thou, Mighty One! and where thy seat') from *Remains of Henry Kirke White* (1807 edn): **1** 74, p. 23
    The Dance of the Consumptives from *Remains* (1808 edn): **130** 40–41, p. 69
    The Hermit of the Dale (1811): **420** 73, pp. 213–14
    The Hermit of the Pacific, or The Horrors of Utter Solitude (1822): **215** 1, p. 105
White, Walter (as 'W.')
    Hope For All (1846), **329** 16, p. 199
Whittier, John Greenleaf
    The Seeking of the Waterfall (1878): **462** 6, p. 218
Whyte, Samuel
    Elegy I (1770): **1** 55, pp. 21–22
Wiffen, J[eremiah]. H[olmes].
    tr. of *Gerusalemme Liberata* as *The Jerusalem Delivered of Torquato Tasso* (1824–25): **176** 23–24, p. 93; **219** 131–32, p. 111; **286** v 513, p. 142; and **296** xxvii 2, pp. 161–62
Williams, Helen Maria
    A Paraphrase on Psalm lxxiv. 16, 17, also known as *The Benevolence of God* (1786): **167** 53–56, pp. 86–87
    Duncan, An Ode (1791): **55** 7, pp. 45–46
    Part of an Irregular Fragment, Found in a Dark Passage of the Tower (1786): **296** cxviii 21, p. 182
Williams, Isaac
    The Spiritual Husbandman from *The Baptistery, or The Way of Eternal Life*, Part IV (1844): **296** xxii 9–12, p. 160
Williams, Robert Folkestone
    The Young Napoleon (1833): **286** i 31, p. 136
Wilson, John
    mentioned: *Preface*, p. 13
    The City of the Plague, from *The City of the Plague, and Other Poems* (Edinburgh, 1816): **84** 15–17, pp. 54–55; **216** 26, p. 107; **316** i 5, p. 193

Dirge from *City of the Plague*: **216** *26*, p. 107
Solitude from *City of the Plague*: **26** *1*, pp. 39–40
The Isle of Palms (Edinburgh, 1812): **47** *35*, p. 44; **153** i *58*, p. 73; **209** *379–81*, p. 103; **286** vii *180–81*, pp. 144–45; **296** ix *1–2*, p. 153, and xxxv *9*, p. 165
The Scholar's Funeral from *City of the Plague*: **296** [Epilogue] *117–18*, p. 185
Waking Dreams: A Fragment (1817): **286** i *12–13*, p. 135

Wither, George
Epithalamia: or Nuptiall Poems (1612): **257** *83*, pp. 121–22

Wollstonecraft, Mary
Letters Written During a Short Residence in Sweden, Norway, and Denmark (1796): **26** *23*, p. 40

Woodley, Rev. George
Britain's Bulwarks; or, The British Seaman (Plymouth-Dock, 1811): **296** cv *23–24*, p. 179
Cornubia (1819): **167** *69*, p. 87
Mount-Edgcumbe (1804): **2** I i *7–8*, pp. 24–25

Wordsworth, Christopher
The Druids, **161** *9–10*, p. 78

Wordsworth, William
mentioned in *Preface*: by T. himself, p. 4; as canonical author, p. 12; alluded to in T.'s *To the Queen* (1851): **216** *4*, pp. 106–7; addressed in a poem by Hemans (see entry under her name)
A Farewell (1815): **241**, Prologue *6*, p. 115
An Evening Walk, Addressed to a Young Lady (1793): **1A** i *8*, p. 17; **296** cxviii *21*, p. 182
Artegal and Elidure (1815): **209** *143*, p. 101
Descriptive Sketches taken during a Pedestrian Tour among the Alps (1793; revised 1820): **2** III ii *78*, pp. 29–30; **209** *151–53*, p. 101; **296** v *5–6*, p. 153
Elegiac Stanzas on the death of Frederick William Goddard (1807): **209** *10*, p. 99
Elegiac Stanzas on the deaths of George and Sarah Green (written and privately but widely circulated in 1808; first formally published 1839): **257** *87*, p. 122
Epitaphs Translated from Chiabrera (1810): **296** cv *1–2*, p. 179
Gipsies (1807): **209** *451*, p. 103
Inside of King's College Chapel, Cambridge from *Ecclestical Sketches* (1822): **127** *67*, p. 67
Laodamia (1815): **427** *33*, p. 216
Lines Left upon a Seat in a Yew-tree (1827 version): **296** xcv *15–16* and *51–52*, p. 175
Ode: Intimations of Immortality from Recollections of Early Childhood (1807): **164** *263*, p. 85
Peter Bell, a Tale in Verse (1819 version): **223** *18*, p. 112; **289** *6*, pp. 145–46; **473** *4* and *242*, p. 224

Presentiments. Written at Rydal Mount. (1835): **420** 57–58, p. 213
Salisbury Plain (1794): **1** 60, p. 22; **4** 101, p. 35
Song at the Feast of Brougham Castle (1807): **286** vii 277, p. 145
Sonnet ('I watch, and have long watched, with calm regret') (1819): **217** 31, pp. 108–9
Sympathy (1827): **296** xxx 22–23, p. 163
The Blind Highland Boy (1803): **330** 128–30, p. 200
The Borderers (1842): cited by Ricks, **87** 26–27, p. 56
The Brownie's Cell from Part 1 of *Memorials of a Tour of Scotland* (1820): **277** 61, pp. 130–31
The Contrast: The Parrot and the Wren (1827): **386** 3, pp. 208–9
The Earl of Breadalbane's Ruined Mansion, and Family Burial-Place, Near Killin (1831): **296** xxxv 1–2, p. 165
The Emigrant Mother (1807): **296** xx 1–2, p. 158
The Excursion (1814): **9** 8–9, p. 37; **163** 6, pp. 81–82; cited by Ricks, **257** 87, p. 122; **296** xxvi 5–7, p. 161
The Female Vagrant (1798): **174** 4–7, p. 91; **296** xx 1–2, p. 158
The Fountain (1798): **241**, The Sleeping Palace 1–2, p. 116
The Green Linnet (1807): **159** 91, p. 75
The Prelude (1798 version): **299** 12, p. 186
The White Doe of Rylstone (1815): **161** 6, p. 78; **296** xxvi 5–7, p. 161
To a Small Celandine (1807): **128** 24 and 33, pp. 68–69
Water-Fowl (1827): **127** 20, p. 66
We Are Seven (1810): **286** [Prologue] 9, p. 133
Written In a Blank Leaf of Macpherson's Ossian (1827): **127** 9, p. 66
Yew-Trees (1815): **3** ii 24, p. 34
tr. of *Aeneid* Book I (1832): **215** 3, p. 106

Wrangham, Francis
tr. of sonnet 149 of Petrarch's *Laura* (later incorporated in the *Canzoniere* as Poem 182) beginning 'Amor che 'ncende 'l cor d' ardente zelo', as *Love and Jealousy* (1817): **163** 17, p. 82

Wright, John
The Retrospect; or Youthful Scenes (1825): **62** 6, p. 48

Wyatt, Thomas
Complaint of the Absence of His Love (1557): **95** 38–39, p. 60
In Spain (c. 1539): **163** 34, p. 83
Tagus Farewell, first published (1557) as *Of his returne from Spain*: **313** 59–62, p. 191
The mournful Lover to his Heart with Complaint that it will not break (1557): **227** 23, p. 113

Yalden, Thomas
 tr. of Ovid's *Art of Love*, Book II (1709): **296** xx *1–2*, p. 158
Yearsley, Ann
 A Poem on the Inhumanity of the Slave-Trade (1788): **296** xi *15–16*, p. 155
Yeman, Alexander
 The Fisherman's Hut, in the Highlands of Scotland (1807): **167** *53–56*, pp. 86–87
Young, Edward
 mentioned: *Preface*, p. 12
 A *Paraphrase on Part of the Book of Job* (1719): **3** i *33–34*, p. 32
 A Poem on the Last Day (Oxford, 1713): **160** *77–78*, p. 77; **161** *89*, p. 80
 Epistle to Lord Lansdowne (1713): **151** *14*, pp. 72–73
 Satire VII. To the Right Honourable Sir Robert Walpole from *The Love of Fame, the Universal Passion* (1728): **296** lxxxvi *13*, p. 173
 The Complaint: or, Night-Thoughts on Life, Death, & Immortality (1742–45): **3** i *2–4*, pp. 30–3; **3** i *87–88*, p. 33; **164** *215*, pp. 84–85; **209** *146*, p. 101; **257** *83*, pp. 121–22; **289** *6*, pp. 145–46
 The Foreign Address, or The Best Argument for Peace (1734): **296** lxxxvi *13*, p. 173
 The Merchant. Ode the First. Strain the Fifth from *Imperium Pelagi. A Naval Lyric.* in his *Imperium Pelagi. A Naval Lyric* (1730): **2** I i *90–92*, pp. 25–26

This book need not end here...

Share

All our books—including the one you have just read—are free to access online so that students, researchers and members of the public who can't afford a printed edition will have access to the same ideas. This title will be accessed online by hundreds of readers each month across the globe: why not share the link so that someone you know is one of them?

This book and additional content is available at:
https://doi.org/10.11647/OBP.0161

Customise

Personalise your copy of this book or design new books using OBP and third-party material. Take chapters or whole books from our published list and make a special edition, a new anthology or an illuminating coursepack. Each customised edition will be produced as a paperback and a downloadable PDF.

Find out more at:
https://www.openbookpublishers.com/section/59/1

Like Open Book Publishers

Follow @OpenBookPublish

Read more at the Open Book Publishers BLOG

You may also be interested in:

The Anglo-Scottish Ballad and its Imaginary Contexts

David Atkinson

https://doi.org/10.11647/OBP.0041

 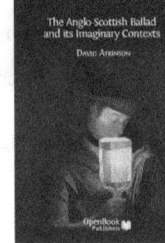

Dickens's Working Notes for *Dombey and Son*

Tony Laing

https://doi.org/10.11647/OBP.0092

An Anglo-Norman Reader

Jane Bliss

https://doi.org/10.11647/OBP.0110

www.ingramcontent.com/pod-product-compliance
Lightning Source LLC
Chambersburg PA
CBHW050207240426
43671CB00013B/2248